A Survivor's Duty

Surviving the Holocaust
and Fighting for Israel:
A story of Father and Son

The Holocaust: History and Literature, Ethics and Philosophy

Series Editor

MICHAEL BERENBAUM (American Jewish University)

A Survivor's Duty

**Surviving the Holocaust
and Fighting for Israel:
A story of Father and Son**

Gabriel Laufer

Boston
2018

Library of Congress Cataloging-in-Publication Data

Names: Laufer, Gabriel, author.

Title: A Survivor's Duty: Surviving the Holocaust and Fighting for Israel: A story of Father and Son / Gabriel Laufer.

Description: Boston, MA : Academic Studies Press, 2018. | Series: The Holocaust : history and literature, ethics, and philosophy | Includes bibliographical references.

Identifiers: LCCN 2018006731 (print) | LCCN 2018007530 (ebook) | ISBN 9781618117847 (e-book) | ISBN 9781618117823 (hardcover) | ISBN 9781618117830 (pbk.)

Subjects: LCSH: Laufer, Gabriel. | Children of Holocaust survivors— | Israel—Biography. | Holocaust, Jewish (1939-1945)—Hungary—Budapest— | Personal narratives. | Budapest (Hungary)—Ethnic relations.

Classification: LCC DS135.H93 (ebook) | LCC DS135.H93 L378 2018 (print) | DDC 940.53/18092 [B] —dc23

LC record available at https://lccn.loc.gov/2018006731

© 2018 Academic Studies Press
All rights reserved.

ISBN 978-1-61811-782-3 (hardback)
ISBN 978-1-61811-783-0 (paperback)
ISBN 978-1-61811-784-7 (electronic)

Book design by Kryon Publishing Services (P) Ltd.
www.kryonpublishing.com

Cover design by Ivan Grave

Published by Academic Studies Press in 2018
28 Montfern Avenue
Brighton, MA 02135, USA
press@academicstudiespress.com
www.academicstudiespress.com

To my beloved Liora, who did not live to see this book completed, and to our family members who were murdered in the Holocaust.

The survivor's duty is to bear witness for the dead and for the living. He has no right to deprive future generations of a past that belongs to our collective memory. To forget would be not only dangerous but offensive: to forget the dead would be a kin to killing them a second time.
—**Elie Wiesel, Night (1)**

Table of Contents

Acknowledgments	viii
Notes on Transliteration and Formatting	xi
Foreword	xii
June 1942: Imprisoned in the *toloncház*	1
July 1942: Budapest	17
August 1942: Leaving Gyula	27
August 1942: Püspökladány, Hungary	41
September 1942: Gomel, Ukraine	59
September-October 1942: When Man Becomes a Horse	64
October-December 1942: Stary Oskol	77
May 1967: Dark Clouds over Israel	85
May-June 1967: The Six-Day War	109
Summer 1967: Messianic Days (or so we thought)	143
January 1943: Near Stalingrad	155
1968-1970: The War of Attrition	182
October 1973: The Yom Kippur War	206
November 1944-May 1945: Dachau and Mühldorf, Germany	265
May 1945: Liberation	313
July 1945: Home at Last	330
1945-1949: Budapest	346
July-August 1949: Escape from Hungary	354
June 1982: A War of Deception	362
Works Cited	390
Index	396

Acknowledgments

The urge to write this book was triggered by my visit to the Hall of Names at the Yad Vashem Holocaust History Museum in Jerusalem. The round hall lined with bookshelves along its walls is the repository of the Pages of Testimony, the biographical details of the known Holocaust victims: one or two pages for each one. Seeing the vast number of black binders on the shelves was breathtaking. But the huge void of empty spaces set aside for the binders which will contain the testimonial pages of the yet unknown victims was far more striking.

More than 70 years after the Holocaust we know the names of "only" 4.7 million victims. More than one million of the Holocaust's Jewish victims remain unaccounted for. Entire families and their communities were wiped out. No one was left to name the victims or identify them on the rare occasion that a picture of a person who once lived was found. Street after street of houses that were formerly occupied by Jewish families were seized by their gentile neighbors who were quick to erase evidence of former ownerships.

The generation of Holocaust survivors is nearly gone and my generation, the so-called Second Generation Holocaust Survivors is rapidly diminishing too. Soon there will be no one left to tell the stories of the victims and of those who survived. Thanks to Yad Vashem I understood my duty to tell the stories of my father, his family, and their community.

My research took me through old villages in Hungary, concentration camps in Germany and battle-fields in Israel. Along the way I met people from all walks of life and various cultures. Some spoke only Hebrew, others only Hungarian, German or English. But they all had an important story to tell. I visited large archives like the US Holocaust Memorial Museum, Yad Vashem in Jerusalem, the Holocaust Memorial Center in Budapest, the Memorial to the Murdered Jews of Europe in Berlin, the US Library of Congress and smaller ones like the Memorial Museum of Hungarian-Speaking Jewry in Safed,

Israel or the Virginia Holocaust Museum in Richmond. Each one of them had at least one piece that fit perfectly into the big puzzle that I assembled. More importantly, these institutes are the dam that holds off the growing flood of "Alternative Facts" and "Fake News" that attempts to re-write the history of the Holocaust or simply deny that it ever existed. I am grateful to these institutes, the visionaries who founded them, and the dedicated people who nourish them daily with their wisdom, time, and money. I pray that their work will protect us from the torrent of lies, misinformation, or plain ignorance.

I am also thankful to the International Tracing Service archive in Bad Arolsen and the archive at the Dachau Concentration Camp Memorial Site for their numerous and accurate responses to my queries.

Ultimately, this book is based on the memories of living persons, on the clues my father left to me and others, those that my mother told and, of course, conversations with those who are still alive. I spent countless days with my cousin Tamás Gróf and his wife Erika Siegfried-Thompson traveling in Hungary between ancient Jewish cemeteries, synagogues, and family homes. Tamás's prescient memory of family relations and events helped me mesh the archival facts with the lives of real people. His translation from Hungarian of documents, long letters by my father and our grandmother during and immediately after the Holocaust transported me to another world. Through his introduction I met Dr. Tibor Várkonyi, a resourceful Budapest lawyer, who knew where to find lost information like the birthdate of my half-sister Judit who was murdered in Auschwitz at the tender age of three and tracked down a nobility award bestowed by the Emperor Franz Joseph I on one of my ancestors.

I am thankful to my sister Noemi Schaefer for guarding precious family documents and helping me navigate through the maze of Israeli bureaucracy.

Thanks are owed also to my cousin Erzsébet (Zsóka) Kiss who shared with me numerous family documents and letters that survived the Holocaust, the communist regime in Hungary and the ravages of time.

Thanks to my family member Ágnes (Ági) Palócz and my uncle István Dénes. They are the last survivors of my parents' generation and the only remaining people who knew my father and mother as children, teenagers and as young Holocaust survivors.

I would be remiss if I did not thank those who guided me through the writing process with direction, ideas, and writing skills. Above all, I thank my late wife Liora who walked with me along most of this journey, traveling to Germany to visit the remnants of my father's concentration camp, his childhood home in Gyula, Hungary, the memorial of the victims of his family, and the home of my early childhood in Budapest. She read my numerous attempts at writing this story and helping me find my voice. Sadly, cancer took her at the prime of her life.

I thank my children Aharon Laufer, Tammar Stein and Dan Laufer for reading and re-reading my manuscripts, wisely critiquing and editing it, until it finally met their exacting standards. No one can be more blessed than having such smart children.

I am indebted to my friends Prudence (Prue) Thorner and Lydia Harris for their tireless efforts editing and re-editing the manuscript and their thoughtful recommendations.

Thanks also to Veronika Farfan-Fürész and Leslie Gabor for editing the Hungarian content of the manuscript.

Last but not least I would like to thank my dear friend Marcie Solomon for being at my side in the long process of publishing the book and directing me to the Academic Studies Press where I met Alessandra Anzani and Ekaterina (Kate) Yanduganova who performed the heavy lifting of the publication of this book.

Notes on Transliteration and Formatting

To maintain authenticity, I chose to follow the Hungarian spelling convention. For example, Tokay wine was spelled Tokaji wine, street names were capitalized as "Andrássy út" rather than Andrássy Út, and last names were written ahead of first names, e.g., Kenéz Tibi rather then Tibi Kenéz. When necessary, the correct pronunciation was indicated in the text.

I italicized all quoted conversations to indicate that they were reconstructed from memory or assumed to have happened based on my knowledge of some or all of the participants.

Foreword

Our family's story was shaped in fire. Two generations, my father's and mine, participated in some of the most significant events in Jewish history: the Holocaust and then the rebirth and growth of the state of Israel.

The Holocaust ravaged our family: my grandfather and four of his siblings, my half sister and her mother were murdered in Auschwitz, and my grandmother was shot on the banks of the Danube by Hungarian fascist thugs. Eight siblings of my wife's grandfather perished in various concentration camps. My father barely survived.

But then, three years after the Nazi surrender came the miracle of Israel's founding, the rebirth of the Jewish nation. I grew up in Israel. My generation was often called the first generation of redemption.

It would not be an exaggeration to compare the heavy blow of the Holocaust to the destruction of the First and Second Temples in terms of the loss to Jewish demography, learning, and culture. The six million dead were not merely people; they were rabbis, teachers, philosophers, scientists, poets, writers, artists, lawyers, doctors, accountants, businessmen, or children who lost their chance to make their mark. Their wisdom, talents, memories, potential inventions, medical cures, and economic growth died with them: a loss to the Jewish people and to the world.

My father, a Holocaust survivor, lost his first wife, infant daughter, and his parents, he witnessed the unimaginable collapse of the Hungarian army on the Don River Bend north of Stalingrad while suffering the vicious brutality of his Hungarian army commanders; he endured the horrors of slavery in a German concentration camp and the degeneration of post-war Hungary into a Stalinist dictatorship. He fled this new tyranny to Israel with his new wife at his side and me, their baby, on his back.

Like so many Holocaust survivors, he hardly spoke about his past. He kept the memories of his torment and losses to himself. But they remained vivid in his frequent nightmares. For me and my younger sister, his dreadful past was the "elephant" in our home; it was there, we knew it was horrific, but we ignored it. Psychologists can offer many theories for his silence. But without a doubt, my sister and I did not really want to know. We hardly asked about his childhood, his adulthood in Hungary and the Holocaust, worried that we might stumble on an embarrassing or horrifying piece of history. Like many young Israelis in those days, we were embarrassed by our father's victimhood. And when we did ask, we were satisfied with brief and laconic answers, just like bees and storks are all that children want to know about sex.

We often lose sight of the miracle that is the state of Israel. There is no other country founded in the twentieth century that made so much of itself. Whereas new African and Asian countries rise, gain independence and then fail to form stable governments and societies, and while Israel's Middle Eastern neighbors are ruled by autocratic regimes that promote ideologies of bigotry and hate; this tiny Middle Eastern democracy within less than seventy years has become a vibrant economy, a cultural and scientific hotbed, the home of Nobel laureates, some of the best universities on Earth, hatchery of multiple billion-dollar startups, and by necessity a powerful army, all the while springing metropolitan cities out of the desert sand and absorbing masses of broken refugees from the entire world.

It took half a millennium from Joshua's conquest of Canaan to reach the high point of King Solomon's kingdom. Modern day Israel has reached greatness in less than a century. The territorial expanse after the Six-Day War was comparable in Jewish history only to the size of King Solomon's empire.

I became an officer in the Israeli Defense Force barely a generation after my father's liberation from a German concentration camp. Along with men of my age and reservists my father's age, I served during the victories of the Six-Day War and the Yom Kippur War. In 1967, at age nineteen, I experienced desperation when powerful Goliath-like enemies tightened a noose around the neck of our young nation. Then, within hours on a sunny day in June, our David-like nation flung its slingshot—a daring and imaginative air attack—to deal a powerful blow to the Goliaths.

But in 1982, I also saw deceptive and thoughtless Israeli leaders take our country to a war in Lebanon that could not be won but that would sink us into a quagmire from which we have not yet fully emerged even decades later.

Much has happened in our family too. I cannot avoid trying to see through my father's eyes the marvel of the family that grew out of the seed of his own survival. He was left for dead on a bunk in a German concentration camp, delirious in the terminal stages of typhus. A day after his German captors fled, an American army doctor, Dr. Michael Shimkin, arrived and saved him and nearly two hundred of other dying prisoners. Had Dr. Shimkin arrived only a day or two later, they would have been dead.

In the course of history, only a few generations were fortunate to witness a stellar revival of a nation and victories as I did, or be cursed to live through defeat and disasters as my father did. Yet, my father died without ever telling his story and I am aging without having told mine.

Memories of our experiences and their lessons belong to our children and the generations to follow. We owe them our stories. I am my family's last surviving witness to many of these events and the only store of information for the rest. It is my duty, as the Passover Hagaddah and Elie Wiesel would say (1), to tell our story.

To learn about my father's past I contacted and visited archives in America, Hungary, Germany, and Israel, searched records of family members in three continents, read a vast volume of literature in three languages, interviewed relatives, gathered pictures from old albums and visited sites. And when documents and testimonies could no longer fill the gaps, I filled them with what I believed to be the most plausible accounts.

I pray that our stories will be source of inspiration and pride to our children and the generations to come. I hope that my father, wherever he may be, is smiling at this book with approval.

Let his memory be a blessing.

June 1942: Imprisoned in the *toloncház*

> *"I assess the power of a will by how much resistance, pain, torture it endures and knows how to turn to its advantage."*
>
> —Friedrich Nietzsche

Despite the hot summer that overwhelmed Budapest's streets and choked the residents in the tall apartment buildings and the elegant stores, László Laufer[1] cell in the infamous Mosonyi utcai tolonchàz[2] prison was damp, dark, and cold. The intense summer heat could not penetrate the thick brick and concrete walls. The large complex was completed in 1888 as part of a new Hungarian prison system. It was intended as a "collection" facility and was considered at that time as one of the most advanced prisons in Europe. Although it had central heating and electricity, it was never designed for comfort. But in 1942 conditions deteriorated even below the minimum that was acceptable the previous century. It was overcrowded and run down.

The *tolonchàz* was a quadrangle of four brick buildings built around an inner courtyard where prisoners got their daily walk. The gallows at the center of the courtyard reminded them that not everyone would be leaving the prison through the front gate. Those who resided in cells facing the yard knew that the gallows were indeed in use—quite often.

Each of the grim looking buildings was three stories tall with rows of cells arranged along long corridors. The cells were sealed with large steel doors. A small window at the top of each door was covered by a steel plate that could be opened only from the outside. Guards would occasionally lift the plate to peek in. Small openings at the bottom were barely wide enough to slide bowls with meals or remove the night pots that were emptied once a day. Even those openings were closed from the outside by steel plates.

---

1 My father, Dr. László Laufer. His name of endearment Laci is pronounced "Latzy."
2 *Tolonchàz* is a Hungarian term for detention center. Mosonyi utcai tolonchàz (pronounced "Moshonyee Outzayi Tolontzhaz") means "the detention center on Mosonyi Street."

The cell windows were protected with heavy steel bars. The whitewashed glass plates beyond the bars allowed some natural light in but deprived the prisoners of the little joy they might have from looking out. Once inside, prisoners were isolated from the outside world.

The cells were originally designed for single occupancy. But as the prison population grew they were modified for double occupancy. Although the cellmates had less space, they enjoyed some relief from the eternal boredom and despair with each other's company.

The large prison was within walking distance of the Keleti pályaudvar.[3] Many of the prisoners could hear the frequent whistles of the trains carrying carefree travelers in and out of Budapest and dream about exotic trips. Centrally located, the Mosonyi utcai toloncház became the ideal place to hold the ever-growing number of political prisoners and Jews. They could be easily removed from their offices and thrown into this enormous prison that swallowed them without a trace. *Tolonchaz* was Budapest's version of the Bastille in Paris, the Tower of London or Lubyanka in Moscow during their heydays.

Laci never told me that he had been in prison, though apparently, it was never a secret. His cousin Ági[4] knew about it. "Everyone knew," she told me. Laci did tell me that during the war – that's how he referred to the Holocaust – while in prison, he heard one night the gallows being prepared outside his cell. He was certain that they were being readied for him.

At that time I did not dare ask him why he was in prison, what prison or why he thought that he might be executed. I just assumed that this was another anecdote in a larger tale that took place in the alien world of concentration camps rather than downtown Budapest.

Laci also told me that our friend Mr. Miller (or Miller úr, as he called him in Hungarian) shared the cell with him. I knew Mr. Miller. He was a jeweler in Hungary but in Israel he was a part-time clerk for Új Kelet, the Israeli-published Hungarian paper. Miller taught me how to fold sheets of paper into airplanes, birds, and even a salt and pepper holder.

I stumbled on Laci's imprisonment account when reading his file in the archives of the Budapest Bar Association.[5] The file told the story of a young

---

3   The Eastern Railroad Station, pronounced "Kelety Payaoudvar."
4   Ági (Ágnes) Palócz, my first cousin once removed from Syracuse NY. Her father, Sándor Neumann was my paternal grandmother's brother. Ági was 16 years old at the end of the Holocaust, surviving by hiding in Budapest.
5   The files and other family documents in Hungary were located by Dr. Tibor Várkonyi, a Budapest lawyer.

and bright lawyer who was prevented from getting a law license by the discriminatory Jewish Laws.[6] Instead of the customary three year training period, Laci was forced to work as a law associate for seven years, until he was drafted into the Hungarian Forced Labor Battalions.

Three years later, after surviving the war and returning to Budapest, Laci could finally apply for a law license. The archived file included a declaration that his felony conviction and imprisonment in *tolonchāz* should not disqualify him because his crime, helping a Hungarian Jew to return from Germany to escape his fate there, was no longer a crime in post-war Hungary. He received his law license a few months later, ten years, rather than three years after graduation from law school.

The statement is concise, written in a lawyer's matter-of-fact language. It does not describe his first night in jail, alone, scared, desperate, and worried for his family. *"Men keep their feelings to themselves,"* he often told me. I can imagine his feelings though, all too easily.

A month earlier Laci was a free man, a Law Associate in the large law office of Dr. Lipót, a well-known Budapest lawyer. Today he was a convicted felon with 364 days remaining of his one-year sentence. The little cell had two bunk beds, his at the bottom, a small metal chair and a table bolted to the floor. The few rays that penetrated the whitewashed windows through cracks in the paint were all the sunlight that would enter his cell facing the inner courtyard.

On the upper bunk was Miller úr, a short, slim, white-haired man with a small white mustache. Miller was the jeweler who sold Laci the diamond engagement ring he gave to Lili[7] and soon after, their two wedding rings.

The diamond ring was a true artwork, one of Miller's best. The large, nearly perfect, glittering diamond was held by four branches that split from the ring itself making the solitary diamond appear as if it floated above the ring. Four rows of tiny diamonds decorated all four branches. Using nearly microscopic letters Miller engraved Lili's name on the inner surface. Miller had to prepare several models before Laci accepted this one.

---

6 Starting in 1938, Hungary began enacting anti-Jewish laws, better known as the Jewish Laws, aimed at restricting Jews from participation in various professions and enterprises. The first law limited the number of Jewish professionals including lawyers in Hungary to 20%. A year later, the Second Jewish Law reduced that number to 5%, the proportional representation of Jews in society. Since the number of practicing Jewish lawyers far exceeded that limit, new Jewish lawyers, including Laci, could not be admitted to the Bar. An early version of these laws, the Numerus Clausus (1920), limited enrollment of Jewish students in Hungarian universities.

7 Lili was my father's first wife, neé Liliá Rozenzweig.

Laci remembered Miller úr's arrest. He was prominent and well-liked in the Jewish community. Miller was the least likely person to be accused of aiding the enemy in a time of war. The case was discussed in Lipót's office even though he was not a client. It was egregious and demonstrated the tactics that the László Bárdossy government, one the most anti-Semitic governments in Hungarian history, was using against Jews. Bárdossy enacted the Jewish Laws that severely limited the participation of Jews in the Hungarian economy, outlawed marriage or even a sexual relationship between Jews and non-Jews. Bárdossy authorized the deportation of 16,000 Jews to Ukraine that was already under German occupation where they were slaughtered by the SS *Einsatzgruppen* (killing squads) near the town Kamianets-Podilskyi. (2)

Miller had been in the Mosonyi utcai tolonchaz since January. He was arrested on Sylvester Night.[8]

Even for Hungarians, who love a good party, Sylvester stands out as a unique party night. Little children stay awake until past midnight to welcome the New Year. Adults, Gentiles and Jews alike, celebrate by drinking, dining, and dancing. The ongoing war that the Bárdossy's government declared on the Soviet Union and the just-declared war on the United States barely diminished the intensity of the celebrations at the dawn of 1942. Siding with Germany, Hungarians felt that the German victory over Russia was imminent. They had already recovered territories they lost in the Great War and the gains of the new war would be theirs to share. The war on the US, most people agreed, was just politics to please the Germans. It would never amount to anything. Even the Jews who were suffering under the wrath of this anti-Semitic government felt hopeful. Of course, the new Jewish Laws were a serious blow and the ongoing hostile policies were a burden. But compared to the Jews of Poland, Czechoslovakia, Austria, and Germany who were confined in ghettos, deported to concentration camps and murdered by the thousands, the Hungarian Jews in Budapest felt they were safe.

Miller was returning home with his wife well past midnight after partying with friends in a restaurant on the Duna-korzó,[9] the beautiful strip of elegant restaurants and hotels along the Pest side of the Danube. From their table they could see on the Buda hills on the opposite side of the river, the illuminated Castle, and the Royal Palace. London, still fearing attacks by

---

8   The Hungarian popular name for New Year's Eve, it is derived from the name of the Catholic Pope Sylvester, the saint of the last day of the year.
9   The Danube promenade

German bombers, was dark that night. Paris under German occupation was depressed. But Budapest, the loyal Germany ally, had nothing to fear. All the lights were on that night.

After a wonderful dinner, washed down with sweet Tokaji wine and aromatic pálinka,[10] dancing the Csárdás to gypsy music and toasting champagne at midnight, Miller and his wife walked home along the Danube, past the magnificent Parliament building, enjoying the crisp cold night.

After passing Margit híd,[11] they turned onto the Nagykörút[12] towards Nyugati Pályaudvar,[13] leaving the Danube behind and then turned left towards Pozsonyi utca, one of the main streets of the new and mostly Jewish residential neighborhood. Their apartment was down the street on the fifth floor of an apartment building. Miller liked to brag that he could see the Danube from his balcony.

Despite the late hour, their custodian was standing at the open front door, the lobby behind him illuminated. It was unusual to see him out that late. The old man liked to retire early, even on Sylvester nights. But before the Millers could greet him, the concierge waved his hand towards someone across the street. Miller turned around. Two men wearing long dark coats and wide brimmed hats emerged from a parked black car with their hands in their pockets.

There were rumors of night raids by the secret police in Budapest along with accounts of people who vanished from their homes. Of course, few witnessed such raids and those who did, did not speak.

In a polite but firm tone, one of the men asked Miller to identify himself and then, without specifying any charge, told him that he was under arrest. The second man pulled him by the arm to the car, brutally pushed him into the back seat, and slammed the door. The two then sprang into the front seats and sped away.

Mrs. Miller remained standing on the cold sidewalk stunned, choking with tears. The concierge took her arm gently and led her into the warm lobby, closing the front door behind them and mumbling some apologies.

The side windows of the secret police car were covered by drapes. Miller could not and did not even try to see where he was being taken. But after speeding through empty streets the car stopped and his door was opened.

---

10   Distilled fruit brandy, usually plum, pear, apple, cherry or apricot.
11   Margit híd—"Margit Bridge" in Hungarian, pronounced "Margeet Heed."
12   Nagykörút—"Great Boulevard" or literally, "Big Ring Road" in Hungarian, pronounced "Nady Keuroot."
13   Nyugati Pályaudvar—"The Western Railroad Station" in Hungarian, pronounced "Nyugati Payaoudvar."

Miller recognized the building on Andrássy út, one of the most elegant streets in Budapest. He was about to enter the Secret Police building. The inscription at the entrance to Dante's Inferno flashed through his mind, "Abandon Hope All Ye Who Enter Here."

Without a word, the two men flanked Miller on both sides and almost carried him through the front door into the empty lobby. A sleepy policeman at the front desk waved them in. They took the steps down. The rumors were true, Miller thought, suspects were taken to the basement. The building was quiet. They entered a long corridor lined with rows of doors on both sides. The sounds of the steel-toed shoes of the two agents broke the quiet in the brightly illuminated corridor. Miller watched in horror the many doors they were passing. Who were the people locked behind them?

They reached the door of his cell. One of the men pulled a large key ring from his pocket, opened the door into a small cell and pushed Miller in. Miller heard the key turn and the sound of steel-toed shoes fading away. Less than an hour passed since he left the restaurant on the Korzó with his wife. What happened to her, he wondered, was she arrested too? He sat down slowly on the thin straw mattress covering a steel plate attached to the wall. He looked around the cell but nothing made sense. He was frightened and confused. The walls of the narrow cell were closing in on him. He tried to think what could be his crime. His mind was blank.

For three days, he did not see a person or talk to one. His meals were pushed in through a slot in the door and empty trays taken away. The only sounds were heavy steps along the corridor or the guards or agents bringing in new prisoners. One night, he heard a prisoner scream briefly.

On the fourth day, the door opened and Miller was taken to his first interrogation. The interrogation did not make sense. He did not understand why the interrogator asked so many questions and what their purpose was. When one interrogator was replaced by another, the new one repeated the same questions. Miller was exhausted, hungry, and scared.

After a week in jail, he was led for the first time to the shower and was handed a clean suit. He recognized it as his own. It was brought from home. Did his wife bring it in? *"Put it on when you're done showering,"* ordered the guard. *"Your trial is today."*

Nothing made sense, not even his crime of aiding the enemy at a time of war. He had not seen any foreigner since the war had broken out. He never traveled outside of Budapest and he did not speak any language other than Hungarian. He did not even listen to the BBC like some of his friends.

But then in the courtroom the prosecutor called his only witness, Mr. Szöllősi Árpád. Miller recognized the slim tall man. Szöllősi wore a perfectly tailored suit, his shoes shone, and his dark hair was meticulously combed. His appearance projected importance. Szöllősi was the director in the Ministry of Interior. He visited Miller's store last month.

When Szöllősi entered Miller's store with his wife, he demanded to see Miller. They were looking for diamond rings. Very quickly Mrs. Szöllősi set her eyes on a beautiful ring with a large diamond surrounded by seven smaller ones. Miller remembered that ring well.

But then Szöllősi pulled Miller to a corner, introduced himself and asked that the ring be given to his wife as a gift. Miller did not mind bribes. It was not unusual to extort Jews, particularly rich store owners. Miller despised those who demanded bribes but he saw it as an inseparable part of business, like insurance. But this was excessive. And there was no favor offered in exchange. Giving away that diamond would erase his profit for the entire holiday month. He tried to plead with Szöllősi, offered another excellent diamond, but Mrs. Szöllősi would not relent. Finally she stormed out the store angrily. Szöllősi followed her, calling Miller a "dirty Jew" and promising that he would hear from him.

Szöllősi stared briefly at Miller as he walked by him to the witness stand. Miller thought he saw a hint of a smile. Szöllősi spoke briefly. His testimony was sufficient to send Miller away for three years.

The next day, Miller was lying on the upper bunk in his cell in *tolonchaz* when the door opened and a new prisoner was pushed in.

That night his new cellmate was dragged out half asleep by two guards. The poor man could not even say goodbye. Soon, loud sounds of pounding hammers came from the inner court. The gallows were being readied for execution. From his upper bunk, through cracks in the paint on his window Miller could see his cellmate being dragged by the same two guards to the gallows. Minutes later, he was dead.

Miller remained alone in his cell. Szöllősi's curse followed him through the prison walls. Alone for months in his tiny cell, he feared that he too might hang on the gallows; until Laci was pushed in.

Four weeks before joining Miller, Laci was sitting at his desk in Lipót's office. Working for Dr. Lipót was depressing. Without a license, or prospects for getting one, Laci could not argue in court, have his own clients, write contracts or provide counsel. He was allowed to prepare court cases for younger and less capable lawyers, who were lucky to be born a Gentile. They used his work to win cases and promote their own careers. With their permission, he could sit with them when meeting clients that he himself brought to the office or write drafts for contracts that they then presented as their own without changing a word. When other young lawyers already had their own private offices, Laci still had to share an office with two young graduates of the Budapest law school who were not even in high school when he got his law degree.

That morning, his office door opened and two men wearing dark suits and Borsalino hats walked in without knocking.

"Is Dr. Laufer here?" one of them asked.

When he introduced himself, they asked him to join them. Flanked between the two, he was paraded through the waiting room and past the waiting clients. Mr. Lipót stood at his office door, visibly embarrassed. The two detectives intended that.

The walk with the agents was short. Lipót's office was near the courthouses and the central police station. Two of his colleagues passed him while walking between the two agents. They ignored him. Association with someone in the hands of the secret police could be dangerous.

Laci tried to speak to the agents, but they remained stone-faced and quiet. *"You will find out soon enough,"* was their only reply when asked where were they going and why. Laci could not remember any violation or any interaction with the authorities that could cause his arrest. But real guilt no longer mattered in Hungary, particularly if you were a Jew.

They arrived at the police station that he knew well. He was led to a small waiting room. The windowless walls were lined with wooden benches. The only decorations were two framed pictures hanging on the opposite wall. One was of Admiral Miklós Horthy, the Hungarian Regent, and the other of Prime Minister Bárdossy. Both faces were gravely serious.

He stepped into the room, the door behind him closed and the two silent detectives disappeared. There were two other doors to the room, closed as well. One of them must have led to an interrogation room. No sound came through these heavy doors. The white paint was peeling in the corners and the ceiling, but the room was clean. Laci knew about the interrogation rooms in this police station. He visited the station often for work and to meet clients. But he had never been in this part of the building. Prisoners' lawyers were not allowed there.

Hours passed, he was thirsty and hungry. He was arrested before lunch. He never ate breakfast but made it up at noon, but not today. He still had his watch; the agents did not take anything from him. The associates at the office had already left for the day. Lili must be expecting him home for dinner. Did anyone in the office tell Lili that he would not be home tonight?

Their daughter Laufer, Judit[14] was nearly a year-and-a-half old. She was a chubby little girl with black curly hair, and a twinkle in her eyes. Laci called her "Snow White," the beauty with charcoal dark black hair, blue eyes and snow-white skin. Judit loved running all over their apartment, climbing everywhere. She could even count her fingers on one hand.

Every evening she met him at the door when he returned from work, her arms raised, ready to be picked up and thrown in the air. Laci used to tease her. *"Tell me, Juditka, what would happen if I throw you in the air twice but catch you only once?"* She always laughed but Laci doubted she understood the joke.

He was dozing off, still sitting on the bench when one of the doors opened. A plain-clothes officer introduced himself as Captain Kovács. It was a common Hungarian name and Kovács looked the role of a Hungarian officer: tall, broad shoulders with a prominent *"handlebar"* moustache.

With a booming voice but very politely he invited Laci into the adjacent room and asked him to sit at one of the two empty chairs facing a desk. Kovács took the other chair facing Laci. He pulled out a cigarette, offered one to Laci and lit them. They smoked quietly for a moment when a prisoner in prison uniforms carried in two trays, one for Kovács and one for Laci. Kovács' tray had a steaming bowl of chicken soup, a plate of mouthwatering gulyás[15] with nokedli,[16] a small bowl of cucumber salad in cream and a slice of apple strudel. Laci's tray had a bowl of watery potato soup. Kovács started slurping his chicken soup praising its great qualities and watching Laci eat slowly his tasteless potato soup.

"Tell me, Dr. Laufer,"[17] started Kovács, *"In the last two years, have you been to Ipolyság?"*

Laci understood now why was he arrested. Approximately a year earlier, Lipót sent him to Ipolyság, a small town 100 km north of Budapest (now Šahy in Slovakia), to meet one of Lipót's colleagues Dr. Varannai István. Lipót did not explain Laci's assignment other than to meet Varannai at the courthouse.

"You must already know the answer if you brought me here," replied Laci.

"Indeed we do. But we need some more details."

"What is that you still don't know?"

---

14 Pronounced "Yoodeet."
15 Gulyás—the Hungarian spelling for goulash, pronounced "Gouyash."
16 Nokedli—small handmade Hungarian dumplings.
17 A law degree in Hungary conferred on its recipient the title Dr.

"You are not making this easy," said Kovács. "We already have your case fully prepared but we wanted to make sure that we do not make an error that might hurt you."

"Isn't it what courts are for?" Laci asked.

"Okay, let's see. Did you meet with a lawyer named Varannai in Ipolyság?"

"If you ask, you must know."

"Okay, did Varannai introduce you to a person named Kenedi Richard?"

Laci remembered meeting Varannai at the Ipolyság courthouse. He was Lipót's colleague and visited the office often. Varannai sat at a corner table in the court café together with a middle-aged disheveled man who was introduced as Mr. Kenedi.

Kenedi arrived from Germany a few days earlier. He was a Hungarian citizen who lived in Berlin for the last twenty years. The previous month he noted that both his German visa and Hungarian passport expired. Normally this would not be a problem, Hungary and Germany were allies, but Kenedi was a Jew. The Hungarian consulate in Berlin told him that to renew his German visa he would need to return to Hungary. They would not renew his passport either. But they gave him a temporary travel document valid for one-way trip to Hungary.

Once back in Hungary he discovered that as a Jew he could not get a new German visa. He also tried to renew his passport, hoping to travel to Switzerland instead. But under the pretext that Hungary was at war and needed all its men, his passport application was denied as well. With nowhere to go, Kenedi returned to Ipolyság, his childhood hometown.

In Ipolyság, Kenedi reported as required to the local police to apply for a residence permit. But this too was denied because there was no one left in Ipolyság, relatives or friends, who still remembered him and could vouch for an unemployed man, with no property or family, and a Jew to boot. Ironically, his passport was denied in Budapest because the nation needed him while his residence in Ipolyság was denied because he had been out of the country too long and was no longer considered a Hungarian. He was ordered to leave town within a week. Kenedi became a man without country.

Laci was surprised that Kovács knew about Kenedi and even more so that he had any interest in him. Kenedi was not a resident of Budapest. He was a refugee with no family, no assets, and no means to survive in Hungary. He came from Germany, a friendly country, where he lived for many years, and therefore was unlikely to be suspected as a spy. Was Kovács interested in him just because he was a Jew? Even if that was the reason, then what could Laci be blamed for?

"*Yes*" admitted Laci. "*I met Kenedi. Why would that be of any concern to the Budapest Police?*"

"*Right now I am the one who is asking questions. Let me help you. Did you recommend that Kenedi relocate to Verebély?*"

Laci's mind wandered back to the café in Ipolyság. He and Varannai were trying to find a place for Kenedi to go. He wanted to leave Hungary but was not allowed to, while at the same time his hometown would not let him stay. He had five days left before his legal stay expired. Once his permit expired, he would put himself and his hosts at the risk of arrest.

Kenedi was desperate and incredulous. He understood that his problem could not be resolved legally because the law contradicted itself.

But Lipót's office helped several refugees to relocate before and Laci knew that in some towns the local police was still hospitable to Jews. Verebély (now Vrable, Slovakia), a small town just north of the Danube was one of them. Laci knew the town well. Lili was born there. He even knew a lawyer there, Dr. Gönczöl Richárd.

Kovács's voice brought Laci back from his thoughts, "*Did you recommend that Kenedi relocate to Verebély?*"

"*I didn't recommend anything.*"

"*If you didn't recommend anything then how did Kenedi know about Dr. Gönczöl?*"

"*How am I supposed to know? He told me that he must leave Ipolyság because the police there would not give him residence papers and I told him that he must follow police orders.*"

"*Ah, we are making progress. You told him to leave Ipolyság.*"

"*No, I did not. The chief of police told him that.*"

"*But you told him to follow his order.*"

"*Is that a crime? Is that why I am here?*"

"*No it's not; it is what you told him next.*"

"*What is that?*" wondered Laci.

"*Look, I do not want to spend the whole night here. We know that you helped Kenedi forge residency documents. I do not care if you admit it or not. If necessary, Gönczöl will do that for you.*"

"*Are you telling me that you are accusing me of forgery? I have not been to Verebély in years.*"

"*Really? Didn't you visit Mr. and Mrs. Rozenzweig a few months ago?*"

"Oh yes, they are my in-laws. We visited them with our daughter. It was purely a family visit."

"Or could it also involve a little business? I'll tell you what, we just happened to have a cell open up downstairs. Hospitality is good here. Please stay overnight and we will continue tomorrow."

Laci was not prepared for the shock of spending a night in a little holding cell in the basement of the police station. He often met clients after a night there. They were disoriented, tired, and shaken. But he was too young and inexperienced to understand them. A colleague once told him that every trial lawyer should spend a night in jail, just to be able to understand his clients. Even after seeing so many clients after a night in jail, Laci was not prepared for the distress and shock of being thrown in and hearing the door slammed behind him. He felt trapped and helpless. He was no longer free to come or go, read, speak, eat or sleep as he chose. He had no friends there and did not know the rules. He was locked up for as long as Kovács wanted, a day or a week. He knew that the laws did not protect him. And thoughts of his personal disaster were followed by thoughts of Lili and Judit and what would happen to them tonight, tomorrow, the day after.

His colleague was wrong. Spending a night in a jail cell would not prepare a trial lawyer to empathize with his clients. All he would experience is the physical discomfort. A "guest" for a night would experience none of the psychological desperation, uncertainties, and the fears that accompany an indefinite imprisonment.

Finding himself alone in a jail cell was depressing. But at least he did not share the cell with another, potentially violent, criminal. He was hungry, thirsty, tired, and hurt. He now realized that he would be accused of forging Kenedi's papers. He met Kenedi once. He only suggested that he travel to Verebély to meet Gönczöl. Gönczöl was not a Jew but Laci considered him a trusted friend of Lili's parents. But the government was trying to isolate Jews and remove them from positions of influence and leadership by any means possible. Arresting Jews and jailing them served that purpose. Gönczöl must have been arrested after meeting Kenedi. Was it possible that Gönczöl was pressured and was now trying to save himself by shifting the blame to Laci?

Laci's first night in jail started early. At nine o'clock lights were off. His high, barred window faced the street. Standing on his bunk he could see a few clerks leaving their offices late and hurrying home. And then the streets were empty. A lone streetlight cast a yellow spot on the pavement. He counted the passing minutes. He tried to think of his meeting with Kovács and his possible defense when he would meet with him in the morning and then in court. He was sure that he would be accused of a crime, tried, and convicted. His only question was what crime and how long the jail time.

After a night that felt like eternity, the sun came up. A few rays emerged from behind the buildings facing his cell. A prison guard opened a steel door in the corridor. Laci could hear his heavy boots hitting the bare concrete. He stopped by Laci's cell, looked at him through the bars as if he was a monkey and kept walking without a word.

Half an hour later the same guard returned carrying a tray with two slices of dry bread, some jam, a slice of bacon and a cup of tea.

Hours passed by. No word from Kovács. At noon a guard brought a new tray with lunch: potato soup, a slice of roasted pork, mashed potatoes, and a slice of bread.

Late in the afternoon, a guard showed up with a note from Lipót. He already notified Lili of the arrest and made sure that she had all she needed. Laci should not worry about her and Judit. They were all right. His office is working on Laci's release, they were doing their best. "*Be strong,*" he offered.

Another night arrived. Laci had not left the cell since he arrived. He was still wearing the same clothes he wore to the office the day before. He had not washed or shaved. There was no running water in his cell. Other than his bunk, a night pot, and a tin can of water his cell was empty.

Days went by. No word from Kovács. No word from Lipót. Other than the guards and an occasional prisoner being escorted in or out of his cell, Laci did not see a human being or speak to one. Without anything to read, time crawled at a snail's pace. Laci never imagined that days could be that long. Minutes felt like hours. But he had now time to think about the events that had got him here, about Lili and their little daughter Judit. He was no longer sure if he would be accused of anything or simply be kept indefinitely, forgotten and neglected.

One morning, a cheerful guard opened his door. "*Good news, Dr. Laufer,*" he said. "*You are leaving us.*" Seeing the door open was a relief. At least he was not forgotten.

He was leaving, but not for home. A prison truck waited at the back exit. He was ordered to climb into the back cabin. It was a prison cell on wheels. The door was locked and the truck drove away.

The ride to Ipolyság took two hours. Through the prison truck's portholes Laci could see the road passing by. He had been on that road before, riding the bus, and he remembered it as long and tedious. But now despite the truck's crude conditions, the ride felt pleasant. Being outside his jail cell after days of solitary confinement, hearing sounds, seeing people and other cars along the road was exhilarating. For a moment he forgot his helplessness and the apathy that was overcoming him. The world outside continued its flow as usual. He hoped that at the end of this trip he would rejoin that world.

The jail in Ipolyság was similar to that in Budapest, as if the same architect designed both. But unlike Budapest, Laci now had a cellmate, a thief, also awaiting his trial.

The trial in the Ipolyság court was brief, only one witness, Gönczöl. Varannai, who was hired by Lipót, was Laci's lawyer. Gönczöl was dressed in a freshly pressed and clean suit and a tie, such a contrast to Laci's appearance. But Gönczöl was the prosecution's witness. He told briefly how he was instructed by Dr. Laufer to buy papers for Laufer's client Kenedi and how Laufer paid for that. He then said how glad he was that thanks to a routine round-up, Kenedi was arrested by the Verebély police. Gönczöl apologized for what he did, asking for forgiveness.

Lili and Laci's father, Sándor[18] Laufer, sat in the courtroom behind him. Lili tried to whisper a few words but the guard ordered her to stop. Laci only hoped that they did not believe Gönczöl's lies.

His sentence, one year in jail, was decided by the judge while still on the bench—without any deliberation. As soon as the short verdict was announced, Laci was handcuffed and carried away. He could not talk to Lili. He only saw her wiping a tear, while Sándor remained stone faced.

He knew that Lili will now depend on Sándor. He resented it. He did not expect that at age of twenty-eight he and his family would still have to depend on his father. Had he not been a Jew, he would have been a lawyer running his own practice by this time. And now he was a convicted criminal. He might never become a lawyer.

Late that afternoon Laci entered the arched gate of the notorious *toloncház*, not as a lawyer visiting his clients but as a convicted criminal. He was taken to a small office where he was registered and assigned his number. From there he was escorted to a shower room and ordered to undress. His dirty, crumpled clothing and other possessions were collected in a large canvas sack that was tied with a string and taken away. He was then ordered to shower. The warm water and the coarse soap felt luxurious. After drying up with a small and coarse towel, he was deloused, and then, while still naked, taken to the

---

18 Pronounced "Shaandor."

prison barber who shaved his head. Finally, he was taken to the storeroom. Two prisoners behind a counter gave him prison underwear, socks, striped uniforms, and a pair of clogs. The aspiring legal associate from Lipót's office was now officially a prisoner.

Lying on the bottom bunk in the *toloncház*, Miller above him, Laci recalled the last few weeks. A routine meeting with a client turned into a nightmare. Miller, speaking to him from the upper bunk, reminded him that he was now in prison.

Laci settled into the new routine. Every morning at five the ceiling lights went on and a guard checked on the prisoners through the window in the door. At seven o'clock two prisoners rolled a cart through the corridor and collected the night pots through the bottom slot in the door. With the stench barely cleared, another group of prisoners rolled in breakfast. Morning walk was usually at 10. Groups of 50 prisoners were taken to the inner court and ordered to walk in circles along the walls, watched from the roof by armed guards. Walks were cancelled when it rained. After an hour they were returned to their cells where they remained until the next day. Lunch was served at noon and dinner at six. Lights were out at nine.

The prison did not provide any reading material. Once a month prisoners were allowed to receive one book from home. They could share their books with their cellmates. Miller had four books.

One night Laci and Miller woke up to the sound of pounding hammers. They knew what those sounds meant. Heavy boots of the night guard sounded in the corridor getting closer to their cell. Were they coming for Laci or Miller? But the guard passed them and opened the adjacent cell. A few minutes later, the boots sounded again walking in the opposite direction. This time they were accompanied by the sound of a pair of wooden clogs making their last steps.

Through the cracks in their window paint they saw the illuminated gallows. Two prisoners in striped uniforms finished attaching two ropes and left. Another door opened and two prisoners were dragged out. Laci could not watch them die. He lay on his bunk and plugged his ears.

Morning came as usual, at six. After breakfast, the cell door was opened and a guard ordered Laci to follow him. It was unusual for a prisoner to leave his cell that early. The gallows were ready, Laci thought, but they had not used them in the morning.

They walked through two gates that were opened as they approached and then closed behind them; they went downstairs and entered a small office on the first floor. Behind the desk sat a prison official dressed in jacket and tie. Across the desk sat Lipót, smiling broadly.

Laci looked at him in disbelief unable to speak. Was he going home?

After a moment that felt like eternity, the prison official broke the silence and ordered him to follow the guard and collect his belongings. Lipót had managed to get him released before his time was up!

Laci stood outside the front gate of the Mosonyi utcai toloncház. He was unshaved and thin, dressed in the same suit he wore more than a month earlier. Lili and Judit were waiting for him on the sidewalk. As soon as Judit saw him she ran to him with her arms up ready to be lifted and thrown in the air. She had not forgotten her Dad.

July 1942: Budapest

Böske's[1] small apartment seemed like a palace to Laci when he entered. It was an expensive apartment in an exclusive fashionable neighborhood. After weeks on a bunk bed in the Mosonyi utcai toloncház in the shadow of gallows, even a shack in Csepel[2] would have looked like a palace. Laci's mother, Böske, together with Lili, had furnished it lavishly and tastefully. A hearty breakfast waited on the table. Freshly cut salami and gyulai sausage[3] on a tray along with blocks of cheese. Slices of freshly baked soft white bread filled the breadbasket next to two jars of homemade apricot and plum jams. A strong coffee brewing in the kitchen contributed to the warm symphony of aromas that filled the welcoming space.

When Lili opened the door, Böske left the kitchen and ran to hug Laci. "*I knew that Lipót will get you out,*" she said with tears filling her eyes. "*He never abandons his friends. Dad was sure you would be out soon. We never doubted that you did the right thing.*"

After a long bath, Laci sat down with the three generations of Laufer women for a late breakfast. As usual, Böske, a plump woman with sharp facial features that Laci inherited, controlled the conversation. When she spoke, even the usually chatty Judit kept quiet: Böske was greatly respected and admired.

Nearly twenty years earlier, during the rapid inflationary years when the old Austro-Hungarian Korona diminished in value from moment to moment, Böske insisted that Sándor buy this apartment.[4] Böske never made secret that it was also her idea to buy the lumberyard in Gyula as well as the adjacent house that her great uncle Adolf once owned.

---

1 Laufer, Berta (Böske)—pronounced "Boeshke."
2 Csepel—an industrial working class neighborhood in Budapest.
3 Gyula (pronounced "Dyoola") was Laci's birth town but also the home of one the best Hungarian sausages.
4 It was on Pasaréti út, a residential Budapest neighborhood with houses surrounded by yards and trees.

"Laci," said Böske, "I spoke to Lipót when he came to pick up Lili and Judit and told him that I will not let you go to the office today. You would not believe it; he laughed and said that you do not need to come in until Monday. That means that he is keeping you despite your conviction."

"It is very kind of him, Mama. But I was arrested because I helped his client. He owes me at least that little favor."

"I know that. But he got you out of jail, gave you four days off to recover, and most important, kept your job. Other lawyers are letting their associates take the fall."

After breakfast, Lili invited Laci for a walk.

They left the building and turned into a little park just around the corner. They found their regular spot under a tree at the edge of the park and sat down. They remained quiet for a while. It was unusual. They have not seen each other for more than a month. Laci hugged Lili but she was tense, clearly her mind was elsewhere.

Finally, hesitantly, she broke the silence. She had bad news, far more serious than his legal troubles or his prison term.

Laci sat quietly unable to imagine what that could be. Was it his parents' health, her own, or God forbid, Judit?

"You got a letter from Honvédség.[5] They want you," She finally summoned the courage to utter.

"Am I being drafted for Munkaszolgálat?[6] Impossible! There must be an error. They are only drafting Jews and Gypsies from rural areas. They are not touching anyone in Budapest."

Lili knew that. But the order was sent to Sándor's address on Béke sugárút in Gyula.

Sándor had immediately called Lipót who also thought that Laci's draft was a clerical error.

"He even called Kenéz Tibi in Gyula and asked him to check if this draft notice is legitimate," Lili explained, her words coming out in a gush. Sándor had begged Lili not to tell Böske, not until Laci was back.

Tibi a lawyer and an old family friend, had gone to see the főispán of Békés County[7] (the County governor) who assured him that this was not an error. Since the war with the Soviets was intensifying and the Hungarian losses were

---

5 Honvédség (pronounced Honveedsheeg)—"Home Defense," as the Hungarian Army was called.
6 Munkaszolgálat (pronounced Moonkasolgaalat)—"Work Service" in Hungarian. The army-run forced labor battalions set up primarily for Jews and Roma.
7 Főispán (pronounced "feuishpaan")—the governor of a county.

growing rapidly, many counties including Békés were given new recruiting quotas. The főispán's office knew that Laci lived in Budapest. But since Laci grew up in Gyula he remained eligible for this draft. The draft that was sent ordered Laci to report next week.

"So that's how Lipót got me out of jail," Laci observed bitterly, "so that I could report to the army next week."

"Yes, but Kenéz got you one thing. He could not get you out but he got the főispán to postpone your date until mid-August. You now have nearly a month with us, sweetheart."

They started walking back home holding hands. The bright sun that only an hour ago caressed them had turned into a burning flame. They were quiet, immersed in thoughts. Laci was thinking what this draft could mean to him and his family. Hardly any information had come back from his Gyula friends who were already serving in the Hungarian Labor Battalions.

Newspaper articles were cheerful and optimistic. They made the war look like a game that would be decided by square kilometers occupied and casualties inflicted on the enemy. They reported a rapid advancement of the German forces together with the Hungarian Second Army through the Steppe, the Ukrainian wide plains, towards Voronezh and the Don River. Together with the German Fourth Panzer Army, they already captured Voronezh and were heading towards Stalingrad. The Hungarian Army was described as an integral part of the Blitzkrieg (lightning war) strategy where German tank divisions stormed through the vast plains, capturing one city after another followed by the Hungarian infantry that cleared the resistance still left behind. After they captured Stalingrad, the headlines predicted, the road to Moscow and the natural resources in the Urals would open up. Victory was in sight. For those not involved directly, these projections were exciting. War was great.

But Laci also heard rumors that the papers did not report. There were heavy casualties, suffered mostly by the poorly trained and ill-equipped Hungarian Army. In a small country like Hungary it was difficult to hide thousands of families who had lost a son or a father and the maimed men on the streets, some blind and disfigured and many, too many, begging for money and food.

Laci knew of two Jewish families who lost a son serving in a Labor Battalion in Ukraine. Very few letters arrived from the front and so far none of the Gyula recruits had returned on leave. Casualties could be much higher. And although by law his draft was limited to one year, he feared that the same arbitrary law that put him in jail would also find a way to extend his service.

This picture of Sándor and Böske in Piazza San Marco in Venice (1936) shows that Laci and his sister Évi inherited their sharp facial features from Böske. Sándor, whom as a child I imagined as tall and slim was in fact short and plump with a round smiling face, hardly the rigorous father that Laci painted to me. It seems that Böske was the strict parent.

At least in in his prison cell he could count down the days of his sentence. And certainly the gallows' appetite for fodder was much smaller than the Russian guns'.

Maybe the family, he thought, should return to Gyula. At least there Lili and Judit could live in the big house with Sándor. And unlike Budapest, where

One of only two pictures I have of Judit. It is undated; I can only guess that her age is 12-18 months.

they already experienced occasional food shortages, food in Gyula would be plentiful. They had a large yard, if needed they could grow their own food, raise their own chickens, and what they could not produce they could find at a local farm. It would be good for Judit to be in the country, surrounded by nature, and with her grandfather. It might help her overcome the separation from her father.

But what would Lili do in Gyula? It was a small town where she had no friends. Laci's mind was racing with many problems and too few solutions. Maybe she could help Sándor run the lumberyard office. Now that Böske was staying in Budapest to help Évi, Laci's sister, who was pregnant, Sándor might be happy to have another pair of hands.

Böske was seating in the kitchen when they returned, holding Judit on her lap and helping her eat her favorite dish, rice in milk, sprinkled with sugar and cinnamon. With her little spoon Judit fished the rice out of the milk one grain at a time and sucked it with joy, as if it were candy. The smell of roasting veal and onions filled the apartment and drew Laci to the stove like a magnet. Small round potatoes boiled in a pot of water next to the skillet. The meal was nearly ready. Böske handed Judit over to Lili, drained the boiling water into the sink, put the potatoes in another skillet with melted butter and stirred in thinly chopped fresh parsley adding its fresh smell to the aromas of her cooking.

The table in the kitchen, covered with white tablecloth, was already set for three adults. It was simple but elegant with Böske's best plates, silverware, and the most elegant cloth napkins. A large covered pot stood at the center of the table. Slight condensation on the outside indicated that it was filled with cold soup. It was not quite the season for plum soup and too late for sour cherry soup. It had to be apricot soup, a refreshing sweet and tart appetizer or dessert. Böske must have cooked it the previous night and chilled it overnight.

As they were sitting down to the table, Lili reached in a small cabinet and pulled out a bottle of barack pálinka[8] with three shot glasses. "*We have something to celebrate. Right?*" she announced happily and filled the glasses.

Laci was wondering how Lili could keep such carefree attitude knowing what was coming. Böske lifted her glass with one hand while wiping a tear with another. Laci inhaled the perfume-like apricot aroma before drinking it in one quick swig.

Lili ladled into their bowls the yellowish soup with large apricots grown in their yard in Gyula. The cold sweet soup was refreshing. Laci tried to set aside his worries and enjoy this wonderful meal with his beloved family.

The conversation around the table was deliberately carefree. Judit giggled as Lili played with her, trying to distract herself. Laci told Böske about Miller's misfortune, about Kovács who interrogated him, and the cell in the *toloncház*. Böske asked about the food and the bed and the showers and if anyone had lice. Laci did not tell her about Miller's first cellmate, the gallows, last night's executions, or his own fears that he could be the next.

The conversation animated Judit. She waved her hands to draw attention and then accidentally hit her bowl and spilled the remaining milk and rice on the floor. Lili rose, wiped the floor and when she returned to the table she carried three small bowls with chestnut puree topped with a generous heaping of whipped cream from the icebox in the corner, Laci's favorite dessert.

---

8   Apricot brandy

It was late afternoon when Laci and Lili woke up from their nap. Judit was already standing quietly at the door in her long nightgown, waiting for her parents to wake up. When she heard the sound of her mother getting out of bed, she knocked quietly on the door.

"*Hi, sweetheart, come in and hop into the bed,*" called Laci.

Without a word, Judit rushed in and jumped on the bed next to Laci and curled up under the sheet covering him. "*Train, train?*" she asked using one of the few words she already knew.

Laci, laying on his back, pulled the sheet over their heads put her on his knees, started rocking them as if they were inside a train compartment and started singing her favorite song.

Megy a gőzös, megy a gőzös Kanizsára,[9]
Kanizsai, Kanizsai állomásra.
Elől ül a kicsi Judit,
Ki a gőzöst, ki a gőzöst oda viszi
(The train is going, the train is going to Kanizsa
The station, the station of Kanizsa,
At the front sits little Judit
Who is driving, who is driving the train)

They played the train game for some time. Meanwhile, Lili dressed up in a sleeveless summer dress, put on a pearl necklace and matching earrings. When she was ready, she stood at the door and announced that they were all going out to have ice cream.

Judit jumped out of the bed and started dancing in joy. She already knew that when Mama wanted ice cream, it meant going to her favorite place, the Gerbeaud. Judit ran to her room and pulled out a dress that was an exact match to her mother's. Within minutes they all were at the door.

Böske was already gone. Quietly, while all were resting she slipped out and walked to Évi's house as she did every afternoon.

Laci, Lili and Judit took a tram to Váci utca, one of the most elegant streets in Budapest. Despite the ongoing war, its stores were still beautifully decorated and shoppers were still hunting for luxury goods. The sun was already low in the sky, but the heat radiating from the buildings on both sides of the street kept the air hot. Young couples strolled arm in arm, inspecting the store windows

---

9 An old Hungarian children song. Records of at least one version date back to 1904.

and enjoying the afternoon as if there was no war, no compulsory labor service, no war casualties or prisoners in the *toloncház*. Judit walked between Laci and Lili, holding their hands.

They entered Vörösmarty tér, a large square named after the renowned Hungarian poet. A large statue of Vörösmarty sitting on a throne dominated the square. A small park behind it featured a fountain with two lions. Judit had no interest in any of these. She was heading through the square to a large, blindingly white, building with its ground level decorated with awnings. Elegantly dressed patrons sat at small tables sheltered by the awnings from the sun enjoying the best cakes and ice cream in Budapest. This was Gerbeaud, the epicenter of Hungarian patisserie.

Judit pulled her hand out of Laci's and ran towards the café. Laci and Lili watched her arrive at the patio, stop and look back to confirm that her parents were following her. When they reached the cafe, the headwaiter stepped out to the street to greet them by their name and even bowed to acknowledge little Judit. Judit already knew the routine. She offered him her hand and the waiter took it delicately as if she was a princess. "*Kezét csókolom kisasszony,*"[10] he said, gently kissing the tips of her fingers. Laci laughed in surprise at this new trick as they were led to their table under an awning facing the street. Laci and Lili loved watching people parade by.

A waiter approached them and asked, "*The usual?*"

"Today we are celebrating," Laci said, "*so please add whipped cream to Judit's ice cream and to our coffees as well.*"

Within minutes the waiter returned holding a tray balanced in one hand held over his head. He maneuvered among the tables as if the tray was weightless and when he reached their table he lowered it gently showing its delightful content.

In front of Lili he placed a white cake covered with a layer of white chocolate and laced lines of dark chocolate. "*Eszterházy cake for Madame.*" Next to Laci he placed a layered chocolate cake covered with a shiny layer of hardened caramel. "*Dobos cake for you, Doctor.*" Laci took his teaspoon and tapped the top of the cake lightly as if it was a drum. Finally he put a small silver bowl in front of Judit who was waiting patiently for her turn. The pink strawberry ice cream ball and white vanilla ball were barely visible under the mountain of whipped cream.

Soon their drinks arrived, a large glass filled with bubbly red soda for Judit and small cups with strong coffee topped with small floating icebergs of whipped cream.

---

10   "*I kiss your hand, young lady.*"

"You know, last night I would not have dared to dream that tonight I would be sitting in Gerbeaud with you and Judit," said Laci.

"I already knew last night that you are coming home. But I was too scared to believe it."

"Did Judit miss me?"

"Of course, but after a few days you could not tell unless you knew her. Every morning your mother took her out to play in the square. I think she spoiled her with a few ice creams and taught her the 'Kiss your hands' routine. In the afternoons we all went to the wave pool on Margitsziget. But at night she cried for you. It was hard putting her to bed. Almost every night she had nightmares. She was scared and was calling out for you."

That evening, after Judit went to bed, the three adults sat outside on the balcony to enjoy the evening breeze. In the distance, a Gypsy band played at one of the restaurants. Faint sounds of joy and laughter came from the park across the street where teenagers congregated after dark. The balcony lights were turned off to keep mosquitoes and moths away. A rising half-moon illuminated the treetops with an orange glow. Laci smoked, consumed by his thoughts and worries.

Lili watched him silently, knowing that he was contemplating how to break the bad news to his mother. Finally, like ripping off a Band-Aid, he blurted out that he was called up for Labor Service (Munkaszolgálat). Lipót had told him this morning, he said, trying to protect Lili from Böske's wrath.

There was silence.

Böske looked at Laci in disbelief. In the dim light coming from the street Laci could see her turn pale. She fully comprehended the terrible implications of this draft. She was not a woman to be fooled. Lili pretended to be surprised, looking down and clasping her hands.

Finally Böske spoke in disbelief. It was impossible, she sputtered. The army was only drafting Jewish men for the Labor Service from the countryside. Laci lived in Budapest. He could not be drafted, she insisted, there must be an error and Lipót should fix it.

Laci agreed with her saying that he too had claimed the same when Lipót told him about the draft. But Lipót already tried all he could do. He even asked Sándor asking him to see the főispán in Gyula. But all the főispán could do was to postpone the reporting date until mid-August.

"Apparently the casualties at the Russian front were heavy and the Army raised the recruiting quotas."

"So does it mean that you will be sent to Ukraine?" Böske asked worriedly.

"From what I heard, they sent the Kolozsvár and Nagyvárad recruits to Ukraine. (3) Do you remember my classmate Diósi Imre? (4) His brother Lajos was drafted early in June. When their train stopped in Gomel, one of his friends met a soldier he knew from Gyula and asked him to mail a postcard for him. I heard that story just before I was arrested but did not think much of it."

"Where is Gomel?" asked Lili breaking her silence for the first time.

"I am not sure. Near Minsk, I think. It is in that part of Belarus that was controlled by the Soviets and now is German."

"How far is it from the front?" asked Böske, trying to cut through the irrelevant chatter.

"I don't know. I don't even know what the MUSZ[11] are doing there. For all I know they may be rebuilding the bombed city."

"If that is the case, why do they need to recruit Jews from Gyula? Couldn't they use men from Gomel? It is their city after all."

"I really don't know, Mama. There's no point in speculating. I may also be sent to the West, away from the front, to work on a farm helping Hungarian farmers."

---

11 MUSZ—short for *Munkaszolgálat*. The abbreviation "MUSZ" was widely used to describe the Forced Labor Battalions. The servicemen in those battalions were called *muszos* (pronounced "moososh," that is, those who belong to the MUSZ). However, for simplicity, the servicemen will also be called MUSZ throughout this text.

August 1942: Leaving Gyula

Laci was called up to serve as a second-class service man, not quite a soldier, but not a civilian either. He might not have known it but he certainly suspected that commanders of many of the MUSZ units, particularly those in Ukraine, resolved to actively destroy their own servicemen. (5)

Imre Diósi, one of the last men to leave Gyula for the Labor Service, wrote that when he left there were no young Jewish men left in town, only women and old or sick men. They had not heard from his brother or most of his friends who were drafted in June, *"not a single letter, not a single sign of life."* (4 p. 9) At the door, his mother hugged him and said *"I know that I am seeing you for the last time,"* And when he hugged his father in the train station just before boarding the train, he promised, *"if there is only one person who survives all of it and returns, it is going to be me."*

Laci, Lili, and Judit left Budapest to return to Gyula on Saturday. Laci was due to report for duty ten days later.

Judit was giddy. She was looking forward to her first train ride. On the way to the Keleti pályaudvar to catch their train to Gyula she babbled *"train, train,"* trying to imitate her favorite song.

Their taxi stopped in front of the large and striking building. Statues of James Watt, the man who revolutionized the steam engine, and George Stephenson who built the first steam locomotive engine looked down at the arriving and departing passengers from the tall arched façade. The chaotic commotion scared Judit who started crying. Lili held her in her arms while Laci unloaded their suitcases. Böske meanwhile found a porter who loaded their luggage on his cart.

They walked through the vast main hall. A large timetable on the wall showed that their train would leave in twenty minutes. Peddlers who sold everything from newspapers to shoe laces to poppy seed cakes filled up the air with their yells promoting their ware. Near the entrance to their ramp stood a shoeshine man, leaning on his tall, throne-like chair. He was an old man wearing a tall hat. His curled up mustache gave him the appearance of a permanent smile. Seeing Judit crying, he invited her to sit on the empty throne. Judit's smile returned as she took her seat. The shoeshine man pretended to polish her shoes making her laugh loudly.

"*We must go.*" Laci interrupted the fun, giving a pengő[1] (6) (7) coin to the shoeshine man.

Their first-class car was the furthest away from the steam locomotive, at a comfortable distance from its smoke, coal ash and noise. Böske and the porter were already at the door. Although not traveling with them, Böske climbed in the car, found their compartment and sat with them, trying to savor their last few minutes together. The porter carried their luggage and placed it on the racks overhead. Heavy feelings of foreboding hovered in the air.

The unknown was too much to bear. Laci was on his way to the front. The security of his small family was no longer up to him. It was now on his father's shoulders. The political uncertainty in Europe and in Hungary and the ever-increasing anti-Semitism were a constant source of worry. Now, with Laci's upcoming military service they seemed even more intimidating.

Lili was not looking forward to this trip. She never liked Gyula. It was too small for her taste and too provincial. She loved Sándor but she dreaded living with him for so long without Laci at her side.

The conductor blew his whistle and Böske, holding back her tears, hugged Judit and Laci one last time and got off the train. The conductor slammed the car's door and the train started moving slowly, leaving behind Budapest. Judit stood on her seat, her face affixed to the window. Soon they were in a vast flat land covered with wheat, corn, and sunflower fields, traveling through the fertile Hungarian Low Land. Gyula was at the far end of this Hungarian breadbasket.

Though they had no way knowing it, this was the last time Laci would see Böske. By the time he returned from the Russian front and German concentration camps nearly three years later, she would be dead, shot by Arrow Cross thugs along with the other residents of a Swedish-protected house on Tátra utca 20/c.

Five hours after leaving Budapest, the train stopped in Gyula station, a small red brick building with a red shingle roof that Sándor built thirty

---

1 Pengő—the Hungarian currency at that time. A post-war hyperinflation, the worst the world had ever known, destroyed its value. At the end of July, 1946 prices increased daily by an average of 158,486 %. The pengő was replaced by the forint.

years earlier as a railroad construction manager. He came to Gyula from Babócsa, a small town on the Croatian border, for this job, met Böske and married her.

When he saw Judit leaning out the open window and waving excitedly at the few people standing on the tarmac he ran towards their car reaching it just as the train stopped. Judit was the first to step out, right into his arms. He lifted her up in the air making her squeal in joy. She was his first grandchild and he adored her. He then put her down, reached into his pocket and pulled out a wrapped candy. Judit remembered his candies. She took it cheerfully and got busy unwrapping.

Sándor waited patiently until the candy was safely in her mouth and then took Lili's hand and kissed it. He was the consummate Hungarian gentleman, always bowing to ladies, holding the door for them and kissing their hands. Then Laci and Sándor hugged each other and Laci kissed Sándor on both cheeks. A bystander watching the happy reunion would never suspect their anguish.

A porter climbed into the train, collected their luggage and arranged it on his cart that he then pushed through to a small courtyard out front where a horse buggy was already waiting. Gyula had few automobiles and although Sándor could afford it, he never owned one. Twenty years later, Laci would be the first in our family to take driving lessons. The porter loaded their luggage took the reins and headed out along a wide, oak tree-lined road leading towards Laci's childhood home.

When they arrived, Erzsi néni (aunty Erzsi), their live-in maid, was waiting by the door of their single-story house. Erzsi, a short, plump woman, wore a white headscarf and an apron. She moved into the maid's quarters at the back of the house shortly after Sándor built it, when Laci was fifteen years old. She had been with them through good and bad times: when Laci graduated high school and went to Szeged Law School, when his little brother Gyuri died from appendicitis, and when Laci and Lili married. Erzsi never had children of her own. Laci, Évi, and Gyuri were like hers, and Judit, whom she now met for the first time, was her granddaughter too.

Erzsi ran to the buggy with open arms before it even stopped. She picked up Judit. Judit, surprised, could not decide if she should cry or laugh. But a candy in Erzsi's hand convinced her that she had a new friend.

The buggy driver tied the reins to a tree and carried their suitcases into the house. Three rooms opened from the living room. To the right was Sándor and Böske's bedroom; to the left were what used to be Évi's room and the boys' room. Laci, as if by habit, walked to the boys' room. It would become Lili and Judit's quarters after he left in ten days' time.

The living room was pleasantly cool. The thick brick walls and the drawn curtains kept the heat of the afternoon sun out. The large cherrywood dining table at the center of the room was covered with a white hand-embroidered tablecloth and set for a late lunch with beautiful Herendi[2] porcelain plates and Czech crystal glasses. These precious dishes and glasses were kept in a locked cabinet and taken out only on special occasions, on Böske's orders. Matching linen napkins were meticulously folded into triangles under the silver knives. A big glass bowl on the table was already filled with plum soup. When Laci and Gyuri were boys, Erzsi would send them to pick plums for soup, cakes, and jam. Laci wondered who picked the plums now. Soon Judit would be able to do it. A large basket was filled with freshly sliced white bread. Wonderful smells of Laci's favorite dishes came from the kitchen.

Standing in the living room by the lavish table, with an ample lunch being readied in the kitchen, one could think that times had not changed. Sándor's business was still robust; the local synagogue was still a lively center of Jewish life, though most of the young men were already gone. Food in Gyula was still abundant and life for non-Jews was still good.

But even in little Gyula, where neighbors used to be like family, anti-Semitism was already vicious. A Schwab owner of a local swimming pool hung a sign at the entrance of his facility declaring "No entrance to Jews and dogs." (4 p. 4) Many Schwabs, even those who lived in Gyula for generations, were aligned with the Nazis. In coffee houses frequented by the Fascist Arrow Cross members, anti-Semitism and bigotry were discussed openly. No one dared to object or antagonize the violent thugs. The hospital's chief doctor was arrested and tried for listening to the BBC short wave radio. Outside the Laufer living room, dark clouds were already rolling in.

After lunch, they all retired to their rooms.

Laci and Judit were the first ones up after a short nap. They tiptoed out quietly, leaving Lili asleep. Through the back door they sneaked to the large backyard. From the back porch they could see the yellow plum trees still loaded with fruit. A few ripe apricots still hung out of reach at the top of the apricot tree. Birds would eventually eat them. The vegetable garden was lush and verdant. Large green and red peppers hung from some of the plants and vines of pickling cucumbers grew on wooden trellises. On the kitchen windowsill,

---

2   Herendi—a Hungarian luxury porcelain manufactured in the town Herend.

Erzsi had recently put a batch of pickling cucumbers in salt brine, covered with a bunch of dill and a slice of white bread. In two days, they would be ready and Erzsi would store them away in the basement for the winter along with delicious Gyulai sausages, ham, bacon, canned fruits and vegetables, and jams. In the fall she would add crates of apples after sorting out the bruised ones, as well as bags of potatoes, beets and onions.

Beyond the large garden stretched Sándor's lumberyard. It once belonged to Adolf, Böske's great uncle. Sándor bought it more than twenty years earlier after making money in several clever deals.

Adolf had died a few years after they moved to the house by the lumberyard. Laci and his family used to sit next to Uncle Adolf during Friday night, Saturday and high-holiday services, by the east wall of the synagogue, where seats were reserved for the rich donors. Adolf always arrived wearing a black suit, top hat and a large medal hanging from a gold chain. A plaque on the east wall reminded all congregants that Adolf Czinczár was the congregation's president when it was built.

Laci did not remember ever speaking to Adolf. He just remembered Sándor and Adolf greeting each other briefly yet politely when they met at the synagogue. When Laci was a child they visited Adolf's beautiful house where he lived alone after his wife died. Laci did not like Uncle Adolf and suspected that Sándor did not like him either. Böske once told Laci that the medal Adolf always wore indicated that he had a noble title he received from Kaiser Franz Josef, the Emperor of Austria and King of Hungary, Croatia and Bohemia. Adolf's large front door was engraved with a crest showing on one side an oak tree with a thick root structure, and two snakes curled up on a winged stick on the other side. It was the Hermes staff,[3] Böske explained, a symbol of commerce to show that Adolf was a merchant. The oak tree, she added, symbolized that Adolf was a wood merchant.

There was also a gold Star of David in the center of the crest and four Fleur de Lis signs below it. Strangely Böske did not say anything about them.

---

3   The Hermes (Mercury) staff or the Caduceus with its two snakes was carried by Hermes who among his many duties was also the protector of merchants (and thieves). The Asclepius, the older symbol of medicine has only one serpent wound around a rough mast. It was carried by the mythical Greek physician Asclepius to whom the serpent represented youth and renewal because of its ability to shed and renew its skin. The World Health Organization chose the Asclepius as its symbol. It is not clear when the Hermes staff came to symbolize medicine. It may have been as early as the seventh century AD, when Hermes was also associated with alchemy.

While the Star of David was self-explanatory, Laci always wondered about the Fleur de Lis. Maybe they marked Adolf's four daughters who converted to Catholicism? The Fleur de Lis was not just a symbol of the French Monarchy; it also symbolized the Virgin Mary. It would be appropriate then to have four of them for the four converted daughters and one Star of David for Adolf's only son who remained a Jew, at least for a while.[4]

The lumberyard that Sándor purchased from Adolf was large. Broad stacks of unprocessed oak and pine lumber filled most of it. On the left was a large shed with machinery, saws, wood planers, joiners and in the corner, Sándor's office. Laci and Gyuri used to play "bújócska"[5] in the yard, careful not to be seen by Sándor who worried that one of the wood stacks would collapse on them. Laci now shuddered at the thought that Judit would also want to play in the lumberyard, a father's perspective.

Just beyond the lumberyard was Dezső's house. Judit and Laci could see its red shingle roof. Dezső, Adolf son, inherited his parents' house and the portion of the lumber yard that Adolf kept for himself. His four sisters left Gyula for Budapest many years ago. Ferenc, Dezső's son, was Laci's age, almost to the day. He was his classmate in the Jewish school when it still existed and then in high school. They used to play together in the yard and walk to the Jewish school near Kossuth tér, the main square just a few blocks from their house. But Sándor ordered an end to their friendship when Dezső and his family became Catholic, just like his sisters. Sándor started calling them Ocher Israel.[6] Laci never understood what it meant, but he knew it was bad.

Adolf, Dezső and their family were an important part of Gyula and its history. Their ancestor, Dávid Czinczár, came to Gyula more than 150 years earlier as one of the first Jews to settle there. I found records that in 1799 Dávid was forced to pay a "Tolerance Tax" of two forint per household member per year for the privilege of staying in Gyula as Jews. Standing with little Judit on the back porch and looking at Dezső's house, Laci must have wondered if Ferenc or Dezső were also drafted to the Hungarian Labor Battalions. Were their noble connections and Catholic conversions sufficient to get them out of the draft?

---

4   When I visited Gyula in 2011 I saw that crest on the large tombstone of Adolf and his wife in the Jewish cemetery. They were both buried under the title "gyulai" that is equivalent to "Von Gyula." Five Hebrew letters under their names were proof that they were buried as Jews. The plot below the large tombstone was large enough to include Adolf's children who, as I discovered, inherited the title as well but whose names were not added to the tombstone.
5   "bújócska"—hide and seek in Hungarian (pronounced "buyotshka").
6   Ocher Israel—enemy of Israel in Hebrew.

Judit snatched Laci away from his thoughts by pulling on his hand. She wanted an apricot but the lowest branch was still too high. A sole ripe apricot hung above her head, Laci lifted her up, she picked it and jumped to the ground running back to the house giggling. She entered her mother's room, pretending clumsily to be quiet, and placed it on her pillow near her closed eyes.

Late in the afternoon, Sándor returned from the lumberyard and suggested that they all go for a walk. Lili and Judit dressed in their flowery summer dresses, and Laci and Sándor in white short-sleeved pressed shirts and light colored pants. They strolled down Béke sugárút towards the canal that crossed the city. They reached the small bridge connecting them to the downtown and Kossuth tér and stopped, leaning on the railing, to watch a row boat passing below heading towards a small dock near the bridge.

"*Juditka, sweetie, do you want to come with me on a boat ride?*" Sándor asked.

Laci and Lili remained on the bridge watching Sándor take a rowboat and jump into it as if his weight and age disappeared. Laci did not remember Sándor being so playful when they were children. Obviously grand-parenthood changed him; it certainly made him behave younger.

The dock hand lifted Judit and placed her on the seat next to Sándor who was already untying the boat. The boat turned upstream, moving lazily under the cover of the lush trees leaning over the canal on both sides.

A light dinner was ready when they returned; a large platter of cold cuts, cheese, jam, pickled peppers stuffed with sauerkraut and, of course, home pickled cucumbers. Laci asked for sour cream. Erzsi laughed, she knew it was his favorite dish along with a thick, buttered slice of white bread. When he received his bowl, Laci picked up his teaspoon and asked Judit, "*Do you know when cream is really good? Look, I will dip my spoon. If it remains standing, it's excellent.*" He dipped in the spoon and it remained standing. Judit watched puzzled, not quite sure what to make of this.

After dinner, Lili took Judit to their room, and Sándor and Laci went to the back porch and sat by the little table. Sándor brought a bottle of pálinka. Its label said that it was the winner of that year's Gyula pálinka competition. Though Kecskemét, a town west of Gyula, was the pálinka capital, Gyula's pálinka was just as good. Sándor filled two shot glasses and they savored quietly its perfume-like aroma.

A few years earlier, Laci was invited to referee in the local competitions. At the end of the day he was drunk. The organizers must have noticed because he was never re-invited.

After a few moments of pleasant quiet Laci asked Sándor to show the draft letter. Sándor pulled out a single page form letter printed on cheap paper with names and dates scribbled in handwriting. The form had already passed through many hands, folded and unfolded many times. It was stained and disintegrating at some of the folds.

Laci unfolded it carefully. A large stamp at the right hand corner next to the signature of a lieutenant confirmed that this was an official letter. It was marked on the top by three large letters, SAS.[7] Laci's name, László Laufer, was on the first line. He was ordered to report on Monday, July 24, 1942 at the Gyula train station for compulsory labor service for the protection of the homeland as prescribed by Act II of 1938. The notice did not spell out the duration.

After Laci finished reading, Sándor started describing his efforts to reverse this call. But it was a SAS call that was prone to abuse and had little flexibility. (8) The only thing he could get from the főispán was a one-month delay. Laci would need to report on August 24 directly to the recruiting base in Püspökladány, a small town north of Gyula. Even bribes, that often gave excellent results, did not help much this time. The orders, or the quotas, must have come from much higher.

They remained silent for a while. The nice summer breeze carried the smell of fresh cut hay from the farms surrounding Gyula. Farm smells were part of their lives, fragrant blossoms in the spring, earthy hay in the summer and the somewhat pungent smells of apples pressed for cider in the fall. They listened to the loud sounds of the cicadas courting their mates and their next-door neighbor who was playing old Hungarian folk songs on his violin. They wished that the magic of that beautiful night would last forever.

"*How do you think I should prepare?*" Laci asked after a while. "*I can't carry gear, food or provisions for a whole year. The army is going to supply me anyhow.*"

"I would not count on the army to supply you properly. Your friends who left in June actually packed quite seriously. They took good boots, warm socks, winter underwear and a good coat. I would bring a good pocket knife, matches, candles, spare bandages, and maybe some dense food such as salami, lard or jam."

Lily joined them quietly and asked Laci to go back to the house and kiss Judit goodnight, tell her a story and sing her a lullaby.

Laci kissed Lili gently on her cheek and left her with Sándor.

---

7   SAS—short for *Siess, Azonnal, Sürgős*—"Hurry, Immediate, Urgent" in Hungarian

August 1942: Leaving Gyula

Judit was lying in her little bed in their bedroom. A small light in the living room illuminated her dimly through the open door. She was dressed in a long striped pink nightgown. Her blanket was at her feet. It was still too hot for a blanket but it would cool down before dawn.

Laci sat down by her bed, stroking her black hair and started telling a story about an imaginary girl whose name was Tiduj, Judit spelled backwards. Tiduj's day events matched Judit's exactly. Laci told Judit how Tiduj went on a train ride with her father Ical and mother Ilil from Budapest to Gyula to meet her grandfather Rodnás. Before boarding the train Tiduj's shoes were polished by a shoeshine man who put Tiduj on a tall chair. By the time Tiduj's train arrived to Gyula, Judit was asleep.

The next morning, Laci dressed in a grey suit and blue tie walked downtown to Kenéz Tibi's office. Tibi was among the few lucky young Jewish attorneys. He got his license just before the First Jewish Law was enacted. Though only two years older than Laci, he was a full-fledged practicing lawyer and Laci was not. Before earning his license, Tibi had been an associate in Keppisch Frigyes's office and remained there after becoming a lawyer.

Frigyes was a prominent member of the congregation and personal friend of the főispán. But even Frigyes could not convince the főispán to release Laci, Tibi confirmed. He observed that the prominent young Jews were the first to be called up. (9) This was unusual because in the past, the wealthy and the well-connected found ways to get out of military service. At first Tibi suspected this was intended to remove the young leadership. But quickly, the draft was expanded to include nearly all Jewish men in rural Hungary, even men well beyond the legal age limit of forty-two or men with serious physical limitations.

Laci already knew all that from Sándor. He had come to Tibi to hear if he knew anything about those who had already left. And just as importantly, did he know how to prepare?

Tibi confirmed that the Diósi family recently got a card from Imre's brother [8] from Gomel.

He also knew that recruits from Gyula were ordered to report to Püspökladány, a large military base sixty miles north of Gyula. Some relatives of recruits traveled to the Püspökladány base and found there their family

---

8 Diósi ended up working initially in Kiev. In 1944 he tried to join Polish partisans but they did not trust him. He then fell in the hands of the Soviets where he remained a POW until 1948.

members. Some even saw recruits board cattle train cars headed to Kassa[9] on the Czechoslovakian border, the last stop in Hungary on the way to Ukraine.

But Tibi did not know where the trains went after crossing the border. Other than Diósi's letter, no one in Gyula heard from any of the recruits, not even those who left more than two months earlier. But at least there were no death or injury notices either.

Tibi was concerned by the treatment of the recruits. Several local Jews who returned from Püspökladány reported that even days after arriving, their recruited relatives were still dressed in their civilian clothing. The army only issued them military caps, yellow armbands to mark them as Jews and military ID cards marked with large letters "Zs".[10] They were sleeping under the open sky in a large yard; food was scarce and truly bad and they had to eat their own food that they either brought from home or smuggled in across the fence.

Some recruits claimed that they were told that they would be issued uniforms at the front and that food would be better there.

Laci doubted that. It was unlikely, he thought, that the army would send trainloads of uniforms and winter clothing to the front when they could easily issue them here. He would need to pack his own winter clothing and food before leaving home, just as Sándor recommended.

Tibi agreed and suggested that Laci also take some money, possibly reichsmarks, the German currency and pengő and hide it properly. There were thieves, even in the army, he warned.

Tibi also told Laci that many of the recruits were deprived of their privileges as officers or decorated soldiers and were treated worse than privates. The discriminatory labor service system deprived most of them[11] of their ranks, honors and the right to wear uniforms. Although Laci was trained while in law school as an artillery officer, he could not expect to enjoy any privileges either, Tibi warned.

Gyula in the summer was beautiful and time was flying. Neither the war nor the ever-increasing virulence of the anti-Jewish decrees could cloud the blue skies and the bright hot sun, nor could they tarnish the beauty of fields covered as far as the eye could see with yellow wheat. Nor could worry of the

---

9 Kassa—now Košice in Slovakia.
10 Zs—the first two letters of Zsidó, "Jew" in Hungarian, pronounced "Zhido."
11 My maternal grandfather János was also drafted to the Labor Service. But unlike Laci he retained his officer rank and served in a location near Budapest. A photograph with my grandmother shows a smiling man in officers' uniform. His round face and plump body are evidence that he did not suffer of malnutrition.

future spoil the fragrances of late summer bloom and peaches ripening on the trees. Warm mornings were the time to take Judit for a swim in the Castle baths that were still open to Jews. Pleasant afternoons were perfect times for Laci, Lili and Judit to go out on a stroll in Kossuth tér that always ended at the ice cream stand just off the canal bridge. Soft summer evenings were Lili and Laci's opportunities for romantic dinners in a restaurant overlooking the canal. They savored these precious moments they had for themselves. They did not dare count how many were left.

Knowing how Laci treated my mother, his second wife, I know that he would have tried to hide his feelings of doom from Lili, but I suspect that Lili understood the upcoming calamity anyway. Deep in Laci's heart he feared that Lili would not be able to cope with the uncertainty of his own fate and of her and Judit's future, the ever-increasing violence of society and the hardships of war that would eventually hit home. But he also trusted her and knew that her strength and wisdom would guide her. And there was Sándor too. Laci was a proud man and wished that his family did not need to depend on his father, but he fully trusted him to watch over his family.

By his last weekend at home, the impossible puzzle of packing for an unknown length of time in unknown conditions in one backpack had been solved to his best ability. His most treasured purchase were his boots, custom-made by Sándor's shoemaker, ankle-high with leather soles. Strips of steel were nailed to the soles at the toes and heels as if they were horseshoes protecting the soles from wear. The shoemaker even provided him with replacement metal strips, should the first set wear out. The shoes were completed a few days early and Laci broke them in, walking in them for hours. The sounds of the steel strips hitting the pavements of Gyula's streets could be heard blocks away.[12]

When I was a child, Laci told me that his discolored toenails were the result of frostbite he suffered at the Russian front. I did not understand the severe consequences of frostbite. It could be deadly, particularly at the toes where blood circulation is low and therefore is difficult to heal. Toes become exposed by the lack of proper footwear and once exposed they

---

12   Nearly a quarter of a century later, when I prepared to leave for military service, Laci insisted that I get new boots and break them in. Just like Sándor he warned me that my feet would be the most vulnerable part of my body. They must be protected at all cost. Good boots may save my life, even more so than food or a coat. Washing my feet every night, he warned, was a more important ritual than brushing teeth. Of course I did not know then that several Holocaust survivors wrote that many died when their feet were injured, infected or frozen.

must be quickly treated and rested. None of this was possible in the forced labor battalions. Many MUSZ died from frostbites that turned gangrenous. I wish I had asked Laci when I still could how he escaped with only toe discoloration.

Attaching steel strips to his soles to protect them seemed an excellent idea at the time. However, decades later, analysis of the factors that tilted the balance in favor of the Russians in Stalingrad showed that they enjoyed several advantages that on the surface may seem minor but in the winter of 1942 made a decisive difference. The highly insulating felt boots that the Russian soldiers and civilians wore was one of them. By comparison, the German boots had iron-nailed soles. While they were certainly more robust, they accelerated conduction of heat from the foot to the snow and ice on ground and thus promoted the onset of frostbites. (8 p. 182) On balance, the decision to protect his soles with metal strips worked to Laci's advantage. He did suffer minor frostbite, but without proper foot protection he would have likely died during his first winter in the Labor Service. Sándor was right when telling Laci: "*the Army does not march on its stomach. It marches on its feet.*"

Laci's last night at home was somber. The packed backpack rested in the corner of their bedroom. Judit, sensing that something was amiss, turned naughty. She ran through the house and the backyard trying to attract attention. To lift everyone's spirit, Erzsi prepared one of her best meals. She even decorated the dining table with candles and wild flowers. Sándor brought up from his cellar an old bottle of red Bika Vér[13] wine and a bottle of five puttony (a mark of the highest quality) sweet Tokaji Aszú wine. Dinner was a feast: little cheese rolls, cold plum soup with heavy cream, fine little salads, Laci's favorite pork roast, roasted potatoes, poppy seed and almond cakes, and a delicate cherry strudel. Laci wished he could fill his stomach with more roast, more soup and more of these extraordinary cakes. He knew that by the next evening, he would be lucky if he got any meal at all.

At night, Lili curled up next to him. Neither could sleep. Judit tossed in uneasy sleep in her crib. Once again they tried to speculate about his destination, the length of his service, re-thinking the wisdom of moving Lili and Judit to Gyula, wondering whether she should return to her hometown Verebély where her mother, father, and two sisters, Edit and Anna, still lived. Laci reminded her how impossible it was with her younger sister Anna still living with her parents. There was no room there for Lili and Judit.

---

13   Bika Vér—"Bull's Blood" in Hungarian.

The Gyula train station was nearly empty. It did not have even the slightest resemblance to Dante's gates of hell. There were no devils with horns and large bat-like wings; no large snakes or beasts. When they entered the station Laci and his family saw only two farmers sitting on a bench, with bags of produce at their feet. They waited, like Laci, for the train to Debrecen where Laci was to take a connecting train to Püspökladány. There were no other young men in the station. The Army had already taken them, the Jewish men to the Labor Force and the eligible Gentiles to the war. Most Jews and Gentiles would never return.[14]

---

14 When I was a teenager Laci told me that moments before boarding that train Sándor told him that he could avoid this service by converting to Catholicism. Sándor had already made all the arrangements and all Laci had to do was walk back home and meet the priest. Laci hesitated for a moment and then told his dad that he could not do that. He would not give up his beliefs and his tradition for the safety and comfort of home.

As a teenager, I was unimpressed by this story. After all, this was what all heroes in books and movies did. I was convinced that I would have done the same. Fifty years later I am not so sure anymore; certainly not after I learned the price that Laci paid to live by his beliefs and principles. I wonder, however, whether Laci recognized at that moment the full gravity of his own decision.

Had he decided after conversion to stay in Gyula, obtain his law license and open his law office, he would still have been deported to Auschwitz on June 26, 1944 along with all Gyula Jews still remaining in town. Racial laws (similar to the German Nuremberg laws) that were enacted after the Nazi occupation of Hungary on March 19, 1944 classified as Jewish, anyone who had at least three Jewish grandparents. Laci would not have escaped deportation nor would he have been able to save Judit and Lili.

But there could be another narrative. After conversion, Laci, Lili and Judit could have decided to return to Budapest where Laci would have resumed his work in Lipót's office, obtained his law license and opened his own office. Many Budapest Jews escaped deportation to Auschwitz, though they did not escape hardship. After the formation of the Arrow Cross Fascist government on October 15, 1944 and until the liberation of Budapest by the Red Army on January 19, 1945, tens of thousands of Jews were murdered on the streets, including Böske. Thirty thousand were deported for slave labor in Germany, including Evi's husband, and thousands more died from hunger, disease, the cold and Soviet shelling.

Nevertheless, odds for the survival of a Jew in Budapest during the rule of the Arrow Cross party far exceeded the odds for survival in the Hungarian Labor Battalions in Ukraine, German concentration camps and of course, the odds of surviving both.

One can never tell how their fate would have been decided by chance and determination, but had Laci converted on that day and returned to Budapest, he and his family might have survived.

Laci finished his story by telling that when he looked at his father's eyes there was a tear; he had never before seen Sándor cry. Sándor then hugged him and said that he knew this would be Laci's answer.

This was one of the few occasions Laci bared his soul for me to see.

The train to Debrecen rolled in and stopped. Laci hugged Lilli one last time, threw Judit up in the air one last time, hugged Sándor and boarded the first class compartment. For one last time he paid for his own trip with cash. He might as well enjoy what his cash could still buy.

August 1942: Püspökladány, Hungary

The train to Püspökladány had a third class car set aside for soldiers in uniform and new recruits. A military police officer at the door was not surprised to see Laci in a long sleeved heavy cotton shirt and a heavy winter coat hanging on his arm. He had seen many summer time recruits board the train dressed for the cold Russian winters. They were mostly Jewish conscripts of the Labor Force. Regular conscripts knew the army would supply them with winter clothing and boots. They traveled light only to discover later that the army-issued gear, boots, and clothing would wear out within months of reaching the front, that the army would not be able to resupply them and that many would die during the harsh Russian winter from the lack of proper clothing.[1] (8 p. 218) Ironically, the Jewish recruits who were forced to bring their own winter gear were better prepared than the fighting soldiers.

When Laci boarded the train, the MP uttered an anti-Semitic slur and directed him to the back of the car where the Labor Force recruits were segregated.

Ten other recruits were already sitting on the only two wooden benches allocated to them. Many more empty benches were available in the car but the MP saw to it that they did not sit there.

Laci sat on the floor leaning on his bag, his heart heavy. It was not the anti-Semitic remark he just heard or the humiliation of being forced to sit on the floor when the car is empty. He was used to being harassed as a Jew. To overcome the Numerus Clausus[2] (9 pp. 30-32) rules that were enacted in Hungary even before Germany enacted its first anti-Semitic laws; he had had to excel in everything he did as a child and a teenager, whether in academics or sports. Once out of law school, despite graduating at the top of his class, his

---

1 By mid-fall twenty percent of Second Army soldiers had worn-out clothing and forty percent worn-out shoes.
2 The Numerus Clausus Act of September 22, 1920 stipulated that the number of Jewish students in institutes of higher education be limited to six percent which represented the proportion of Jews in the general population.

religion prevented him from becoming a lawyer. He already spent time in jail for helping another Jew escape persecution.³

But now, for the first time, it was not Laci's career or his honor that were challenged. He could handle that. This time, he was anxious because his well-being and even his life might be in danger. His only daughter might never see him again. What would Lili do? How would he survive? Could he overcome hunger indefinitely, the bitter cold at the Russian front? Would he be shot? Was it a good idea to turn down his father's offer to convert?⁴

The other MUSZ at the back of the army car were cheerful. Laci was not sure if they were covering up their fears or simply oblivious to what is coming. One of them tapped him on his shoulder claiming that he knew Laci from somewhere. He introduced himself as Endre Schwartz⁵ (3 p. 76) from Békéscsaba.

---

3   When I once slacked in school, Laci shamed me by telling that through elementary, middle and high school all his grades were As. He was even the best sprinter in high school and earned the nickname "Loufi," possibly because "laufen" in German means "to run."

   Laci would have graduated *Summa Cum Laude*, he told me, and with a perfect score he would have been entitled to receive the Regent's Ring. But in his last year in high school his physical education teacher gave him a B, spoiling the perfect record and his right to Regent Horthy's ring.

   I doubted this story until I got his matriculation records for the academic year 1931-1932 graduating class from the archives of the Roman Catholic Gymnasium of Gyula. Laci's name on the list was italicized along with the name of another student. Both earned "straight A" records, including Physical Education! Laci's name on the list was distinguished in one more way. It was marked by the letters "izr." for "izraelita," the polite Hungarian word for Jew.

   Remarkably, Laci's cousin Ferenc was also listed. His name was not italicized and was not marked by the letter "izr." Instead it was distinguished by the nobility title "gyulai" that was granted to his grandfather Adolf nineteen years earlier. Ferenc earned only one A, in a subject called "behavior." Even in Physical Education he only scored a B.

4   Very few train rides are as memorable as the one that takes a young man from his home and civilian life to his first military base to start a-long service. I still remember my own ride from Haifa to the IDF recruiting center near Tel Aviv. Like Laci, I was still dressed in civilian clothing, anxious and somewhat frightened. But I only can imagine Laci's anxiety and fears on his way to serve an army that he knew was hostile to Jews, in a faraway war in a hostile land, leaving behind a wife and a little daughter.

5   Endre was to become Laci's close friend, during their service together, after the war in Hungary and later in Israel. I remember Endre as a thin man with a leathery, well-tanned face. He was a surveyor and spent most of his time out in the sun taking part in some of Israel's large development projects in the Negev desert and the drainage of the Hula swamps in the upper Galilee.

   He often brought us exotic gifts, probably as an honorarium for free legal services from Laci. Two of them stood out; a magnificent coral from Eilat on the shores of the

The ride from Debrecen was short. Military signs at the Püspökladány station directed arriving soldiers to their assembly points. Military trucks were parked in a lot just behind the fence. Several gendarmes with large rooster feathers decorating their caps directed new recruits to their assembly areas while yelling obscenities and occasionally whipping a recruit with a switch or a nightstick.

The MUSZ assembly point was located at the far end of the station. Just like on the train, they were segregated in a remote corner from the other recruits. More than a hundred MUSZ, brought from towns like Gyula, were already sitting on their bags and waiting. Most, like Laci, were wearing boots and carrying heavy coats.

Throughout the station, groups of recruits were assembled into new military units. As soon as the number of new recruits in a group reached thirty, they were marched to a waiting truck and taken to the base. But the army did not seem to be in any hurry to collect the more than a hundred new labor recruits.

Hours passed. Occasionally a gendarme came by, ordered them to fall into formation, three rows deep and counted them. On one occasion, a MUSZ asked for water or food. Instead of an answer, the gendarme cursed and ordered him to pick up his backpack, hold it overhead and run ten times the length of the station.

By early evening train traffic slowed and the station was emptying of soldiers and recruits. Only the MUSZ, whose number increased to a hundred and fifty, were still waiting. Finally three gendarmes arrived and ordered them to fall into formation with their bags on their backs and then marched them out of the station. There were no trucks waiting for them. Thirsty and hungry, they began their march to the base, five miles away.

A gate at the end of the road between two tall guard towers marked the base entrance. When they reached it, the guard raised the bar and saluted the gendarmes. They walked through the base and reached a large field. The barbed wire surrounding the base marked on one side of the field, tents that

---

Red Sea and a gigantic live catfish wrapped in wet burlap that he brought from the Hula swamps. Both sparked my imagination because only a few people traveled in those days to the far ends of Israel.

Endre Schwartz was mentioned in Dantsig's book. The overlap between Endre, Laci and Dantsig suggests that their stories must overlap at least for part of their time in the Labor Service.

An undated picture of my father, Laci, in his artillery officer uniform, most likely at the end of his reserve artillery officer training while still in Law school. It was a perfect picture of a young man proud to be a Hungarian officer. The similarity between Laci and my youngest grandson Henry is striking. Laci would have been ninety-three when Henry was born. The genetic code has a long memory.

appeared to serve some official functions marked another side and barracks marked the other two sides.

The field that might have been before the war the parade square looked now more like a squatters' camp with hundreds of men dressed in rumpled civilian clothing. The men, some wearing military caps and yellow armbands,

(9 pp. 305-306) looked as if they had lived on that field for weeks. They were unshaven, dirty, and the military caps that some wore rendered them comical figures: neither civilians nor soldiers. Most were huddled in small groups shouting at each other in what appeared to be lively discussions. Others were sitting around small bonfires that illuminated the darkening field busy cooking meals or boiling coffee. Others were simply lying on the ground with their bags as pillows, either sleeping or smoking cigarettes.

The new group was marched to a corner of the field that remained relatively empty. The gendarmes that led them to the base stepped aside and an army officer stepped forward and introduced himself as István.

In a short address he clarified that they were not considered soldiers by the army. They were only laborers, property of the Hungarian Army and they belonged to battalion 106. Since they were Jews who could not be relied on to protect their homeland, they would not be issued uniforms. Wearing the Hungarian Army uniforms was an honor that they had not earned. They would be issued military caps with no insignia and yellow armbands to mark them for what they are: Jews. They needed no training to learn how to dig holes in the ground or to shovel snow from roads and therefore they would be shipped to the front as soon as a train became available.

István delivered his speech in a booming voice, his shoulders pulled back and his chest thrust forward, clearly deriving great pleasure from the authority he had over the new recruits. His impeccably pressed uniform and the shiny boots that glistened to impress actually proved that he was an office soldier, a pencil pusher who was never in the field and never would be. His job was to send others to the front for the dangerous job of defending their nation.[6]

Before dismissing them, István ordered them to assemble at 05:30 am for roll call.

Laci and Endre sat down just where they had stood. Their new company was assembled from many little towns around Debrecen. They did not know anyone. They sat quietly feeling as if the descending darkness also permeated their hearts.[7]

---

6   I met many "pencil pushers" during my service. Some of them never left Tel Aviv; others reached as far as the main field command in Sinai, but were still a hundred miles from the front line. I could recognize them instantly. They even smelled different, always fresh from the shower, smelling of soap and deodorant. They also tended to be better dressed and better equipped!

7   My first night in basic training was memorable too. We arrived at the training base from the recruitment center where we were issued our uniforms, boots, a military beret with a large,

Only twenty-four hours and two short train rides separated Laci from a world to which he no longer belonged. Meals, shelter, uniforms, or even arms were no longer included among his rights. He realized, with a sinking feeling, that Tibi's predictions were accurate and started asking himself if he could survive. Could anyone survive? Who was his enemy, István and his colleagues, the Russians if he ever got to the front, any of the MUSZ around him? If he wanted to survive, he would need to protect himself from all that plus dangers he did not even know yet.

His thoughts were interrupted by Endre who stood up as cheerful as if he were at a party. He was hungry and he was not prepared to go to sleep hungry. He had some sausages in his bag and this night was as good as any to eat them. He even was prepared to share with Laci.

Grateful for pulling him out of his dark thoughts, Laci offered to share his sausages, some goose fat, dried bread, and jam.

They each pulled out their goods, ate them in silence and tucked the rest back into their bags. They tied the straps of their bags to their hands and fell asleep. Both slept through the night, hearing or seeing nothing. When they

---

brass, shiny, diamond-shaped insignia marked with a large letter "T" (for *Tiron*, the Hebrew word for recruit). There was nothing more humiliating in my service than wearing the beret with the diamond-shaped insignia.

Then there was another humiliation. Our new military ID cards carried our newly minted ID numbers that we were ordered to memorize and shout loudly when ordered. Mine, 988163, was on that day among the highest in the entire army. Veteran soldiers could tell just from the first three digits "988," that I was a "T." When we all passed the "memory test" and shouted our numbers loudly enough, we received vaccines and then marched to the mess hall.

With our large kitbags on our backs we were lined up in a long corridor leading to the mess hall. Our new commander, a young corporal, barely six months older than us, pointed to a horizontal bar hanging from the ceiling at the end of the corridor. Each one of us was to jump, grab it and perform three pull-ups. Those who failed were sent to the back of the line. Some of us could not even reach the bar. But by the end of the six weeks training, we all could meet the pull-up standard that was by then raised to five.

We spent most of the night practicing how to make the bed and assemble our military gear that did not yet include arms. Some were brought to tears when their bed was turned over by the corporal for the fifth and sixth time because the blanket stretched over the sagging mattress did not bounce the coin he tossed on the bed. We got our rifles a week later after a swearing-in ceremony.

I do not remember the corporal's name. I barely remember his face. But I do remember his uncanny ability to find among us those who could be brought to tears. For six weeks he was preying on them. Suicide rates among new recruits of the IDF during those years were so high that the military eventually felt compelled to change the practices of basic training. At least one Tiron killed himself during my basic training.

woke up, the sun was just rising. Both their bags were open, missing much of their food. Most of the men in their group were still sleeping but others who were waking up were already shouting that their bags had been opened in the night and that food was stolen.[8]

As the MUSZ were getting up and assessing their damages, several military policemen stormed into the courtyard screaming orders. Laci checked his watch. It was 5:30. They were ordered last night to be ready for roll call but most men were still asleep. Wielding sticks, the policemen began beating the sleeping men. Blows were flying indiscriminately. Aching, some bleeding, the startled MUSZ jumped to their feet making an effort to line up in somewhat orderly rows.

Once the group was assembled, one of the MPs shouted at them for disobeying orders. They had just lost breakfast. The hungry men were left standing in formation watching how several recruits of other companies hauled in large vats with steaming liquid and crates of bread loaves. The vats and crates were placed on a folding table that was brought out from one of the nearby barracks.

Laci and Endre, standing next to each other, watched how each company on its turn marched to the vats, and by the order of one of the MUSZ who was wearing a special cap lined up and received their breakfast: a bread loaf and a cup of coffee that was poured into a tin cup that each was carrying.

Eating the sausages last night was not such a bad idea after all, Laci thought. For one, he was not that hungry and more importantly, the food would have been stolen if he had saved it.

They remained standing for three hours. Many wished they could use the latrines, some were already feeling the effect of hunger after more than a day

---

8   While I always had plenty of food to eat during my military service, I too experienced the shock of midnight theft. Our first night's sleep in basic training was brief but when we woke up, many discovered they were missing army issued items, a blanket, a rifle cleaning kit or a mess kit. One of the worst sins a Tiron can commit in basic training is losing army-issue equipment, and the worst sins of all is losing or damaging his rifle. Any minor loss led to a court martial, seven days in the brig and of course a fine to compensate the army for its loss. Losing a rifle could send a Tiron for months to an army prison. During roll call, our corporal asked if we encountered any "Equipment Make-Up." It was a new terminology, a euphemism. Our equipment was not stolen. The graduating Tiron class who occupied the adjacent barrack was merely "making up" their own equipment losses. There was only one rule to "Equipment Make-Up": it was taboo to do it within your immediate unit.

A week before our graduation, a new Tiron class arrived. They too learned during their first night the lessons of "Equipment Make-Up."

without food. The military policemen took turns watching them. The MP on watch sat on a nearby bench smoking a cigarette while the others left to the base to have breakfast.

At nine o'clock, two soldiers carrying a large folding table walked into the field and placed it near the assembled company. Another soldier carried in chairs that he placed behind the table. Finally an officer accompanied by another soldier carrying forms arrived. Both sat by the table and ordered the MP to line up the recruits for registration.

When Laci's turn arrived, he was asked to produce his call up orders. The officer examined the papers and noted that he was ordered to report in July.

"*It says here that you were to report in July. Why are you late?*"

"*I got an administrative relief order, sir.*" Laci replied.

"*By whom?*"

"*By the főispán of Békés County, sir.*"

The officer flipped through piles of forms but could not find a confirmation.

"*I cannot find such record. For now I will register you as a new MUSZ but we will investigate it and if you were absent without permission, you will be punished severely,*" the officer said as he passed Laci's records to the clerk besides him.

The clerk pulled from a box a blank card that was marked boldly on one side by the letters "Zs," he filled in Laci's name, date of birth, his last home address and the issue date. He then pulled out a form printed on a thin paper that he handed to Laci with a hollow metal disk.

"*This will be your Dögcédula.*[9] *(S pp. 21, 43) Fill in the form and fold it to fit in this can. Close the can hard to seal it and hang it on your neck with a string. When you croak ("dögöl" in Hungarian), as all of you certainly will, someone will take it back to your wife so she can look for someone better than you.*"

Laci returned to his group. It was past noon when all were done registering. A smell of food from the nearby mess hall drifted to the courtyard. They were not called to have lunch. At this rate, Laci thought, the labor force will be starved to death even before reaching its work site.

At 2 pm a new military policeman ordered them into formation and took them for a physical exam to determine who was fit for hard labor. "*A doctor will check you out and if you are sick, old, or weak, you will be reassigned or dismissed,*" he promised.

---

9 Dögcédula—"dog tag" in Hungarian, pronounced "Deugtzedoolah."

The man standing next to Laci whispered, "*I know I will be dismissed. I am 55 years old. The law limits recruitment to 42 year old and younger.*" (5 p. 13), (3 p. 19)

They were ordered to gather their packs in one pile. The MP appointed one of the new MUSZ to watch it, another one as their group leader and then to the orders of their new group leader they marched to the infirmary building that was marked by a large red cross.

Once again, a large folding table was brought out and set up in front of the building with two chairs behind it. It was then covered with a blanket as if it were a tablecloth.

They remained standing in formation in front of the table until two officers wearing armbands marked with a red cross walked out of the building and sat behind the table.

"*Get undressed and keep your clothes in your hands,*" ordered one of the two.

Several of the servicemen hesitated, but a nightstick blow to the head of one of them erased their remaining modesty.

They stood naked, facing the table and the female nurses who stood at some of the windows in the infirmary, pointing fingers at them and chuckling.

One by one they were paraded in front of the officers, ordered to stand to attention and then turn around. The man who was standing next to Laci tried to protest that he was fifty-five, well past the legal draft age.

"*You look forty. To me that's all that matters,*" was the doctor's reply.

A MUSZ standing behind Laci approached the table and showed a fresh scar across his abdomen from a recent hernia operation. "*The best cure for this operation is service at the front and a shovel,*" was the doctor's decision. (4 pp. 13-14)

Not one of the new MUSZ was declared unfit. Not even the person who was limping on his two deformed legs. (9 p. 310)

When they were dressed again, the MP led them to the supply room where each was issued a military cap without any insignia, a yellow armband marking them as Jews, as if their civilian outfit was insufficient to set them apart from the rest of the army, a tin cup, tin plate, an aluminum spoon, a fork but no knife.

"*Welcome to Honvédség,*" announced the MP. "*You now have all you need to go to the front. In case you were unaware, you are now Company 106/12.*"

Just when they returned to the parade square, a few MUSZ were hauling out steaming vats and large boxes of quartered bread loaves. It was dinner, their first meal after two days of military service.

It was meager and bad. The soup was watery and lukewarm. The quarter loaf of bread tasted as if made of sawdust. The teaspoonful of margarine spread on it did not hide its foul taste. Thankfully the dark tea was sweet.

Before retiring for their second night's sleep, they posted their own company night watch. They had learned that danger loomed everywhere. Everyone was a suspect, anytime; MUSZ of other companies, soldiers on base, even their own company commanders would not hesitate to steal from them.

The following days, new recruits trickled in at a slow but steady rate. By Friday, more than a thousand MUSZ filled the courtyard to capacity. Every morning two or three policemen arrived and ordered them to assemble in formation and after a roll call, drilled them in military marching routines until noon. The rest of the day they were free to move around the courtyard mingling with MUSZ of other companies and exchanging rumors, such as when would they receive their assignments, where they might be sent, how many MUSZ had already been killed, where the current front was, whether Hungary was winning or losing the war, was Horthy's son killed, murdered or was his plane crash a few days earlier just an accident? (10)[10]

Occasionally, several civilians came to the fence at the edge of the yard and asked to see a certain MUSZ. Laci remembered Tibi's story that some family members knew that their loved one would be at this base; somehow they found its location and the fence that bordered the parade square and took the train from Gyula to visit them, bringing food and letters. He wished that Sándor or Lili would come too. One of the visitors, a man from Gyula that Laci recognized, could not find his loved one but when he saw Laci, he left with him a bag filled with food and promised to call Sándor.

On Friday morning, after roll call, a company of fifty armed soldiers led by ten officers marched into the courtyard. The MUSZ, intimidated by the forceful march moved out of the way. The company reached the center of the square and then broke down into ten squads, each with its own officer and soldiers. The commanding officer of the group, a captain, ordered the MUSZ to fall into formation by their companies. The MUSZ in the parade square fell silent and slowly formed their companies. But several still continued chatting, surprisingly unaware of the commotion.

The Captain watched in silence for a minute and then without a word he waved his baton towards one of the squads. Their officer shouted a command and his soldiers scattered around the yard hitting MUSZ not yet in formation with their rifle butts, aiming at their heads and backs. Some of the

---

10 István Horthy—the son of Miklós Horthy, Hungary's regent—was a fighter pilot. He was killed on August 20, 1942 on the Russian front in an unexplained plane crash.

beaten MUSZ dropped to the ground unconscious, but the yard turned silent. The Captain sneered, obviously pleased:

"I am glad we got your attention. Looks like some of you understand only the rifle butt language. In thirty seconds I want all companies lined up in formation five rows deep with your bags at your feet. You do not want to be out of formation when time is up. Now!"

In a quick dash, MUSZ began lining up in their companies. One of the captain's associates, a mean-looking corporal stood by him and was counting time aloud:

"Thirty, twenty-nine, twenty-eight..."

At the end of the count, all companies were lined up except for two MUSZ who were still running from one end of the courtyard towards their companies at the opposite end.[11]

The Captain, with great delight ordered the two MUSZ to approach him. "It appears that you need private lessons on how to obey orders," he gloated.

Standing in attention with his company Laci could see the two turning pale.

"Get the whip," ordered the Captain.

One of the soldiers ran forward holding a long leather whip. Laci recognized it as a horse whip.

"I feel lenient today, this is a twenty lash offense but I will settle for ten. Take off your shirts."

Hesitantly the terrified MUSZ started unbuttoning their shirts.

"I don't have the entire day for you," the captain yelled and motioned with his baton to the soldiers with the whip.

"Teach these swine Jews what it means to disobey an order in Honvéd!"

Swiftly the soldier tore off the first MUSZ's shirt, raised his whip and in a sudden motion swung it against his bare back. The strike left a streak of blood on his back and the MUSZ screamed.

---

11 Punctuality was important also in my basic training. Most times it was simply part of the day's routine: The Tiron had to be on time for morning roll call, inspection, practice, dinner or bedtime. Being late, even by one second, generated for the offending Tiron an extra night watch, a run around the parade square or a midnight inspection of his bed and gear all set up in the parade square.

But exercises in punctuality were also a mean method of punishment. At times, an individual, or the entire company, were ordered to run to a tree or a building, touch them and return in 10, 20 or 30 seconds. The trouble was that the distance to these objects could not be covered in that short time even by the national running champion. Punishment for not meeting that time could range from a new running assignment to even more distant objects in less time, night watch, twenty or thirty push-ups or sit-ups.

"*Stop this whining, you pig, if you do not want the punishment to double. And count aloud the blows. Be sure not to make a mistake,*" the captain ordered

By the tenth strike, the MUSZ fainted.

The second MUSZ, realizing what was coming dropped to his knees and begged for mercy. The Captain kicked him and ordered him to stand up and doubled his punishment. The soldier continued whipping the MUSZ even after he fainted. Four MUSZ were ordered to carry their unconscious comrades to the edge of the square where they were laid down.

The first rule of survival in the Labor Service, Laci learned, was written with the blood of the first victims: do not stand out, always blend in.

The ten companies, less two unconscious MUSZ, were now standing in attention. All were silent. The Captain turned around facing the end of the parade square and stood at attention, his back stretched like a board and his chest extended forward. A colonel wearing the gendarmerie's cap decorated with a dark rooster-feather marched in. After exchanging salutes with the army captain, the colonel turned to the recruits to address them.

"*Labor Servicemen, (3 p. 36)*[12] *today you will travel to the front. Our brave soldiers are spilling their blood fighting the Soviet army. Your job will be to support them. You will clear their roads, dig their trenches and haul in their supplies when horses are tired or no longer available. But do not think for a moment that you are true soldiers. You are just MUSZ. You did not earn the privilege of wearing the uniforms of our great Army. But this is not an excuse to slack off. It is about time you Jews learned to work and not just exploit your neighbors. It is about time you got out of your old Jewish habits of stealing and embezzling. You will be at the front. It is dangerous there and I hope that many of you will pay with your own blood and lives for what you and your parents stole from Hungary for generations.*"

When finished, the colonel turned to the Captain, exchanged salutes and marched out of the yard as pompously as he walked in.

Once he disappeared, the soldiers with their commanding officers reattached to the MUSZ companies. For the first time each company had its own commanding squad that would accompany it to the front.

One by one the companies were ordered to pick up their bags and march out of the square, through the camp and towards the train station. Once again they paraded through the city. It was nearly noon; hundreds of citizens lined the street watching a pathetic army head to the front.

---

12 A similar address was made by a major general before Dantsig's unit departure.

More than a thousand men, some barely able to march, were heading to the front where two of the world's largest and strongest armies were fighting each other. They were wearing crumpled civilian clothes, most of the men were unshaven, and all looked tired and dispirited. Each of them carried a large bag that had no resemblance to military gear. Despite the heat, most were wearing heavy coats, and most striking, they carried no weapons, not even sticks. By contrast, their commanders were dressed in impeccable military uniforms, carried rifles, but no backpacks and no winter clothing.

The citizens of Püspökladány were already used to these parades. Some watched quietly, possibly disappointed by the disgrace displayed by the army they once admired. Others felt sorry for the humiliation of loyal Hungarian citizens, their personal suffering and for the terrible waste of their extraordinary talents. But many, too many, yelled obscenities wishing the Jews harm and death. One old woman, feeling sympathetic to the Jews marching to the front, tried to hand out candies but a gendarme accompanying the march jumped and pushed her to the ground.

A long cattle train was already waiting at the station when the first MUSZ company marched in. Three passenger cars at the back of the train were reserved for the commanding squads. About fifty gendarmes in dress uniforms holding bayoneted rifles lined up along the train. There was no mistaking it: the gendarmes in their dress uniform were not heading to the front. They were only feeding the ever-growing appetite at the front for human flesh. But only a fraction of the bodies loaded on that train would become "cannon fodder." The rest would be wasted by the brutality and bigotry of their own commanders and the terrible winter that was sure to follow the waning summer.

Each company was divided into two boxcars, fifty MUSZ in each. Gendarmes tossed several loaves of bread, a few buckets of water and several empty buckets for latrines into each boxcar. Once all on board, the boxcars' heavy doors were slid closed and bolted from the outside.

They waited for hours inside their locked dark car. Only one small window near the ceiling allowed in a little light. The train was not moving. Watching through the steel bars across the window Laci could see the setting sun. Shabbat, the Jewish day of rest, was arriving. At home Lili and Judit were lighting Shabbat candles. Soon Sándor would walk to the synagogue for the short Friday night service. When Sándor was back, they would have Shabbat dinner. The food would be festive but even young Judit would stop her happy chatter when she saw Laci's empty seat at the table. Cramped inside the boxcar, Laci and Endre found a spot on the floor next to a wall and sat down next to each other with their bent legs resting on their bags. Others continued scrambling, pushing and shoving as they tried to capture a little floor space for themselves.

Through this mayhem the sound of a loud deep voice chanting an ancient Jewish song emerged. It was surreal to hear this song inside the chaotic boxcar. The rich voice, carrying the melody of the sacred song, was a contrast to the shouts inside the car, to the armed gendarmes still guarding outside and to the stench of fifty men crowded for hours in a boiler-like compartment.

The MUSZ who were still scrambling for a place to sit stopped. Those who already sat turned quiet and looked up. At the far corner stood a slim, slightly hunched, bearded man, slightly older than Laci and wearing a black yarmulke (skull cap). His voice took over the boxcar. The MUSZ watched him as if hypnotized.

"I know him. This is Csengeri Imre,"[13] Endre whispered to Laci. "I know him from Békéscsaba. He is our tailor."

Rays of the setting sun that penetrated through the little window behind Csengeri illuminated his face. Against the background of the darkening boxcar, the brightly illuminated face seemed as if it was glowing. Csengeri, standing with his arms folded on his chest and his eyes closed was visibly floating to another world far beyond the armed gendarmes.

Laci closed his eyes listening to the words of *Lecha Dodi*, the traditional song welcoming the Shabbat at the start of the Friday night service. Csengeri's melody also floated Laci to the synagogue in Gyula. He could see Sándor sitting at the front row, near the east wall and Rabbi Adler Ignác,[14] singing the same words in the same melody. It was a love song to the incoming Shabbat likening her to a bride and to a queen.

Csengeri reached the last verse welcoming the Shabbat into the boxcar and to their hearts singing "Come in, Shabbat, Come in, Shabbat, Shabbat the Queen." All the MUSZ stood up, turned towards the bolted door and bowed while joining him: "Bo'i Shabbat, Bo'i Shabbat, Shabbat Ha'Malka."

---

13   Csengeri Imre, born on March 14, 1909, died in Mühldorf on April 17, 1945, 16 days before liberation of the camp. (Archives of Dachau concentration camp www.kz-gedenkstaette-dachau.de)

14   Rabbi Adler was deported to Auschwitz on June 26, 1944 with the rest of the Gyula Jewish community where he died. The small street on the side of the old synagogue was named after him. The old synagogue building now serves as the Béla Bartók conservatory.

Through the bolted doors Shabbat entered the boxcar. One of the MUSZ picked a loaf of bread from a box near him, blessed the food, broke a piece for himself and passed the rest around for the others to break off a piece. At home, their families were breaking off pieces from a challah, a rich braided white bread filled with raisins.

Through the walls of their car they could hear the song repeating in the adjacent boxcars and the whistle of the locomotive as the wheels of the train began rolling towards Ukraine.

The train, heading in a north-west direction, was slow. It only moved when tracks were available due to its low priority cargo. When the Shabbat morning sun rose, the train reached Budapest. Laci, who could not sleep, climbed on his bag and stood by the little window. Looking through the bars and barbed wires he saw the city he so loved for one last time. The train crossed the Danube and in the distance he could see the Lánchíd[15] where not long ago, he, Judit and Lili strolled, and Margitsziget[16] where they spent magical afternoons swimming and playing.

The doors remained locked the entire day keeping the hungry and thirsty MUSZ trapped. The little air entering the single window did not do much to abate the heat or clear the stench from the latrine buckets.

AUGUST 30, 1942

On Sunday morning the train stopped and for the first time in nearly two days the doors were unbolted and slid open. The MUSZ, aching from long squeezed sitting, thirsty, hungry, and tired from sleepless nights, slowly climbed out of the boxcars into a vast train station. Large signs announced that they were in Kassa, the last stop in Hungary. This ended their hopes that they might complete their service in a Hungarian farm or factory. Their destination from this northern border town could only be Ukraine.

Their eyes were still adjusting to the brightness when a gendarme standing at the open door of their boxcar holding a nightstick and wearing a pistol at his belt ordered them to fall into formation with their bags at their feet.

Their army commanders got out of their comfortable passenger cars stood aside and watched in amusement. Within minutes the MUSZ companies were lined up and more gendarmes entered the station joining their comrades.

---

15   Lánchíd—"The Chain Bridge", pronounced "Lantzheed."
16   Margitsziget—"Margaret Island", pronounced "Margitsiget."

Two station conductors hauled in a large box and put it down facing the MUSZ who stood at attention. Finally, a gendarmerie captain in dress uniform marched in and stepped up on the box. After reviewing the lineup for a minute or two he started to speak. Despite his loud voice, Endre and Laci who stood at the far end of the lineup had to strain to hear him (3 p. 46).[17] But the message was clear.

This was their last stop on Hungarian soil. Like all Jews, they were carrying valuables in their bags to trade. But once at the front, they would meet German soldiers who would confiscate their valuables. The Germans are greedy, the captain assured them; they would want everything for themselves. It was the MUSZ's patriotic duty to leave their valuables in the hands of trusted Hungarians like himself and his gendarmes rather than letting them fall in the hands of foreign soldiers.

So once again Tibi, back in Gyula, was right and so was Endre. The gendarmes would rob them, Laci thought, as the Captain continued insisting that they turn in any currency, gold, diamonds, jewelry, or even expensive food items they had.

Putting a pious expression on his face, the Captain offered them "an opportunity" to do what he was sure they would understand was their patriotic duty. This was their only chance to do what was right. If they missed it, his face hardened, the gendarmes would search their bags and punish severely anyone who tried to smuggle valuables out of the country.

Good thing he prepared for that, Laci thought. His backpack contained some clothing, candles, and a few sausages. He could give them up if he had to. But he also had currency, pengős and reichsmarks that were sewn into the seams of his pants, and hidden in a cavity the shoemaker had prepared in the heels of his boots. Standing in the back row behind a taller MUSZ, Laci was barely visible to the gendarme. Slowly he pulled out two sausages and placed them on his bag. He regretted losing them but he knew that this food would not support him for too long anyways, but it could distract the wrath of the gendarme. He was glad that he and Endre consumed most of the food they brought from home during the train ride.

After waiting for a few minutes, allowing the MUSZ to voluntarily offer up their goods, the gendarme standing in front of their company began collecting his loot. Stopping in front of a large man at the center of the front row, he whispered menacingly:

---

17   Dantsig describes a similar account of MUSZ companies being violently robbed by Hungarian gendarmes while the army commanders were watching from the side.

"Where is your treasure, my friend?"

The MUSZ handed him two cans of food.

"You must be kidding. Do you really think I believe that this is all you've got?"

In a blink, like a striking snake, he pulled a knife out of a sheath on his belt and with a single continuous motion sliced off the man's left sleeve along his coat's shoulder seam. Then with a second strike, he cut off the right sleeve. As the sleeves were sliding off, several German reichsmark bills emerged from the shoulder paddings.

With a large grin, the gendarme pulled the money out and then the knife swung again, striking the MUSZ in his face, leaving a deep cut from the middle of his left cheek to his chin.

"Where is the rest? Give it to me now if you do not want to have your other cheek sliced too!"

Holding his bleeding cheek with one hand, the terrified man pointed to his other shoulder pad.

"What about your shoes? Should I cut them too?"

The MUSZ slowly removed his shoes as well.

For an entire hour, gendarmes were walking between the rows of the MUSZ companies robbing them of the few valuables that could save their lives at the front or during the upcoming harsh Russian winter, beating and injuring those who resisted or did not have anything to offer.

The Gendarme searching Laci's company was just reaching the back row when a whistle was blown. The captain stepped on the box again and ordered the MUSZ back to the train. Climbing back into the cattle cars, the robbed and beaten MUSZ looked back one last time at the country that betrayed them, the country that they once loved and that most of them would never see again.

The train continued its slow motion towards the front, stopping often on side tracks. On a few occasions the doors were opened and the MUSZ were allowed out to rest or wash in a nearby stream. Bread and water were distributed on alternating days. After five days on the road they reached Nazi-occupied Poland. At one of their stops, while still locked in their boxcar, they saw a group of skeletal men dressed in rags and wearing wooden clogs repair a narrow road that ran parallel to their tracks with shovels and axes. (3 p. 37) Their shaved heads accentuated their bony faces and their large expressionless eyes.

In the distance they saw a camp surrounded by barbed wire and tall watchtowers. A German soldier in a dark uniform, carrying a rifle and a whip, stood on a small mound at the side of the road, watching his slaves. Through the bars of their window they tried to speak to the workers. But when one of them tried to answer, the German officer got off the mound and lashed him with his whip while barking orders and obscenities in German. The rest of the workers continued toiling without raising their heads or acknowledging the MUSZ.

The MUSZ, despite their own hunger, have never imagined that human beings can be starved and worked to death. Persistent rumors were circulating in Hungary that the Germans built concentration and even death camps for the Jews in German-controlled territories in occupied Poland. The rumors seemed to the Hungarian Jews exaggerated and even preposterous.

A day later, even deeper in Nazi-occupied Poland, the MUSZ saw a similar group working on the tracks near their train. This time they spoke with the MUSZ, in Yiddish. They were Polish Jews from a nearby concentration camp. Was it Majdanek or Sobibor? (4 p. 25)[18] Despite their hunger, the MUSZ threw bread, sausage, and bacon that the prisoners quickly collected and hid under their rags. The MUSZ now saw two of these camps and a few of their inmates. The rumors in Hungary were true after all. But they would not return to Hungary in time to tell and their letters home would never be delivered.

Despite their ever worsening experiences, even the MUSZ could tell that the Hungarian Jews still fared better than the Jews in most of Europe. Despite the large deployment of Jewish men to harsh, highly discriminating, labor battalions; the ever-increasing severity of the Jewish Laws and the growing virulence of anti-Semitism the life of Hungarian Jews in 1942 was still better than the mortal threats they witnessed. It would be two years before the start of deportation of Hungarian Jews to Auschwitz and the complete destruction of most rural Jewish communities. But then the destruction will be harsh and swift.

---

18 Diósi's train passed through Krakow and Lublin. He too encountered weakened prisoners working while an SS officer supervised them. His path is consistent with passing near Majdanek and Sobibor. Similarly, Dantsig saw emaciated prisoners along the way to Ukraine and he and his comrades gave them food.

September 1942: Gomel, Ukraine

SATURDAY, SEPTEMBER 5, 1942

On the ninth day, early in the morning, the train stopped. They had reached their destination. The station sign written in Cyrillic characters announced "Гомель." One of the MUSZ translated it—Gomel. The only card the Diósi family got came from here. They were in Ukraine. Less than a year earlier this was still part of the Soviet Union.

The exceptionally long train ride they had experienced was not unusual. Almost all the soldiers of the Second Army spent eight or more days traveling to the front (8 p. 204) contributing to their exhaustion and low morale. Trains were delayed for fuel shortages, tracks sabotaged by partisans, or simply mined. But the MUSZ were singled out for the harshness of their travel conditions, little food, water and hygiene.

When the doors opened, one of their commanding soldiers from Püspökladány was standing on the ramp and ordered them out and into formation.

Back home, early September was still summer, but in Gomel the morning already felt like fall. It was cold, cloudy and the light drizzle made everyone feel gloomy.

Within minutes they lined up with their bags at their feet. Tired, hungry and thirsty from the long trip, the cool morning felt even colder. Those carrying coats were glad to have them. The soldier in front of them did not speak. He just stood and watched them standing to attention for an entire hour. Fortunately, the morning sun started to clear the sky and the air was warming up.

At eight o'clock, the rest of their commanding staff, led by their captain, left their comfortable train cars, marched in and spread among the companies with five soldiers standing in front of each company. Four of the five in front of Laci's company were privates armed with handguns and nightsticks. The fifth, a dark-skinned corporal, armed with only a handgun, was looking fresh as if he had not traveled for the last nine days.

When all were lined up, the captain stepped on a small podium and introduced himself as Captain Baky. He was their new master. Their lives were in his hands and like the officers before him he made it clear that he did not value those lives.

When Captain Baky stepped down from the podium, their corporal turned to them and announced:

"My name is Hegedűs.[1] You heard Captain Baky. He thinks he is God, but I am the Devil. My four aides are Bálint, Kőrösi, Kobak and Balázs. Now pick up your bags and be ready to march."

The MUSZ companies marched out of the station and into a badly damaged city. (11) Almost every building outside the station showed signs of battle. Some had large holes from tank shells, while others had a wall or a roof collapsed by a cannon shell. Many were pockmarked by hundreds of bullets. But surprisingly, only a few buildings were fully collapsed.

The streets they passed were mostly cleared of rubble and occasional carts drawn by horses passed by carrying farm produce. Almost all the stores were empty, their windows broken, obviously looted either by German soldiers who were the first to pass through, Hungarian soldiers that followed and now occupied the city, or possibly by the townspeople themselves.

Laci read about the German Blitzkrieg—the lightning war that caught France, Belgium, Holland, England, Poland, and the Soviet Union by surprise. He knew that German Panzer tank units stormed through Gomel earlier that summer and that Hungarian infantry units behind the armored German units helped clear the city of pockets of resistance. In some street corners he saw military posts manned by one or two soldiers flying the red-white-and-green Hungarian flag.

"Do you know what the colors of the Hungarian flag mean?" Laci asked Endre who was walking next to him.

"Doesn't red stand for strength?" replied Endre.

"Yes, white for faithfulness and green for hope." It was an empty symbol. There was no strength, no faithfulness, and definitely no hope for the MUSZ.

Many locals lined the streets to watch them. Their faces were expressionless. They recognized the units as part of the occupying Hungarian army but they also knew they were not true military units. They were Jews. Laci, marching next to Endre, wondered if the citizens feared the MUSZ for being part of the occupying army, pitied them for being essentially slaves or hated them for being Jews. Their faces did not betray any of these emotions.[2]

---

[1] Hegedűs ("violinist" in Hungarian), pronounced "Heguedush."
[2] I too marched through occupied enemy territory: as a civilian visiting the West Bank in 1967 after the Six-Day War, as an artillery officer in 1973 on the Egyptian side of the Suez Canal and in 1982 on my way to the outskirts of Beirut.

September 1942: Gomel, Ukraine

After marching for nearly four hours, crossing the Sozh River and a swath of rural farmland they arrived at an abandoned military base that served as a Soviet army vacation camp until its capture by the Germans. (3 p. 39) The red sign above the gate, still showing a few Cyrillic letters, was broken and columns on both sides still bore the Communist hammer and sickle. But a Hungarian flag flew at the entrance and at the main parade square, visible from the gate. Several rusting carcasses of destroyed Russian tanks, still scattered within the base, were evidence of the swift Blitzkrieg battle that had taken place there.

In less than three weeks, between June 22 and July 9, 1941, German troops occupied parts of the Ukraine, Belarus, all of Lithuania and Latvia. They reached Gomel by the end of August of that year. It was this stunning success that convinced Hungary to join Germany in the war in the hope that they could make a quick territorial grab. Now, a year later, the fast-moving German army was bogged down near Stalingrad and the Hungarian Army was suffering heavy losses.

Just past the gate they saw a group of MUSZ clearing the rubble of a destroyed barracks building. They were lifting up large concrete chunks, wood beams, and cinder blocks and loaded them on a cart that stood with its tugs on the ground. Another cart was just returning empty after its load was dumped. Instead of a horse, four MUSZ tied to its tugs were pulling it. Two Hungarian soldiers standing nearby smoking were watching them and laughing. (12)[3] Both were armed and both held whips. Laci noticed that the MUSZ who had to pass near the two while carrying heavy concrete chunks tried to avoid eye contact and were running fast on their return empty-handed.

They reached an auditorium at the opposite end of the parade square. It was a large hall, its cinder block walls covered with graffiti, some in Russian hailing Stalin, German hailing Hitler and Hungarian hailing Horthy. The roof seemed to be intact but a cold breeze blew through the shattered glasswindows. The concrete floor covered with blankets and bags of the MUSZ of other companies was barely visible. Only a few MUSZ were inside, sitting

---

I too have seen the expressionless faces of the defeated and I wondered what was hiding behind the stone faces. They were always the same blank stares that could mean hate, submission or shock. I do hope for the sake of the Ukrainians that they could find room in their hearts for some pity for the poor MUSZ marching by.

3 MUSZ replaced horses even when the horses were fully capable pulling the wagons. At stops, the horses were given fresh water while the MUSZ were forced to drink water from puddles on the side of the road. German and Hungarian officers stood by laughing and taking pictures.

in one of the corners busy boiling water on a small wood fire that burned uncontained on the floor. They must have been left behind to watch the belongings of their comrades.

Hegedűs, who did not march with them, was standing in a corner. Fresh and as elegant as he had been in the morning, he was yelling at them to reach him, drop their bags in a pile and line up outside. He had no plans to feed them lunch, allow a break or even let them drink after the long march. As they scrambled, Hegedűs picked one laborer and ordered him to stay behind to watch Company 106/12's pile.

They marched again through the base, past the group of working MUSZ and toward the fence at the edge of the base. A long expanse of barbed wire stretched between concrete posts. A long deep ditch ran along the fence and ended just where they were standing. More than a hundred shovels and a few pickaxes were leaning on the fence in a neat row.

"Here we are," announced Hegedűs. "Let's see what you pigs can do. You see the ditch; it needs to continue until it surrounds the entire base. It must be wide enough for two people to pass by each other when inside and deep enough to show no more than their heads when they stand up straight. The group before you did a hundred and fifty meters every day. You are fresh, you just arrived from home; you can do a hundred and seventy meters today. If you finish before dinner, you will eat. If not, then too bad. If you are lazy like typical Jews, you may not even sleep before the next stretch of a hundred and seventy meters starts tomorrow."

The MUSZ spread along the fence to pick tools. Laci and Endre picked a shovel and a pickaxe and positioned themselves at the edge of the line of working MUSZ trying to be out of Hegedűs's sight and the reach of his whip.

What started as a cool morning turned into a hot day when the sun rose high in the sky. After observing the MUSZ briefly, Hegedűs left the hard work of watching to his lieutenants—Kőrösi and Bálint and retired to a cooler place.

Sitting on two empty crates of ammunition, Kőrösi and Bálint seemed to enjoy the sun for a while. They waved their whips trying to generate cracking sounds, smoking and laughing. Occasionally, probably out of a deep sense of duty, one of them strolled along the long row of MUSZ, yelling orders and profanity and flogging someone at random for no obvious reason.

During one of these reviews, Kőrösi passed near Laci and Endre. When he noticed Endre standing up to clear dirt from his eyes, he swung his whip without warning and hit him in his face.

After four hours of work without break, a new section of the trench was cut into the ground. Thanks to the soft ground soaked by the summer rains, digging moved fast. The section was nearly complete both in depth and width. But it still was too short. Pacing out its length and counting aloud, Bálint determined that it was only eighty meters long, barely half the required length. But to their surprise, he ordered them to line up in formation and they walked back to the auditorium where they were allowed to drink water and rest briefly before returning to work.

They completed digging that day's section just before dinner.

The meal was familiar, watery soup with some cabbage and a little meat, a chunk of dark bread, and hot dark tea. The Püspökladány cook must have traveled with them to Gomel, Endre joked.

Trains continued to arrive. The auditorium floor that was already full when Laci's company arrived miraculously absorbed an additional few hundred MUSZ. Conditions became unbearable, barely enough room for all to lie on the floor at night, inadequate sanitation, running water, or toilets. But soon all were about to depart.

September-October 1942: When a Man Becomes a Horse

WEDNESDAY, SEPTEMBER 9, 1942.

After three days of digging trenches, the 106/12, along with seven other companies, was ordered to move. Following the usual breakfast of dense bread, a teaspoon of jam, and a lukewarm diluted coffee, more than eight hundred men, mostly from Transylvania, lined up in formation with their bags on their backs and then marched through the gate and lined up on the road leading away from Gomel. Nearly a hundred large wagons; all covered with tarps that hid their cargo and each drawn by a pair of horses were already waiting.

The wagons seemed battered, their side planks unpainted and coated with splashed mud. This was clearly not their first trip. On a bench at the front of each wagon sat the drivers. They were all soldiers. Laci and Endre recognized Bálint, Kőrösi, Kobak and Balázs among them.

Despite the heavy-handed censorship in war-time Hungary that prohibited mentioning any losses (8 pp. 186, 217) and despite the intense German propaganda that described a rapid progress towards Moscow, Laci, like most Hungarians, knew that the army that was sent to the Russian front was ill-equipped and poorly trained. But what in Budapest seemed like a joke about the Hungarian cavalry riding to battle on horses waving their sabers against the Russian tanks became a sad reality in Gomel.

But in fairness, the Russian infrastructure in the captured territories was rudimentary, without sufficient paved roads and railroad tracks to allow movement needed to supply the vast armies at the front. Therefore, supplies in limited quantities had to be pushed by horse-drawn wagons through unpaved roads, leaving soldiers poorly fed and often with insufficient or no ammunition. Even fodder for horses was lacking and so horses needed to draw cannons had to be left in the rear, leaving the cannons immobile and largely ineffective. (8 p. 213)

Laci noticed that the lead wagon had been modified with an additional bench, high above the wagon's tarp. The bench was covered with a canopy and was facing backwards. Captain Baky sat in it and monitored the preparations. How odd, Laci thought, that the leader of the convoy would choose to lead his convoy facing backwards.

"*Looks like a mezzanine in a theatre,*" (3 p. 41) Endre laughed while pointing to the elevated bench.

"He probably can see the whole convoy from there."

"Quiet there," interrupted Hegedűs. "*Attention!*"

The eight companies turned quiet and the MUSZ stretched to attention. The wagon drivers got off their benches and lined up standing to attention near their horses. Then Baky climbed off the "mezzanine" and positioned himself in front of the companies. Standing at ease, his narrowed dark eyes scanned the MUSZ as if trying to measure them up. His large black mustache was curled up like a corkscrew. The thin smile on his face radiated contempt. Captain Baky, a poor peasant from the "Low Land (*alföld*)," now commanded lawyers, doctors, accountants, journalists, businessmen and best of all, Jews. In civilian life they would have called him a *paraszt*,[1] but here they belonged to him.[2] With a whip in his hand, it was his time to enjoy it.[3]

"*We are heading to the front,*" Baky announced. The MUSZ's mission was simple, to accompany the convoy that carried food and ammunition to its destination. They were to help the horses if they could not pull the wagons, and replace them if they were injured or if they died. The convoy was to reach its destination at any cost, even the MUSZ's lives. "*Almost any cost,*" Baky added smugly. The lives of the horses and their energy had to be preserved. They were precious military property. (5 p. 32)

---

1 Paraszt—"peasant" in English, but also a dismissive word describing a boor or a hick.
2 Actually Horthy and his newly appointed Minister of Defense Nagy Vilmos tried to improve the condition of the MUSZ but mid- and low-level command sabotaged their efforts.
3 My basic training commander was an uneducated corporal barely older than us. At the age of nineteen, he was already bitter; he saw his life as a dead end: an undesirable military assignment followed by a lousy job in civilian life. He resented us. We were the symbol of everything that he would never be. We were the Academic Reserves, the future engineers of the IDF, almost guaranteed to become commissioned officers, most likely to spend our military service in a nice office rather than running on the dunes with new trainees week after week.

But at that moment we were his subjects. We had to obey him. And he used this power. His treatment of some of my friends was abusive. Luckily, military laws and his commanders restrained him; he almost crossed the line but he knew where to stop. Baky, his peers, and his command staff were unrestrained.

The wagons carried fodder for the horses, but very little food for the MUSZ, after all they brought their own food from home, Baky smirked. He then ordered them to divide into squads of six, a squad per wagon and asked for volunteers for his own wagon's squad."

Several MUSZ raised their hands.

"*What fools,*" whispered Laci to Endre, "*Let's try to get to the back of the column. If nothing else, we will be the last to arrive to the front.*" Csengeri was already standing behind the last wagon when they reached it.

The convoy started its long way to the front on a flat paved road passing through a wide plain, part of the Ukrainian steppes. The sun was shining and the going was easy. The two drivers on Laci's wagon were busy with their own conversation and ignored the MUSZ walking behind.

Ukrainian farmers working in the fields stopped to watch the passing convoy must have wondered why the wagons, each drawn by two able horses, could not at the very least carry the heavy back packs of the six civilians that followed it on foot. A farmer standing near the road waved to the drivers and the MUSZ and when the last wagon passed him and its drivers were out of sight, he pulled something out of his pocket and threw it to Laci. It was a potato.

Shortly before sunset, the lead wagon with Baky in the mezzanine turned off the road into a clearing at the edge of a pine forest. The other wagons followed and lined up in three parallel rows. When Laci's wagon came to stop, one of the drivers got off and pointed to him.

"*You, jump on the wagon. There is a small tent in the corner. Take it off and build it with your friends.*"

Laci climbed on the wagon opened the back flap of the tarp and crawled in. At the corner he saw the folded tent. But next to it was a crate of potatoes, sausages, a few loaves of bread, and several cans. So there was food on the wagon. Maybe there would be dinner tonight, he thought, but maybe not. With no second thought, he picked two potatoes and a sausage and hid them in his coat's pocket, praying that they were not counted and noticed missing.

While Laci and his squad were building the tent in the space between two wagons, the two drivers climbed into the wagon and started preparing food. Laci watched them start a small kerosene burner, open a can that they placed on the stove. The smell of boiling canned meat permeated the air. The hungry MUSZ stopped for a moment mesmerized by the aroma that tortured them more than it pleased.

"*Why are you staring at me?*" yelled one of the drivers. "*You want to eat? Even the horses have not eaten yet.*"

The drivers finished their dinner just as the tent was completed. They tossed the empty can overboard and Csengeri jumped to pick it up hoping to scrape the bottom. But before he could even straighten his back, a whip cracked and Csengeri fell to the ground holding his head.

"This can was not meant for you, scum of the earth," yelled the driver. "Field rats need to eat too. The squad will get food when we decide so. But for you there is no food tonight. Now leave the can on the ground and go back to work."

When the tent was built, the squad stood in attention to have it inspected. "Looks good," announced one of them. "I feel generous tonight; here are two loaves of bread and half a pack of margarine. Be sure that this lasts until tomorrow's dinner. This should be sufficient since only five of you eat tonight. After all, your friend tried to steal food. As you can see, we catch all the thieves."

They sat down and started slicing the bread. The drivers sitting on a folding cot in their tent watched them carefully to be certain that Csengeri did not get his share.

When the MUSZ were done, the drivers entered their tent and closed the flap behind them. The MUSZ were left to sleep under the starry sky. (5 p. 35)

Sitting by Endre Laci noticed that Csengeri was standing alone, leaning on the wagon and watching the MUSZ finishing their dinner. He approached him, reached into his pocket and pulled out a raw potato.

"Just eat it and be sure no one knows," he whispered and returned to Endre.

After getting themselves ready for the night, Laci suggested to Endre that they go out of the camp to relieve themselves. Once out of sight, he sat on the ground, pulled out the sausage and a potato and split them with Endre.

They ate silently listening to the sounds of people talking and horses snuffling accompanied by the love songs of crickets in the fields and angry barks of distant dogs.

"Look at these stars, Endre," Laci broke the quiet. "I wonder if my little Judit is now sitting on the porch in Gyula with Lili and looking at these same stars. Two weeks ago, as we were sitting on the porch, Lili told Judit the story about the Big Dipper constellation ("Göncöl Szekér" in Hungarian) and showed her how to use it to find the Pole Star. I wonder if Judit remembers that."

"Did you know that Göncöl Szekér is also part of the Hungarian mythology, not just the Greek? Göncöl Szekér means "the Dipper Cart." This was the cart that the táltos[4] used to carry medicine to cure the sick."

"I wish the táltos was carrying medicine for us too."

---

4   Táltos (pronounced "Taaltosh")—a Hungarian mythological shaman.

Their first night in the field was mildly pleasant. The skies were clear, the air cool and their stomachs full. If this was the worst, they would be OK after all.

THURSDAY, SEPTEMBER 10, 1942.

They woke up well before dawn to the sounds of roosters crowing. Soon, barking dogs and a couple of donkeys joined the symphony. As if to complement them, one of their wagon drivers opened his tent's flap and started howling orders. Quickly all the MUSZ squads scrambled to collect their belongings and get ready for roll call.

"I wonder what's our driver's name," said Laci. "Did you notice? They haven't bothered to introduce themselves."

"I heard the other driver calling him István," Endre answered.

"Well, then what is the other driver's name?"

"Attila?"

The six MUSZ lined up on time for roll call, standing in a row behind their wagon. Soon after, István emerged from his tent and gave them instructions for the morning routine.

First, the horses were to be fed, then István and Attila's tent was to be folded and loaded on the wagon, then the MUSZ were to wash and get ready for departure. There was no breakfast—the bread from last night should be sufficient. Morning departure would be at 8 am.

When he finished he pointed to one of the MUSZ, "You, what's your name?"

"Feri, Lakatos Feri."

"Great, Feri, you are now the squad leader. Be sure the squad obeys you and follows the rules. You will get extra rations for your work, but you will be punished if you miss any of my instructions. Dismissed."

After roll call and inspection by Attila, Feri marched the MUSZ to the "field kitchen," a large steaming pot on a stand with a few burning logs underneath and a folding bench with crates of cut bread next to a bowl of jam.

One of the "cooks," a MUSZ, was doling out ersatz coffee from the pot into the tin cups that the MUSZ were holding. Occasionally the ladle missed its target and the hot liquid hit an outstretched hand.[5]

---

5   Military meals in the field are far from an enjoyable picnic. I saw field kitchens operate during my military service. The experience was invariably bad.

   In fairness, cooks in the field have a difficult task. They need to feed hundreds of hungry, tired and impatient soldiers in a short time. Like the entire unit, their kitchen must be mobile, rebuilt and then torn down at every stop. Hot pots must be cooled before packing and dirty

At eight o'clock the convoy of wagons was lined up on the road. Much to his relief, Laci's wagon was still the last. Baky at the front was shouting orders but he was too far off for Laci and Endre to hear him. They were just glad to be out of reach of his swinging whip.

They started moving with the rising sun to their left. "*We are heading south,*" Endre concluded. "*The front is to our east, so at least for now we are not heading towards the front.*"

They continued on the road for a few miles. Baky, on the mezzanine facing backwards watched the wagons and the MUSZ while the convoy was led by his deputy, a sergeant named Horváth György.

Laci's squad was walking behind their wagon carrying their bags on their backs. After a short uphill section they saw the lead wagon turn off the road into the forest.

"*Our easy going is coming to an end,*" predicted Endre. "*I bet this will be a dirt road and that will turn muddy after the first rain.*"

They entered a forest of tall pine trees that blocked the sun. Cool and misty air filled their lungs. The narrow dirt road was just barely wide enough to fit the wagons. Long deep marks along the road showed that the road was well traveled. Some of the deepest tracks marked the spots where wagons were stuck in the mud during rainy days. It was quite a wonder how such a narrow dirt road that could barely accommodate a horse-drawn wagon had turned into an important supply road.

The going was getting harder, but the idyllic forest and the cool air made it feel easy. Occasionally they stopped by a creek to quench the horses, and their own thirst.

---

dishes washed using a meager water stream from a tanker, all the while surrounded by mud, rain, blowing sand or dust raised by moving vehicles. Meals must be ready even when fresh supplies fail to arrive and must be waiting for the units returning from their mission early or late. Invariably, my military meals in the field were made up of canned food that was heated up in large vats standing over large gas burners, cut up vegetables, slices of ancient bread and a hot drink, coffee or tea. We joked that meals in the field weren't cooked. They were opened.

Receiving food in the field was just as difficult. Rain or shine, we lined up in front of a folding table that was the serving counter, wearing our full gear, helmets on our heads, rifles hanging on our shoulders, two long handles of our "mesting" dishes (The Hebrew version of the English term "Mess Tin," two deep rectangular aluminum dishes, each with a long handle. When not in use, the two dishes folded together to form a rectangular box.) in one hand and a plastic cup in the other. When the mesting plates were filled up, the weight at the end of their long handles pulled them down. Trying to balance the dishes often caused the rifle to slide off my shoulder, the helmet to slide off my head and cover my eyes, or the hot coffee in my other hand to spill.

"You know, I recognize some of the mushrooms we see along the road," said Endre. "I know that some are edible."

"Are you sure? If we get poisoned here we won't survive it."

"I know, but I definitely recognize some of them."

When Baky disappears behind a curve, they slipped out of the line and picked a few mushrooms.

The others quickly learned to recognize these mushrooms and picked some for themselves. By day's end, the squad of the last wagon was much less hungry.

They continued walking behind the wagon until sunset. By Endre's estimate they covered another thirty kilometers. The first wagon turned into a large clearing followed by the other wagons. Tracks of wagon wheels, scattered cans, horse manure, and even a broken wagon wheel indicated that this clearing was used regularly as a campsite.

Once again, Laci volunteered to unload the tent. Instead of a sausage he now took a can of meat.

At midnight, heavy rain woke them up. Almost immediately the ground turned muddy and the deep wheel tracks in the ground turned into little rivers. Crawling under the wagon did little good; the tiny rivers followed them turning their blankets, clothes and coats into muddy soggy traps.[6]

---

6 I was an artillery officers' cadet during the 1971 winter. Much of our training included firing live artillery ammunition at the artillery firing range at the northern Negev desert.

Military field exercises are hard: long days with hardly any rest, night practices, rough camping style accommodations and exposure to the weather. But the harsh winter of 1971 made them even harder.

One of these field exercises fell on a cold and rainy spell, an unusual event in the arid and warm Negev. Temperature at night fell below freezing. One night it even snowed. We were equipped for winter training with water-resistant boots and coats, sleeping bags and small two-person tents. We even got daily three warm meals. But nothing could shield us from the thick yellowish desert mud that stuck to our boots and splashed on us by moving vehicles, the cold wind, freezing rain, and worst of all, the nights in a tiny personal tent built over cold muddy swamps. Combined with the fatigue, that exercise turned into a nightmare.

Every morning we tore down our camp and climbed on our mechanized cannons, moving to our new assignment holding on to the freezing steel structure, loading up the heavy iron shells with our bare hands because our gloves were too slippery.

At night, when we reached our new bivouac, even before building our new camp we had to complete the daily maintenance of our cannons. The barrel had to be cleaned and the tank wheels greased. The grease nipples facing out were easy to grease. But there were also nipples facing in between the treads. They could only be reached by crawling under the tank in the mud.

FRIDAY, SEPTEMBER, 11: ROSH HASHANAH EVE, 1942.

A grim grey dawn ended the night's misery. Tired from lack of sleep, shivering in their wet clothes, wearing heavy water soaked coats and carrying their backpacks that were weighed down by the wet blankets, the MUSZ lined up for another day.

With their soggy shoes sliding on the slippery ground, Laci and his squad at the rear needed to push their wagon back to the road while the horses pulled. The mud was slippery and their shoes had no traction while the horses' hooves were just grinding the mush. The effort felt hopeless.

After bringing the wagon back to its position behind the entire convoy they watched how several squads near the front were still struggling to get their wagons in place. Baky, sitting on his mezzanine on top of the lead wagon seemed from a distance to be indifferent. But then as if he suddenly made up his mind, he climbed off his seat and walked, clearly agitated, to the wagon just behind his.

"Look," cried out Endre, "*they released the horses of the second wagon and they are tying up the MUSZ to the harness.*"[7] (3 p. 44) (9 p. 313)

"*They cannot be serious,*" Csengeri said loudly, "*the MUSZ cannot pull such a wagon. They barely can carry themselves after being starved for days.*"

"You shut up," yelled Attila, from the front, "before I show you how you too can pull a wagon."

Finally the last wagon was back on the road and the convoy started moving. But cold drizzle and thick mud slowed their progress. With each step the horses' hooves and the MUSZ's boots sunk in the brown paste and when they were finally pulled out, the rain filled up the holes, making the mud even softer and stickier.

Often a wagon wheel got buried and stuck in the mud. The drivers tried to release it by steering the horses to the left and then to the right. But when they failed, MUSZ squads from that wagon and others were ordered to dig a long

---

After completing maintenance and passing inspection, we could finally pitch our tents trying to avoid all the little rivers running in old and new tracks of tank chains.

Looking up one night to the cliff where Avdat, the ancient Nabbatic city near us, once stood I saw a red flame flickering in one of the caves. It was a nomadic Bedouin warming up by the bonfire. I was so jealous and I am sure he must have wondered at the insanity of sleeping in the open field in such a night.

We were wet and covered by mud for days. Several of my comrades suffered frostbites. But surprisingly, not one of us caught a cold.

7   Dantsig and Braham give an account of wagons pulled by the MUSZ tied to the harness as if they were horses.

trench around and ahead of that wheel to help it roll out while Baky and the drivers yelling and beating the poor men.

During one of these stops, as if from nowhere, Sergeant Horváth appeared riding on a horse and pulled up along the stuck wagon swinging his whip and lashing the MUSZ who were digging in the mud with spades.

"You lazy bastards," he shouted. *"Drop off your gold filled bags, your coats, anything, and lift up that wagon until it moves. You are here to work. I'll kill you if the wagon is not out in a minute."*

Then he rode up to the next wagon and lashed its MUSZ as he ordered them to help the other squad to lift the wagon out of the mud.

The twelve MUSZ lined up around the edges of the wagon near the stuck wheel and started lifting it while another MUSZ collected broken branches off the road and stuffed them into the space below the raised wheel. Finally, resting on a solid bed of twigs and branches and with the horses pulling, the wheel started rolling. As it did, one of the MUSZ fell to the ground yelling in agony.

"I wonder if his leg got stuck under the rolling wheel," said Csengeri from the back of the last wagon. *"If he broke it he will never make it back home."*

"Up on your feet," they heard Horváth yelling while lashing the agonized MUSZ with his whip. *"I saw actors like you before. I call them 'artists'. If you are not on your feet in ten seconds I will shoot you."*

Assisted by his friend, the MUSZ stood up. Unable to put weight on his crushed foot he was hobbling on his healthy foot. In agony, he put on his heavy coat and backpack, supported by a friend and under the watchful eyes of Horváth he lined up with his squad behind the wagon. The convoy was again on its way.

After a few miles, the flat terrain turned hilly. What was before a difficult drive became nearly impassable. Occasionally a horse lost its footing and its wagon stopped. Unable to pass it on the narrow road, all the wagons behind it had to stop too. The progress of Laci's wagon at the back of the convoy ground down to a near stop. Horváth could not contain his anger. Together with another sergeant on a horse they lashed mercilessly the horses and the MUSZs.

The convoy reached the top of its first hill. The road curved onto a flat plateau and shortly after started moderately downhill. After the long climb, moving downhill felt almost effortless. Men and horses breathed a little easier and walked a little faster. But then the slope turned steeper and the effort of pulling the wagons uphill was replaced by the struggle of keeping them from rolling freely downhill.

They reached a sharp curve around a steep slope. The wagon in front of Laci's started turning slowly trying to avoid the abyss at the other side of the road. The horses pulled to keep the wagon on the road when one of them slipped and fell to his knees.

The horse neighed. It sounded like a squeal and then the wagon drivers and its MUSZs screamed. Laci could not see anything through the thick fog but he could hear a whip hitting the horse and then István's shouting orders.

They walked to the wagon to help. It was tilting dangerously to the right, barely avoiding the steep slope at the edge of the curve. The horse on the right was on his front knees, and the MUSZ were lined up with their backs against the side of the wagon pushing to straighten it. The drivers of that wagon were standing by the reins of the fallen horse trying to release him. When they finally got him free they inspected its foot. It was broken.

"Go and help those bastards," yelled Attila to his squad from the driver's seat.

They dropped their bags and coats at the edge of the road and joined three other squads pushing to right the wagon. With more than twenty men pushing from one side and the single horse pulling on the other, the wagon slowly emerged from the ditch dug by its right wheels and gradually rolled back to the center of the road where it remained standing with only one horse. The injured horse remained lying at the edge of the road panting in agony.

Appearing like a ghost from the thick fog, Horváth rode to the wagon, got off his horse and examined the injured beast and then pulled out his rifle. A single shot ended the horse's misery.

"*Tie the MUSZ to the empty reins and be ready to move in two minutes. I want to get off the road before nightfall,*" he shouted, as he rode back into the fog.

They were back in motion; it was not even midday and they already had one seriously injured MUSZ and one dead horse. The dangers of this journey were sinking into their minds. They were far from the front, they might never encounter enemy, and yet their casualties could exceed those of the fighting forces. Each rock on the road, a muddy patch, or a curve could be a death trap, worse than a landmine. And this didn't even count the ever-present threat of Horváth or his deputies.

Past noon the rain stopped, the sky cleared, and the convoy stopped in a valley near an overflowing creek. The sound of the gushing water combined with the misty scenery of wet pine trees was idyllic. But the exhausted MUSZ, eager to eat and rest, did not notice any of it. They removed their backpacks and found rocks elevated above the mud to sit or even lie down. Despite the warmth of the season and their hard work, they were shivering in their wet clothes. Their commanders, the wagon drivers, climbed into the wagons and started preparing their own lunch. There was none for the MUSZ.

"*Let's try to find some berries or mushrooms,*" suggested Endre.

Leaving Csengeri to watch their bags the squad members spread into the forest scavenging for food. The wet valley was fertile. Large wild raspberry bushes were blazing with clumps of red shiny berries and lush caps of yellow mushrooms peeked from underneath the thick beds of pine needles. Soon they gathered enough for a foraged lunch.

While they were eating, a MUSZ from another squad passed between the wagons searching for a doctor. The search did not last long. Ironically, there were more doctors among the MUSZs than among the fighting units. Some of Hungary's best physicians were employed in the Labor Battalions as horses. Torturing to death Jewish doctors was a higher priority in the wartime Hungarian army than saving lives of wounded Hungarian soldiers. (3 p. 20)

They scaled three additional hills before reaching their night camp. Two MUSZ and three horses were crushed to death when their wagons ran out of control on a steep descent. The corpses of the dead MUSZ along with the horse carcasses were left at the side of the road. They will feed the wolves, Horváth declared.

After building the driver's tent in the new night camp, feeding the horses and receiving their daily rations, Laci and Endre were preparing for another wet night out on the muddy ground when Csengeri asked them to join him for the evening prayer. It was Friday, but it was also the Eve of the New Year, he reminded them. The next day will be Rosh Hashanah, the first day of the Jewish calendar.

Tradition says that on Rosh Hashanah all Jews are judged by the Heavens for their deeds during the past year and their fate for the upcoming year is inscribed: "Who shall live and who shall die, who at his predestined time and who not at the predestined time, who by water and who by fire…"[8] But their fate is not sealed until Yom Kippur, ten days later. Repentance, prayer and charity may bring forgiveness.

Rosh Hashanah in Laci's childhood home in Gyula was marked by a festive and yet somber service in the synagogue. Joy and woe are blended together in most Jewish festivals, bridegrooms break a glass as part of their

---

8 The Unetanneh Tokef prayer was written in the eleventh century by Rabbi Amnon of Mainz and recited during the Rosh Hashanah and Yom Kippur morning services.

wedding to commemorate the destruction of the Temple, and believers fast on the day before the festival of Purim to commemorate the three-day fast by Queen Esther, the protagonist of the Purim narrative. But Rosh Hashanah is unique in its dichotomy between joy and sorrow; joy for the upcoming New Year is overshadowed by trepidation for the upcoming Yom Kippur.

After a short evening service in their synagogue, Sándor and Laci used to walk home along the dark Béke sugárút, Sándor's arm resting on Laci's shoulder as if hugging him. The moon is always absent on Rosh Hashanah and the poorly illuminated street seemed to be darker than usual. At home Böske and Évi hugged and kissed each one of them as they wished each other a Happy New Year. Behind them, in the living room, the large table would be set for the festive dinner that always started with apple slices dipped in dark, autumn honey. The honey and apple expressed their hopes for a round, full sweet year. After Sándor blessed the wine, the fruit, the bread and the New Year, Erzsi néni would bring out Böske's chicken soup. It was always the best chicken soup of the year. She would simmer it for hours on low heat, barely boiling, skimming off fat, adding herbs, checking and tasting until she declared it perfect. Then she cooled it, "to let it rest", and reheated it just before Sándor and Laci arrived.

After the soup came a roast, accompanied by mashed potatoes and *tzimmes*, a sweet Galician-Jewish carrot stew dotted with raisins. The Jews of Gyula who thought of themselves first as Hungarians and only then as Jews tried to distinguish themselves from the mostly orthodox Galician Jews. But they still served the Galician tzimmes on Rosh Hashanah. They "washed down" the dinner with sweet Tokaji wine and honey cake.[9]

If honey-dipped apple was all that needed to guarantee a sweet year, Laci thought as his mind drifted back to Csengeri who was assembling his Minyan, the ten man quorum required for a service, they would not have been sitting here in the damp valley by the large wagons and smelly horses, exhausted, hungry and scared that the next day one of them might die in a gory accident.

They all stood up and joined Csengeri when he started chanting in his rich voice the sacred words of the Rosh Hashanah eve service, *"Tik'u Ba'Chodesh Shofar, Ba'Kesse Leyom Chagenu."*[10] They had no shofar to sound but they

---

[9] Laci used to rave about Böske's chicken soup. It had just the right amount of fat, he told me. And when the fat floated to the top it formed little yellow translucent rings. *"You could tell if it was a bad soup,"* he told me with a smile *"if it had just one large ring at the top. It was too fatty."* But on Rosh Hashanah there were always many rings in Böske's soup, like hundreds of little gold coins.

[10] "Sound the Shofar on the first of the month, when the moon is covered, for our festival".

did not need one. Csengeri's voice penetrated the thick clouds overhead and reached to heaven above.

"Today marks the first day of Tishrei,[11] the 5703th year since the creation of the world," Csengeri announced before pulling out his evening bread ration and blessing it as if it was a challah.

There was no sign that their prayers were heard. The first night of the new Jewish year was as wet and cold as the previous night, the last of the expiring year. They spent it lying shivering in deep mud under thick and wet clouds.

---

11   Tishrei—the first month of the Jewish calendar.

October-December 1942: Stary Oskol

The convoy reached its destination in late October, a large supply depot near Stary Oskol in Russia. (3 p. 46) Their trip from Gomel took them through more than nine hundred miles. They passed near Chernigov that only fifty years earlier was a major Ukrainian Jewish center. Eight hundred Jews were still living there in June. SS infantry troops that followed the German Panzers rounded up all the Jews of Chernigov a few months earlier, lined them up in the marketplace and machine-gunned them down. Only one Jew survived to tell the story.

Past Chernigov, the convoy turned east towards Nizhyn that less than a century earlier was a center of the Orthodox Chabad Jewish movement. A Nazi purge turned Nizhyn *Judenfrei*—free of Jews.

From Nizhyn the convoy passed by Kursk that within a year would become the site of Germany's last strategic offensive and the largest tank battle in history.

Many MUSZ did not reach Stary Oskol. Some were killed by accidents, by the hardships of performing as "human horses," beatings, or executions by their commanders. Many died from the secondary effects of beating or injuries, such as broken bones or infected wounds that would not heal. Many died from a combination of causes, blistered feet that became infected or normally mild diseases, such as the flu, that their weakened and malnourished bodies could not fight off. Whatever the cause, many of their commanders were mostly indifferent and some even promoted and accelerated the rate of casualties.

Although the tests endured by the MUSZs during this long journey were not nearly as harsh as the tests that still awaited them in the coming months and years, the natural selection between the strong and the weak, the determined and the apathetic, the resourceful and the unimaginative was already taking its toll. Although luck played a role, it tended to favor those who did not rely on it exclusively.

At the depot, the MUSZ unloaded the wagons and carried the cargo on their backs to the large warehouses. When done, they were marched into town.

A large, heavily damaged theatre stood at the center of the town. (3 p. 47) They sat down on the front steps with their bags at their feet. Old signs in Russian on the wall behind them announced the title of the last movie that was played there. It showed a woman in a blue skirt and white shirt, her long brown hair blowing in the wind, standing in a wheat field holding a large red flag with the communist hammer and sickle symbol. Behind her, muscular men were harvesting the wheat with sickles.

The destruction in the town was extensive. Like in Gomel, the war did not discriminate between rich or poor, large buildings or small. It destroyed everything along its path. Most buildings appeared vacant; their residents either killed or fled with the retreating Red Army. Stores were looted and their windows shattered. A faint stench of rotting corpses, animals or humans, still persisted in the air.

With time to sit, look, and reflect, Laci was thinking of the destroyed lives that each vacant window represented. Even if the inhabitants behind those windows survived, they were now refugees, their property lost, their jobs and income gone, and their future uncertain. How long would it take for the city to rebuild? Who would rebuild it? The Nazis? The Soviets?

"*What do you think our next assignment will be,*" Endre interrupted his thoughts. "*Join the convoy on its way back, remain here to repair roads, or go to the front to dig ditches?*"

Endre did not wait for an answer. Noticing that Attila was gone, he stood up, casually strolled around the corner and disappeared. Minutes turned into an hour and then two. Laci began to worry that Endre might not return. But then he was back.

"*I have a surprise for you,*" he whispered to Laci. "*Remind me tonight to show you what I got.*"

Darkness fell rapidly and with it came the night chill. Finally, Attila returned and ordered the squad to join him. They entered the dark theatre, and scrambling through people lying on the floor he led them to the opposite corner where most of their company was already setting up for the night.

"*This is your company,*" he said. "*Stay with them until you get new orders. Too bad we missed dinner but maybe we will have breakfast tomorrow. Oh and by the way, we are in a war zone. You are not allowed to turn on any lights, no candles, no fires,*" he said as he disappeared in the dark.

They settled near a wall, Endre opened his bag, pulled out two fur hats and gave one to Laci. "*I went to tour the city and dug through building ruins,*" he explained, "*I found these two hats in a collapsed apartment building.*" He then reached into his bag again and pulled out a large slab of bacon.

When they prepared to settle down for the night, they noticed that at the far end of the theatre, several MUSZ were burning candles and cooking food.

"Interesting, Endre." mused Laci. "*Do you think Attila just made up the rule about maintaining the dark inside the theatre?*"

"He might have. But it really doesn't matter now. I'm ready to sleep."

Several gunshots followed by screams and shouts woke them up after midnight but then quiet returned and they fell asleep again.

In the morning they saw on the street outside the theatre a row of six dead MUSZs, each with a gunshot wound to the head. A sign attached to each of the bodies explained that they were executed for signaling their location to the enemy by lighting candles.

Later that morning the 106/12 company was assembled in front of the theatre along with two other companies.

It was their first roll call as a company since leaving Gomel. Of the eighty MUSZ that started the deadly supply march, only seventy were standing there. The human toll was visible to them for the first time. Csengeri, who had seemed the weakest when they started, was still with them.

Captain Baky was standing in front of them.

"So you are the tough ones," he started. "*You may end up regretting that you are still alive. But don't worry; I will take care of it. I promised to return to Hungary eight hundred and forty pairs of shoes, with or without their owners. I already have in my wagon forty pairs. I would like to introduce your commanders for your next mission, Sergeant Horváth and his deputies, Privates Attila and Mátyás. But of course you will never call them by their names,*" he added as he waved towards the two standing next to him, both armed with rifles and whips.

After the roll call, the companies left the theatre heading towards their new assignments. A wagon with two horses was assigned to each company to carry their equipment. But as before, the MUSZ were still carrying their personal gear on their backs.

They left Stary Oskol on a narrow road heading south passing through farmland. By early evening they reached a little kolkhoz. Attila guided their wagon off the road onto a recently harvested field near a small farmhouse. A plump woman wearing a headscarf stood at the door with her three little children watching quietly as the wagon stopped in her field. The MUSZ unloaded it and prepared an overnight camp.

Their dinner was meager as usual: coarse bread, a slice of bacon, and some jam. Horváth, Attila, and Mátyás retreated to their tent for their own dinner. There was no tent for the MUSZ. A large barn behind the house that could easily house their company was declared off-limits by Attila.

When Attila and Mátyás disappeared in their tent, several MUSZ walked out to the field. It was a harvested potato field, but fortunately, they still found some.

Two MUSZ dared to walk beyond the field and into the kolkhoz to trade with the farmers. In the morning, they showed proudly two packs of Russian cigarettes. Endre speculated that they traded away their evening bacon.

In the morning they continued their march. The Russian woman with her three children stood again at the door of her house waving them with a relief a cheerful goodbye.

They continued for several days, passing through Chernyanka, Novy Oskol and then south to Volokonovka. Each night they stopped near another kolkhoz or village that remained off limits to the MUSZ. But the fields provided them generously with potatoes, turnips, and beets.

Volokonovka, their last stop along this march, was a little town of about ten thousand people, an administrative center for the kolkhozes surrounding it. From the edge of the town they could see that a multistory building was partially collapsed and many houses in the outskirts were burned or damaged. Burned vehicles were still littering the roads. Surprisingly, the fields looked unharmed and most of the kolkhozes undamaged. Despite the war, and despite missing most of their young men, farming communities managed to successfully grow crops and harvest them.

The company camped outside the town and the MUSZ set up tents for the company kitchen, equipment storage and of course for Horváth, Attila and Mátyás. There were no tents for the MUSZ, not even in this semi-permanent camp. Although night temperatures were still moderate, occasional rain soaked them, depriving them of sleep.

Four members of their company were assigned to kitchen duties and an additional three as butlers to their commanders. Normally, only officers of the Hungarian army were allowed butlers. But the Forced Labor battalions were not an ordinary army.

The MUSZ assigned to the kitchen were the luckiest, being close to the source protected them from hunger. The rations issued by the army to the labor battalions were meager but still nutritionally sound. But by the time they trickled down to the MUSZ through the distribution channels they were depleted of most nourishing items such as meat, fat, and sugar, often stolen by their own commanders who then traded the goods with the locals for vodka, or even with the MUSZ themselves who paid for what was rightfully theirs. Since most their valuables were already spent or robbed, MUSZ started paying with coupons (*bónok*), (9 p. 306) simple notes scribbled by MUSZs to their families at home instructing them to pay the bearer with cash or other valuables. Often, a *bónok* was presented for collection long after the death of the issuing MUSZ. And to add to the tragedy, the family did not even know that their MUSZ will not return.

The following day the 106/12 company marched eastward to its worksite carrying shovels, rakes and wheelbarrows. Along the way they were joined by the other companies under Baky's command who camped nearby with wagons.

They stopped at the head of a road leading eastward from Volokonovka to Alexeyevka, the seat of the Hungarian Second Army's headquarters. (8 p. 215) Their new task was to repair the road that was damaged by the heavy German Panzers on their way to Stalingrad, by bomb explosions, freezing ice, or simply old age. It was a forty-mile-long stretch that would keep them working for many weeks.

Each morning they were woken before sunrise. After breakfast, they marched to the next section that was further east than the previous section. Just before sunset they stopped work, polished the shovels and rakes as if they were rifles and after inspection they returned to camp. The march that was short on the first day became longer as they progressed towards Alexeyevka.

Although work was hard, it was much easier than pulling the convoy and largely not dangerous. The fall weather was cool and getting cooler, it often rained but they were not in danger of freezing, at least not yet. Their commanders were often harsh and did not hesitate to beat their subjects, but as long as the work progressed well they refrained from sadistic exercises such as pointless calisthenics lasting for hours.

Often supply of gravel or asphalt did not arrive on time and the MUSZ were allowed to enjoy a few days of relative rest. On most Sundays, they stayed in camp to rest while their commanders went to Volokonovka to drink and to buy cheap love, paying with food stolen from the MUSZ. Some of the most enterprising MUSZ used these free days to connect with the locals. Many found friends among the Russian farmers who adopted them like their own sons, possibly as a substitute for their real sons at the front. Often after visiting with their acquaintances, they returned with small treasures such as a warm piroshky (a Russian dumpling), a chunk of smoked ham or a small pie.

Other MUSZ ventured to the adjacent fields searching for potatoes and roots, while others used the time to recover from injuries or illnesses.[12]

The free days allowed many MUSZ to write letters to home. The military mail service was irregular and heavily censored. (9 p. 316) Letters, unlike the valuable bónoks, were often destroyed or simply lost. (3 p. 56) Sometimes a car would stop by their unit and the driver agreed to carry letters, at other times it was a soldier on foot. But always, a letter had to be ready in the pocket for delivery.

The promise to deliver a letter was rarely free. Not only because the carriers demanded compensation, but also because the senders wanted to motivate the carriers by the promise of payment by the recipient. Still, many letters were not delivered. Occasionally the carriers robbed the recipients. In some cases, the carriers convinced the recipients that they were returning to the front and would be happy to carry back a package, for a fee, of course. Many packages "disappeared" together with the fee. But on rare occasions, a returning soldier brought back goods and valuables to the serving son.[13]

When the road repair progressed several miles, the camp was relocated closer to the work site. It was already mid-November and almost overnight winter took over. The endless fall rains turned into snow and night temperatures fell below freezing. This rapid change spelled a death sentence to many MUSZ. Without proper clothing, shelter, and sufficient blankets, many suffered frostbite and some froze to death in their sleep outdoors.

After several MUSZ died in their sleep under the open wintery sky, Baky decided that it was time to let the rest move into the barns near their worksite.

---

12   Like many children, I was picky with food. I really liked my mother's mashed potatoes, they were rich and tasty. But she prepared them often, too often, until I grew tired of them. One evening I left my potatoes on my plate. Laci noticed and ordered me to eat them. "*They are sacred,*" he told me. "*They saved my life when I was in Ukraine. Often for days on end, potatoes were the only food I got. I found them in the fields or got them from generous farmers. I would have died if not for the potatoes.*"

   That evening I struck a deal with her—if she would allow me to leave one food item on my plate, no questions asked, I would eat everything else. We agreed on spinach; potatoes were not even an option.

13   Before leaving home for my basic training, Laci pleaded that I write a postcard every day; even if I had nothing new to tell or even if it was just one line, then number the cards in the order sent so they could determine if any of the mailed cards was missing.

   Knowing that I may not be able to write daily and that mail pickup is irregular, I used my weekends to write cards in advance for the entire week and then carried the pre-dated and numbered cards, ready to mail.

The 106/12 company found a large barn that they shared with several horses. (3 p. 7)[14] They used hay they found in the barn for mattresses and combined it with mud they gathered in the fields to build a small stove at the edge of the barn that they fired with small branches and straw. Without a chimney, the fire filled the barn with smoke. But it provided sufficient heat to boil water, roast the potatoes they scavenged, and to dry their shoes and coats. Combined with the body heat of sixty people and several horses under one roof, the stove kept the barn comfortably warm even on bitterly cold nights.

When nights grew longer and workdays shorter, the MUSZ assembled near the stove, warming up, cooking, telling stories, singing, and even listening to a flute that someone brought from home. Despite the hard work, at nearly all weather conditions, these weeks in November and early December were almost tolerable. The food supplements they scavenged and the shorter workdays allowed many to regain weight, recover from earlier injuries and illnesses, and even boost their morale.

But winter had no mercy; snowstorms were getting longer and more frequent. The vast steppes were coated with a thick permanent white blanket. Road repair work was no longer possible and Horváth assigned the MUSZ to clear snow instead. Even during the most intense blizzards, the MUSZ, dressed in torn clothing, some without coats, were ordered outdoors with shovels to clear the road and pile the snow into mountains along the edge of the road. Those without shovels were handed rakes and ordered to stand along the road and in intersections acting as human road signs to direct the nonexistent traffic. They stayed outdoors from sunrise to sunset even when the hardy Russian farmers chose to stay indoors. Many lost their lives during those futile and senseless tasks.

Even when the skies cleared and the sun came out, the environment remained hostile. The strong wind that traveled uninterrupted along the vast plains chilled the air and blew the dry snow as if it were sand. There was no escape from the flying ice dust and from the bright sunlight that was reflected by the white surfaces.

Cold weather and snow were not the only killers. Germs and viruses were their companions. Crowded living conditions, proximity to horses, lack of basic sanitation, and weakened immune systems brought diseases.

---

14 The name of Dantsig's book, *Be-tsel Susim*, "In the Shadow of Horses" in Hebrew, was chosen because of the many nights during the 1942 winter, which the author spent in barns shared with horses.

Almost everyone suffered from colds, influenza, pneumonia, and diarrhea. But what at home could be brushed off as a simple malady turned deadly here.

Those days in the barn were the last before the front in Stalingrad collapsed, and the Hungarian army suffered disastrous losses and one of its worst defeats in history.

May 1967: Dark Clouds over Israel

When I turned 19, the liberation of the concentration camps was only twenty-two years behind us. In Israel, where survivors with tattooed numbers on their arms were a regular sight, the *Shoah*[1] was still a raw memory. But to me and the *Sabras*[2] of my age that was an ancient history, as remote as the destruction of the Temple. It was a narrative that could happen only to the Diaspora Jews that we the Sabras viewed as weak and spineless, unable or unwilling to stand up for themselves, their women and children. We, the new Jewish breed, were different.

Until May 15, 1967, that is. For the first time in my own memory, our existence as a nation and as individuals was brought into question. Suddenly, the word *Shoah* was uttered again, and this time we, the Sabras, along with the survivors of the previous Holocaust, were the targets.

Israel's 19th Independence Day was celebrated on that day which fell exactly one week after my 19th birthday. As a teenager, I used to agonize that had I been just one week younger, I would be among the more than one hundred Israeli children invited as guests to the home of Israel's president, Zalman Shazar. Every year I saw their pictures in the papers shaking hands with him, showered with gifts and most importantly, missing school the day before the holiday. I was so close, so deserving, and yet so far.

On that Independence Day, these lucky guests received their best birthday present ever. They joined the President at the dignitaries' stand erected in the center of Jerusalem to watch the annual military parade. I could see them in my mind, some wearing white cotton shirts, blue canvas pants, and khaki "Tembel" sunhats,[3] others in military dress uniform, shaking hands with

---

1. *Shoah*—the Hebrew word for the Holocaust.
2. *Tzabar*—a Hebrew word for the "Sabra," describes a native-born Israeli. The Tzabar is also a cactus pear and the cactus plant that grows it. They are conspicuous in Israel. The human Tzabars, or the Sabras, were viewed, like the cactus pear, as prickly on the outside but sweet on the inside.
3. *Tembel*—in Hebrew "silly" or "fool." The cone-shaped Tembel hat became a symbol of the Israeli pioneers and then of Israel itself as depicted by many cartoons.

the Prime Minister, Levi Eshkol, and the Chief of Staff General Yitzhak Rabin; and then sitting smugly behind the president watching the parade with cold soda bottles in hand.

But I was born in Hungary one week too early. Instead of sitting on the dignitaries' stand, I was in my parents' flat in Haifa and like most Israelis, listened to the live radio broadcast. In 1967, my parents Laci and Zsuzsi[4] still did not own a television set. Israel was a much simpler country then.

That year was Jerusalem's turn to host the annual military parade that rotated among the three largest cities. As in previous years, it was the highlight of the day's festivities. Born from the ashes of the Holocaust, the new Jewish nation could not be prouder of its military might. The Nazi victims, those who were portrayed as the "lambs led to their slaughter," those who were viewed as helpless, a passive human mass, now had a mighty army. Their sons were generals, tank commanders, battle ship captains and fighter pilots. Even their daughters carried arms. Thousands of Israelis traveled by bus or train to see the parade and those who did not, followed it on radio.

The Israeli Defense Force (IDF) was believed to be the strongest army in the Middle East and as we would soon learn, among the strongest in the world. This army proved its strength in the War of Independence in 1948 and the Sinai Campaign in 1956. This was the army that participated in countless incursions across the borders of four neighboring hostile Arab states. This was the army that stood on the wall holding back the armies of four neighboring Arab nations.

But on that festive day, not a single Israeli could imagine that the most critical test yet of the IDF lay only three weeks away. That within a week, we the confident Israelis, would seriously fear that a new Holocaust was upon us. And with the exception of some Israeli generals and several ministers, no one could hope that after fearing a new Holocaust, the IDF would score in a short war, only six days long, a victory of biblical proportions.

The pleasant late spring morning turned into a hot scorching day. This was not unusual for the season. Previous Independence Day parades also took place in heavy Khamsins.[5] Hot winds from the Jordanian and Iraqi deserts carried red sand. Khamsins in Jerusalem, located on mountains at the edge

---

4 Zsuzsánna Laufer (neé Zsuzsánna Dénes), "Zs" is pronounced in Hungarian like the "Zh" in "Dr. Zhivago."

5 Khamsin—an Arab word describing an extraordinarily hot and dry day with eastern desert winds. Folk tales suggest that the word derives from the Arabic word "khamsun," meaning "fifty," thereby implying that there are fifty such hot days in a year.

of the Judean desert were particularly vicious with temperatures higher than along the shore and the blowing sand denser. Remaining at home listening to the radio was not such a bad predicament after all.

In the weeks before, while I was preparing for my mid-term exams at the Technion, Israel's equivalent to MIT, many of my high school friends who already started their mandatory military service were practicing for the parade, marching nightly along Jerusalem's Yafo Avenue.

Like my peers, I started my military service at age 18. But unlike most of them, I was transferred to the Academic Reserves (AR) corps after a short basic training and assigned to study Aeronautical Engineering at the Technion. The ARs were ordinary students as well as IDF reserve soldiers. We were called up for military training during our summer breaks and had to set aside two afternoons a week for other military activities. We were training to become officers when we resumed our military service after graduation. And like all Israeli reservists we were also subject to mobilization during an emergency.

Although Jerusalem was the Israeli capital, Israel was not totally free to hold a large military parade. Jerusalem was a divided city, half-Jewish and half-Arab, half Israeli and half Jordanian. Barbed wire fences marked the border between its two parts. Only UN officials, occasional foreign reporters and some clergy were allowed from one side to the other through a checkpoint at the heart of the city, the Mandelbaum Gate. The uneasy quiet along this urban border was broken occasionally by Jordanian snipers taking aim at a careless border guard or a heedless citizen.

To contain these occasional flare-ups, the two sides of the city were declared demilitarized zones, free from heavy weapons such as tanks or overflies by military jets. To avoid any pretext that could spark a conflict, Israel had to limit the parade to foot soldiers and light military vehicles. It was a low-key parade, but in Jerusalem nevertheless. For two millennia Jews turned toward Jerusalem in prayer and now it was the host of a Jewish army military parade.

When the live broadcast began, my best friend, Rafi, was already dressed in his pressed flight school cadet uniform, proudly wearing the broad white stripes on his shoulders that marked his status. Rafi, the son of two Polish immigrants, Holocaust survivors, was exactly a year away from earning his "wings." In my eyes he was already an Air Force pilot. I was jealous. Not only was he flying planes regularly, having long ago passed the solo exam, but he was to parade with the most selective unit in the IDF, ahead of the paratroopers and even ahead of the commando units. He was among the darlings of

Israel, a role model for every young Israeli male and the heartthrob of every young female.

Lining up for the parade, a few units behind the flight school cadets, was the famed infantry brigade, Golani, where one of the squad commanders was Me'ir, another of my high school classmates. His olive color uniform, the brown shoulder tags showing an oak tree, and his black, over-the-ankle boots distinguished him from other "low-class" infantrymen.

Behind Me'ir's unit marched the sailors of the Israeli frigate Eilat, all dressed in Navy whites. Among them was another of my friends, Chaim. We had been in school together since the first grade. Chaim was a mischievous troublemaker. A little scar above his left eyebrow was a souvenir from one of his many fistfights.

Sharply at 10 o'clock, the commentator stopped at mid-sentence. Two trumpets announced the arrival of the President, the highest post in the country, the personification of the nation. Laci, who admired Mr. Shazar for his modesty, commented with pleasure, "*L'exactitude est la politesse des rois*" ("punctuality is the virtue of kings"). My father had a French or Latin quote for every occasion.

The radio broadcaster reported that everyone on the dignitaries' stand, including the prime minister, cabinet ministers, the chief of staff, members of the Knesset, diplomats (and of course the lucky 19-year-old guests), jumped to their feet as President Shazar emerged from his modest Citroen limousine and walked to his seat, turned towards the Israeli flag and the Army band began playing the national anthem, Hatikva, "The Hope," a somewhat melancholic song describing the two-millennia-old hope of the Jewish nation for a homeland of its own.

When the president sat down, Prime Minister and Minister of Defense Levi Eshkol, walked to the microphone to deliver his holiday pronouncements. Eshkol was a member of the old Israeli establishment that consisted mostly of Russian Jewish immigrants. This ideological group parted with Communism decades earlier in favor of Zionism and its members were among the early waves of immigration to the desert and swamplands of Palestine.

Eshkol, a short, bespectacled man, looked like a grocery store clerk. Having been the finance minister for more than a decade and presiding over one of the worst recession in Israel's history, he was highly unpopular. As was the custom, Eshkol was also the Defense Minister. Few believed he had the necessary skills, but with the security challenges being perceived as minimal, no one objected.

After losing his first wife, Eshkol had recently married a much younger woman and soon became the target of salacious jokes taking aim at his strange marriage. The black humor highlighted the bitterness of many Israelis and the sense of despair that resulted from the long and deep recession.

As expected, Eshkol's uninspiring speech, delivered in a thick Russian accent, was brief. He tried with little success to reassure his countrymen that the financial difficulties would end soon. They responded by an old joke, calling on the "last person to leave the country to please turn off the lights".

The Army Chief of Staff General Yitzhak Rabin followed Eshkol. Rabin, a Sabra, spoke very slowly, every word carefully measured, more like a university professor than an army general. In his characteristic deep, raspy voice of a chain smoker and in perfect Hebrew, he told the nation that despite continuous Syrian aerial incursions and artillery attacks from the Golan Height on the kibbutzim in the Jordan valley below, Israel's security had never been better. The IDF and the Air Force were more than prepared to meet the challenge. The strength of the IDF was the best deterrent to any attempt on Israel by any neighboring nation; a lesson the Syrians learned from the last air skirmish where they lost six of their MiGs. Rabin ended his reassuring speech by projecting that a wide-scale war in the region was unlikely in the coming years.

How wrong he was.

That night, Israel held its first Hebrew Song Festival, a nationally broadcast competition for the next national hit. An unknown young singer, Shuli Nathan, captured everyone's hearts singing in her angelic voice a song about Jerusalem, a city adorned by gold and bronze but divided by a wall that passes through its heart.

> Jerusalem of gold, and of bronze, and of light…
> The city that sits secluded
> And in its heart is a wall.

The wall in the heart of Jerusalem was meant to be the barbed wire entanglement fence partitioning the city between Israel and Jordan and keeping Israelis away from their holiest site, the Western Wall.

The song, Jerusalem of Gold by Naomi Shemer, was commissioned by the mayor of Jerusalem. It was not part of the competition but overnight it became part of Israel's and Judaism's cultural heritage. A month later, a monumental event would prompt Naomi Shemer to update the song with a new stanza.

The Song Festival ended close to midnight. Just before going to bed I listened to the last news brief of the day, the Egyptian Army mobilized some units across the Suez Canal into the Sinai Peninsula. The announcer noted that just like Jerusalem, the Sinai Peninsula was a demilitarized zone and that the additional forces in Sinai were in violation of the 1957 armistice agreement between Israel and Egypt.

I did not think much of the announcement. As a condition for Israel's withdrawal from the Sinai Peninsula after capturing it in 1956 during the Sinai Campaign, the desert was to remain arms-free with a UN peace-keeping force monitoring it. Without a doubt, I thought as I was falling asleep, Egypt would be ordered by the UN to withdraw these additional forces.

MAY 16, 1967

The next morning I took the bus as usual across town to Naveh Sha'anan, the mountaintop neighborhood where the Technion was located. It was full as usual and the speakers on its ceiling carried music from GALATZ, the popular military radio station. Unlike the national radio channels that usually carried talk shows and classical music, GALATZ was lively. Songs from last night's Song Festival filled the air. They had all the qualities of new hits.

At 8 am, six sharp beeps marked the top of the hour. Imitating the BBC, the beeps were used to mark the exact time and the start of the news broadcasts. The deep voice of Moshe Hovav penetrated the air with the regular morning greeting and then went on to repeat last night's news. Hovav, a veteran radio celebrity, was usually the broadcaster of the 7 pm prime time evening news. Having him read the morning news was unusual it suggested that a serious event, often bad, was about to be reported.

Indeed, the follow up to last night's news was that overnight, Egypt moved additional troops into Sinai including infantry and heavy armored vehicles in blatant violation of the demilitarization rules.

The bus became a mini Israeli parliament. Everyone had an opinion and everyone expressed it loudly. Almost no one had the patience to hear out his neighbor and hardly anyone noticed that just before signing off, Hovav announced the arrival of an urgent news item: Radio Cairo welcomed Israel's aggression and predicted that the long awaited battle in which Egypt would destroy Israel was coming. These threats from Cairo, I marveled, were in sharp contrast to Rabin's speech only a day earlier.

The mood in the bus changed abruptly from the high spirits carried over from yesterday's holiday into a new reality of concern and worry.

Sharp mood swings were not unusual in Israel. Almost everyone either served or had an immediate relative who served in the military. Border skirmishes and casualties often had personal impact. A routine condemnation of Israel by the United Nations was taken as a personal insult and a win in an international soccer match were taken as a personal victory.

But the harsh tone coming out of Radio Cairo, blaming Israel with aggression and calling for a war was uncommon. The last few skirmishes along the northern border were largely associated with Syria's attempt to divert the sources of the Jordan River. But Egypt, with the largest army in the Middle East, was not openly aggressive and most importantly, its army was kept at arm's length away from Israel. The aggressive tone now coming from Radio Cairo was more befitting Damascus Radio.

Six months earlier Egypt and Syria had signed a defense treaty. Was it possible that Egypt considered the skirmishes with Syria as relevant to the treaty that required them to respond? It did not make any sense. The skirmishes along the Syrian border were not a direct threat to Syrian security. They were a far more serious threat to Israel. Could it simply be a test of the demilitarization rules in Sinai that would eventually be stopped by the UN or by the Soviets? We did not know then that the Soviets were in fact the instigators of this new escalation.

I got off the bus at the bottom of the hill that was crowned by the Aeronautical Engineering building. It was a magnificent building designed by one of Israeli's top architects. Its location at the highest point on campus and its beauty reflected our belief that we were the most prestigious engineering program in the school and the entire country. The breathtaking view of the Haifa Bay from the large deck just outside the library provided all the distraction necessary to ignore any textbook even at the height of the exam season. Most classrooms had full-length floor-to-ceiling windows facing the bay and the mountains beyond. The students were situated with their backs to the window in the belief that the professors were better able to resist the temptations of the view.

When I reached our classroom, breathless after climbing the steep hill and the steps that meandered through the park that decorated the slope, I found a few of my classmates already sitting in their regular places loudly dissecting the recent news.

We were a class of sixty-five Aeronautical Engineering students; the largest class in the department's seventeen-year history. We all studied an identical curriculum during our first two years. We attended the same classes on the same schedule. And we were all men. Very few women had any interest in engineering, let alone Aeronautical Engineering. One female that started with our class dropped out after two months.

Only ten of my classmates were my age. Of them, nine, like me, were in the AR corps, and like me they were preparing to become the future aeronautical engineers of the Israeli Air Force. The others were at least three years older, having completed their mandatory military service and in some cases additional years of service. They were reserve paratroopers, infantrymen, or officers. Two were Air Force pilots. The pilots were greatly admired. To be sure that they would be recognized as such, they wore Air Force-issued jackets with fur collars in the winter and Air Force-issued aviator shades year round. The glasses were the most recognizable symbol, even more so than the large black aviator watches. The recent downing of six Syrian MiGs added glory to all pilots, particularly those who flew the Mirage, the elegant French-made delta-winged supersonic plane. Mirage pilots were the superheroes of the nation and two of them were in my class!

Just before class, as usual, we discussed recent events. Some hardliners argued loudly that Israel should send warplanes to attack the Egyptian forces before they dug in the Sinai Desert. Egypt violated the demilitarization agreement, they argued and Israel should do the same while it still could. But the cool-headed thought that Egypt was just posturing. This was the Middle East after all. One of our two pilots sat quietly. But then, he was always quiet, almost passive.

But even the moderates wondered if this mobilization of Egyptian forces into Sinai would force Israel to mobilize its own reserve units. Some worried that they would be called up just when mid-term exams were coming up.

In 1967, Israel was a very small country of fewer than 2.4 million Jews surrounded by significantly larger Arab countries. Although most citizens of these countries were poor and uneducated, Egypt, Syria, and Jordan could easily maintain regular armies numbering altogether more than half a million soldiers armed with the most modern Soviet- or British-made weapons, including more than 950 combat aircrafts and 2,500 tanks. By contrast, Israel could barely keep a regular army of 50,000 soldiers consisting mostly of young, inexperienced conscripts.

To offset this overwhelming numerical disadvantage, Israel built a well-trained and easily mobilized reserve force. Regular exercises of these reserve units included execution of very clever mobilization systems. In an emergency, reserves could be mobilized "silently" through a pyramid scheme where each reservist was called up by a member of his own unit, either by phone or in person. The newly recruited reservist, before reporting to duty, served two other members of his own unit and so on until the entire unit was mobilized.

By today's perspective it feels quaint to think of one reservist knocking on the door of another. It speaks volumes both to the tiny size of Israel, the deeply intertwined webs of connections, and the very true sense that everyone was in this together.

The silent mobilization was intended to avoid panic, to conceal the Army's actions and just as importantly, prevent the escalation that could come if the enemy chose to mobilize forces as well.

But on rare occasions, units could also be called up by an open emergency mobilization system. Each unit was assigned its own call-up code-name. In an emergency, the call names of the various units were broadcast repeatedly on all radio channels. When a unit's code name was called, all its members were required by law to stop everything, immediately pack up and report to their assembly point using any means of transportation. Most public transportation systems were required to provide free rides to mobilized soldiers.

My unit's code name was "Night Owl." It was, in my opinion, a humiliating code name. Even the least imaginative spy would think of my unit, if it were ever called up, as a group of students and not as a fearsome fighting unit. The IDF might as well have called us "Quill and Ink."

Embarrassing code names aside, these mobilization schemes were well tested and proven highly effective. Israel could have all its reserve units fully mobilized and equipped within 24 hours and in their positions in less than 48. Such quick deployment, however, could take place only if highways, railroads, bridges and call up centers were not destroyed by a surprise air or artillery attack. Unfortunately for Israel, nearly all its infrastructure was within artillery range from at least one hostile border. The enemy did not need to mobilize to deal Israel a crippling surprise attack.

When fully mobilized, the reserve Army could reach as many as 210,000 servicemen. But even at full strength the IDF was outnumbered by a two-to-one ratio. With such a small army, Israel could not operate more than 300 combat aircrafts and 800 tanks. It made for a very disturbing outlook when attacked simultaneously by all three neighboring countries. The feelings of "the few against the many" and the vulnerability of the small territory were amplified by the still raw memories of the Holocaust.

Israel's best hope and almost the only viable strategy for surviving and winning simultaneous threats was to engage each of them separately, using highly mobile forces that could be quickly transferred from one front to another. At least here, Israel's small size and consequently the short distance between the fronts presented a strategic advantage. With most of its forces concentrated in any one front, the IDF could expect a localized numerical advantage, and with a better trained army, also a strategic superiority. But to achieve such superiority Israel had to take the initiative and attack each adversary separately while hoping that the other neighboring countries did not join in before the current front was successfully decided. Furthermore, the engagement on any front and the entire war had to be both quick and decisive. With most of its working-age men and many of the women called up, Israel's economy would be seriously crippled if a war lasted too long.

That morning, the darkest of scenarios appeared to be materializing as the alignment of Israel's arch-enemies, Egypt and Syria, seemed to be coming together. Our only hope was that Jordan would not join that alignment. But even without a Jordanian threat, we were losing our strategic advantage: because we did not take the first initiative, two active and dangerous fronts were forming at the opposite ends of the country.

Although I was through only six weeks of basic training, the IDF already thought of me and my AR friends as potentially useful in times of emergency. We, like the other reservists, kept at home a set of military uniforms, boots and personal gear. But like most of the ARs, I was certain that even if there were large-scale mobilization we would be spared. The Army needed us to study without interruption, we argued. We were its future engineers.

Classes ended as usual at mid-afternoon. As I boarded the bus for the ride back home, Shuly Nathan's voice streamed through the radio speakers, singing *Jerusalem of Gold*. Shuly's high-pitched voice and the beautiful melody made it feel like a prayer.

When I reached home, my sister Noemi had already left for her daily afternoon swim practice. At age 15, she was emerging as an Israeli swimming star. She already held several Israeli national youth records in her specialties of 100 meter and 200 meter backstroke. An album on our coffee table was full of her pictures and newspaper headlines. She was no longer Noemi Laufer; she was just "Laufer."

I sat down to complete my daily homework assignments while listening to GALATZ. My parents were still at work in Laci's downtown law office that specialized in filing reparation claims on behalf of Holocaust survivors, mostly from Hungary, Germany, Romania, and Czechoslovakia.

Ironically, while both Zsuzsi and Laci were eligible for reparations, they believed that accepting them would be equivalent to forgiving Germany for the Nazis' atrocities. For years they won lump sum compensation and generous pensions for their clients, while refusing to file on their own behalf. Only weeks before the final deadline they decided to file at last.

I was munching on my favorite snack, Bamba, a popcorn-like bite, when the music on GALATZ was interrupted: General Indar Jit Rikhye, the commander of the 3,400 member UN peace-keeping force in Sinai, had been summoned to the Egyptian Army liaison office in Gaza where he was handed a message from the Egyptian Army Chief of Staff requesting him to withdraw his forces from the Peninsula. There was no official comment from the Israeli government.

This was awkward, I thought as the brief ended. Indar Jit Rikhye should be the one summoning the Egyptian commander and ordering his troops to leave Sinai. The Egyptians were violating the armistice agreement, not the UN. The situation was becoming more unsettling. I could not imagine that the UN would accept that onerous demand. They were put in place to resist exactly such demands.

Laci and Zsuzsi were home early that day. They already heard the news. Laci took off his jacket and tie and put on his knee-length khaki shorts and slippers and dropped into his comfortable armchair. After drinking his daily glass of tomato juice with a dash of black pepper and a slice of lemon, he turned on the radio full volume, as he always did when expecting important news. I could not tell if the high volume was an early sign of hearing loss or a sign that he should not be interrupted. Zsuzsi went to the kitchen to fix a light dinner of omelet with green peppers, two slices of white bread and butter. She brought it in on a tray and joined us.

At exactly seven o'clock Moshe Hovav was on the air again, repeating the Egyptians' request for the withdrawal of the UN forces. Although the request was addressed to the UN Secretary General U Thant, Hovav explained, the decision was up to the UN Security Council where the US had a veto power. Meanwhile the Israeli cabinet was holding an emergency meeting and Egypt continued moving forces into the Sinai. The latest estimate suggested that 200 tanks were already in the Peninsula. Despite the blatant violation of the armistice agreement between Israel and Egypt, there was no reaction from the US, Europe or the Soviet Union.

The news broadcast ended. Laci turned off the radio. A heavy silence replaced the loud, reverberating voice of Hovav. Slowly Laci rose from his armchair, his face expressing deep concern, went to the bar behind him and poured three glasses of vermouth over ice, our favorite evening drink.

I knew that Laci and Zsuzsi tended to see life more pessimistically than I did. To them, the entire world was anti-Semitic, ready to get the Jews in general and Israel in particular. Since their childhoods they had witnessed ever-worsening conditions for European Jews, rapid growth of German aggression, capitulation of most of Europe to German aggression, development of violent policies against Jews in much of Europe, including their homeland Hungary, and finally, the loss of everything they ever had, careers, property, family, freedom, dignity, health and nearly their own lives. I knew that Laci, and often Zsuzsi, would assume the worst and still believe that things could get even worse.

But in my mind and the minds of many Israelis of my age, what was possible in Europe was no longer possible in modern Israel. I could not comprehend how Laci and Zsuzsi could draw parallels between Egypt and Germany, or the threat to the Jews in Hungary and the current threat to Israel.

As if reading my mind, Laci broke the silence predicting that the reserves will be called up. He agreed with Hovav that the US might veto a decision to withdraw the UN forces. But even if those forces remained, he did not think that a mere 3,400 UN soldiers would forcefully prevent Egypt from filling up the Peninsula with their own units.

"The UN will not, but what about the US?" I asked.

"The US? They will not start a nuclear war over a local conflict. Why would they? And even if they did, what can they do? The Sixth Fleet is nearby, but it carries mostly planes. They hardly have any ground forces. The few marines they have cannot fight the two hundred Egyptian tanks in Sinai."

"But this is not a local conflict. We are an important ally and so is France who supplied us with the Mirages."

Laci's pessimism did not disappoint me. He downed his vermouth, poured a second one, lit up a cigarette and settled in his armchair to reflect.

"You might be right," he finally said, "but I still think that the cabinet will call some reserves up tonight. They have to. We no longer have the advanced warning we expected if Egypt chose to attack. They will be at our throats in the south and so will the Syrians be in the north. This does not look good."

I sat on the couch watching Laci's face taking on a far-away expression. Blue smoke rose from the cigarette that he held between his index and middle fingers. His eyes turned glassy as he traveled to another world to which I had no access.

Now that I am in my sixties, I think more about my father and those moments and wonder, where was he? Behind those glassy eyes Laci's world was much more evil than any world my mind could create. In that world not being able to imagine the worst was a fatal mistake. Many did not survive the Holocaust because of it. Laci was not going to make that mistake.

After sitting quietly for a while, Zsuzsi asked me to join her for a short walk in the neighborhood. We walked to the door and Zsuzsi picked up Bobby's leash. The old dog jumped from his mat in the kitchen and ran to the door ready to join us.

Bobby was an old Tibetan terrier. Zsuzsi liked to think that she adopted him, but in truth, Bobby adopted us. One evening, several years ago, we heard a scratch on the front door of our ground floor apartment. When Zsuzsi opened the door, she saw a little graying dog looking at her as if to say: "May I come in?" He was disheveled, dirty, tired and had no collar or a tag. She let him in, gave him some water, food and a bath. When done, Bobby lay down in a corner behind the refrigerator as if declaring "I'm making this my own place." Bobby stayed with us for the rest of his life.

We crossed the yard and walked down the quiet street. It was a beautiful late spring evening. Darkness was already descending; the skies were clear and the setting sun turned orange. We liked these walks along the quiet streets; the intoxicating smell of the new blooms on the mimosa trees induced the right mood for conversations. Zsuzsi loved this time of the day when the setting sun painted everything in a deep golden glow. She called it the Golden Hour. Maybe it was this lovely light, but at that moment neither one of us felt the looming crisis too threatening.

"*You know, Dad may be right. The situation is not good,*" she said after we walked silently for a while, "*but I still don't think it will turn into a war. We have shown last month such superiority over the Syrian air force, Nasser, Gamal Abdel will think twice.*"

I agreed with her. Or was it just wishful thinking?

The streets were dark when we returned home, the few mercury streets lamps shed a cold white light that barely illuminated our way. When we entered the living room, it was filled with cigarette smoke; Laci was immersed in one of his detective novels, a cigarette burning between his fingers. A long strand of ash hung from the edge of the cigarette, curving downward ready to fall on his lap.

Noemi just returned from her swim practice, oblivious to the recent news. She was hungry and tired.

MAY 17, 1967

Early the following morning I woke up, as usual, to the thud of the morning paper delivered at our door. I slipped out of bed, picked up the paper and settled in Laci's armchair. It was "his chair," but he was still asleep after another night of nightmares haunted by memories from the German concentration camps and Hungarian Forced Labor Battalions. More than twenty years were still not sufficient to heal his scars. Almost every night, after having trouble falling asleep he would go to the living room, sit for a while, take a sleeping pill and return to bed. But the nightmares were stronger. The pill kept him asleep only for a few hours until another night terror woke him up.

I stared at the bold headlines announcing that Egypt demanded removal of the UN Forces from Sinai and that more than 60,000 Egyptian troops and approximately 200 tanks were already there. But a smaller headline on the back page saying that a limited call-up of reserves was ordered was to me far more relevant.

It was still too early to turn on the radio for the morning news. Though radio broadcasts started half an hour earlier with a brief morning prayer followed by the news summary, I knew that even the slightest sound would wake everybody.

I continued reading. Commentators tried to guess the motives behind Egypt's actions. One of the commentators noted that Anwar El Sadat, Egypt's Vice President, had returned a few days earlier from an unannounced visit to Moscow. No details were given about the nature of his trip. Such visits usually ended without a joint announcement. As one of the largest client states of the Soviet Union, Egypt received many favors but also assumed in return many commitments to their patron state. That commentator was wondering if the current events were not part of an agitation initiated by the Soviets. But if so, the question remained: why and how far would they let it go? That commentator was the first to note that if this process remained unchecked it could lead to an all-out Israeli-Arab war. He indicated that since Israel could not absorb the first blow without risking its own existence, if Egypt continued accumulating forces in Sinai, Israel would have to consider a pre-emptive strike. Other commentators still speculated that this tension would dissipate quickly simply because no Arab state was militarily ready to engage in a full-scale war with Israel.

Laci and Zsuzsi joined me before seven o'clock. Noemi already left for her early morning swim practice. I turned on the radio as the morning news broadcast started. It was not encouraging. There were discussions at the UN headquarters in New York trying to determine the UN response to the crisis. Commentators speculated that the UN would resist the Egyptian demands and that eventually Egypt would have no choice but to withdraw. But meanwhile, Egypt continued gathering forces in Sinai. The radio confirmed the newspaper headlines that Israel had begun a limited call-up of its reserves. However, the scope remained small and was intended mostly to demonstrate that Israel would not remain idle against this threat. Laci was somber. He did not comment until the news and the weather forecast ended.

"I am very concerned about the lack of a more assertive UN response," he said. "They are part of an international agreement between Israel, Egypt, and the world. They are obligated to keep Egypt out of Sinai. At the very least, they need to consult with Israel if they want to modify the agreement. There was no word of any contact between the UN and Israel."

"The UN is pro-Arab; they have no strong interest in remaining in Sinai. I don't believe they will ever ask us," Zsuzsi replied.

"So what if the UN left Sinai?" I asked. "Our border is far from the Suez Canal. Even if Egypt pulled their forces closer to us, they cannot supply an army so far from their bases, and besides, we have an excellent air force." I saw no reason for this hysteria.

"Indeed, except that we can deploy only 50,000 men of our regular army against the 200,000 Egyptians," Laci said. "And only if the Syrians and Jordanians stay out. If we mobilize our reserves, who will run our buses, bakeries, banks, or factories? We have never mobilized reserves on such a scale for more than a few hours. Our reserve army is only great on paper."

"What do you mean?" I asked indignantly, annoyed with this hand-wringing doom and gloom. "Don't you remember a couple of years ago the Army tested the emergency call-up system? It worked perfectly. Why won't it work this time again?"

But my father wouldn't be soothed.

"Gaby, don't you understand? We cannot sustain ourselves with most men tied up in the desert, sitting on their tanks and waiting for Egypt to make the next move. The streets will be deserted if all men between the ages of 18 and 55 just disappeared? Not to mention most unmarried women."

Of course he was right. For once, I was left without a quick rebuttal.

The first lecture at Technion was at 10 am, Strength of Materials by Professor Lefkowitz. Lefkowitz, among the oldest of Technion's faculty, emigrated from Poland in 1948, just after Israel declared its independence.

He was an Auschwitz survivor and the tattooed number on his left wrist was visible when he wore a short-sleeved shirt—though that was rare.

When I entered the classroom only five students were present. This was a low turnout even for Lefkowitz's classes. "*Where is everybody?*" boomed Lefkowitz when he entered. He too recognized that some of his few regulars are missing.

"*We're all on the Academic Reserve,*" someone said "*the rest were called up last night.*"

"*And if we get called up, you know we're doomed,*" another of the students half-joked.

Lefkowitz did not laugh. His sense of humor was strange. All knew that Lefkowitz had survived Hell and that he had lost his entire family. But his survival and that of other Holocaust survivors was never seen as an evidence of extraordinary strength, wisdom, or tenacity. Just the opposite, his losses, the tattooed number on his arm, his heavy Polish accent, his rigid European habits, and his strange humor were all symbols of weak people and their inferior culture.

The next class was not until 1 pm and Matty, one of my AR friends, and I headed to the Mensa, the student cafeteria. Lunch was ordinarily the busiest time there, long lines stretched from the buffet to the top of the stairs and even to the main lobby. But today, the line was deserted and the single cashier was sitting and filing her nails. One of the headlines of the evening papers on sale near the entrance explained it all. The earlier announcement of a limited call up of reserves was now at the top of the front page.

"*It does not seem to me such a 'limited call-up'*" Matty commented.

We quickly picked up our lunch and sat down. The Mensa was eerily empty and quiet. Even during the summer break there were more students. We were uncomfortable sitting alone in the empty cafeteria. We felt left out, as if getting called up for war was some wonderful party that only the popular students were invited to. We finished our lunch quickly and headed back to our building.

We entered the library. The old librarian, Mr. Mendzsicky was at his desk. He smiled at us, evidently happy to see customers. Mr. Mendzsicky, a mild-mannered elderly man was as much a part of the department as the library itself. He knew all the students and faculty by their first name. He remembered all the graduates, from the first class on and often their current places of employment. With such a memory, no wonder he knew the location of every book and magazine in the library. I often wondered if he also read the books in his library. He certainly understood the science.

We sat at one of the tables. I tried to read one of the monthly aeronautical magazines but I could not concentrate. Overnight the campus had turned into a ghost town. Laci was right; calling up the reserves was easy, running a country without its workforce was the problem. Even the Technion would not be able to offer classes, even if faculty were available, without students.

I arrived after classes at the bus stop but the bus was late. When it finally arrived, the driver apologized that Eged, the national bus company, had too many drivers called up and many of its buses requisitioned by the army to transport troops. Eged was now operating on a holiday schedule and even that might be difficult to keep.

The ride back was quick. Traffic along the road was sparse and with few passengers the driver could skip many of the stops. When I got off the bus at the Carmel Center, the Merkaz, most stores were open but the foot traffic was greatly diminished. The center that was busy most afternoons with shoppers, patrons sitting in street cafés sipping espressos or enjoying an ice cream, was deserted.

The sight was eerie but it did not feel like the prelude to a war. War, I thought, had to be chaotic: vehicles running urgently from one place to another, sirens being tested, panicked housewives running to stores to stock up groceries. And yet, this was the sign of an upcoming storm.

MAY 18, 1967

The new morning brought another round of dire news. Overnight the UN Secretary General U Thant declared that he would not relocate his forces to Gaza or Sharm El-Sheikh. Instead, Nasser could choose between two options: either keep the UN forces in the Sinai in their current position or have them withdraw all together. Israel, who was a side to the armistice agreement, was not even consulted.

This was shocking. Israel looked at the UN peace-keeping force not just as a buffer between the IDF and the Egyptian army but also as a guarantee for free shipping through the Red Sea to Eilat. The UN forces in Sharm-el-Sheikh near the southern tip of Sinai controlled the Straits of Tiran, the narrow passages from the Red Sea to the Bay of Eilat and to the southern Israeli port of Eilat Israel's maritime gate to the Far East. One cannon in Sharm-el-Sheikh could easily block passage of any ship through the straits. Without the UN in Sharm-El-Sheikh, Israel's shipping in the Red Sea would no longer be secure.

We listened to the news in disbelief. "*I don't get it,*" Zsuzsi said, "*U Thant does not have the authority to make such a decision. We had a deal.*"

"*Yes, but I have seen commitments like this broken before,*" said Laci. Zsuzsi murmured her agreement. She and Laci were thinking of the Munich Agreement where Chamberlain practically handed over the Sudetenland to Germany in return for Hitler's promise not to invade the remainder of Czechoslovakia and Poland. "*Do you know how long Hitler's promise to Chamberlain lasted?*" Laci asked,

"*Oh Dad, please, don't bring up World War II again. Things are different today.*"

"*Really? I hope you are right. The Munich agreement lasted less than six months before Germany invaded Czechoslovakia. Less than a year before the Nazis overran Poland. At least now we had eleven years. So, you are right, today is different. Eleven years is more than six months.*"

"*Are you comparing what is happening now to the start of World War II?*"
"*Who knows? We did not know then that those events would lead to another world war. But if things get out of control, who do you think will come to help us? Who cares if the UN leaves Sinai, other than Israel and Egypt of course? Do you think we can protect ourselves if the Syrians joined Egypt? Or even worse, if Jordan, Saudi Arabia, Iraq, Lebanon? You think like a Sabra.*"

"*It is different, Dad. We have an Army. We have weapons, tanks, cannons, jets.*"

"*What's so different? Didn't France have cannons, tanks, and airplanes? Didn't England have tanks, cannons, and airplanes? Together they looked stronger than Germany and yet, France was overrun by Germany within weeks, the British got surrounded near Dunkirk and barely managed to escape. Who knows, had the Americans not joined the war, England might have lost too and I, you, Noemi and Mom, none of us would be here today. Yes, having an Army is good. But if the UN leaves Sinai, I think we may end up like France and England in 1940.*"

That morning at Technion, classes were nearly abandoned. Even Professor Bentov who just returned from the US after years at Carnegie Mellon University was drafted. Bentov's teaching assistant, a young graduate student in a wheelchair, rolled in.

After classes, the entire Technion AR corps assembled in the large field behind the Sports Center that, like most places on campus, faced the Haifa Bay. The hills of Mount Carmel behind us were still green after a rainy winter. In a month, the dry summer season would scorch the grass, turning it golden brown. The Haifa Bay to the north was blue. The white rock of Rosh HaNikrah,

50 miles further north, was clearly visible. It marked the Israeli border with Lebanon. The snow-covered cap of Mount Hermon towered above the range of Mount Galilee. It looked so close and yet it was outside Israel, in Syria. On a clear night, a Syrian on that peak could see the lights of Haifa. To the east stretched the Jezreel valley with its manicured green fields. The border with Jordan lay just beyond that valley. The smallness of Israel was painfully obvious from this training field. Wherever one looked a border was visible. Only the Egyptian border was beyond the horizon. But even it, while out of sight, was very much on our minds.

The ARs began assembling into their platoons, each representing an academic year. I, together with the first year students, was still a private. The fourth year ARs were already commissioned officers.

Despite being a military gathering, we all wore civilian outfits. Military uniforms were required only for the Tuesday afternoon military drill sessions.

"*Attention!!!*" boomed a large voice. A red-haired officer wearing a military uniform and the ranks of a Second Lieutenant stood in front of the partially assembled platoons. The huge baritone voice emerged from his large chest. This was "Gingy" Diamond, a teaching assistant in our department and the only graduate student still in the AR corps. Gingy was the somewhat derogatory nickname of red-haired persons, but this Gingy wore it with pride. He hardly ever mentioned his real name.

Gingy was a very colorful man, the editor of the student paper, where he imposed his personal sense of humor, a fixture at all student parties. His large belly was evidence of his love of good food and good life. But beyond eating, Gingy loved to be the center of attention. Today as the oldest member of the corps and the highest ranking among us, he was our unofficial commander. I could tell that he enjoyed shouting orders to more than 500 ARs.

"*Attention!!!*" Gingy shouted again. "*In 30 seconds I want everyone assembled in their platoons.*"

Though no one took Gingi too seriously, platoons were formed nevertheless. The ARs were eager to hear the latest word, even if it came from Gingy. Pleased with his unusual success, Gingy stood in front of the platoons stretched out, pulling his shoulders back, extending forward his large belly that was barely contained by his uniform shirt.

Even the beautiful afternoon sun could not dissipate the tension. The threat that Nasser may be returning to Sharm-El-Sheikh was on everyone's minds.

An Egyptian jet could reach Haifa from its Sinai base in Bir Gafgafa in Sinai in less than half an hour and a Syrian jet from Damascus in ten minutes. But all Gingy had to say was that our regular commander, Lieutenant Yoram, was on his way to the Northern Command to get orders for our deployment.

"Maybe Laci was right and the threat is real," I thought. "Could it be that like Czechoslovakia in 1938, the world has given us up for a little peace of mind and soon we will be overrun by the enemy?"

Before dismissing us, Gingy ordered us to reassemble the next day at 8 am.

Laci was already sitting in the living room reading the third special edition of the evening paper when I reached home. "Look," he said, "not only that the UN is leaving the Sinai, but unnamed sources in the Defense Department claim that the Egyptian forces that are now entering Sinai are carrying poison gas. Ever heard about Jews being gassed? Do you still think that I am out of line thinking that history might repeat itself?"

He was right. It did not look good at all. But I was not prepared to concede.

"What do you know about gas warfare? Have you ever worn a gas mask?" he continued. "Have you done it in the desert on a hot summer day while running uphill with your gear? And what if they spread their gas on a city? All it takes is one flyby by a MiG to wipe out thousands. Look, Gaby, this is truly serious." He turned quiet; his eyes fixed into an imaginary point in space.

I remained silent. In boot camp we tried on a gas mask for a few moments. We walked with the mask on into a small chamber filled with tear gas, removed the mask, took one deep breath and then put it back. Laci was right, it was almost impossible to breathe through the mask. It got even worse after taking a breath of tear gas. My eyes were filled with tears, my nose with mucus and I was coughing. I couldn't wait to be allowed out of the chamber and remove the mask. I wondered how anyone could wear a mask for a long period of time, let alone fight with it.

If the Egyptians had poison gas, would the Syrians have it too? Would the ARs be called up? What would I do if I was at the Syrian front and they used gas? I was no longer worried. I was actually scared stiff. I could not believe that we celebrated Independence Day only a few days earlier.

On the evening news the anchor announced that the Syrian army was observed shifting to high alert. The IDF announced that all its forces were on high alert as well. Although no official announcement was made, observers speculated that by now, half of the Israeli reserves had been called up and were either in their planned positions or on their way. The mood in Israel was somber. Essential services such as transportation and power were strained to the limit by workforce shortages.

The broadcast ended. I interrupted the quiet that followed. "*I think we will be called up.*"

"*I was afraid it would happen.*" said Zsuzsi as she entered the room carrying Laci's dinner. "*Have you heard anything definite? Where will you be?*"

"*No, I don't know anything but starting tomorrow at eight, we must report to the AR's gathering place twice a day.*"

"*I suggest you pack your bag,*" said Laci. "*If they announce tomorrow morning that you are deployed, you may not have time to pack properly. But be sure to pack light but take many socks, your feet are your most important asset in the field and you need to care for them well.*"

Was that one of his lessons of the Holocaust? I was not sure that I agreed with him. I had blisters before but I never thought that had anything to do with dirty socks.

Later that evening, the national radio station cancelled regular programming and brought instead commentators to analyze the developing events. One of them, General Chaim Herzog, became a national celebrity through his commentaries during that period. But that night only a few people in Israel recognized that name. Herzog spoke slowly in a soft voice; each of his words was measured carefully and pronounced in a strong British accent.

"We are entering a very uncertain time…" Herzog started. (13) "We are surrounded by enemies and to a nation of Holocaust survivors this all may seem as a return to our darkest days."

It was the first time I heard anyone, other than my father of course, draw an analogy between our present threat and the Holocaust.

But Herzog did not go on air to further depress our dispirited nation. He then described his visit to the Negev desert where he witnessed the calm and confidence of our soldiers facing the Egyptian army and urged us to trust the wisdom of our generals.

It was reassuring to hear Herzog. But I was not sure that I believed him. Although I never before heard an IDF officer or spokesman lie or exaggerate a report, I knew that if the situation was indeed as dire as Laci and I thought, no one from the IDF would admit it.

MAY 19, 1967

The morning brought more bad news. It felt like the world was using the nighttime to plot against Israel. In New York U Thant ordered UN forces withdrawn from the Sinai. Egypt poured forces into the Peninsula and beyond, amassing them in the Gaza Strip and along the Negev border.

Although this was a Friday with no classes at the Technion, I had to be there by eight for the AR morning formation. Heading out to the Merkaz, the Carmel center, traffic was thin. Few people waited at the bus stops along the island in the middle of the Merkaz, most of them children heading to school.

Two middle-aged men dressed in rumpled military uniforms, carrying small backpacks rushed towards the only bus waiting: two new reservists rushing to join their units.

At the corner of Derech HaYam, the road leading down from the mountain to the coastal highway, stood a large group of younger reservists trying to hitch a ride with one of the rare private cars passing by. With some luck, they could get a ride to Tel Aviv, or even better, directly to their military base in central Israel or the Negev.

Hitching rides was the favorite mode of transportation by Israeli military personnel, men, women, young or old. On most Fridays almost all soldiers on leave looked for a ride back from their bases. But this was not a normal Friday.

A small car stopped by the soldiers. I felt for the driver, his car's door was almost torn off its hinges as more than ten men tried to squeeze into the two or three available seats.

I looked around. I was the only healthy 19-year-old man walking on the street in civilian clothing. I almost felt naked without a uniform. I truly wished I were called up too. I started worrying that war would break out and I would be left out. Despite my minimal training, I knew I belonged in the Army.

My bus was half an hour late. An old driver, well beyond military service age opened the automatic door and gave me a disapproving look as I boarded. I nodded to him apologetically telling him that my unit was just about to be called up. "*Good luck then,*" he said smiling back at me.

At eight o'clock sharp, Gingy marched on the field behind the Sports Center. He seemed to have grown two inches; his sharply creased uniform looked as if he spent the entire night pressing it. His wide shoulders were pulled farther back and his large belly stood out even further ahead. His face projected an all-knowing expression: he had information of great importance that five hundred men were anxious to hear. Gingy lived his entire life for this moment. He was a great actor and this wide field was his stage.

"I don't know if the news I have are good or bad," he started. "Egypt is pouring troops into the Sinai, Syria is on emergency footing and if you have not heard yet, the UN is moving out."

"Come on," Matty, my friend, whispered to me, "please don't give us all this nonsense. We heard the morning news too."

"As you all noticed, the IDF has mobilized most of its reserves," continued Gingy. "We are one of the most important units the IDF has. We are the intelligent ones. We can think!"

"As if it really matters," Matty whispered again.

"We will be mobilized tomorrow morning," Gingy finally uttered the one sentence that mattered.

A loud cheer emerged from the AR formation. I remained quiet. I had mixed feelings of anxiety and pride, worry and eagerness. I could not cheer. But I was eager to go and be part of what we now thought would become a war.

I was immersed in my thoughts on the ride back home. I did not hear the radio blaring as usual, I did not notice the passengers or the road and I did not mind the strange, almost hostile looks I was getting for not being in service. I was thinking of Laci and Zsuzsi. How would they respond? What would we do? How long would the war take? What would happen to me? Matty? My other friends? Would I see any combat?

Weekends were short in Israel: only Friday afternoon and all of Saturday. I loved Friday afternoons. They always started with Zsuzsi's specialty lunch, chicken soup with plenty of noodles, a grilled steak, boiled spring potatoes sautéed in butter and parsley and for desert her wonderful "Bird Milk."[6]

The smell of the slowly boiling chicken soup greeted me when I arrived. Zsuzsi was in the kitchen preparing the Bird Milk. I took a teaspoon and tasted the smooth, yellowish liquid. It was still warm. The sweet vanilla flavor was heavenly. Zsuzsi once again outdid herself. But my mind was elsewhere. How to tell my mom that I would leave tomorrow? How would she and Laci react?

But she knew. She could read my mind.

"Is it tomorrow?" she broke the quiet.

"Do you know where are you going or what you will be doing?"

"I have no idea. They will tell us tomorrow, I guess."

---

[6] Bird Milk ("Madár Tej" in Hungarian)—sweetened vanilla milk and cream with "clumps" of foamed egg whites floating on top.

Our lunch was quiet. My parents, Noemi and I sat around the table eating our meal without a word. I was preoccupied with my own thoughts. It was my first deployment. I was not afraid, perhaps because I did not quite understand what war was. To me war was nothing more than gallant men running in an open field with rifles in hand killing their ugly looking enemy.

I will never know what went through Laci's mind.

May-June 1967: The Six-Day War

MAY 28, 1967

Although it was Saturday, I was up early, too excited to sleep in as usual, eager to go. Logically, I understood that wars are dangerous. But I was too young to emotionally comprehend the danger. I clearly remember that I was not afraid. I wanted to do my part. My personal well-being seemed to be detached from the well-being of the country.

My olive-green uniform was already prepared by my bed along with my black over-the-ankle infantry boots. My kitbag was packed with some toiletries, a change of clothes, flashlight, batteries, military mess kit, sewing kit and even textbooks should I have spare time to study. Zsuzsi and Laci were still asleep. Noemi, who on most Saturdays was up early getting ready for another swim meet was asleep too. All sport competitions were cancelled. I quietly slipped into the kitchen to prepare breakfast. I turned on the radio at low volume hoping to get the most recent newscast. Papers were not delivered on Saturdays because of the Sabbath.

I was preparing my breakfast when the kitchen door opened quietly and Laci joined me, still in his pajamas and slippers. He sat down by the table and lit up his morning cigarette while I poured a cup of dark coffee for both of us and sat down next to him to listen to the first news broadcast.

The newscaster began by announcing that US President Lyndon Johnson met with the Israeli Foreign Minister Abba Eban at the White House, and that the US would not intervene militarily on behalf of Israel to resolve the blockade of the Straits of Tiran. Johnson reaffirmed, though, the support of the US and the commitment to Israel's rights to security but offered no immediate actions or timeline.

"So, Abba Eban was in Paris and President Charles De Gaulle told him that Israel should not act unilaterally to resolve this crisis," Laci said grimly. "In other words, De Gaulle preferred to see the Arabs attack Israel first. Then Abba Eban flew to London and Prime Minister Harold Wilson told him how sympathetic the British were, though not enough to do anything about it. And now Johnson is telling us we're on our own."

"Dwight D. Eisenhower promised in 1957 that America would guarantee passage of our ships through the Straits of Tiran and now Johnson is saying that it's up to us to take care of it. France and England were our allies in the Sinai Campaign and now they're telling us to wait until the Arabs attack us. What did I tell you Gaby? Promises are only promises. I've seen it before. At least they're sympathetic. Twenty years ago they couldn't care less when the Jews were taken to Auschwitz."

My Dad was right. I too was disappointed with what I thought was an unfair response by Johnson, Wilson and De Gaulle. The Arabs received weapons and support from the Soviet Union. They had more jet fighters than we did; more tanks and more soldiers; they were the ones who provoked the present situation. Why should we stand by and wait for them to attack? But I didn't like Laci drawing parallels with the Holocaust. Our situation was vastly different.

"Tell me, are you fully packed, ready to go?" he changed the topic.

"Yup. It's about time they called me."

"You're right to feel that way. But please be careful. The army probably needs you, but that doesn't mean you have to be a hero. Do what they tell you. But please don't jump ahead. I know you like standing out and volunteering but war is not the time to do that."

I resented his words that morning by the kitchen table but I understood his advice better years later, after encountering real danger. He did not preach cowardice. Just the opposite, he knew that I had to go not just because of my orders but because my conscience demanded it. I had his blessing and he was proud. But he was a survivor. He instinctively knew and understood what I learned as a military commander: to accomplish my mission but to minimize or, if possible, avoid danger and losses. Casualties are an unavoidable consequence of war, but good commanders win wars while suffering fewer casualties than their enemy.

Nearly all the ARs were already assembled when I arrived. More than twenty buses and transportation trucks were parked at the edge of the large field. The atmosphere was festive. The ARs, all in uniform, were standing in small groups exchanging jokes and chatting. I joined one of the groups. Matty, standing with his shirt untucked and with no beret on his head was analyzing the morning news simultaneously with three other equally sloppy ARs, each trying to overpower the other by yelling louder.

"*Attention!*" Gingy interrupted the conversations through a megaphone.

Gingy did not disappoint. He looked as if he spent the entire night shining his boots and pressing his uniform. Even the beret on his head had a sharp crease in the middle making it look like a wedge. I am not sure if it was my imagination, but his large stomach and broad shoulders seemed to have grown yet again since the previous day.

We were heading to Tzemach military base at the southern tip of the Sea of Galilee, he announced, where we were to get our gear and assignments.

Tzemach was one of the emergency deployment bases scattered across the country. It consisted of offices and large warehouses that were set up to quickly register and equip reserve units heading to positions along the Syrian border only a few miles away.

I wondered about the wisdom of putting such a vital facility within range of the Syrian artillery, but I also recognized the value of having tanks and cannons near the front thereby sparing long distance transportation along narrow roads vulnerable to congestions and aerial attacks.

Our equipment was World War II surplus: a Czech rifle,[1] an ammunition pouch with twenty rounds, a tin canteen, three coarse military blankets, two sets of battle uniforms, a backpack, and 24-hour military rations. To top it off, we received British army helmets. British soldiers wore these helmets during World War One! In the IDF only women in basic training wore those flat helmets with the wide round rim whose main utility seemed to be protection from rain and other objects falling from above. Combined with the antiquated rifles, the helmets made a clear statement: the IDF did not take us seriously.

Night was falling by the time all of us received our gear. Although the official blackout was still a week away, the main streetlights were kept off and most windows were already covered with blankets or dark sheets. With little light escaping through open doors the base turned into a ghost town. With nothing better to do, we gathered in small groups and started opening our rations, sharing canned bully beef, bean, corn, and old hard crackers[2] that had probably been passed down through generations of soldiers until one of us decided to break open the sealed package. Our improvised dinner was interrupted by Gingy and his megaphone, ordering us to reassemble.

"*You will be assigned to various settlements in the Jordan Valley and the eastern shore of the Sea of Galilee,*" he announced. "*Many of their men were mobilized and the few who were left behind are the only defense against the well-fortified Syrian Army on the Golan Heights and the hills above us. You will be*

---

1 The Czech bolt action rifle (VZ.98N) was developed between WWI and WWII. It had a 5 round, 7.62 mm (0.3") internal magazine. By comparison, the Syrian infantry was using the Kalashnikovs (AK-47) automatic rifle with twenty round magazines.
2 We called them biscuits.

divided into groups of twenty; each assigned to reinforce a settlement. You will be picked up by a representative of your settlement. You will likely participate in their fortification efforts, provide night watch and other guard duties, and if, God forbid, the Syrian army moves to the valley, you will help the local defense units and the IDF push them back. Good luck. Chazak Ve'Ematz."[3]

Several trucks and minibuses were already parked in the nearby lot, among them a minibus that took me along with Matty and 18 other ARs to Sha'ar HaGolan.

Kibbutz Sha'ar HaGolan is located in the Jordan Valley less than a mile from the intersection of three borders: the Israeli, the Jordanian and the Syrian. Looking east, the settlers of Sha'ar HaGolan faced two enemy territories only a mile away: Syria to the north and Jordan to the south.

The kibbutz was established thirty years earlier together with its neighboring Kibbutz Masada. On May 1948, one day after Israel's declaration of independence, Syrian artillery began shelling both kibbutzim and Syrian infantry gathered along their fences. Lacking reinforcement and fearing that both settlements might be overrun by the gathering troops, the local command ordered the settlements abandoned and evacuated the women and children to Haifa. The abandoned settlements were captured, looted and burned down by the Syrians.

Reinforcements arrived at Sha'ar HaGolan and Masada a day later and both settlements were recaptured. Nevertheless, the members of both kibbutzim remained for decades the source of criticism and ridicule, similar to the stigma of shame that was assigned to the few Israelis who surrendered during that War of Independence.

Like many kibbutzim in the 1960s, agriculture was Sha'ar HaGolan's primary source of income. Its factory of plastic pipes that would become its main source of income was still small. Its tropical crops of banana, avocado and date thrived in the hot and water rich Jordan Valley and its magnificent groves stretched from its fence to the international borders. During harvest time, trucks lined up along the dirt roads at the edge of these fields to load crates of expensive fruits for next day delivery to Europe.

Syrian soldiers on the hills overlooking the kibbutz could not possibly ignore the lush green of the groves, the beautiful white houses with red-tile roofs surrounding the large central green lawn. When the wind blew from the

---

3   *Chazak Ve'Ematz*—"Be Strong and Resolute," Deuteronomy 31:6. A blessing given by Moses to the Israelites before crossing the Jordan River to capture the Promised Land.

west, it must have carried the sounds of children playing and the aroma of a large farming community to the Syrian hills. The poor farmers of the Syrian village of Tawfiq on the slopes above Sha'ar HaGolan must have watched with envy the modern farming enterprise and the rapid growth of a settlement that nineteen years earlier had been in ruins.

In the violent years since the War of Independence, Tawfiq became the base for Syrian artillery and commando attacks against the kibbutzim in the Jordan valley below. Often, armed commandos from Tawfiq slipped across the river to attack farmers working in the groves along the border. Tawfiq was the target of a major Israeli raid in 1960 in retribution for continuous Syrian attacks. Usually, such raids brought some peace and quiet for a little while before harassment resumed. With tensions between Israel and the surrounding Arab nations growing, members of the kibbutzim along the Syrian border began developing hopes that an upcoming war might remove that threat.

When we got off the mini-bus at the mostly dark kibbutz, I could not avoid noticing the menacing dark hills in the east and the few, faint lights from the tiny village on the slope above.

We were housed in two shacks at the edge of the kibbutz. These were the first to be built in 1948 when the kibbutz was resettled. Until we arrived they served volunteers, mostly from Scandinavia, who spent time enjoying the experience of kibbutz life while paying for it with free labor as farm hands. With tensions mounting, many of the volunteers left. The shacks were minimally furnished: iron beds covered with straw mattresses, tables, chairs and small storage crates.

MAY 29, 1967

Early in the morning, a tall curly haired *kibbutznik*,[4] wearing blue shorts and blue tee shirt woke us up and asked us to line up outside.

After apologizing for missing us the previous night and introducing himself as Chico, the regional security commander, he thanked us on behalf of the members of Sha'ar HaGolan for taking part in their security efforts and preparations.

Chico acknowledged that we were serving in the military but offered to dispense with formalities if we contributed our share just like the other kibbutzniks. That meant that during the day we would be paired with

---

4   *Kibbutznik*—a member of a kibbutz.

kibbutzniks to dig trenches along the fence or to fill sandbags and at night, we would be assigned to three-hour watch shifts.

He then invited us as guests of the kibbutz to take our meals in their communal dining room during our stay and even to collect some civilian work outfits from their supply room. When he was finished we joined him for breakfast.

The single-story dining room stood at one end of the rectangular central lawn. It was the largest building of the kibbutz and doubled as an auditorium, a dance hall on Friday nights and a meeting room. The patio at the front was the center of social gatherings and the lobby wall a message board. It reminded me the social role of the well in biblical villages.

When I entered I was greeted by the sound of nearly a hundred men and women[5] eating and chatting, the mix of smells arising from eggs fried in oil, chopped onions, and fresh vegetables. It was similar to a military mess hall albeit this one was slightly more elegant. Long Formica-topped tables were lined up in rows, four chairs at each side. A large bowl of whole tomatoes, peppers, unpeeled cucumbers, and onions stood at the center along with a basket of day-old[6] sliced rye bread, olive oil, lemon juice, smaller bowls of margarine, marmalade, pitchers of coffee, hot chocolate, and tea, and a large bowl for waste. Kitchen staff pushed in the aisles carts with plates of fried or scrambled eggs, distributing them to diners who were meticulously cutting up vegetables into small cubes and mixing them with olive oil and lemon juice.

Cutting vegetables for salad was a serious ritual in nearly every kibbutz. Years later, my father-in-law, Dudi, who lived most of his adult life in Kibbutz Degania and later in Kibbutz Beth Oren, told me that while many kibbutzim were split over socialist ideology, the true divide was between those who swore by the finely cut salad and those who believed that the coarse salad, the so-called "Donkey Salad," is the best. But no matter the culinary school, cutting the perfectly shaped salad was a matter of personal pride. Cubes had to be perfectly square and uniform in size. For the next three weeks, I watched with fascination the variety of cutting techniques developed, mostly by the older members, to achieve perfection even with dull knives.

I sat down with Matty next to an old kibbutznik named Zvi. While fully concentrating on his salad, Zvi told us the sad story how Sha'ar HaGolan was

---

5   Kibbutz children were raised in a communal childcare center where they had their own dining facilities.
6   When I once asked Chico when we would get "today's bread," he replied "tomorrow."

abandoned in 1948. Over my next three weeks in the kibbutz, I heard several versions of that story. But in each, the teller was one of the handfuls of members who would rather die than abandon the kibbutz. Even nineteen years later, and with the kibbutz flourishing, the event was still traumatic and the new threats stirred up old memories. Zvi, like the other story tellers, ended his story with a sigh. Clearly if war were to break out, this time Sha'ar HaGolan and Masada would not be abandoned, no matter what.

On the way out from the dining room I overheard kibbutzniks discussing the latest news. Jordan, our neighbor just a mile to the south, allowed the Saudi and Iraqi armies to cross through its territory and position themselves along the Israeli borders. "*I won't be surprised,*" one of them said, "*if tomorrow morning we see Iraqi tanks rolling down the hills and into position just outside our bananas. What is Chico going to do about that?*"

Outside the dining room, Chico was already pairing up the ARs with kibbutzniks and assigning them tasks. Matty and I were assigned with Kobi, a young muscular farmer, to dig trenches along the eastern fence facing Tawfiq. We walked to the storage room, picked up shovels and pickaxes and headed to our section.

The fence surrounding the kibbutz was tall and topped with barbed wire. It was clearly designed to hold off personnel but not tanks. Behind the fence was a freshly raked dirt road and beyond the road was a large banana grove with heavy, green banana clusters hanging on the plants.

I asked Kobi why there weren't any anti-tank measures. Didn't they worry about tanks?

"*Of course we do,*" he answered. "*But if tanks reach the fence line we're dead anyway. Holding them off with a barrier would make little difference. We're counting on the air force to hold off tanks or armored vehicles until our tanks can arrive and finish them off. But we do worry about individuals and small commando units. They can penetrate through the border and reach the kibbutz undetected.*"

Pointing to the raked road just behind the fence he explained that it was designed to show footprints. There were similar raked dirt roads running along the border. They were patrolled every morning by trackers who looked for new foot prints that would indicate an incursion and freshly raked every evening before dark. "*And no matter what you do,*" he warned looking at all of us, "*do not dare set foot on this road. Your footprints may trigger a huge manhunt and if they find out that it was one of you…*" he stopped without elaborating.

Inside the fence was a partially dug trench. The fresh dirt piling up along its fence side suggested that this was a new addition to the kibbutz's line of defense.

"*We decided to dig trenches along the fence and from the fence to inside sections of the kibbutz,*" Kobi continued.

"*Chico and some of the old guys who were here in 1948 worry that we might be attacked by infantry who arrive under the cover of artillery. They think if we have a trench system we could hold them off and be protected from the artillery fire.*"

Matty started laughing. I knew why. He was thinking about our Czech rifles and our rudimentary training. I didn't think it was funny. I couldn't imagine myself standing in a trench with the British helmet on my head and a rifle that could only fire five rounds before needing to be reloaded by inserting the rounds one by one, all the while, crazed soldiers running towards me firing their automatic weapons and artillery shells exploding everywhere.

I doubt that Kobi noticed Matty's scoff because he just continued, "*To provide such protection, the trenches must provide cover to a standing man and sufficiently wide to allow one person to pass by the other. As you can see we've already started digging but with so many being mobilized, we had to stop. Hopefully with you we can finish the trenches in time.*"

We started digging. The ground was dry and hard. The last rain in the valley had fallen several weeks earlier. Breaking it up with the pickaxe was hard but after removing the top layer the dirt was moist and soft. Reaching the full depth of the trench was not as hard as I had feared. Being in a valley had some advantages, I thought, digging trenches in Tawfiq must be much harder with all the rocks dotting the mountain-side.

But soon the fresh cool morning air gave way to oppressive Jordan Valley heat. The heat blasted by the sun in the clear sky was absorbed by the dirt underneath us and the bare mountains above us and radiated as if we were inside a gigantic oven. Blisters started popping up on my untrained hands and my arms burned in pain.

I stopped to catch some air. Kobi was digging his shovel into the ground, raising the dug dirt and turning it over onto the pile at the edge of the trench in a precise rhythm. It was almost like watching a dancer. The sun that already burned my skin had no effect on him. I don't think he even sweated.

Kobi looked up and noticed I was watching. "*Drink some water,*" he advised.

"Tell me," I asked, trying to take a short break, "Is that Tawfiq on the slope up there?"

"Yes. But there are hardly any villagers there anymore. Syrian commando units, artillery and intelligence officers took their houses. Then two or three years ago, IDF paratroopers raided the village, blew up several buildings and killed some of them."

"So what is it now, a military base?" asked Matty.

"Possibly, they've fired artillery at us from a little wadi[7] behind the village. There's probably several artillery and infantry units there with spotters sitting in the village."

"Do you think they have other posts around here?" I asked.

"Without a doubt; look, you see the deep valley to our right that cuts through the plateau? This is the Yarmouk River, it flows into the Jordan. There's a military base there. There are many more up on the plateau above Tawfiq. They have plenty of army locations around us."

We continued working quietly until Kobi called for lunch break. It was hard, my body and mostly my hands were hurting. But looking at the section we already dug I felt satisfied, proud that I could contribute to the defense of the kibbutz. At the bottom of my heart I knew it wasn't much. I tried to convince myself otherwise.

We returned after lunch to our shacks for an afternoon break. The entire kibbutz turned quiet between noon and 2 pm. Kibbutzniks returned from the fields for lunch hurried to their rooms. Although they were not air-conditioned, the drawn shades, fans and some clever water evaporation devices kept them cool. Even the tough kibbutzniks needed to hide from the heat.

The sun was past its zenith when we returned to the ditches. Moving to the west it illuminated the mountains to the east like a projector in a theatre, casting new shadows that accentuated their contours. The well-illuminated bare hills looked as if they were a stone's throw away. I could easily discern the houses of Tawfiq that reminded me of houses I often saw in the Israeli Arab villages.

Despite having rested, Matty and I were tired and listless. By contrast, Kobi continued digging as if his day just started. He tried to drive us harder but after two hours of sluggish work he took pity on us and declared the end of the day. Before sending us back to our shacks he ordered us to report to the kibbutz security headquarters for our night watch assignments and to be back in the trenches at 6:30 am the next day. As I turned to head back to the kibbutz I noticed that Kobi's newly dug section was longer than mine and Matty's sections put together.

---

7   *Wadi*—an Arabic word for a dry riverbed, often used in Hebrew with the same meaning.

After a shower we met at the security office that was located in an underground bunker at the edge of the central lawn. The "office" at the bottom of a flight of stairs consisted of a desk with two telephones, a two-way radio, two chairs, and a small bookcase filled with binders stacked in haphazard order. Chico was seated at the desk holding the handle of one of the two phones at his ear and shouting in what appeared to be a loud but friendly conversation. When he ended the conversation, he asked that we sit outside on the lawn for a briefing.

The mature trees around the lawn cast long shadows that cooled the air. With blooming shrubs between the trees, the lawn looked like a manicured park. Joyful shouts of teenagers playing soccer at the far end were in sharp contrast to the menace from Tawfiq and the Golan Heights above. Several parents walked with their children from the daycare houses to their own rooms for their daily afternoon family gatherings. Others were already sitting on lawn chairs next to their rooms enjoying homemade cookies and soft drinks.

"Once again, thanks for being here," Chico started. "*I am sure that by now you appreciate the weight of the load we carry: hard work at day and long shifts of watches at night. I know you are tired from your first day. It will get easier.*" He then proceeded to assign our shifts. Of the three shifts, the ARs got the second and third, the hardest, of course.

After dinner, we gathered on the lawn to enjoy the warm and dry breeze of the Jordan Valley. Families retuning from dinner passed by and each one invited one of us to join them.

"Hi, I am Behira," a middle-aged woman introduced herself to me. She looked like a typical kibbutz woman: her appearance dictated partly by ideological principles of communal living, partly by hard work under the bright sun and partly by the economics of the kibbutz. She was short, robust and her graying hair cut short. Her well-tanned, wrinkled face with no makeup made her look ageless. Like nuns, Kibbutz women gave up much of their feminine chic but gained instead a facial glow derived from content and a deep sense of self-fulfillment.

"*Please join us, Prime Minister Eshkol is about to speak, we have a radio in our room so you can sit with us to hear him.*"

Even Behira's name, although rare, was typical to a kibbutz. She was born in Czechoslovakia as Klara and to fit in when she joined the kibbutz, she translated it literally to Hebrew, just like Golda turned into Zahava and Herschel into Zvi.[8]

---

8   *Zahav* is "gold" and *Zvi* is "deer" in Hebrew

I was happy to join them. I already missed home.

Behira and her husband Shaul were among the founders of Sha'ar HaGolan, she told me as we walked to her room. They had seen attacks by Arab gangs before the state was established. They were among those who had to abandon the kibbutz when the Syrians reached the fence in 1948. They were there when terrorists from Syria raided them and lived through years of Syrian artillery shelling and. they stood at the fence watching when Israeli paratroopers raided Tawfiq. But that was nothing compared to what was happening now. Unlike before, they were worried not just for their own well-being but for the entire country. *"We are so glad you are here,"* she said. *"The whole country pulling together is what makes us great."*

We reached Behira's room. It reminded me of the dorm rooms at Technion. It was on the ground floor of a two-story building. We entered through a little patio that faced the lawn into a small living room. Most of the wall space was taken by packed bookcases. Glancing at them briefly, I noticed the Communist manifesto by Karl Marx and a biography of Lenin—not surprising for an ideologically strict kibbutz.[9] But the shelves also included classical novels in Hebrew, German, and what I assumed to be Czech.

On the little table at the center of the room was a small platter with cookies and as we walked in, Shaul came out from the little kitchenette in the back carrying a tray with glasses and a bottle of grapefruit juice. Like Behira, Shaul was a typical kibbutznik. He wore checkered slippers, the same as his neighbors, and I was certain that he too had brown boots under his bed and grey wool socks to match Behira's.

Our timing was impeccable. Shaul just finished introducing himself when the announcer of Israel's main radio station started introducing Eshkol.

To most Israelis, Eshkol was the face of the severe recession that was still in full swing. Unemployment had reached twelve percent and jokes were abundant about him and his policies.

A soft-spoken man who loved telling anecdotes in Yiddish, Eshkol was viewed by many Israelis as the typical "Diaspora Jew." A spineless little merchant bent on pleasing the Gentiles, always ready to strike a deal with the more powerful.

Traditionally, the Israeli Prime Minister also held the portfolio of the Defense Minister. But many Israelis were concerned for quite some time that this non-charismatic politician might not be able to fill the shoes of

---

9 Sha'ar HaGolan was part of the leftist HaShomer HaTzair movement.

David Ben-Gurion, his predecessor. By contrast, General Yitzhak Rabin, the Chief of Staff or Moshe Dayan, the Army's Chief of Staff during the IDF victory in the 1956 Sinai Campaign were viewed as the new breed of Jews: strong, decisive Sabras who would not hesitate to act when necessary and whose actions were swift, courageous and successful.

As Eshkol was introduced, I pictured a bespectacled, hesitant technocrat sitting in front of the microphone, leafing through his prepared manuscript that he would read in a thick Russian accent which he had despite living in Israel for more than fifty years. A short plump man with a little mustache and bald head, he was certainly not the image of a fearless leader. But I hoped that his government would be decisive and that his upcoming speech would carry a strong message.

My hope didn't last long. From the start Eshkol sounded feeble and hesitant as if succumbing to his own fears. He started by describing the results of an inconclusive government meeting. Shaul, Behira and I exchanged worried stares.

As he was reading from his script, the flow of his speech was broken abruptly and he started stuttering. Shaul later told me that he heard Eshkol ask someone in the studio in Yiddish *"what's written here?"* It was a handwritten note inserted in the last minute into the typed text.

Rather than describing a clear path, his speech stated the obvious, that Israel viewed the closure of the Straits of Tiran very gravely, that our military would continue to remain on alert and his plan for the next day would be to brief the Knesset, the Israeli parliament. Although he confirmed that the government was confident in the power of the IDF to overcome any aggressor and restore Israel's rights to sail through the Straits of Tiran, the tone of his talk and his stuttering portrayed an indecisive Prime Minister, a Diaspora Jew who stammers in Yiddish when frightened. Eshkol was the exact opposite of the defiant and bellicose Nasser who was challenging the IDF and gathering support in the Arab world.[10]

The apartment and the people on the lawn outside fell silent. Sha'ar HaGolan and the entire State of Israel were stunned. The terrifying threat from across the borders and the lack of active support by Western nations, who were assumed to be allies, were magnified by the sudden realization that Israel's leadership was incapacitated by fear and incompetence.

---

10 In historic perspective, that hesitant speech is viewed as a blessing in disguise by portraying Israel as weak and fearful thereby contributing to the self-confidence and reduced alertness of the Arab armies at the opening hours of the Six-Day War.

"This was how I felt in Czechoslovakia when the Nazis took over," Shaul broke the silence. "Living in Sha'ar HaGolan I definitely felt fear before. But I always had the conviction that we know what to do, even when we lacked the resources. Now this little merchant from a little village near Kiev seems to be terrified by the Arabs and by the lack of Western support. What does he intend to do? Jump on the next ship and sail away? I wish we had Dayan in the government. He would have courage now."

"I heard some women mention Dayan's name as a possible Minister of Defense," added Behira. "I'm not sure if now is the time to replace Eshkol, but morale is so low. Dayan might change that."

I was surprised that Shaul mentioned the Holocaust. I knew that he and Behira emigrated from Europe before the Holocaust. In my mind they were the new Israelis, the fearless pioneers who knew it was time to leave Europe and who settled the barren land of Palestine, fought off the Arabs while turning the swamps into paradise. They were tan, muscular farmers, and yet well-educated and thoughtful. The Holocaust to them, I thought, was no more than a historic footnote.

But the fate of Czechoslovakia lay heavy on Shaul's mind.

"Czechoslovakia had a treaty with France and the Soviet Union," Shaul reminded me. "Counting on those treaties, Czechoslovakia agreed to give up part of its territory in return for a promise of peace with Germany. The Czechs had a strong army of their own but they trusted their allies. Six months later Germany broke its promise, annexed the entire country while France and the Soviets stood by."

"Now we are threatened by Egypt, Syria, and possibly Jordan, Saudi Arabia and Iraq," Shaul continued the comparison, "and the US, France, and Britain promised to support us if Egypt brought its army into the Sinai or blockade Tiran. Like the Czechs, we have a strong army but they are telling us to wait. And what do we do in response? Like the Czechs, we agree to wait. If Israel doesn't act now, we will end up just like Czechoslovakia in 1939. We will be slaughtered and the world will sit and watch."

I could not believe my ears. I expected Laci to say something like this. After all, he was a Holocaust survivor. But coming from Shaul, this comparison was disturbing. This could be far more serious than I thought.

Several groups were huddling on the lawn discussing the situation and Eshkol's speech when I walked back to my room. As in many political discussions in Israel, loud voices were expressing opposing opinions. Everyone had a solution. But everyone also agreed that this time the situation was different.

MAY 30, 1967

Someone I did not recognize woke me up by tapping my shoulder and telling me that it was my turn to go on watch. Matty was already sitting upright in his bed rubbing his eyes. It was 1:30 am. We dressed quickly, grabbed our rifles and the ammunition pouches, lit cigarettes and walked to the Security Office to meet our watch partners.

Several ARs were already there sipping black coffee and eating a slice of brown rye bread covered with strawberry jam. A middle-aged kibbutz member, probably the shift commander, sat behind the desk listening intently to the phone that he held in one hand and a cigarette in the other.

I took some coffee, walked out of the bunker and sat on the bench near the entrance. The night was warm and a large receding moon rising in the east, painted the hills across the Jordan River in a cold white. The kibbutz was asleep. The quiet was interrupted occasionally by a barking dog.

Everyone arrived by 2 am and the shift commander assigned ARs to the kibbutzniks. I was assigned to Zvi, the man who sat with me at the table at breakfast. He carried a light Uzi submachine gun. I could see the laughter in his eyes when he saw my Czech rifle. "*I remember having Czech rifles in 1948*," he mused. "*We used its heavy butt to crack nuts.*"

We started walking towards our section near the animal barn. It was Zvi's regular section and he led the way.

After walking for a while, Zvi interrupted the quiet to ask what I thought of Eshkol's speech.

I admitted that it was terrible and that I thought Eshkol was scared. The contempt in my voice was loud and clear.

"*You know, having a leader who hesitates before going to war isn't such a bad thing,*" Zvi answered after digesting my reply for a while. "*It tells you he understands that lives will be lost. And that he's aware that we could also lose. I'd rather have a leader who hesitates than a leader who drags his country into a poorly thought-out adventure.*"

I recalled this conversation fifteen years later, almost to the day.[11]

---

11 On June 6, 1982 Israel invaded Lebanon in what was later known as the First Lebanon War. Although there were provocations from Lebanon they did not justify an invasion. The then Prime Minister Menachem Begin declared the war based on deceitful arguments by his defense minister Ariel Sharon. Two weeks later I reached the outskirts of Beirut with my unit in time to hear Begin declare victory in what he described as a "War of Choice."

Three years later, Israel was forced out of most of the captured territories by incessant terrorist attacks that cost the lives of hundreds of Israeli soldiers, holding on to only a

But that night, near the cattle barn I was not ready to agree with Zvi.

"*This situation isn't our own doing,*" I argued. "*We need to respond decisively. We can't wait much longer.*"

Zvi was unconvinced. "*What is the hurry,*" he argued, "*once a soldier is killed he is dead, he cannot be brought back to life.*"

Zvi's opinion was not unique in Sha'ar HaGolan. The Socialist ideological movement that created the kibbutz was pacifist in nature, the exact opposite of the ideology of the movement that brought Begin and Sharon to power.

I tried to convince Zvi that as we were waiting, the Egyptians continued digging themselves in along our Sinai border and that by keeping our reserves deployed we were damaging our own economy.

Zvi just laughed when he heard my arguments. They were exactly what the press was claiming he explained. He would have hoped to hear more insightful arguments from an engineering student, he added. It was a slight but I was not offended. Despite the harshness of Zvi's words, he spoke kindly and patiently, like a grandfather to his naïve grandson. I admired him for having lived in a frontier kibbutz for most of his life, for carving this land out of a hostile environment and adversarial neighbors. I was eager to hear how someone who lived for decades under Syrian guns could be so reluctant to go to war.

"*You agree that most of our military strength is derived from the reserves?*" Zvi asked. I nodded silently. "*They benefit from the extra time. They can train, refresh their skills, check out their equipment and repair what was damaged during the long storage time in warehouses. They will enter the war in a far better shape after having had a couple of weeks to prepare.*"

"*And as for the damage to our economy,*" he continued, "*you're right, but think of the damage to our economy if the war doesn't go well. Or even if it does go well, do you think that the cost of a successful war would be lower than the cost of waiting? You're from Haifa, right? Imagine that a single Syrian bomber penetrated our defenses and blew up the oil refinery near Haifa. Eshkol and the government have it right,*" he concluded. "*Slow and steady, thoughtful and careful, I like it.*"

This was a prophetic argument. Six days later, a single Syrian MiG fighter was shot down near Haifa as it was preparing to bomb the refinery. Fifteen years later, I witnessed the destruction of large oil storage tanks in an oil terminal near Sidon in Lebanon. Thick clouds of black smoke covered the skies tens of

---

narrow strip north of its border. In May 2000, Israel abandoned unilaterally even that narrow strip.

miles away for more than a week. It was not difficult then to imagine the devastation in Haifa had the refineries been blown up.

I told Zvi that after Eshkol's talk Behira and Shaul felt as if they were back in pre-Holocaust Czechoslovakia.

Zvi was not surprised. He agreed that we're having a difficult time and there been many similarities to Czechoslovakia of 1938. But that didn't mean we needed to react before having explored all of our alternatives. He reiterated that the damages from a war, no matter how successful, would likely exceed the costs of a few more weeks of waiting.

I didn't give up, "I can see Nasser sitting in Cairo and laughing at the coward Jews and their frightened leader Eshkol."

"And why should that matter? We're either prepared and will win or we're not. How Eshkol is being perceived by Nasser has no effect on the outcome. If anything, I can see how they are lowering their guard and making our work easier."

"Just the opposite, they're smelling blood and we're encouraging them to attack."

"If that's what you think, then we certainly should take our time and wait. That will allow us to be better prepared. Imagine if the Egyptian or the Syrians attacked us before we had our reserve units along the borders. Just look at these hills. How long do you think it will take the Syrian tanks to get here if they faced no resistance, an hour, two hours, maybe half a day? All that stands now between them and us is your Czech rifle, my Uzi and their belief that we have a significant force waiting for them in the valley. Other than your ARs, not a single new reserve unit was deployed near us."

We checked back at the security office at dawn. Zvi didn't convince me, but our shift passed quickly as we argued with each other. I returned to bed to try to catch a quick nap. In less than an hour I was due back in the trench for another day of digging. But Eshkol's speech and Zvi's arguments kept me awake.

We headed back to the trench after grabbing a cup of coffee and a slice of bread with jam in the dining room's patio. Like most kibbutzniks, we did not want to waste the cool hours on breakfast. We preferred to return to the cool dining room later in the morning when the sun was high in the sky.

Matty and I continued digging. Yesterday's blisters popped and burned my hands, but my arms and back felt much better.

Matty's transistor radio rested on a dirt pile at the edge of the trench and was tuned to GALATZ. Patriotic songs streaming from the radio provided rhythm to our work but did nothing to improve our mood that remained depressed since the previous night.

The seven o'clock news broadcast brought responses and reactions to Eshkol's speech. Radio broadcasts from most of the Arab world brought ridicule and predicted a swift destruction of Israel. Radio Cairo promised to throw the Jews into the sea. What seemed in the past to be a joke looked that morning like a real possibility.

Comments by various Israeli pundits and European observers described confusion and concern in Israel. Mothers and wives of reserve soldiers were planning a demonstration in Jerusalem to call for the resignation of Eshkol from his role as the Minister of Defense. Some were calling for the appointment of Moshe Dayan as the new Minister of Defense. But since Dayan was a member of the opposition party, commentators thought that the likelihood of such an appointment was slim.

That night after dinner, I returned to Shaul and Behira's room. They have become a bit like my adoptive parents while I was in the kibbutz. When I arrived, Chaim Herzog just began his second daily commentary. He analyzed the strength of the Syrian army relative to the Israeli army and found its balance of power in our favor. He reminded the listeners that the Syrian army's command was appointed based on political merits rather than military, and that regimes in Syria changed at least once a year through coups that left the army demoralized. Furthermore, Damascus, the Syrian capital, was the closest of all Arab capitals to the Israeli border. This had to be a consideration both for the Syrian generals and their patrons in the government when contemplating whether to join the war.

It was comforting to hear Herzog. The convincing logic by an IDF general and his calm tone were in sharp contrast to the uncertainty and even fear that was projected by our Prime Minister or the hysteric broadcasts from the Arab stations.

Shaul was the first to break the silence. The morning paper reported that several rabbis in Tel Aviv marked sections of city parks as potential cemetery sites. I was not certain what marking parks as cemeteries entailed, was it merely blessing the land? Marking it with strings? But it certainly meant that certain government officials thought that if war broke out casualties in Tel Aviv could exceed the capacity of all the existing cemeteries.

Despite the many hostilities during Israel's brief history, the total toll of lost lives was in the single-digit thousands. But if the projection of casualties in the next war exceeded the capacity of existing cemeteries, it had to mean that they were exceeding tens of thousands or even hundreds of thousands. It was a clear indication of how grim things looked in Tel Aviv.

I was thinking again about the conversation with Zvi the previous night. If the number of dead could exceed tens of thousands, how many wounded could there be? Where would they be treated? Hospitals would run out of capacity even more quickly than the cemeteries. Zvi was right; the cost of war could be too high to bear even if it ended in victory.

The following news broadcast did not mention of the conversion of city parks into cemeteries. It focused on a large demonstration in Jerusalem, mostly of mothers and wives of deployed soldiers, calling for the resignation of Eshkol as the Minister of Defense and appointment of Moshe Dayan as his replacement.

"You know," Shaul said, "*Israel seems like no more than a large ghetto. Like the Jews in the ghettos in Europe, we're fenced in, our tormentors are sharpening their butchers' knives just outside the fence and the world is watching indifferently from a safe distance.*"

I was exhausted after the night on watch followed by digging in the hot sun. After dinner I returned to my room to rest before my next night on watch. I missed a special news announcement reporting an unscheduled trip of King Hussein of Jordan to meet President Nasser in Cairo to sign a five-year bilateral defense treaty that was identical to the treaty between Egypt and Syria. In it, the Jordanian forces were put under the command of an Egyptian general. It was now official: should any of the three nations surrounding Israel be attacked, the other two were committed to join. With units from Saudi Arabia and Iraq already in Jordan, Israel was facing armies from five nations.

The new threat from Jordan was significant. While the Egyptian border was in the Negev desert, far from any significant population center, the Jordanian border was barely ten miles from Tel Aviv, within reach of even mid-range cannons.

Even more importantly, only barbed wire entanglement fences separated the Jordanian East Jerusalem from the Jewish Western side. Snipers could fire at residents in their own bedrooms. Small cannons and mortar launchers could turn West Jerusalem into a wasteland.

Though Lebanon to the north remained silent, Israel could expect an attack along that border as well. Although Lebanon was not actively hostile no one doubted that if the opportunity presented itself, Lebanon would jump in to grab the nearby city of Naharia or even Haifa. The IDF had to allocate forces to that seemingly peaceful border as well. The noose was tightening; good options were diminishing, and hope fading.

That night I patrolled again with Zvi.

"So what do you think about the Jordanians joining forces with Egypt?" I asked.

Of course he didn't like it but he surprised me by saying that in his opinion, Sha'ar HaGolan and Israel itself had been in a much worse situation back in 1948.

I wondered how could that be, though Sha'ar HaGolan and Israel were smaller in 1948, so were the Arab armies then.

"Hell, we barely had chance to organize an army when we were attacked after we declared Independence," he reminded me. "The IDF was mostly made up of the Haganah and the Irgun[12] who didn't speak to each other. We hardly had any weapons because the British were actively searching our Sliks.[13] We had no serious air force, artillery, or armored units. Meanwhile, Syria and Egypt were already independent states for quite some time and had armies and equipment, and they were much larger, tens of millions of their people against our six hundred thousand Jews."

It was compelling, but the ratios still didn't favor us, I thought. The Arabs still outnumbered us, their armies larger, their equipment better, deadlier, and the Soviets supported them openly while we were standing alone.

As if reading my mind, Zvi conceded that our current danger was enormous and we might not have a second miracle like we had in 1948.

We continued our patrol along the fence near the cattle barn. Twice an hour we returned to the security office to register, take a cup of coffee and smoke a cigarette.

"Tell me about Sha'ar HaGolan in 1948," I asked. I didn't dare ask him why the kibbutz was abandoned, because it was such a sensitive topic. But I was eager to hear from someone who was there.

Zvi understood. "We were barely two hundred members and we only had a few Czech rifles, like yours, and STENs,"[14] he started. "The Syrians attacked first Tzemach, the base that you saw a few days ago. It was captured after a heavy fight and they were coming in our direction. We asked for reinforcement but it was tied down in Deganiah which was attacked too. Had we decided to fight, the Syrians might have captured and killed us all and the members of our neighbor Kibbutz Masada. By choosing to retreat, we saved our lives and the lives of our wives and children. The very next day, when the reinforcement arrived, we returned, pushed the Syrians out and took back both Kibbutzim. I think having two live Kibbutzim is better than two memorials to dead ones."

---

12 Haganah and Irgun—two pre-statehood Israeli paramilitary organizations that joined to form the IDF.

13 Slik—a term in the pre-state years describing a hidden weapon depot, often in a basement, between double walls or underground.

14 STEN—WWII-era British-made submachine gun.

MAY 31, 1967

In the morning, digging the trench along the fence, I looked south. The Jordanian red mountains had not changed since the previous day but they looked more threatening. I could almost see the angry eyes peering at us from behind the rocks. Even the heat radiating from these mountains felt like the fiery breath of a dragon.

Kobi must have had the same thoughts, *"Listen to the silence,"* he said, interrupting our work. We put down our tools, turned off the radio and stood outside the trenches to listen and watch.

There was no sound. Animals and other creatures were hiding from the heat. Even birds stopped flying. The silence was mesmerizing. If the Saudis, Iraqis, or Jordanians were deploying on these mountains, they did so without a sound. The contrast between what might happen and this stillness was so sharp that I thought it might just be a bad dream.

We returned to work and the radio brought us back to reality. Women in Jerusalem were demonstrating again demanding that Dayan replace Eshkol as the Minister of Defense. Reports about high-level conversations speculated that Eshkol might form a National Unity Government. For the first time in Israel's history, Menachem Begin, the leader of the right wing Herut Party, could join the coalition government as a minister. If that were to happen, Dayan's party would also join the coalition and Dayan could then become the Minister of Defense.

The radio also reported that Iraq saw the existence of Israel as an error that must be rectified and that the opportunity to wipe it off the map was coming.

Not wanting to be left out, Ahmad Shukairy, the head of the Palestinian Liberation Organization announced that while the PLO would allow those Jews who survived the war to remain in Palestine, he did not expect there will be any survivors.[15]

In the next news item, Germany, in an act of support, agreed to sell Israel twenty-thousand gas masks. Of course that number was insufficient to protect even the army's front units, let alone the civilian population. But it was a harsh reminder that Egypt, after using chemical weapons in Yemen two years earlier, would not hesitate to use them again. It was ironic that Germany, who only twenty-three years earlier gassed millions of Jews, was now offering to protect Jews from the same hazard.

---

15 The Israeli-Palestinian conflict is centered today on the Israeli occupation of the West Bank and consequences of that occupation such as the Israeli settlements there or the roadblocks and check points that Palestinians must endure.

In the evening Chaim Herzog gave a new commentary, starting with an old Jewish tale about the sages of the city of Chelm.[16] According to that story, the citizens of Chelm crossed the river that passed through their city by tying themselves to a log that was pulled across to the opposite side. One day, the log flipped while it was pulled and the passenger riding it was immersed in the water with his feet dangling up in the air. Look at this impatient guy, mused the sages of Chelm when they saw his feet clad in white socks pointing up in the air, he has not yet reached the other bank but he is already drying his stockings. And so is Nasser, Herzog continued, the war has not even started but he is already promising his people to destroy Israel.

JUNE 1, 1967

As speculated the day before, Levi Eshkol decided to broaden his cabinet and invited Dayan and Begin's parties to join what he called the National Unity Government. Although his government already enjoyed a large base in the Knesset, seventy-five out of the hundred and twenty members, the new government included nearly all of them, one hundred and eleven members.

In the evening, when I joined Behira and Shaul for dessert, the radio announced that five hundred volunteers from London and almost two hundred and fifty volunteers from Sweden would leave for Israel to take over jobs left vacant by Israelis called up for reserve duty. This was the first encouraging news item since the beginning of the crisis.

I told Behira and Shaul that I talked with my parents on the phone. My mother was excited that Dayan was appointed the Minister of Defense: she loved him. But my father kept comparing Eshkol to Chamberlain, the British Prime Minister who tried to appease Germany before WWII even though he could not avoid comparing Dayan to Churchill.

JUNE 3, 1967

In his first interview as the Minister of Defense, Dayan was asked if the war would be short or long.

"I cannot predict that," he replied, "but if war breaks out, I know we will win."

---

16 Chelm—a mythological city of fools that is the source of many Jewish jokes and anecdotes.

In his evening commentary, General Herzog remarked that there are only two types of generals: generals who fight the wars of yesterday and generals who fight the next war. *"I can assure you that the generals of our army belong to the second group."*

MONDAY, JUNE 5, 1967

We just returned to the fence from breakfast and I was still standing outside the trench looking towards Tawfiq when two jets flew in our direction at low altitude without a sound. The deafening roar of their after-burners reached us only after they passed overhead.

"*Syrian, MiGs,*" Kobi shouted just as I noticed that instead of the Blue Star of David, their wings were marked with red-white-and-black concentric rings.

But before we could react, a rapid sequence of machine-gun fire came from a third jet following the first two. We recognized its delta wings before we could see its blue and white markings.

"*A 'Mirage,'*" Matty shouted.

Instinctively we jumped into the trenches. But by the time we reached bottom, the three jets were out of sight and their sounds fading.

"*Is this the start of the war?*" Kobi asked when we climbed out of the trenches. We looked beyond the banana groves for any sign of an aerial fight, downed plane or any other military activity. But the quiet returned to the valley. The stillness of another hot day took it over.

A few minutes later, the Israeli radio, Kol Israel, made an announcement that many Israelis would later remember vividly.

"*An IDF spokesman announced that Egyptian forces launched a land and air attack. Israeli forces took actions to repel these attacks. At this time, we have no additional information about the nature of these activities. Further announcements will be made as information becomes available.*"

Soon after the announcement was made, General Herzog came on air. I was surprised. His commentaries were scheduled at night.

"*Nasser decided to take advantage of the Arab unity while it lasted to launch an attack on us. However, I can assure you that they will be taught a lesson they richly deserve,*" Herzog started. He then continued by reassuring us the listeners that just because no announcement was made, it does not mean that Israel had nothing to announce. When Arab radio stations fan mass hysteria, Israel does not need to dispel their reporting and disperse the "fog of war."

So we were in war and we already saw some action. The new term that we had just learned, "fog of war," surely applied to us. We did not see if the Syrian jets were shot down, nor did we see any other military activity, we didn't know who was at war, and oddly enough, I don't recall being scared or worried. I think I was mostly thrilled, very much like during an exciting soccer game. These are the feelings of someone who's never experienced a real war and hasn't seen its losses. I don't believe Laci was thrilled when he heard the news. But I doubt he was scared either. *"We better continue digging,"* Kobi interrupted our cheers. *"If I know anything about the Syrians, they'll start shelling soon."*

An artillery forward observer in Tawfiq up on the hills must have overheard him because a faint thud of an explosion came from that direction.

"It sounds like the 'exit' of a cannon shell." Kobi said. He was surprisingly calm, probably because we were already inside the trenches digging. *"Train your ears to recognize these sounds so you can distinguish between a cannon fire and a mortar launch. Cannons fire in low trajectory and when fired in our direction a shell will hit us in 15-20 seconds. Sound travels one kilometer in three seconds. So if they fired at us from Tawfiq, that's less than five kilometers from us, sound will reach us barely five seconds before the shell hits."*

He barely finished his sentence when we heard a second explosion and saw a smoke column rising from Deganiah to our north.

"Mortar shells fly longer because they follow a high trajectory. So if you hear an 'exit' from a mortar launcher you have at least half a minute, maybe even a minute to find cover." Kobi continued his lesson.

"One more thing, keep your eyes open. It's not out of the question that we see commando, infantry and even armored vehicle rolling down from the hills."

We laughed nervously. What were we supposed to do when we saw those commandos, throw rocks at them? Hit them with the butts of our Czech rifles?

At lunch the kibbutz looked more like a military than a farming community. All adults carried steel helmets and some even carried their side arms, Uzi submachine guns or rifles. Children were kept near their shelters. Carrying helmets or weapons was prudent. But like a fashion show, helmets and side arms also marked the standing of their owners in the security hierarchy.

Helmets in Israel came from three sources, WWI British army surplus, WWII American army surplus, and at the top-of-the-line, Israeli-made helmets that were issued almost exclusively to paratroopers. Unlike the American or British helmets that were secured by a single strap tied under the chin, the paratrooper helmets were distinguishable by their double strap, one from the back of the helmet and one from underneath the temple. Both straps were attached to a chin cup. Unlike the single-strap helmets, the Israeli helmets were tied snugly to the head. Only "protektzia," that is, a high-level connection, could provide such helmets to non-paratroopers. The same "protektzia" could also deliver to its beneficiaries an Uzi machine gun.

When we entered the dining room carrying our British helmets and Czech rifles we were clearly marked as low class members of the security fashion show. Even Zvi, my aging night watch buddy, had a paratrooper helmet and, of course, an Uzi.

A loud radio in one corner of the dining room played patriotic music. Groups at each table were discussing the recent events trying to guess the direction of the war that was now a few hours old. Some, mostly those who carried the paratrooper helmets and therefore considered well connected and knowledgeable, provided details that they labeled as "confidential," or "fresh from the front." The less "connected," particularly those of us with the British helmets and the Czech rifles gobbled up the rumors.

How little did we know! Even in our wildest dreams we did not imagine anything close to the reality that was shaping rapidly in distant places, Cairo, Damascus, and even H-3, a mysterious Iraqi air base in the Western Desert. When we sat down for lunch the war had already been decided. We didn't know all that, but neither did the Egyptian president, the Syrian president, or the Jordanian king. The enormity of their defeat would be revealed much later that night when the IDF would chose to partially disperse the "fog of war."

But we did learn a few true facts during that lunch. One of the MiGs we saw that morning was downed not far from us, and Deganiah was indeed shelled this morning by Syrian artillery from Tawfiq. Several other Kibbutzim along the border north of Sha'ar Hagolan were also shelled, but there were no reported casualties or property damage. the other MiG escaped the lone Mirage and reached Haifa but it was shot down while attempting to bomb the refineries there. There was no word why only one Mirage was available to tackle two MiGs.

The radio stopped playing the music. The dining room turned quiet at the start of the one o'clock news brief. Jordan had joined the war. Jordanian cannons were shelling Jerusalem, Tel Aviv, and various settlements along the Armistice Line. But there were no updates about the progress of the Israeli army or the actual status of the war now in its first day.

The dining room remained quiet. Our worst fears were materializing. We were being attacked on three fronts. Jerusalem and Tel Aviv, two of our major cities, were shelled, Haifa, our second largest city, might have been bombed from the air by at least one Syrian plane. And Jordan was attempting to cut Israel in two by using its artillery in Qalqilia where Israeli territory was only 12 kilometers wide.

In past border skirmishes Israel was quick to announce the outcome of the IDF's efforts—that were almost invariably favorable. Why was our own radio silent about our progress? Was Herzog's "fog of war" intended to confuse the enemy or to obscure our own losses and possible defeat? But then, if we were doing so badly, why did we only see two Syrian MiGs and a tepid shelling of Deganiah? Wouldn't the Syrians jump on the opportunity to hit us harder as we lay bleeding?

Lunch was brief. The need to complete the defense system seemed far more urgent today than the yesterday. All those who could lift a shovel joined us along the fence line, digging feverishly.

Shelling of Sha'ar HaGolan began at 2 pm. Faint cannon "exits" from Tawfiq announced the arrival of shells that within seconds began falling in the banana groves, a few hundred meters from our trenches. A siren on top of the water tower began wailing. We all jumped into our freshly dug trenches to watch if the shelling would be followed by any attempt at an invasion. But strangely, of the few shells aimed at us, only one landed inside the kibbutz.[17]

Within minutes, explosions appeared in Tawfiq. Our artillery did not miss the village.

We watched the duel that lasted approximately an hour. Every few minutes one or two shells from Tawfiq landed in the banana grove and, as if by a reflex, two shells from an Israeli artillery unit near Deganiah landed in Tawfiq. Other than a few banana plants and a deep hole in the middle of the central lawn, Sha'ar HaGolan suffered no damage. Later kids started digging around the hole in the central lawn for shrapnel souvenirs.

After dinner I walked, or more accurately, felt my way across the dark central lawn to Shaul and Behira's apartment. Falling into one of the newly dug trenches in that moonless night seemed to be a more imminent danger than being hit by a Syrian shell. I reached them just in time to hear Prime Minister Eshkol's announcement that fighting had been pushed by the IDF into the Sinai, outside Israeli territory. But the news from Jerusalem was still worrisome, Jordanian cannons continued shelling the city and snipers were targeting its

---

17 After becoming an artillery officer I often wondered why did so few of the Syrian shells hit the kibbutz throughout the course of the war. It was certainly on their target list and it was hit many times before. They didn't even need a spotter to guide their cannons. In the end, I concluded they must have feared the Israeli response.

citizens, inflicting many injuries and deaths. Shelling continued along the Syrian border.

We tried to read between the lines, hoping to guess if the news so far was good or bad when General Herzog's voice came on the air.

"*The first day of fighting is over. Today we opened a new page in the annals of Israeli wars. After responding to hostile movements by Egyptian forces, the IDF moved the war into the Sinai, into Egypt's territory,*" he started.

Hardly any of Herzog's listeners noticed the significance of his opening sentence. Shaul, Behira, and I, along with many of the kibbutz members were still worrying about a Syrian infantry invasion that could wipe out the kibbutz. Had we paid attention, we might have noticed that Herzog was hinting at historic achievements by the Israeli Air Force. One that possibly overshadowed the miracle of Hanukkah, where a small can of oil intended to light the menorah in the ancient Jewish Temple for one day lasted for eight days, or the miracle of Purim, where the plan of Haman, a Persian villain, to exterminate the Jews in Persia was foiled by Queen Esther.

The fog of war, Herzog continued was an obstacle to the Arab generals, not the Israeli generals. Citizens in Tel Aviv surely noticed that despite reports by Radio Cairo that their city is burning, life went on as usual.

Herzog did not mention though that suburbs of Tel Aviv were shelled by Jordanian canons in Qalqilia.[18] But he was probably right when he said at the end that Nasser was a different person that evening from the Nasser who woke up that morning.

We just sat quietly and listened. When Shaul turned off the radio, we could hear the chirping of the crickets outside. In previous evenings, the central lawn outside was filled with shouts of children playing, sounds of animated conversations by families sitting on the porches outside their apartments. Now, the children were being put in bed in their bomb-shelters, many of the men were patrolling along the fences, and the remaining members were huddling around radios hungry for any shred of information. In Sha'ar HaGolan, the end of the first day of the Six-Day War felt like the quiet before the storm. The air was electrified. We sensed that something immense was happening but we couldn't tell what it was.

On my way back to my hut I tried to imagine the heavy battles that were taking place in Sinai. Were Israeli soldiers in trenches fighting off raiding Egyptians? Or just the opposite, Israelis soldiers raiding Egyptian

---

18 Qalqilia—a Palestinian town in the West Bank just east of Tel Aviv's suburb Kfar Saba.

fortifications? Were Israelis being killed right now defending our country? Was Haifa safe? What about Jerusalem?

With a heavy heart I entered the dark room. Quietly I slipped under the blanket, remaining fully dressed with my shoes on as ordered by Kobi. Despite our minimal training and sub-par gear, we were an important part of the kibbutz's defense. I woke up just after midnight. Shelling from Tawfiq resumed. The wailing siren accompanied the incoming shells explosions. I got out of my bed, grabbed my helmet and rifle, and ran to the security bunker. My watch was about to start anyhow. Good timing.

Two suitcase-size military command radios in the bunker were blurting messages in rapid succession that were hard to decipher because of the background static. The only word I understood was "over." Two men holding microphones in their hands sat next to the radios listening intently. I wondered if they understood the conversation or were just pretending. The room was filled with kibbutz members and ARs who stood silently, lighting one cigarette with the end of another. I poured myself a cup of black coffee from a kettle in the corner and lit my own cigarette.

"What's going on?" I asked one of the kibbutzniks.

"Tirat Zvi, just south of here, was shelled earlier tonight. I think we started moving across the border in that area and rumors are that we already captured Jenin[19] and in Jerusalem we captured the UN headquarters, I think it's called the Government House, it was invaded in the morning by Jordanian units and we took it from them."

I didn't believe the story. It seemed like another rumor, no different from the many that circulated in Sha'ar HaGolan since morning. But if it was true, we were a stone's throw away from Jerusalem's Old City and from the Wailing Wall.

One of the radios in the corner announced that Syrian cannons were shelling Ein-Gev, a kibbutz on the eastern shore of the Sea of Galilee. It was a favorite target. It sat on a narrow strip of land between the shore of the lake and the steep slopes leading up to the Golan Heights. The Syrians always fancied the idea of cutting the kibbutz and that strip of land off from Israel and gaining a direct access to the Sea of Galilee Israel's main water source.

I stepped out of the bunker to start my watch duty and joined up with Zvi who wore his paratrooper helmet that barely covered his white hair and held his Uzi in "ready" position. I suspected that his safety catch was toggled to fire.

---

19   Jenin—a town in the north of the West Bank.

We started walking towards our position along the fence. We made up a truly comical pair, an aging man carrying paratrooper gear and a young man carrying aging World War I gear. I was certain that if Syrian commandos chose to raid the kibbutz through our sector, despite our best efforts they would find very little resistance.

The thin sliver of moon rising over the mountains did little to obscure the distant red flashes coming without a sound from the north and the south. They could be from Ein-Gev or even as far north as Rosh Pinah and from Tirat Zvi in the south. But other than those silent flashes there was no sign that a major war was going on.

We kept patrolling, going back and forth along our fence section. Occasionally Zvi found a rock to sit down and *"listen quietly to the night trying to detect suspicious sounds,"* as he tried to put it. I could not tell if this was a genuine security precaution or an excuse to rest. Either way, I welcomed it and enjoyed watching the dimly lit landscape, listening to the crickets or night birds and wondering if we could hear the footsteps of commandos if they would approach us.

We were replaced by the next sentry just before 3 am and returned to the security bunker for tea. Most of the earlier crowd was still there, chain-smoking, trading rumors and analyzing the little information that trickled in. The two military radios continued crackling incomprehensible messages, each ending with "Over" and the civilian radio in the corner was still playing patriotic songs in low volume. The GALATZ radio staff was pulling an all-nighter.

Six beeps at 3 am announced the start of the news broadcast. *"The Chief of Staff General Rabin and the Air Force commander General Hod announced tonight that in Sinai the Israeli forces captured Rafah, Sheikh-Zuwayd, and El Arish and are on their way to Abu Agueyla. But the lead story of the day is that the Air Force dealt a decisive blow to the air forces of the Egyptian, Syrian, and Jordanian armies, attaining air superiority in all three fronts. Four hundred enemy planes were destroyed. The Chief of Staff described the victory as unprecedented."*

The bunker turned quiet. The news was too astonishing to cheer. Only a few weeks earlier destroying six enemy planes was considered a huge victory. The destruction of four hundred enemy planes in less than a day was beyond belief, let alone the capture of vast Egyptian territory.

We looked at each other wondering if what we just heard was indeed the truth. We didn't even hear the announcer continue that fighting with Jordan also went well and overnight the IDF captured Jenin and Latrun, or General Herzog saying that he was justified in repeating Churchill's' quote when he thanked the Royal Air Force during the Battle for Britain "Never in the field of human conflict was so much owed by so many to so few."

I still remember that night. Americans often ask "where were you when Kennedy was assassinated?" For Israelis this intense national moment could be paraphrased by "Where were you when the Six-Day War was decided?"

Just after sunrise nearly all men and some women of the kibbutz were back in the trenches to continue our digging. The valley and the mountains still looked threatening, though the angry eyes I imagined yesterday to be looking at us from behind the rocks had now a glint of fear. Despite the destruction of the Syrian air force, the artillery in Tawfiq was still active and a ground war was still possible.

Although the Hebrew broadcast of the Cairo Radio was still continuing to announce imaginary Arab victories, reality started to sink in. Israel was on its way to one of the biggest victories in Jewish history. And when weighing in the initial odds as represented by the size of the enemy and its resources, we thought, this could stand as one of the most spectacular military victories in human history.

In the evening, Kol Israel announced that Israeli forces captured Abu Agueyla and Jabel Libni in the Sinai. By the end of the second day, IDF forces were already half way to the Suez Canal.

On the Jordanian front, Israeli forces captured the French Hill near Jerusalem and Shuafat, a suburb of the Arab section of Jerusalem. The road to Mount Scopus was open. Once again it was an integral part of Israel.[20]

That evening, while on watch, Zvi and I were wondering if the IDF would capture the Old City and the Wailing Wall, the holiest of holy Jewish site.

I don't think I believed in God. And yet that night I sensed the presence of a higher force. A miracle just happened and another one might happen tomorrow. The Wailing Wall could return to Jewish hands for the first time since the destruction of the Second Temple. I rarely thought of the Holocaust or the two thousand years of Jewish diaspora but both Zvi and I understood that the next day might mark the end of that dark period in Jewish history.

JUNE 7, 1967

Early in the morning, I called Laci and Zsuzsi. Life in Haifa was slowly returning to some semblance of normality.

---

20 Mount Scopus, located in east Jerusalem just north of Mount Olives was until 1949 the site of the Hebrew University and Hadassah Hospital. When the armistice line with Jordan was drawn after the Independence war, it remained in Israeli hands but separated from the Israeli side of Jerusalem. The Mount was manned by a skeleton police force and supplied by bi-weekly convoys escorted by UN forces.

Ten days earlier, strict civil defense regulations went into effect country-wide. Citizens were ordered to clear clutter from their bomb shelters, many of which were built after the Sinai Campaign in 1956, to cover windows, including store windows, with dark screens and to reinforce the glass with crisscrossed adhesive tapes. Car headlights were ordered painted dark blue with only a narrow clear slit at the center. Large public shelters were opened and stocked with water and emergency food, and field hospitals and collection centers were prepared to accept a flood of injured or killed citizens.

To prevent a run on grocery stores, purchase of basic staples such as sugar, flour, and oil was restricted. Radio announcements warned against hoarding but recommended preparing an emergency water supply in buckets and bathtubs.

Civil defense units were called up to enforce these rules. These reserve military units consisting of men who were no longer fit for regular service due to age or physical limitations and were given vast enforcement authority including fines and arrest. Old men wearing khaki uniforms and green berets patrolled the streets day and night.

Laci, a captain in one of these units, oversaw the civil defense of an entire Haifa neighborhood. He was proud as a peacock. Every afternoon since the start of these emergency measures he reported to his headquarters to monitor his squads as they patrolled the deserted streets. But after the destruction of enemy air forces, all civil defense restrictions were lifted and Laci's active military career in the IDF came to an abrupt end.

Streetlights were back on, coverings were removed from most windows, reinforcement tapes scraped off, and the dark paint was washed off the car headlights. Movie theatres reopened but stayed empty; too many men and women were still on active duty and those who remained at home started mourning the early casualties or were just not interested. Though no losses were announced officially, individuals were already getting visits by grim-faced military officers. Death announcements of fallen soldiers began appearing on billboards and in newspapers. Almost everyone in Haifa knew someone who fell or a family member of a fallen soldier. The losses, though relatively few, touched everyone personally. More losses were still coming and continued to come for days.

At the same time, legends of tough battles and heroic fighting began circulating. The despair that was so deep only a week earlier disappeared. Eshkol's infamous speech was only nine days old but already forgotten. Haifa was no longer gripped by fear and anguish, the relief was tinged by grief. Like the rest of the nation, it was a city in mourning.

Without business in his office or a role in the civil defense, Laci stayed home with Zsuzsi, waiting for my calls, listening to an endless stream of commentaries on radio and reading the daily papers and their special editions that kept appearing every few hours.

Matty and I were walking back from the trenches when the radio announced: *"This morning Israeli forces penetrated the old city of Jerusalem. Sharm-El-Sheikh was captured; the Straits of Tiran are open."*

We stood breathless. The main cause for the war, the blockage of the Tiran Straits was now removed. It would have been enough to make us jump for joy. But the Old City, what about the Old City, was it liberated?

After a brief pause the announcer continued: *"the Chief of Staff announces that the Old City of Jerusalem is in our hands, and most of the West Bank. Also, the entire Sinai Peninsula is in our hands."*

When the announcement ended, the broadcast resumed with Shuli Nathan singing:

Jerusalem of gold, and of bronze, and of light,
Behold, I am a violin for all your songs.

I looked at Matty; we both had tears in our eyes. Our last Passover Seder meal, like hundreds of Seders before, ended with *L'Shannah Haba'a B'Yerushalayim Habnuya* ("next year in the rebuilt Jerusalem"). We knew we were witnessing that moment.

I will never know if at that same moment Laci thought of his little Juditka, Lili, and his parents who did not survive the Holocaust? Did he wonder why was he chosen amongst most of his family, the hundreds from Gyula, the hundreds of thousands from Hungary, and the six million from Europe to see this moment?

Not many listeners noticed a few days later that Shuli Nathan was singing a new version of the second verse of *Jerusalem of Gold*:

The words "How did the cisterns dry out?" were replaced by *"Chazarnu el borot hamayim"* ("We returned to the cisterns").

JUNE 10, 1967

During the last two days of the war, the Israeli air force and artillery bombed the Golan. From our post, we saw clouds of smoke rising in the distance and along the ridge in front of us. In response, the Syrian army shelled

Sha'ar HaGolan, Masada, and the kibbutzim to our north and south. We continued digging trenches, though we no longer thought that an invasion was likely.

The war was already settled with Egypt and Jordan but despite the heavy Israeli fire, we did not see Israeli ground troops moving towards the Golan Heights. The Arab members of the UN along with their Soviet patron state requested a ceasefire and an immediate stop to the "Israeli aggression." It was becoming clear that a ceasefire might take effect any moment. We started worrying that the war would end without removing the Syrian threat to the kibbutzim in the valley. As long as one cannon in Tawfiq could threaten children in the kibbutz, as long as farmers working their fields had to carry Uzi submachine guns, the victories of the last five days, however great, seemed incomplete in Sha'ar HaGolan. One of the kibbutz members joined a regional delegation to Dayan urging him not to leave this job unfinished.

The sixth day of the war fell on a Saturday. Shelling and bombing stopped, as if cannons also observed the Shabbat. Early morning reports described heavy fighting in the north and central parts of the Golan Heights. But the southern front facing us was quiet. A commentator suggested that the UN might impose a ceasefire as early as that evening, which the US would help to enforce.

I joined many members of the kibbutz at the trenches along the east fence hoping to see signs of an Israeli invasion. Slight haze covered the slopes facing us. Smoke was still billowing from distant targets bombed the day before. But there was nothing else to see. The war seemed to be fading, leaving Tawfiq untouched. Despite the slight haze, its buildings—looking through binoculars—were all intact. There was no detectable motion. The artillery spotter could still be hiding there. Could it be that the kibbutzim facing the northern and central part of the Golan would be liberated from the Syrian threat and only in Sha'ar HaGolan civilians would continue living under a real threat?

We broke off for lunch in the dining hall in a sour mood, resigned to the fact that Tawfiq would remain Syrian.

Lunch was ending when a faint sound of helicopters emerged from the west. The sound got louder and soon approximately ten helicopters flew overhead towards the Syrian Mountains. We ran to the fence line just in time to see the last of them cross the border and continue flying over the mountains deep into Syrian territory. There was not a single shot fired and not a single MiG showed up to intercept them. We could only guess if they were carrying troops or flying into enemy territory to evacuate casualties. But we were puzzled by the lack of resistance. Could that mean that the part of the Golan Height facing us fell into our hands without a fight?

The ceasefire was announced for 6:30 pm that evening. Only four hours were left to capture Tawfiq and the southern tip of the Golan. From the foot of the hills just north of Tawfiq emerged a column led by a bulldozer that seemed to cut a road into the mountain. The bulldozer was followed by a tank and a column of approximately one hundred soldiers walking behind it in a long line. The bulldozer was not armored. Even from our position we could tell that its operator was unprotected. The few binoculars changed hands between us. When I looked through the binoculars at the soldiers walking behind the tank I could see their rifles hanging on their shoulders. They were not in a "ready" position.

The bulldozer reached Tawfiq just before 6:30 pm. Not a single shot was fired. The entire Golan Height was in Israeli hands. The war that lasted only six days had just ended.

Although the capture of the Golan Heights seemed easy at the southern end of the front, heavy battles took place at the north. One hundred and twenty-seven IDF soldiers lost their lives there, and six hundred and twenty-five were wounded, (14) among them eleven soldiers under the charge of my high school classmate Corporal Yitzhak Hamawi. He was among the twenty-five Israelis left from a battalion that attacked Tel Fakhr, a Syrian fortification at the northern slopes of the Golan Heights.

When their half-tracks could no longer continue (15), their battalion commander ordered them to dismount and split. A group of thirteen men, including Yitzhak and the battalion commander himself began clearing the northern part of the fortification. The remaining men were sent to clear the southern part. When fighting ended, Yitzhak remained the only man of his group still standing. Ten of his men and his battalion commander were dead. Yitzhak was decorated for his heroism.

The next morning, trying to sleep late I was awoken by explosions from Tawfiq. They were too loud to be cannon "exits." When I reached the fence I could still see the last few houses in Tawfiq being demolished. Each explosion blew out the walls of a house bringing the roof to the ground nearly intact. Tawfiq was dead.

Almost exactly twenty-seven years earlier, in a completely different world, General Glaise von Horstenau, a Hitler-appointed German military historian, commented on the lopsided German victory over France. (16) Employing the Blitzkrieg, a new strategy of fast-moving modern tanks supported from the air by Stuka dive-bomber, Germany defeated within six weeks and occupied

Holland, Belgium, and most of France and forced on the British army a hasty and humiliating retreat from Dunkirk.

There are moments in military history, Horstenau noted, when for a short period of time that might last a few weeks, months or years; offensive weapons are superior to those of the defense.

Ironically, in the summer of 1967 Israel enjoyed a brief period of offensive superiority over the much larger Arab armies, using German Blitzkrieg-like strategies including a superior air power that was established in the early hours of the war, to overrun the Egyptian, Jordanian, and Syrian armies.

Unfortunately, Horstenau was right. Within six years, the strategic advantages of the Israeli air force and the highly mobile and effective armored forces were all but wiped out by new ground-to-air missile batteries and hand-held anti-tank missiles acquired by Egypt and Syria.

Germany lost its unprecedented superiority even faster. The turning point of World War II, the defeat of the German Sixth Army along with the Hungarian, Italian, and Romanian Armies in Stalingrad, occurred less than three years after the extraordinary German victories in the west. Laci and his MUSZ unit were caught in the collapse of the Hungarian Second Army in Voronezh near Stalingrad.

Summer 1967: Messianic Days (or so we thought)

It took nearly a week for the IDF to recognize that it no longer needed us in Sha'ar HaGolan. With no other military duties, we volunteered that week to join the kibbutz members in their rush to restore their lives that were put on hold for nearly a month. Fields and orchards that could not be accessed needed watering. Trees and plants damaged by the shelling had to be pruned or removed, and crops that were ripening had to be harvested. But during all that rush we kept our sights on Tawfiq, wishing to visit before we left.

A few days after the ceasefire agreement went into effect; the regional command notified our security officer that the road to Tawfiq and the village itself were cleared and open to visitors from the Valley's kibbutzim. There were no Syrians left in Tawfiq and hardly any in the Golan Heights. All soldiers and most civilians fled, some out of fear of retaliation and some to protect Damascus, only fifty miles east of the new border. Only two villages in the north, Majdal Al Shams and Mas'ada, remained populated by Druze villagers, who, like their brethren in the Druze villages on top of Mt. Carmel and in the Galilee, declared loyalty to Israel.

That afternoon, two tractor-towed platforms were parked at the eastern gate of the Kibbutz. Matty and I took our seats on one of the benches along with many ARs and kibbutzniks.

We headed out towards the neighboring kibbutz to our north, Tel Katzir, and then just before reaching its fence we turned east towards the old ceasefire line. An opening in the fence marked the head of the new road to Tawfiq.

Only a week earlier, merely standing at this fence would have been suicidal. But now, two sleepy IDF reserve soldiers manning the border crossing just waved us through. Some kibbutzniks on the platforms cheered and hugged each other as we started on the new road broken open by the tractor the previous Saturday.

I looked at Zvi sitting across the aisle facing me. Tears trickled down his face. His eyes were open but his mind was elsewhere, possibly seeing the Syrian tanks rolling from these hills nineteen years earlier towards Deganiah and

Syrian commandoes marching towards Sha'ar HaGolan. I put my hands on his lap and he touched them. His hands were trembling.

Shaul and Behira, sitting near me, were holding hands and looking down toward the valley that grew distant as our tractor climbed.

Matty, the eternal cynic, put his hands quietly on my shoulder. I think he was crying. So was I.

Officially we had just left the Land of Israel.[1] For most of the riders, this was the first time outside the country. But to all of us on the two platforms, the elation of the moment was not from the gain of new territory, the defeat of an arch-enemy or an opportunity for spoils of war. It was not even due to the sense of an exciting adventure. That moment, our feeling was of great relief and joy of a new freedom: the freedom from fear. For the first time since it settled on a hostile land, Sha'ar HaGolan was not in the sights of a Syrian artillery spotter. For the first time since its establishment, Israel was free from the threat of Syrian army raids.

Years later, in another war, I noticed that new freedoms often smelled like gun powder, smoke of burning fires, or the revolting smell of decaying dead bodies. But on that moment, the smell of our freedom was of clay dust stirred up by the tractor mixed with exhaust fumes of its Diesel engine.

The lone bulldozer working its way uphill on Saturday in a hurry to beat the UN imposed ceasefire deadline, broke a one-way road to serve one tank and an infantry battalion. It was far from an ideal road and yet, in less than half an hour we were standing on concrete slabs resting flat on the ground. These slabs were once the roofs of Tawfiq's houses.

It's amazing how quickly war can erase any sign of life. Tawfiq, a farming village with very little farming land, was never prosperous. But at one time, hundreds of people lived there herding sheep and goats to graze on the slopes. For generations, men and women formed families, loved or fought with each other, brought children into the world, celebrated holidays and then died.

But only days after its fall, all that was left of Tawfiq were thirty or forty concrete slabs on the ground, concealing anything that the villagers or the Syrian soldiers that displaced them once owned. Two fig trees bearing small green figs and several pear cactus bushes in bloom were all that remained of the

---

1 The Golan Heights were under military administration until 1981 when Israel officially annexed that territory making it subject to Israeli laws. It remains the only territory, other than East Jerusalem, annexed by Israel after the Six-Day War.

village's agricultural past. Even the smell of burned animal dung, typical of Arab farming villages, had already dissipated.

A few days later someone ignited the brush and dry weed on the slopes of the mountain in the hope that the wild fire would explode all undetected landmines. The brush burned for several days turning the golden hills black. As for the landmines, the Golan Heights are still infested with minefields marked by fences and warning signs.

But the most beautiful sight of our visit was below us. The white swan in Hans Christian Andersen's *Ugly Duckling* story, seeing his reflection for the first time, must have felt like us seeing the kibbutzim from above. The beauty that cannot be fully appreciated from below was striking. The Jordan Valley, stretching for many miles to the north and to the south, was covered with square patches of various shades of green, yellow ripening wheat and dark brown soil readied for the next crop. Neatly constructed villages with their red roofed houses dotted the landscape. The international borderline could clearly be discerned: the land to its west was green and to the east was yellow.

Further to the north was the blue Sea of Galilee, the white houses of Tiberias on the opposite shore were clearly visible. Mist rising from the lake covered it with a thin white-blue haze, like the veil of a beautiful bride, dimming the reflection of the sun that was already moving to the west.

Directly below us were Sha'ar HaGolan, Masada and Tel Katzir. Their little buildings looked like matchboxes covered with red roofs. I could recognize the dining room, the central lawn, the building where Shaul and Behira's apartment was. I could even see the teenagers' group playing their afternoon soccer game on the lawn. With good binoculars, the Syrian artillery spotters could probably tell what the kibbutzniks were doing in their rooms if they carelessly left their curtains open.

Shaul and Behira stood alone at the far end of Tawfiq hugging each other, looking down at their beautiful home.

We returned in time for the first funeral of the Kibbutz casualties. A new grave was added to the small cemetery. Thirty days later a small, standard, white marble headstone was erected on it. Like all IDF military headstones, it resembled a large pillow with its top engraved with the name of the fallen, his military rank, the site and the Hebrew and Gregorian dates of his death.

The next day I returned home. I felt as if I were the last one to return. Streets were full again with pedestrians, traffic choked major intersections, almost all stores were open, and business at sidewalk cafes was brisk again.

But signs of the recent war still remained; windows of some stores were still crisscrossed with tape, headlights of many cars were still painted dark blue, entrances to buildings were still protected by walls of sandbags, many men and some women were still wearing uniforms probably returning from war, like me, or heading to a new deployment in the new territories.

The most depressing sign of the war were the billboards at central locations. Instead of colorful movie, theatre and event promotions, they were covered with row after row of rectangular white signs, framed in black, announcing the names of the fallen and the location of their death. Names of sons, husbands, parents to young children, executives of prosperous businesses, teachers, doctors, day laborers, and friends were printed in bold black lettering. Locations of great victories like the Old City of Jerusalem, Jenin, Hebron, Tel Fakhr, Umm Qatef, or El Arish took a different meaning. These billboards displayed the price of these victories.

Haifa was a large sprawling city, and yet it was small. People stopped in front of these boards to watch when new posters were pasted up, covering up others that were only days old. An occasional cry or a moan signaled someone who found out that another friend was not coming home.

Laci and Zsuzsi were not expecting me when I rang the doorbell. I was giddy with anticipation to see their reaction and at the same time very emotional. Zsuzsi opened the door. I was standing at the entrance dressed in my uniform, the kitbag at my feet and smiling. She jumped on me hugging and screaming with joy. Noemi ran out of our room and jumped on my neck too. With the two women hanging on me screaming with joy I could see Laci standing quietly in the corridor holding back his emotions and waiting patiently for his turn. There were tears in his eyes. I never saw him cry. I always thought his eyes were incapable of producing tears. Those were his only tears I ever saw. I did not see Laci crying even when Zsuzsi died. When I finally hugged Laci I felt as if he got slightly taller and his shoulders straighter.

Most Israelis, including myself, were busy resuming normal life, trying to comprehend the meaning of the victory and come to terms with the losses. Newspapers recounted stories of great battles and personal heroisms. Friends exchanged memories and occasionally showed each other souvenirs such as an Egyptian flag, a Jordanian military unit tag, or simply a picture from one of the historic sites that were now part of Israel.

Classes at the Technion resumed within days after my return but without three of my classmates, including one of the pilots. His plane was lost on the first day. Four other classmates were still in the hospital. Two of them rejoined us at the start of the second year.

Michael Hadow, the British ambassador to Israel, noted the absence of mass celebrations and the detached manner in which Israelis reacted to their victory, "They went to war, won, and returned home to business as usual." (15 p. 309)

As an outsider, Hadow might have felt Israelis were dispassionate. We were not. We were mostly sad for our immense losses in human life and the realization that the world, once again, had abandoned us. We were certainly joyous for our victory and the realization that even alone we could protect ourselves. But we could not celebrate while our dead were lying at our feet.

Only a few Israelis noticed and even fewer still remember today that on June 19, 1967, days after the war ended, the Israeli cabinet voted unanimously to return all of the Sinai to Egypt in exchange for peace, demilitarization of the territory and special arrangements to guarantee safe Israeli shipping through the Straits of Tiran.

A similar offer was made to Syria; the entire Golan Heights were offered in exchange for demilitarization and peace; and direct discussions were held with King Hussein of Jordan regarding the future of the West Bank. (17)

The Soviets, eager to maintain the Israeli-Arab conflict, convinced the Arab nations to reject these offers and started re-arming Egypt and Syria at a fast rate. On September 1, the Arab League issued in Khartoum, the capital of Sudan, a resolution that was later known as the "Three No's": "…the occupied lands are Arab lands… the burden of regaining these lands falls on all the Arab States." And that "…there would be no peace with Israel, no recognition of Israel, no negotiations with it, and an insistence on the rights of the Palestinian people in their own country." The resolution effectively became the declaration of the wars to come between Israel, the Arab nations and the Palestinians. (18)

Convinced that the overwhelming victory just won would discourage the Arabs from a new war for decades, most of the Israeli public and its politicians dismissed the Khartoum resolution as irrelevant.

Most Israelis are secular. They feel that their religious obligations are met by merely living in Israel. At the same time they see themselves as direct descendants of their ancient ancestors such as King David who beat Goliath the Philistine, the Maccabees who fought the Hellenistic rulers and won, and Bar Kochba who rebelled against the Romans.

Even before the last of the war's explosions faded away, thousands of Israelis flocked to the new territories looking for the historic sites where their biblical ancestors once lived and fought. Even the most atheistic Israelis were driven by curiosity, a desire to reconnect with their ancient past and not the least by the worry that these sites might be returned to the Arab states soon, just like the Sinai desert was returned to Egypt after the 1956 Sinai Campaign.

Sleepy towns and villages across the Jordanian armistice line overnight turned into major tourist attractions. Stores stocked with Jordanian products could not keep up with the sudden demand for "foreign goods" even when some of those "foreign goods" were repackaged Israeli products. For Israelis starved of foreign travel, those territories seemed like a wonderland. The locals did not speak Hebrew, signs in Arabic made the rundown Palestinian towns look exotic, and even hummus and falafel tasted better there than in Haifa or Tel Aviv. Never before was the Israeli territory so vast, not even during King Solomon's kingdom. Territories captured by Joshua from the Amalekites and Canaanites were recaptured by his descendants from the modern-day Amalekites.

My family and I joined the masses headed to the West bank for a day trip. Packed into our small Cortina, Laci, Zsuzsi, Noemi and myself headed to the military crossing-checkpoint near Tel Megiddo southeast of Haifa. A few soldiers manning the crossing waved us through without even stopping us and less than an hour after leaving home we were in the West Bank—the land of Samaria as Menachem Begin[2] started calling it.

The narrow road meandered through rolling hills covered with olive groves. Occasionally, we passed an Arab farmer leading a donkey, two or three Arab women dressed in heavy dark robes carrying gigantic packages, perfectly balanced, on their heads, or a shepherd herding his sheep on a nearby hill. Other than a few cars, all with Israeli license plates, there were no signs of the modern world: no electrical poles, telephone lines or gas stations. Small road signs in Arabic and English showed direction and distance to the nearest town. We could tell that the hills dotted with little villages had barely changed since the time Jews were exiled. The few Arabs we encountered, all dressed in traditional robes and keffiyehs[3], could be mistaken for members of Issachar or Manasseh, two of the twelve Israeli tribes who had lived on that land three thousand years earlier.

---

2 Menachem Begin, the head of the right wing Herut party and later Israel's Prime Minister, saw the Six-Day War victory as divine and insisted on calling the West Bank by the biblical names of its sectors: Judea and Samaria. The modern-day West Bank settlers use these biblical references to justify their link to the land.

3 Keffiyeh—an Arab headdress.

We reached Nablus, the Biblical Shechem, nestled between Mount Gerizim—biblically known as the Mount of Blessing and Mount Ebal—the biblical Mount of Curse. Most of the traffic in this poor town included livestock, carts drawn by animals, and Israeli cars. Only the main square had several local cars with Jordanian license plates. A side street off the main square led to the Casbah, the picturesque market of Nablus.

Several Arab children swarmed us before Laci even parked the car, yelling excitedly in Arabic. Using sign language and a few Hebrew words we understood, they were proposing to "guard" the car. After haggling with a barely ten-year old child who seemed to be their leader, Laci paid a coin and the boy promised to be there when we returned.

Nearly fifty years later I reflect back on that moment and wonder what has become of those children. They must be in their late fifties. They spent most of their lives under Israeli rule. They hardly can remember Jordanian rule. What was their first impression of the Israelis they met? Did they see us as arrogant and stingy or exotic and generous? They must have children and possibly grandchildren who have only known Israeli occupation. Did they or their children become terrorists or did they just settle into a passive contempt? That morning in Nablus they were eager to earn a coin and too young to hate us. We missed a historic opportunity for peace, and they missed it too. But what could we have done differently that day? We made at least one offer to give up the territories we just captured for the promise of peace. How many nations have ever made such an offer?

The Casbah was a wonderful exotic market. The narrow alleys were lined with little stores displaying colorful spices in large burlap bags, mountains of stacked vegetables, barrels of pickles and olives, sweets with nuts and without, variety of baklava, butchered goats hanging by their feet, some already skinned, some not, fishnet checkered keffiyehs and aquals,[4] white cotton Arab robes and purple brocade female robes, Jordanian cigarettes, kitchen utensils, shoes. The smells, colors, and sounds were intoxicating. Not even the sewage running in a narrow ditch along the center of the narrow alleys, donkeys brushing against us, and little children pulling on our sleeves, begging for coins, could diminish our excitement.

Although white flags or white sheets were still hanging from windows and balconies to indicate surrender, the atmosphere was friendly. Merchants welcomed the crowd and happily haggled with the Israelis, knowing full well

---

4 Aqual—the woven black ring that holds the Keffiyeh in place on the wearer's head.

that even after cutting prices in half they still made a healthy profit. The Israeli pound was welcome everywhere, its value well understood, and for us, even after overpaying, we still felt we had a great deal.

After buying Jordanian cigarettes, *rahat lokum* (Turkish Delight), and colorful sugar-coated almonds we settled in a little restaurant in the market. The menu, already translated to Hebrew and priced in Israeli pounds, offered hummus, falafel, lamb-shishlik (grilled chunks on a skewer), and beef kebab (ground meat on a skewer). It never occurred to us that a meal in a restaurant that only weeks earlier was in enemy territory could be unsafe. It was excellent. We capped it with baklava, sahlab (Arab custard seasoned with rose water, pine nuts and cinnamon), and Turkish coffee.

The boy guarding our car greeted us when we returned and stretched out his hand for tip. He got another coin.

Within a few years, the Palestinian resistance to the occupation grew violent and the Nablus Casbah turned into a hotbed of nationalism and one of the most dangerous spots in the West Bank. Israeli civilians stayed out and military patrols ran frequently into ambushes. In April 2002, at the height of the second Palestinian revolt, two IDF brigades had to be ordered in to re-establish control of the market.

Only a few Israelis could see after the Six-Day War the corrupting effect that the occupation would have on Israel and correctly predict the Palestinian resistance and its consequences. Yeshayahu Leibowitz, a Chemistry professor at the Hebrew University who was better known for his philosophical thinking and critical views of Israeli policies, was among the few.

The large Arab population in the West Bank and Gaza Strip would become a demographic time bomb, he argued. For its own security sake, Israel had to withdraw from these lands. His forecast seemed like a Cassandra Prophecy: a perfectly true warning that went unheeded. He wrote: (19)

"Our real problem is not the territory but rather the population of about a million and a half Arabs in it and over whom we must rule. Inclusion of these Arabs (in addition to the half a million who are citizens of the state) in the area under our rule will affect the liquidation of the state of Israel as the state of the Jewish people and bring about a catastrophe for the Jewish people as a whole."

Many called Leibowitz a traitor. Today many call him a prophet. But after Khartoum's "Three No's" most Israelis refused to let go of any territory.

The abbreviated semester ended two weeks past schedule and I was back to reserve duty, ten weeks of squad leader training in Shivta, an infantry training site in the Negev near the old Egyptian border. Before the war, in addition to being an infantry training base, Shivta also served as part of the Negev defense. The training staff and their trainees were counted by the IDF as a full, well-trained, infantry battalion.

In the weeks leading to the war, training of Shivta's companies was accelerated and those who graduated were kept on base, rather than being redistributed back to their original units. Shivta became the home of a highly trained infantry battalion where even the lowest ranking fighter could already serve as a squad leader. Days before the war the battalion was repositioned to the front and on the first night of the war fought in one of the most critical and well-known battles in Israel's history—the battle of Umm Qatef.

Umm Qatef, fifteen miles inside Egyptian territory, was a well-excavated infantry stronghold with line after line of deep trenches blocking the route to central Sinai and to Ismailia. Those who controlled Umm Qatef controlled one of the three eastern gates of Sinai. At the front, facing Israel, Umm Qatef was protected by a wide and densely seeded minefield. To the north and south, the trenches were supported by heavy sand dunes that prevented access by tanks or armored vehicles. The site was well selected and well protected.

On the night of June 5, the Shivta battalion as part of an infantry brigade under the command of General Ariel Sharon was ordered to capture Umm Qatef by attacking it from the dunes to the north. The battle started at 11 pm and by 2:30 am a third of the stronghold was taken. That was a sufficient opening for a tank battalion to come through and open the central route into Sinai.

The battle of Umm Qatef was pivotal to the progress of the fighting along the central section of Sinai and became a legend. Its tactics became an example taught in future military training. The permanent staff at Shivta who trained us led that battle and recounted those lessons to us first-hand.

Following weeks of training and practicing routines that were tested during the battle of Umm Qatef, we were ready to see the stronghold. The bus ride from Shivta was brief. We stopped on a hill just past the old border that still marked the artificial line between two deserts: the Negev and the Sinai. Vast stretches of an arid plain covered with dark granite rocks and pebbles were bounded in the distance by brownish, sharply peaked mountains. The plain was crisscrossed by narrow grey-green strips of hardy desert shrubs that grew along the paths of dry creek beds. On a few rainy winter days, these creeks filled up with water running off the distant mountains. That bit of water, absorbed in the clay-like ground, was sufficient to sustain these plants for the remainder of the year. The plants in turn were the main source of grazing for the occasional

Bedouin nomad, passing through with their sparse herds of thin goats and a few camels.

We lined up facing a low ridge of hills similar to ours, about two miles away. We stood at attention as our battalion commander Lt. Col. Ben-David arrived in his Jeep.

Ben-David, a tall, muscular career officer, was the battalion commander on June 5. He projected authority, but also kindness. Wearing black ankle-high boots and an olive-green beret, he was easily identified as a regular infantryman. We admired him, not the least because we knew he led his battalion to victory at Umm Qatef. The Russian Kalashnikov hanging from his right shoulder ignited my imagination. Did he take it during the battle? How? From whom?

"The ridge facing you is Umm Qatef," Ben David started in his booming voice. "Can anyone say what's unique about this hill? Is there anything that tells us from a distance that it's well-fortified?"

The grey-green strip running in front of the ridge for its entire length was the answer. We inspected it with our binoculars. It was covered with desert shrubs, the same shrubs that line the creeks, but its edges were sharp and straight. It could not be a river-bed. Rivers run off ridges and mountains, not parallel to them, and riverbeds hardly ever run in straight lines. It was a manmade feature, but why would that be a sign of fortification?

"We saw it in aerial photos before the war and wondered what it could be. We didn't figure it out until after the battle started and we regretted it. Let's see if you geniuses can figure it out."

We had a genius among us. "*Is it a minefield?*" he asked.

Indeed it was, half a mile deep at the point facing us, somewhat thinner at the edges, near the dunes. It was marked by a thin wire with little red triangles to warn the shepherds, Ben David told us. Years of bloody experience taught them to respect these signs and keep their herds out. Even wild animals learned to keep out. Years without animals filled that area with dense desert brush.

Seven Israeli tanks were destroyed when they tried to approach Umm Qatef from the front. Shivta would have benefited before the war by having our "genius" among its ranks.

That minefield was one of the reasons why the Shivta battalion was ordered to walk under the cover of darkness to the dunes at the north and attack Umm Qatef from its flanks without tank support. The Egyptians did not expect an attack from the dunes that they considered impassable. They were caught by surprise when after heavily shelling by the Israeli artillery, six thousand shells in less than twenty minutes, (20) three infantry battalions jumped into the ditches from an unexpected direction.

Umm Qatef fell the following morning.

An Egyptian battalion commander, taken prisoner in Umm Qatef, claimed that the battle was "unfair" and "unbalanced" because they were attacked from their flanks rather than the front (20 p. 71) by more numerous fighters than they could offer.

I returned from Shivta just in time for our family's trip to the unified Jerusalem. Visits to Jerusalem, even before the war, were exciting and emotional. Everything in the city speaks of its history and its religious significance; street names, ancient buildings, modern buildings that by code were required to be built with Jerusalem limestones, the roads paved over the same ancient roads traveled by King Solomon, King Herod, and Roman chariots. Even the pure air, scented by the Jerusalem pine trees, was special. Abraham breathed that same air when he tied his son Isaac to the rock on top of Mount Moriah.

We drove up the road to Jerusalem through Sha'ar HaGai, a narrow mountain pass. Only nineteen years earlier, Sha'ar HaGai was blocked by Arab villagers hiding behind boulders on the hills on both sides of the pass and firing at Israeli vehicles. Access to Jerusalem was reduced to convoys of armored vehicles. Skeletons of some of the destroyed vehicles still littered the pass reminding us of a not too distant past and yet so different from the present.

We reached Jaffa Road, Jerusalem's main artery to the Old City. Almost unnoticed, we passed through the remnants of a wall that once blocked that road and separated the new Jewish city from the ancient city. There was no checkpoint; access was free from both sides. The Israeli Knesset declared the city united and extended Israeli law to all its parts and all its citizens.

We parked just outside the old city's walls and joined the river of thousands of Israelis pouring to the Western Wall, now known as HaKotel HaMa'aravi. We walked side by side, two Holocaust survivors and two Israeli Sabras. We were seeing the same sights: festive Israelis enjoying a sunny fall day, ultra-Orthodox Jews dressed in their traditional black coats and fur hats on their way to pray at the Wall, Arab merchants peddling their wares, armed IDF soldiers standing at street corners, Arab children playing hide and seek in inner courts that opened to the alley. But we carried different memories. Our minds wandered to different places.

My mind drifted back to Sha'ar HaGolan; I could hear the radio announcing that the Temple Mount was in our hands. I could see the image of the Army's Chief Rabbi blowing his shofar at the foot of the Wall. Was he trying to summon the Messiah? Cynics quipped that he was attempting to play that role himself. It did not matter that day. To me and to many others who walked with me to the Wall, the Messiah had already arrived.

I think that on that day, Laci also felt that the Messiah had arrived. When we stood at the Wall and recited the customary *Shehecheyanu*, the blessing that thanks God for sustaining us and enabling us to reach that moment, the glow in his eyes betrayed his emotions.

I wish now that I asked him about that. Which of his memories came to life as he recited the blessing? Was it his father Sándor at their Passover table praying to reach the rebuilt Jerusalem by the following year? Did he think of his little Judit whom he hardly ever mentioned but whom he could not possibly forget? Or his first wife Lili? His murdered parents? Or was it the moment in 1949 when he, our mother, and I got off the ship in Haifa?

Thousands stood in the large square in front of the Wall. It had been cleared by Israeli bulldozers within days after liberating it. Someone in the Army understood that the "fog of war" also allows creating facts without too much scrutiny. No one ever asked whose homes were destroyed by those bulldozers. To most, the square seemed as if it was always there. But old pictures show otherwise: praying Jews standing in a narrow alley facing the Wall.

Thousands of Jewish memories stood with us in that large square: memories of pogroms in Russia, the Farhud[5] in Baghdad, Auschwitz, immigration to Israel through the British blockade, arriving from Yemen in the Operation Wings of Eagles,[6] the War of Independence, Sha'ar HaGai, and terrorist raids from Egypt and Syrian shelling the Jordan valley.

I now understand why the alley had to be turned into a square. Even the new square could barely contain all these memories.

---

5   Farhud—a pogrom against Jews in Baghdad on June 1-2, 1941.
6   Forty-seven thousand Yemenite Jews were brought to Israel between 1949-50 in a massive airlift also known as the "Magic Carpet."

January 1943: Near Stalingrad

There was very little to celebrate on New Year's Eve. Laci and the MUSZ barely survived the last four months of 1942 and the future seemed even bleaker. The dim hope that by the middle of the coming year their labor service would be coming to an end was too remote to cheer about. Surviving the next day's long hours in the freezing blizzards and shoveling snow off roads that no one traveled was a far more immediate concern. And even if they were inclined to celebrate, there was hardly anything to celebrate with, maybe an extra potato or a small piece of bacon saved from an earlier dinner.

Laci and the MUSZs could not possibly know it, but there was a reason to cheer. The war reached its turning point. Most of them would not survive to see the end, but the beginning of the end for Nazi Germany and for the madness that engulfed Hungary was days away. Like a heavy ship, the war in Europe was slow to turn. Only years of hindsight would show that on January 1943, near Stalingrad, the balance tilted against Germany and its allies. Gone were the quick and stunning German victories.

The heroic resistance of Stalingrad's Russian defenders is the topic of academic papers, movies, and high school curricula. It is celebrated as the victory of Russian determination over German might. Outside Hungary it is less well-known that the Hungarian Second Army was destroyed in that battle suffering tens of thousands casualties.

The scale of the Stalingrad Battle is mind-boggling. Twelve armies, six on each side, faced off for months. It is hard to imagine the suffering of millions of men living outdoors in trenches or open fields at the height of the Russian winter, hunkering down to survive bombardments, trying to overcome both their enemy and the weather. Even more terrible are the casualties suffered by all sides: more than two million killed, injured or captured.

It is hard to comprehend what caused the Hungarian Army to bring on itself such a disaster. Contrary to any logic, in 1941 it declared war on the Soviet Union and the USA with whom it did not even share a border. It had no territorial or other demands against these nations and did not even have a well-trained and properly equipped army. (8 p. 147) The little military strength it had was necessary to protect its own border with Romania. At the start of the German invasion of the Soviet Union, even Hitler did not think that Hungarian participation would be necessary or even desirable.

It all changed on June 26, 1941, four days after the start of the German operation against the Soviet Union. Three mysterious planes marked with the Soviet Red Star appeared from the direction of Slovakia and attacked the Hungarian border town Kassa, causing some damage and leaving several people dead and others wounded. One unexploded bomb was confirmed as being Soviet-made. (8 p. 149) The Russians denied any responsibility. Speculations that the bombing was in fact by German planes flying under a false flag to provoke Hungary into joining the war were never confirmed.

Normally, such an unprovoked minor attack would have triggered a comparable retaliation. Instead, through a series of miscommunications between the Hungarian Regent Horthy and his newly appointed Prime Minister Bárdossy, before the day was out, Hungary declared war on the Soviet Union. Four ministers in the Council of Ministers' meeting that was convened that afternoon to approve the declaration of war demanded less drastic measures but Bárdossy ignored them and drafted a resolution that he described as unanimous. In 1945 Bárdossy stood trial for war crimes. One of the charges was this omission.

Despite the wartime prosperity and peace that Hungary enjoyed, the first such period since the end of World War I, its leaders, generals and much of the public were eager to join the war. Some were drawn by the excitement of quick and seemingly easy German victories in Western Europe. Others believed Hitler's promise that the Soviets would collapse within six weeks. Only a few recognized the futility and danger of Bárdossy's decision, not the least of which was Szombathelyi, Ferenc who in two months became the Chief of General Staff: "What will come of this, good Lord!" he wrote "What will come of this? Did we really need this; to jump into this stupidity?" (8 p. 172)

The first unit to be committed to the Russian front was the Carpathian Group that consisted of ninety thousand troops and included some of the elite, most modern and best equipped Hungarian units. But even the best of Hungary's military were inferior to ordinary German or Soviet units. Some of the Carpathian Group's units did not even have their own military vehicles and had to requisition horses and civilian vehicles that were ill-suited for the task and ended up breaking down on their way to the front, littering the roadside and arousing ridicule among the locals.

The first troops left base less than a week after the declaration of war. One week later, enjoying the vacuum left by the advancing Germans, the first Hungarian soldiers reached the banks of the Dniester nearly three hundred miles from their eastern border.

Hitler's promises of quick victory must have felt believable in those days. It is not difficult to imagine the Hungarian press reporting stellar victories or the proud pronouncements by Horthy and Bárdossy trumpeting their own wisdom and good sense. Of course, most of the Hungarian public was blind to the army's shortcomings and could not see the troubles ahead.

By early August, the advance units were showing troubling signs of exhaustion. There are numerous accounts of the deteriorating conditions of the Carpathian Group. One of the most astonishing tales was that of the Bicycle Brigade, a cross between the cavalry and the mechanized infantry. (8 p. 173) The Brigade was assigned to ride their bicycles along with the German infantry. But the Germans were transported in motorized vehicles. After thirty-two days of chasing the motorized convoy without rest, the bicyclists were exhausted. A medical commission sent to examine their condition reported that many suffered from enlarged hearts and ruined lungs. Despite their poor condition and pleadings by their commanders, the German command did not authorize any break for the bicyclists, and as the German losses mounted, they forced them into difficult battles.

At the end of August, two months into Hungary's foray into war, Hitler's promise of quick victory faded away. Some in the Hungarian leadership began wondering if the war they joined so willingly was not a bad bargain after all. Although the public was kept in the dark by the censored press, military commanders and some ministers noticed that the Russian soldiers were resisting harder than Hitler or Bárdossy predicted and their equipment, particularly their artillery, was far better than projected. It certainly was far superior to anything Hungary had.

In late August Horthy dismissed the Chief of General Staff Werth Henrik and replaced him with Szombathelyi who immediately requested that the Hungarian troops be withdrawn "before we plunge further into war."

Extricating the Carpathian Group from the war proved much harder than getting them into it. In September, Horthy took his new Chief of Staff to meet Hitler where he succeeded convincing him that the Carpathian Group had suffered too many losses and too much of its equipment was destroyed making it largely useless. Hitler agreed to a withdrawal in stages, and by Christmas of 1941, nearly all the Hungarian soldiers returned home.

In addition to their physical losses, many of the troops were emotionally scarred with what today would be labeled as Post Traumatic Stress Disorder (PTSD). But hardly anyone in Hungary heard about these casualties or the emotional and personal tragedies. The press only covered the stunning German victories. Losses and defeats, other than the enemy's, were excluded from reporting. (8 p. 178)

No sooner had the Carpathian Group returned than a letter from Hitler arrived demanding the reengagement of the Hungarian Army. What was earlier believed to be a voluntary participation was redefined as mandatory, driven by temporary weather related setbacks. (8 p. 184) The letter was followed by a visit by Field Marshal Wilhelm Keitel in January 1942, to demand Hungarian participation and threatening "severe consequences" if Hungary declined. It was understood by most Hungarian negotiators that the "consequences" could be the loss of territories that Germany helped Hungary gain, or even worse, a German invasion.

During a late January dinner in the upscale Gellért Hotel, Szombathelyi agreed reluctantly to deliver a force consisting of 207,000 troops that would be placed under direct German command. This mostly nonexistent force was to be incorporated into the Second Army. In return, Keitel promised to outfit it at the front with anti-tank weapons and other equipment. Thus began one the biggest tragedies and worst military disasters in Hungarian history.

In less than four months more than 200,000 troops were recruited, trained and equipped for a war against a far superior, stronger modern army. Unlike the great excitement that accompanied the mobilization a year earlier, there were no longer illusions of quick victories or territorial gains.

The first hastily assembled units of the Second Army left on April 1942. Nearly all were shipped by July 1942. They were heading east to Ukraine, a distant and hostile land. Much of their training was completed for service as the backup to the attacking German armies, including mostly maintenance, security and administrative tasks.

That was not how the German command saw their role. During the coming winter they would become an integral part of the fighting forces in the Stalingrad front.

To balance out the demographic burden of this massive call-up, recruitment was spread across the entire country rather than concentrating on selected regions or demographic groups that would have provided a more homogeneous and skillful force. Consequently, most of the recruits came from rural areas. They were largely uneducated, some with no more than six years of schooling, many even without the training to operate a motorized vehicle.

The equipment of the Second Army was outdated and in poor condition. They relied on horses to draw cannons into the battlefield where they promptly became immobile. The Germans did not keep their promise to equip and supply these units, and the little they did deliver was used, old and often defective.

Training of the forces was pitiful. Exercises with live ammunition were mostly limited to firing ranges. Without large empty territories within Hungary, they were unable to practice large maneuvers. Most of the tactics and fighting skills were practiced only theoretically. Because of the short time that was allowed to build and train the units, the soldiers who were pulled together from different cultural and geographic backgrounds were unable to develop the cohesion and strong bonding between soldiers that is critical for successful operation in battle or under tough conditions. (8 p. 193)[1]

How could an entire army be sent to war without practicing maneuvers with live ammunition? It was the worst sort of negligence. Two hundred thousand young Hungarian men were sent to be butchered. The responsibility must lie in the chain of command.[2]

Not surprisingly, the command assigned to the Second Army was not much better than its men. Most high-ranking officers were aging. They drew their war experience from the Great War. They knew little about modern and mobile warfare.

The Second Army was doomed from the start. Even the ride to the front proved to be an ordeal that sapped the energy and morale of the troops. Trains were slowed by partisans who sabotaged the rails, by the fear of landmines, and sometimes by lack of fuel. Rides often lasted eight to ten days or ended far from their final destination in Voronezh. Many units completed the last seven hundred miles of their trip on foot, reaching the front exhausted. (8 p. 205)

These hardships might look similar to those suffered by the MUSZs. Without a doubt, the condition of the average soldier of the Second Army was not enviable. But at least they were given uniforms and weapons and were taught how to use them. They were fed and sheltered, even if in rudimentary

---

1 A significant effort in my military service was devoted by my commanders and later by me to the development of the unit's spirit. Collective punishments and rewards as well as competitions among units were often used to solidify these feelings. It is hard to comprehend how an entire army was sent to war without individual troops trusting their comrades that they will sacrifice their own lives to save their friend's.

2 Practicing military maneuvers with live ammunition at all levels was common in Israel. Despite its small size, Israel made training a priority at all levels and found the space necessary even for training at the brigade level with close aerial and artillery support.

conditions. They were not forced to perform useless and demeaning tasks that would lead to their death and above all, they were not considered and treated as disposable, even though their lives were cheap too.

The Second Army, as part of the massive front facing Stalingrad, was assigned to hold a line along the Don River, from Voronezh in the north to Pavlovsk in the south, hundred and forty miles in total. The Don River, which in antiquity was considered the border between Europe and Asia, became a strategic line that the Soviet army was prepared to hold at all costs to protect the road to Moscow. In the section facing the Second Army the Soviets still retained three bridgeheads on the western banks of the Don, in Uryv, Korotoyak, and Storozevoje that had to be destroyed before the line could be consolidated (8 p. 208). Throughout the summer the Second Army made several failed attempts on these bridgeheads while suffering heavy losses. More than thirty thousand officers and soldiers were killed. (8 p. 209)

The arrival of fall and with it the *rasputitsa*—the seasonal ceaseless rain that turns the landscape into a muddy quagmire—found the Second Army exhausted, demoralized, and unprepared for the heavy battles and the winter that lay ahead.

Remote, desolate places often achieve fame or notoriety when an army commander chooses them as a site for an attack or fortification. Uryv is one such place. Even today, with a population of five thousand, it should barely make mention on most maps of Russia. But Uryv, one of the bridgeheads along the Don *kanyar*,[3] was etched into the Hungarian national memory on January 12, 1943 when the Red Army opened its offensive there by launching a massive attack on the Second Army. (8 p. 221) Thousands on both side found their deaths that day on or near the frozen river.

Uryv, like the other two bridgeheads, was located on a finger of land pointing eastwards. On the map it appears as if an imaginary finger pushed on the Don River eastward, forcing it to bend and flow around the fingertip. A bridgehead on that fingertip enjoyed the protection of a natural moat from three sides. Only the side facing westwards needed protection by firepower.

Choosing Uryv as the site of their first offensive, the Soviets threw three times as many soldiers into the battle as the Hungarian defenders had, and ten times the number of artillery pieces. (8 p. 225) They easily broke that line.

Even the river crossing was not an obstacle, as the Don was frozen solid. The surprised Second Army offered hardly any resistance. Their cannons and

---

3   Don *kanyar*—"The Don Bend" in Hungarian.

rifles jammed up in the cold air after firing only once. By contrast, the Russian firearms were treated with oil diluted with gasoline, and they fired well. Diluting the gun oil delayed its freezing and jamming.

Two days later a second attack near Schucsje sealed the fate of the Hungarian Army. (8 p. 221) On January 17, General Jány the Second Army commander gave an order to retreat. The retreat was largely disorganized. On at least one occasion, soldiers were specifically ordered to break into small units and independently attempt to cross through the Russian lines. (8 p. 223) Thousands died from exposure and hunger as they moved through the hostile winter landscape without any support, resources or training.

Of the 207,000 Second Army soldiers sent to war, nearly 148,000 were killed, injured, or taken prisoners during their twelve months engagement in the Russian front. Of the fifty thousand forced laborers in the MUSZ force, only six or seven thousand returned home. (8 p. 225)

Ironically for Laci, when the Hungarian line collapsed, he was less than eighty miles from Red Army units that two years later, when they captured Budapest, were viewed as liberators. But in January 1943, falling in the hands of the Red Army was far from liberation. It often resulted in an immediate execution or a long imprisonment in a Siberian Gulag.

Rumors about earlier defeat of the Italian and Romanian armies and the collapse of the Hungarian army at the front must have reached the MUSZs. After suffering bitterly at the hands of Hungarian soldiers they must have felt some satisfaction. But surprisingly, many were true patriots and remained loyal to Hungary and its army.

On January 15, while clearing the road from Alexeyevka, Laci and Endre saw the first fleeing Hungarians. Five soldiers appeared from behind a bend on the road, two of them supporting an injured soldier. They were wearing the typical German helmets that covered much of their ears[4] and olive-green uniforms. From the distance Laci and Endre could not tell if they were Hungarian or German.

The previous night, the MUSZs noticed that Horváth and his deputies huddled near the company's wagon whispering to each other. In the morning, when Laci got out of the barn, he saw the deputies loading their personal gear on the wagon along with most of the company's food, and then leading the horses out of the barn and putting on their harnesses. When they noticed that Laci was watching, they yelled at him to return to the barn. It was unusual for

---

4 M 1935 helmets.

the deputies to do a MUSZ's job. But whatever they were planning, the MUSZ were not part of it. When they were done, they ordered the MUSZs to line up for the regular morning muster and sent them out to their usual road work. While on the road, the MUSZ could see the wagon leave, heading away from the front.

When the five stray soldiers reached them, Laci and Endre could identify them as unarmed Hungarians. Their overcoats were dirty and torn. They looked tired, worn down and desperate. They did not project the self-confidence and cockiness that Horváth and his deputies did or any of the Hungarian soldier that Laci and Endre encountered so far. These were beaten and hungry soldiers looking for help.

"Are you coming from the headquarters in Alexeyevka?" Laci asked.

"No, we walked around the city," replied one soldier. "We didn't want anybody to see us. Someone could stop us as deserters and shoot us. There are many more behind us, if they didn't freeze the last couple of nights. Our whole battalion is on the run. Please help us. We must rest. We've walked a hundred miles, slept only one night and haven't eaten in three days. Please."

Laci and Endre decided to shelter them. There was little food in the barn and barely any room to accommodate another five men. But at least it was warm. With temperatures at night reaching -30°F or -40°F, the poor soldiers would certainly die if they were not taken in.

Three days earlier, just before dawn, an artillery barrage woke up the infantry battalion of these soldiers. As usual, they hunkered down in their trenches near the Don waiting for it to end. But this one did not end. Just past sunrise, machine gunfire joined the explosions of shells. Russian airplanes arrived with the sunrise, strafing them with their machine guns. When the planes disappeared, they finally dared sticking their heads out of the trenches only to see thousands of enemy soldiers running towards them firing their rifles and machine guns. The artillery continued bombing until the first enemy soldiers reached the barbed wire fences just yards away, blew holes through them and started running through the narrow mine fields and climbing into their trenches.

"Did you shoot at them?" Endre asked.

"We tried," answered their leader who introduced himself as János, "but after one round our rifles jammed up. They didn't work in this terrible cold. We didn't have artillery either. Even the mines didn't explode. The cold air must've frozen everything solid. But somehow the Russian guns and cannons fired just fine."

With hardly any resistance, the Soviets crossed the river, climbed on the ramps and slaughtered the Hungarians. Hiding in a nook in their trench, the five managed to survive and in the commotion surrounding them they jumped out of their trenches and ran. They heard several shots fired at them and one of them was hit in the leg.

"Didn't you take anything with you?" Endre asked.

"How could we? We weren't prepared for this attack. We thought the shelling was just another one of those. Within half an hour we were overcome by Russians. We thought that if we dropped our rifles they wouldn't kill us."[5] (8 p. 221)

Surviving difficult and unknown conditions requires not only luck but also quick decisions under uncertain and rapidly changing circumstances, essentially a bet. A correct bet could mean another day and another chance to bet. A wrong bet could mean death.

That night in the barn, Laci, Endre, the MUSZs, and their five guest soldiers had to place such a bet. With no commanders to give orders, they could have thought they were free. But they were only as free as a little child lost in a forest in the middle of the night. They were abandoned, facing multiple enemies and threats, without maps, updated information, supply, arms, and proper clothing. All they had in abundance were questions:

What should they do after the collapse of their own army? Even trained soldiers were fleeing the frontline in panic.[6] (3 p. 76) Should they stay put and wait for the frontline to pass them, or walk west toward Hungary?

If they go, how should they proceed without provisions, arms, and ammunition?

If they were caught on the road without uniforms to identify themselves as soldiers, they could be considered spies and executed.

How would they protect themselves from the cold? Even one night outdoors could be deadly. What about wild animals? Wolves?

If they stayed in the barn and waited for the Red Army, at least they had shelter. But would the enemy be more benevolent than their own commanders? They might risk spending years in prisoner camps.

Whether they stay or leave, armed fleeing Hungarian soldiers could be dangerous. They might not hesitate to kill them just to get their clothing, shoes, or food. How should they defend themselves without weapons?

And no matter what they decided, they were Jews! No matter whom they met: Russians, Ukrainians, Germans, Hungarians or Italians would all consider them traitors, deserters, filthy Jews, or simply persons outside the law.

---

5 As much as a Soviet attack was anticipated, when it finally came, it took the Hungarian army by surprise.

6 Similar dilemmae were raised by Dantsig.

The MUSZs were gathered in the barn. János and his friends were sleeping on straw piles that Laci and Endre gathered near the burning mud stove. With Horváth and his deputies gone, the MUSZs could finally rest too. But they had homework to do. Should they leave the barn in the morning and move away from the advancing Soviets? If they chose to stay, how would they protect it and provide for themselves?

There was more wisdom accumulated in the barn than in an average university department but hardly any relevant experience, other than the little that János and his four comrades learned in the last three days.

With no good choices available, the men went to sleep leaving a guard at the door. Without a weapon in hand he was no more useful than a scarecrow.

They woke up at dawn to the sound of low flying airplanes. Peeking through cracks in the walls they saw a long convoy of Hungarian army trucks heading slowly west on the snow-covered road. Three low flying planes, their tails decorated with Red Stars, were diving one after the other towards the convoy, firing their machine-guns. The lead truck caught fire first and stopped as if it hit a brick wall. Two trucks at the back were hit too. The remaining trucks were trapped, unable to turn around in the deep snow or pass the burning trucks. The drivers and the soldiers in the convoy jumped out of their cabins and scattered into the fields away from the barn. The three planes turned and one by one shot the fleeing soldiers too, leaving no survivors. The remaining trucks were left intact, waiting for the arrival of the advancing Red Army.

But the MUSZs hiding in the barn had other thoughts. As soon as the sound of the last plane faded away, Csengeri and Endre went out to search for survivors. With the exception of an occasional explosion of burning ammunition, there was no sound. Nature was still asleep, the few human witnesses too scared to make a sound, and the riders of the doomed convoy were all dead. Within a day drifting snow would cover them until spring when farmers would find their frozen bodies and bury them in an unmarked mass grave.

Other than three burning trucks, the convoy remained undamaged. Several engines were still running and their driver's cabins pleasantly warm. It was a Hungarian supply convoy fleeing the crumbling front.

After nearly reaching the frontline, food, ammunition, coats, shoes, even blankets that could have saved hundreds or thousands of lives were hauled away. In their hurry to flee, the few dead men scattered near the convoy did not even stop to unload their cargo or consider their trucks could become their own death traps. However, with their deaths, they saved the lives of the MUSZs in the barn.

The MUSZs raided the trucks, replacing their worn civilian coats with new military coats, fur hats, and boots. For the first time since their call up, they were well outfitted for the climate and the long road ahead.

"*As usual, these supply guys are the last to arrive and first to run when trouble hits,*" János blurted as he and the other four soldiers collected rifles and ammunition from the dead.

Still unsure how to begin their own retreat, Endre suggested that the MUSZ line up as an organized company, three rows of marching soldiers with János and his group leading them as their commanders.

"*We'll look like an organized military company moving from one assignment to another,*" he explained. "*If we walk individually, the Russians will think we are spies and the Hungarians will think we are deserters. Either way we get shot. As a group, and with five armed soldiers, who look like our commanders, bandits or desperate runaway soldiers will not dare attack us.*"[7] (3 p. 75)

After collecting all they could carry from the abandoned trucks, they lined up in formation, János at the lead, and started on the road to Volokonovka. This was the road they had plowed and repaired for the last few months. They were a thousand miles from the nearest Hungarian border. They only had a vague idea where Hungary was and how to reach it, but at least they had supplies for a few days, they were well-dressed and organized. At that moment they were more fortunate than most of the troops of the Second Army.

Just before nightfall they reached the barn at the edge of Volokonovka that was their home more than a month earlier. The abandoned barn had since lost its door but was still protected against the heavy snowfall that came that night.

Having rifles and ammunition and with heavy snow to prevent anyone from traveling on the road, the new residents of the barn felt sufficiently secure to light a fire using wood they found there. They were cheered by the progress they made that day, nearly twenty miles, by the warm meal they cooked with their rations, the safe and warm place they had, and by the two bottles of vodka they found under a trucks' driver seat.

Heavy snow continued for two days and with no MUSZs to clear it, the road blended with the vast plains. Only two parallel rows of tall sticks and long levees of snow piles marked the location of its shoulders.

With no motorized traffic on the roads, Soviet planes stayed away and only a faint rumble of distant cannons from the east disturbed the magical quiet.

---

7   Several MUSZ units protected themselves from dangers faced by individuals during the retreat by marching in formation, demonstrating that they were an organized military unit even if they did not wear uniforms.

They remained in the barn for three days, content with the food and the pleasant heat of burning wood. They needed rest, but the Red Army was approaching. The roar of the cannons during the day, accompanied by red flashes at night, was getting closer.

On the fourth day they saw on the road three civilians wearing Hungarian Army caps. They were MUSZs from Kolozsvár in Transylvania, drafted in June, the only survivors from a one hundred strong MUSZ company. The rest died of hunger, cold, beatings, and landmines.

"*Landmines?*" Csengeri asked incredulous.

"*Yes,*" answered one of the three who introduced himself as Tibi. Their company was located just behind one of the infantry brigades facing the Uryv bridgehead. During the summer the brigade attacked the bridgehead several times. They started early in the morning with artillery fire. After half an hour of heavy shelling the Russians answered, they could see hundreds of Hungarian soldiers getting out of their trenches, lining up in formation behind tanks and then moving out towards the bridgehead. The Hungarian artillery stopped, but the Russian artillery continued, and then sounds of machine gun and rifle fire joined in. About an hour later, sometimes longer, the line turned quiet and the soldiers returned carrying the wounded. Many of the dead were left behind.

"*It was an ugly sight. So many men who were perfectly fine in the morning came back all broken up, or not at all,*" Tibi said and then turned quiet.

After a few moments he continued. One night, their sergeant woke them up. They lined up in the regular formation thinking that he would take them out for one of his "late night gymnastics," running and crawling in the mud. But this time it was different. One by one he picked twenty MUSZs, lined them up in a separate formation and marched them off towards the infantry brigade. The rest were allowed to return to sleep. Barely an hour later, explosions from the direction of the bridgehead woke them up.

Just after dawn another attack started on the Uryv bridgehead accompanied as usual by artillery and then machine-gun fire. That attack, just like those before, broke up quickly.

But when they lined up later for their morning muster, twenty were missing. They died doing what Jews do best, their sergeant explained smugly, walking through minefields to clear a path.[8] (21)

After a few minutes of silence, János asked Tibi how they got there from Uryv.

---

8   There are multiple accounts of MUSZ forced to clear minefields by simply walking across them.

They were attacked on January 12, Tibi said. The attack started with heavy artillery fire that hit mostly the infantry brigade locations. They were surprised that there was no response from their own artillery units just behind them.

"*We figured their firing mechanisms must have jammed up in the cold,*" Tibi explained.

János nodded.

But then they saw one of the infantry officers on a horse riding away from the front line, screaming "*Run, run, the Reds are coming.*" At first they did not know what to do but then they saw two other soldiers on horses fleeing the area. So Tibi and his two friends figured that they too should take what they could and start moving west.

They had been on the road ever since, not sure how many days; they had lost count.

"*It's been a week,*" János said.

They found some food on some German trucks destroyed by a Russian air raid.

"*That must have been the convoy near our old barn,*" Endre said.

"*Could be, but we saw three other convoys, two of them were Hungarian,*" Tibi answered.

They were ahead of most of the retreating soldiers and, just like Laci's company, they hardly saw anyone. When they reached the first kolkhoz they discovered that houses near the road were already taken by other soldiers who would not let them in. To avoid being buried under the falling snow, they kept walking through the night. The following morning, they found a barn where they stayed through the night. But then they were forced to sleep outdoors the following two nights.

"*I think that there are many refugees behind us and as we continue walking, we will find it more difficult to find shelter and food. I'm not sure how we should go from here,*" Tibi said.

Once again, the slowly growing group of MUSZs and soldiers had to make a decision: stay or keep going? The three new MUSZs added little new information.

The following morning, the sky cleared and the MUSZs lined up on the road ready to march.

When János, who never dreamed he would command a company, ordered "*Forward March,*" their MUSZ company was the best organized Hungarian unit within miles around. They were rested, well-dressed, well-supplied, their wool blankets, rolled into long sausages, were strapped to their backpacks in proper military style, and they were marching as a coherent unit with a united purpose.

Even so, marching was difficult. With each step their feet sunk in the deep, fluffy snow. The bright sun and its reflection from the vast white prairie were blinding and the cold wind raised dust-like snow particles that chafed any exposed skin. They passed through Volokonovka, marching along mostly deserted streets, past destroyed buildings and looted stores. A few people warmed themselves near bonfires that were burning inside some vacant stores. At the other end of the town they met the road to Shebekino. Even on a nice spring day, on a clear road and with nature cooperating, Shebekino was at least three days away on foot. With Tibi's pleading, they decided to take that road.

It was busier and more traveled than the road they just left and showed new signs of the destruction and misery that were awaiting them. Many retreating Hungarian and German soldiers used vehicles and wagons for their escape and were already ahead of the marching MUSZs. Vehicles that broke down or burned by enemy planes littered the roads.

But most disquieting were the signs of a silent but relentless killer, the frost. It was a swift yet merciful killer. An exhausted soldier lay down for a moment, just to catch his breath. It did not take long. His eyes closed briefly and a pleasant sleep took over. Overcome by exhaustion, his sleep turned deep. In his sleep he might dream of home, his wife, his children, or a fire in the hearth. He would not feel how the harsh cold sapped the warmth out of his body faster than the fire in the fireplace would burn a twig. Death snuck on him without any pain or agony.

Corpses of frozen fleeing soldiers dotted the road. Many of the dead appeared as if they were taking a nap. Some lay on their sides in a fetal position with their backpack under their head as a pillow, their faces relaxed and well preserved by the cold air and their eyes closed. They seemed as if any moment they would wake up and continue walking. Only the thin layer of ice covering their faces betrayed the truth: these men would never walk again.

Marching in an organized fashion protected them from that insidious killer. The group would not allow an individual to succumb to a moment of weakness. The frozen corpses belonged to lone individuals. They had no one to urge them forward or drag them out of their sleep if they did lie down.

That day they walked ten miles. Only a few horse wagons passed them along the way, their drivers and passengers too busy in the urgent task of escaping to intimidate a MUSZ company. The occasional pedestrians on the road were too weak to bother them. The big flood of retreating soldiers and vehicles streamed along the main roads leading from Voronezh to Stary Oskol and from Alexeyevka to Belgorod. Mercifully, Russian planes, if they still had any interest attacking the chaotically retreating army, must have done so along the main roads.

Their march was uneventful for the next few days. Every night they found shelter in an abandoned barn. Farmers in the kolkhozes fed them, glad to see them fleeing. To those farmers, the war was coming to an end, feeding the beaten soldiers was a small price to pay to see them gone quickly.

At the outskirts of Shebekino, they met two MUSZs who were heading to Belgorod, forty kilometers away. Belgorod was the largest regional town and the two MUSZs heard that it served as the army's rearward assembly center and that anyone found outside Belgorod would be executed. (11 p. 36)

"*This could be a trap*," said Csengeri. "*We get there; they will take us and make us slaves again.*"

"*True,*" agreed Laci. "*But Budapest must be at least a thousand miles away. It took us ten days to walk fifty miles. At this rate it will take us six months to reach Budapest. We need to find supplies and shelters along the way and pray that no one attacks us for being Hungarians, or deserters, or Jews, or simply tasty meat. Walking home isn't a good plan.*"

"*But right now we're free; at least we have some choices.*"

"*Not really. No one with any common sense is walking across these snow-covered plains. We were lucky to get this far. Here are our only choices: we either let the Russians take us, or the Hungarians. Otherwise, the snow, frost, or wolves will kill us.*"

It was the grim truth, though not everyone agreed.

They reached Belgorod in three days. From a distance, the snow-covered Belgorod looked just like what its Russian name meant: the "White City." But inside, the large crowds of retreating Hungarian, Italian and German soldiers trampled the white snow in the streets and turned it into a depressing dark grey slush.

The large railroad station near the Severny Donets River attracted thousands of soldiers looking for a ride westward, away from the approaching Red Army. Military police officers worked frantically to gather these soldiers and reorganize them into new units that could be thrown back into combat should the high command choose to do so. Officers of military engineering units searched frantically for manpower to load equipment on departing trains. Medics tried to establish field hospitals to accommodate the wounded soldiers that were arriving by the thousands on cargo trains from the front. Shouting, panic, and disorder dominated the area. The few buildings still standing near the station were commandeered for officer housing, command centers, and storage.

At the terminal, the MUSZs met hundreds of soldiers sitting on the icy sidewalks with their few possessions at their feet. Others stood in small groups arguing loudly, trading food for cigarettes, cigarettes for fur hats, and fur hats for shoes. Everything was for sale, including malnourished women.

Military Police officers armed with handguns and truncheons were wading through the crowd plucking one soldier or another and dragging him to an assembly point where new companies were forming. However, some of the most resourceful still found a way to disappear into the masses or to hop on a departing train, even without confirming its destination.

The marching MUSZs entered the chaotic terminal and the trap that Tibi so feared. A military engineering captain standing at the door stopped them and asked János for their assignment papers. János, repeating an answer he rehearsed with Tibi, explained that they were heading to Kharkov on a new assignment. But without official papers the captain was not convinced and assigned them to one of his sergeants who led them to the train-loading unit.

The main hall of the terminal was in surprisingly good shape. With the exception of broken windows it showed no war damage. It was filled with soldiers, some like the MUSZs, assembled in units, which were led by a commander to an assignment. But most soldiers, Hungarians, Germans, Italian, and even a few Romanians, were running around in a loud commotion. At least half seemed to bark orders and the other half tried to avoid them. But all were intent in finding a way to board a train heading west.[9]

In the terminal the MUSZs were assigned to their new commander: Sergeant Pécsi István. Pécsi wasted no time announcing that no one had survived from his previous MUSZ company and that he was looking for the same success with his charges. He ordered them to leave their belongings in

---

9 In a different place, different time, and different circumstances I witnessed a similar chaotic scene of soldiers trying to find a ride home. The IDF offered two modes of transportation for troops returning from Sinai on leave: by air or by bus.

Boarding a Tel Aviv bound plane at Rephidim Military Airport in central Sinai required a boarding pass. But only those who served at the various headquarters got the limited number of pre-assigned passes. The rest, the field soldiers, had to fight in the terminal for the remaining standby passes that were issued only moments before the flight. If they missed that flight, they could wait for the next one or board a bus that left every fifteen minutes for a six to eight hours' ride. Though missing a flight to Tel Aviv was not nearly as traumatic as missing a train from Belgorod to Budapest, to those fighting for the few standby tickets in Rephidim, the anxiety felt similar. Home was beckoning.

a large pile, leave one MUSZ to guard it and then move to ramp three to start loading equipment on the train. *"Be sure you do not lose any member of your company,"* Pécsi warned. *"Someone will be hung for anyone who defects."*

The platforms in the station were filled with logs, bridge components and flotation devices probably intended for crossing the Don, ammunition crates, folded tents, and truck engines. On one platform, they saw hundreds of wounded soldiers on stretchers or sitting while leaning on columns. Many groaned in pain, crying out for help, food, water, or a blanket. Despite their suffering, they were the lucky ones, Tibi commented. *"In a few hours, a day or two at most, they will be out of this hell."*

Loading the trains was extremely hard. Without any hoists, everything had to be lifted into the train manually. The cold air blowing through the mostly open station turned metal parts into frozen blocks that stuck to the ground by the glue-like frozen moisture. Heavy pieces became even heavier with the added coating of ice that accumulated on top. The only relief from this new hardship was the short day; with no electricity the terminal turned dark early and work had to be stopped.

János and his four soldier friends disappeared soon after entering the station. Later that day Endre saw János climb onto a train parked at the adjacent platform and waiving the working MUSZs good-bye. They never found out if the train headed west or returned to the front.

They set up camp at a remote corner inside the main terminal. Although unheated, it still provided protection from strong winds, snow, wild animals, and random looting and intimidation by fleeing soldiers. Neither Pécsi, nor the lieutenant who commandeered their services offered any food or drink. But broken crates scattered in the station provided food, clothing, even alcohol, well beyond their needs.

Late at night, when most of the noise in the terminal subsided, they could hear the faint sounds of cannon fire coming from the east. The front was approaching fast. It was a matter of weeks, maybe days, before Belgorod returned to the Soviet Union.

Day by day, cannon fire became louder. Soon they could hear the explosions even during the day. Despite the hard winter, the Red Army was gaining fast over the crumbling armies facing it. Evacuation of the remaining Hungarian presence in Belgorod, including equipment and other goods, was a priority, and the MUSZs were a critical part of that effort. They were still forced to do hard work but they were no longer tortured: the beating, the imposition of "night gymnastics" and of course Pécsi's threat of hanging MUSZs were strictly forbidden and enforced by his upper command.

Red Army artillery explosions drew near and the terminal emptied considerably. The front had reached them. Departures were reduced to trains heading west, carrying the little equipment still needing evacuation and the dishearteningly large number of injured soldiers that were carried into the station by trucks, horse wagons, or on stretchers by foot.

One night, shells began exploding near the station. Panicked soldiers and civilians rushed into the terminal in search of shelter and first aid. After midnight, Pécsi woke the sleeping MUSZ up and ordered them into a cattle train car at a nearby platform. Two other trains were already leaving the station. They boarded a cattle car on what might have been the last train to leave Belgorod.

Steady snow slowed the train as it had to plow the accumulation off the tracks. But however slow, it still moved faster than the approaching frontline. The harsh weather also prevented Soviet planes from taking off to attack moving trains.

Despite the brutal cold, the temperature inside their car was comfortable, thanks to the body heat of its thirty passengers. With plenty of food and even some room to stretch their legs their ride was almost pleasant.

A motto of experienced soldiers is: "Never run if you can walk. Never walk if you can stand. Never stand if you can sit," and ultimately, "don't be awake if you can sleep." The MUSZs were asleep in the late afternoon when the train blew its horns and slowed down. A sign in Russian announced "Харьков," they were entering the Kharkov station. An hour later, the door of their car slid open.

Kharkov was founded by Cossacks barely three hundred years earlier to defend the Sloboda region from the Tatars and the Russian army. It was a large industrial city, but its name was often associated with the *Holodomor*, the "Great Extinction by Famine." In 1932-33, following Stalin's plans to collectivize the large swaths of land in the Ukrainian plains, grain production dropped dramatically and the little that was produced was taken by Russia. The great food shortage reached catastrophic levels by 1932, causing millions of deaths. Kharkov was hit the hardest with thousands dying in the streets. When the MUSZ train rolled into the station, Kharkov had already changed hands once from Soviet to German control. With the front nearing, it was about to change hands once again. Hardship would not let up.

As in Belgorod, the Kharkov station became a staging place of retreating armies. Remnants of the Italian and Hungarian armies were mingled with each other, and officers were trying desperately to reorganize units either for fighting or for organized retreat, no one knew which for sure.

Long platforms were filled by rows of wounded or dying soldiers lying on stretchers or on the cold pavement under thin blankets. Mixed among them were small groups of healthy looking soldiers sitting on their bags. They showed no visible wounds, they did not speak or move, their faces were expressionless and their blank eyes gazed into a fixed spot in space.

Equipment, hardware, and crates of loot that were most likely loaded by the MUSZ in Belgorod were now lying on other ramps, probably waiting to be loaded again onto other trains that would carry them to the next station that soon would become the new front. Soldiers on foot who escaped the advancing Red Army were arriving in large numbers adding to the chaos and desperation in the station. Like a snow avalanche, the shape of the disaster seemed to grow from one station to the other, the wounded victims, salvaged equipment, loot, or escaping soldiers from Belgorod were joined by new victims, equipment, loot, and refugees generated by the advancing front.

Even Pécsi was losing his determined attitude. After taking the MUSZ to a platform to start loading a train, he disappeared along with his staff, leaving them unattended. He was drunk when he returned the following morning.

The resistance of the German Army along the line east of Kharkov broke. On February 16, the Red Army captured the city, dealing it a new wave of destruction.

A day before its fall, the MUSZs left Kharkov. After working to the last possible moment loading equipment and loot on departing trains, they boarded once again one of the last trains and headed North West, leaving behind the sounds of exploding shells.

After losing Stalingrad, Kharkov and Belgorod turned into Hitler's next "must have" cities. In the following six months, Kharkov would change hands twice again, each round bringing more death, destruction and misery. The German army recaptured the two cities in March. The Red Army, in a swift night attack, took them back on August 23, 1943, saving them from Hitler's order to remove anything valuable and then burn them to the ground. Nearly half a million Soviet and German soldiers died or were wounded in the battles over Kharkov along with thousands of its citizens. Seventy percent of the city was destroyed in these large battles.

After a night-long ride, the train stopped and the door of their cattle car was opened. An Italian soldier stood by the door smiling. They were in Sumy. Pécsi was gone. No one knew if he fled, was reassigned, killed, or remained in Kharkov. They certainly did not mourn his loss, but once again they had no commanders, no duties, no directions, and no clear path for returning home.

The Sumy station was chaotic like the previous stations they saw. A large depot of food that the Hungarian command could not ship back was made available to all soldiers, even the MUSZs.

To escape a new assignment, Laci and Endre quietly left their company, walked to the far end of a remote, mostly deserted, platform and behind a large pile of rubble contemplated their next move.

Trains were entering and leaving the station frequently. Hitching a ride could be easy. It could be their best opportunity, they thought. The Hungarian army was in disarray, most records were lost or destroyed, and commanders had disappeared. Even if they reached Hungary and then home, no one would know if they were discharged or simply walked away. But choosing the right train was a game of chance. They had to find someone who could guide them to the right train.

They walked out of the terminal into a dark street filled with Hungarian and Italian soldiers. The mostly disorganized Hungarians were sitting or standing in small groups smoking and drinking. They jeered at the two passing MUSZs.[10] The Italians were mostly indifferent.

As they turned back to the station, they passed a parked Italian truck convoy. Several drivers were sitting in their cabins, their feet resting on the dashboard; others were standing on the curb smoking, drinking coffee, and chatting.

One of the drivers on the street invited them to join him for coffee and even offered cigarettes. Endre and Laci gladly stopped to smoke and chat, the driver speaking in Italian, and Laci in Latin,[11] while Endre listened and smiled.

The convoy was heading back to Italy, the driver told them. They had been near the Don when the Russians broke through and now finally they were returning home. They should be in Milan in a week.

"You have to pass through Hungary," Laci cried out. "Can we join you?"

"Sure, hop on," he said pointing to the back of his truck.

The bed of the truck was covered with a canvas canopy. Its back flap was lowered and tied to the side-bars to form a fully enclosed space. The driver, who introduced himself as Vittorio, untied the flap and helped them on. In the dim light coming from the outside they saw that the truck bed was filled almost entirely with crates with the exception of a little space that was covered with a mattress. On one of the crates stood a little kerosene Primus stove.

---

10 Though they were wearing standard issue military coats that would make them indistinguishable for an ordinary soldier, they had to wear the yellow armbands that marked them as MUSZ.

11 In 1963 I traveled with Laci to Italy. His excellent Latin was sufficient for most of his conversations there.

"*How about some more coffee?*" Vittorio offered and without waiting for an answer started lighting the Primus, first igniting the kerosene in the little heater cup, then pumping the piston handle on the round tank at the base of the stove. Soon, the yellowish flame turned pale blue accompanied by the hiss of the hot fuel jet feeding the flame. He then handed a little kettle to Laci and asked him to go outside and fill it up with clean snow.

When Laci returned, Vittorio already had a small can filled with ground coffee. The smell of freshly ground coffee was intoxicating. Endre inhaled the smell in deep breaths with his eyes closed.

"*You like it strong?*" asked Vittorio while measuring one teaspoon of coffee after the other into the snow-filled kettle.

While they were sipping their coffee, Vittorio pulled out several dry sausages, cheese, and even white bread. A loud whistle from the terminal announced that a train was departing. Wherever that train might have been going, it could not possibly be as good a ride as the one Laci and Endre just found.

They ate their excellent meal quietly, enjoying the warmth created under the truck's canopy by the burning Primus flame when a knock on the driver's cabin door brought them back to reality. Vittorio turned off the Primus, packed it in a box and tied up the few loose crates. "*We worry about air attacks; we travel mostly at night,*" he said. "*We'll have a long and bumpy ride. Try to catch some sleep on the mattress.*" He then jumped off the truck, tied up the canvas flap at the rear and entered the cabin, ready to drive through the night.

Fully dressed, shoes on and their bags packed, Endre and Laci stretched out on the mattress and immediately fell asleep

Bright sunlight penetrating through small holes in the canopy woke them. The truck was standing still, its engine off. Outside Vittorio was speaking with someone in rapid-fire Italian. They got on their feet and raised the back flap. The convoy was parked near an unusual-looking church. The building, which survived the Nazi invasion, had three cylindrical structures capped with pear-shaped domes, each topped with an ornate cross.

A few civilians standing on upper floor balconies across the street watched them with curiosity. Two plump women, wearing coats that barely covered their well-endowed chests, waved at them. One of them smiled a broad smile exposing a shiny array of silver and gold teeth.

"*I think we are in Romny,*" Vittorio greeted them when he saw their heads peeking out. "*They have all these Russian signs along the road that I cannot read,* so it's hard to tell. We made some two hundred fifty kilometers.[12] Not bad. We will be here throughout the day. I hope you are not in a hurry."

They remained in Romny for three days. Laci and Endre stayed near the convoy, out of sight of Hungarian military police or other Hungarian functionaries. Vittorio's food and coffee supply seemed to be endless. Even with limited cooking implements, one Primus, one large pot and one skillet, he turned every meal into an Italian feast. Lunch preparation started at mid-morning with fried canned meat that Vittorio converted skillfully into meat parmesan, followed by boiling melted snow for pasta that was topped with wonderful tomato sauce. Canned olives with slices of cheese and dry prosciutto were combined into an antipasto that brought the Mediterranean sunshine into the truck.

Bad news waited for them when they reached Kiev a few days later. Vittorio's unit assignment was changed: they were not returning to Italy. The trucks were ordered back to Kharkov and Laci and Endre lost their comfortable ride to Hungary.

Once again they encountered a fork in the road with a few bad options but many new threats. Luckily, they were out of Red Army cannons range. But they were also away from the disarray of a collapsing front and panicked soldiers. Military units in Kiev were organized, individual soldiers, and certainly MUSZs walking without papers were arrested. And, as Vittorio discovered, Jews were not permitted to enter or stay in Kiev. (11 p. 39) They had to find quickly a new MUSZ unit and blend in unnoticed. But how to find one? How to find a unit heading away from the front? How to avoid a unit of new recruits that could remain in service for another year?

Luck is never a sound plan, but when it strikes it could beat any other plan. They were sitting with Vittorio at the side of the road weighing their options when a MUSZ company led by two sergeants on horses marched by. The MUSZ looked weak, tired and poorly dressed; some could barely walk and were leaning on their friends who could barely carry themselves.

"Look, Imre is there," Endre cried out pointing to one of the marching men. It was Csengeri. Endre jumped to his feet, grabbed his bag and inserted himself into the unit just behind Imre. As if reading Endre's mind, Laci joined the company behind Endre waving goodbye to Vittorio. The two sergeants at the front were too occupied smoking and chatting to even notice that their company just grew by two. But with head counts changing daily as MUSZs

---

12   Approximately 160 miles.

fell dead from disease and exhaustion, the sergeants would never realize that two MUSZs chose to join their company. Laci and Endre became part of the 101/35 company.[13][14] One of the two sergeants was Zsoldos György. (22)

Like most MUSZs companies, the 101/35 was afflicted by a typhus epidemic. As winter was subsiding, the deadly disease spread by lice infestation caused by poor hygiene and dense habitation. Hundreds, if not thousands, died from the disease. Many of those who did not die from the disease itself were murdered for being sick. One of the most horrifying mass murders related to the disease took place in Doroshich. (3 pp. 127-128), (11 pp. 42-45)

Doroshich was a small village between Zhitomir and Korosten, approximately one hundred miles west of Kiev. When the typhus epidemic could no longer be ignored, the Hungarian army set up a regional Jewish hospital. The title "hospital" was a charitable description of that institution. Two farmhouses and an abandoned schoolhouse were cleared of their original occupants to accommodate approximately four thousand sick MUSZs. The density in those buildings was unbearable; hundreds were squeezed into the attics. Fistfights erupted between the sick men who were trying to find enough space to lie on the bare floor. Medicine was non-existent and the few Jewish doctors and orderlies assigned to run the "hospital" were helpless. Without bathrooms and with such high density, even the simplest hygiene could not be maintained. Stench, dirt, human excrement, and lice dominated. Hundreds of corpses were simply carried out and stacked like firewood against the outside walls.

And then came the night of April 28, 1943, the last night of Passover. One of the farm buildings caught fire from its four corners simultaneously. The quiet night turned into mayhem of cries and shrieks. Some of the sick trapped inside tried to push the doors open, but the doors were bolted from the outside. Others, who managed to escape through the attic windows, were gunned down by guards who were waiting outside.

More than four hundred died in that fire.

What disease and fire could not do, commanders of the MUSZ force like Zsoldos did. His actions are remembered because he was tried on February 9,

---

13 Laci's September 29, 1945 letter to the Budapest Bar Association.
14 I could not find out how Laci actually joined the 101/35. Like many MUSZ companies in Ukraine, the 101/35 was reconstructed after the Soviet breakthrough in Stalingrad by assembling members of collapsed companies. Twenty months later the 101/35 reached the Budakalász station near Budapest and transported to Dachau, Germany where its members, including Laci, became slaves of the collapsing Nazi regime.

1946 by the Hungarian People's Court for war crimes. (21 p. 194) The title of his verdict simply reads "Bathed his MUSZs in Ice Water".

The charge against him read:

"In early 1943, the operation of the 101/35 company was in the area of the Horczyk camp in Ukraine. Other companies were stationed in that camp as well and Zsoldos had some responsibilities over the MUSZ. The large majority of the MUSZs in that camp were sick with typhus or related diseases.

Sergeant Zsoldos continuously maltreated them, hitting them with nightsticks, bully sticks, whips and kicking them. He outdid this maltreatment when on a spring day he ordered a cleansing bath. With an outdoors temperature of -10°C and chilling wind, he ordered all the healthy men and all the sick that could still stand on their feet outside. Five hundred men, most of them weakened by typhus and other diseases, were taken to a creek half a kilometer from the camp. There he ordered them to undress, run for 15 minutes and then he ordered the sweating men into the ice-cold creek.

After the bath, he lined them up still naked and inspected them one by one, and only then they were allowed to dry themselves and dress. After the bath, the condition of many of the sick worsened. Many died."

The People's Court sentenced Zsoldos György to 15 years of prison and hard labor.[15] (23)

Laci never told me if he gave testimony or attended this trial. But he did tell me that he attended several executions of war criminals.

With the arrival of spring, water from melting snow and heavy rains accumulated on the flat muddy plains and formed pools that attracted swarms of mosquitos to breed and multiply. Mosquitos were everywhere, day and night, filling the air with their annoying whine. There was no escape, nowhere to hide. Even smoky bonfires could not repel them.

Then Endre remembered his grandmother's recipe, a tar-like paste she used to smear on his face and hands when he was a child. With a pocket-knife he peeled the bark of beech trees and boiled them in water for hours until the solution thickened and turned black. The Ukrainian mosquitos, like the Hungarian, disliked the paste and from that day left the MUSZ alone.

---

15 Although the sentence appears light relative to the magnitude of his crimes, at least it represents the intention of the new Hungarian government to wash its hands clean from the atrocities committed by their predecessors. For a period of two years there were approximately 23,000 war crime trials in Hungary alone. Many of these trials were carried out without a specific underlying law and by judges without proper qualifications and credentials.

They spent the summer in Korosten unloading trains arriving from home and re-loading the cargo on trains heading to the front. In August that pattern reversed; trains from the front were unloaded and their cargo was loaded on trains bound to Germany. Looting took precedence over supplying the front or evacuating wounded soldiers. The front was approaching Kharkov, approximately 400 miles to their east, for the last time. Realizing that the German army would never return to that city, Hitler ordered anything that could be moved hauled away: machinery, trucks, building materials. Boxes marked with the Soviet hammer and sickle were carried away in trains marked with swastikas.

A few trains arriving from Kharkov were parked on remote platforms under heavy guard of armed SS soldiers. No one was allowed near those platforms or to even stare too long at them. No one knew for sure if they carried captured secret weapons or looted treasures. But much of the loot stolen from Kharkov was never found.

Work in Korosten was hard, the commanders harsh and the rations meager, but life was almost bearable. Working near trains carrying supplies and goods provided ample opportunities. A can of meat could be traded for a bottle of Vodka, a sausage for a pack of cigarettes. Even letters could be sent home by returning Hungarian soldiers. Lili, Sándor, and Böske must have received at least some of Laci's letters and tried to send him letters and packages.[16]

August 24, 1943 was an ordinary day for most of the 101/35 company, except for Laci and Endre. It was the anniversary of their draft. If the law, or just simple decency, meant anything, by noon of that day they should have been walking out of the recruiting center in Püspökladány to catch a train to Debrecen and then to Gyula.

This had to be a sad and dispiriting anniversary. Laci was logical; he must have known that his conscripted service would not end when promised. But in the dark cold nights in the Ukrainian steppes he must have dreamed about that day. Standing on deserted roads during snow blizzards with a shovel in his hands, he must have pictured his train entering the Gyula station, Sándor and Lili waiting on the platform with little Judit between them, her face

---

16 Böske wrote in one of her last letters from the Swiss safe house on Budapest's Pozsonyi Str. 39 V/3: "My heart aches for my only son because I do not know how he is doing or whether he received the package I sent and the letter the boys have written to him."

covered by a huge bouquet of red flowers that she barely could hold. And like any recruit anywhere in the world, he must have counted the days.

With the "last day" come and gone there was no other "last day" to expect. His service became an open-ended, endless torture. How did he keep his hopes up to ever return home? Where did he draw his strength from? He must have understood that the system was set up to crush him well before his time came. Did he consider dying? Death could be swift and painless, a dip in the cold river, a gunshot to his head, a fall under a train. He had more options for quick death than for maintaining that hard life. Only Judit could keep him alive. She was waiting for him. She would never forgive him if he did not return, nor would Lili, Böske, or Sándor.

Four hundred miles to the east, one of the fiercest battles of the war had just flared up. The German army that earlier that summer tried again to reach Moscow was now defending Kharkov against a fierce Red Army offensive that started the night before and was about to push them out. Forever.

On November 6, Kiev was also liberated by the Soviets. Later that month, the front reached the Zhytomir and Korosten line.

On the day Kiev fell, the MUSZ began a new march westward towards Pinsk in the northwest.

A new winter was coming. The roads and the plains, as far as the eye could see, turned white. Their worst enemy, deadly frost, was back, surpassing diseases, lice and insects. But these MUSZ already survived one winter. They were resourceful, adaptable and they had good shoes, coats, clothing, and hats. But they were hungry again, the food they gathered while loading trains was gone and the fields around them were bare.

They passed Pinsk in December. Pinsk was once proportionally one of the largest Jewish communities in Eastern Europe. When the Nazis occupied it four years earlier, twenty-seven thousands of its thirty thousand inhabitants were Jews. When the MUSZ passed through, Pinsk was already Judenfrei. A year earlier, the entire ghetto was deported. Ten thousand of the deportees were murdered in one day. (24)

They continued marching through icy terrain and icy roads finally reaching Brest-Litovsk, a small town on the Bug River that now marks the border between Belarus and Poland. Brest, as it is called now had been a center of Jewish life since the fourteenth century. Important Hassidic learning emerged from Brest.

Soon after invading the Soviet Union and capturing Brest, the Nazis began murdering the city's Jews by ad hoc executions. Approximately five thousand were killed on July 10, 1942 in a forest outside the city by the SS Einsatzgruppen, traveling SS units formed to carry out mass murders of Polish intelligentsia and Soviet resistance, but mostly Jews. To account for and identify the remaining Jews, the occupying Nazi government required all Jews ages fourteen and older in Brest to carry locally issued "passports" bearing the holder's name, age, place of birth, names of parents, and photograph. (25) Six months after the invasion the Nazi established a Jewish Ghetto in Brest, forcing the remaining eighteen thousand Jews into it.

On October 15, 1942 the entire Ghetto was liquidated and burned; all occupants were rounded up, loaded on cattle car trains, transported to a large killing site near Bronna Góra, lined up along wide pits and shot. A monument near the site commemorates them among a total of fifty thousand victims.

The MUSZs reached Brest on December 22, 1943 where they marked the first day of Hanukkah near the ashes of the burned ghetto. (26) They remained in Brest through most of the winter digging graves.[17]

On March 19, 1944 Germany invaded Hungary. The alliance of convenience between the two nations had turned into an occupation. Company 101/35 was still Hungarian but now it was controlled by Germans. Strangely, the German army in the east chose to treat its Jewish slave labor more humanely than the Hungarians. While elsewhere in Europe Jews were exterminated, in Brest they were protected. Their work was hard but not deadly, their food was simple but life-supporting, and the weather was getting warmer.

The annexation of Hungary was the last Nazi territorial gain of the war. The Red Army was advancing west and in June the Allies landed in Normandy starting to push the Germans east. On July 28, 1944 Soviet troops liberated Brest. Unit 101/35 marched westward again, closer to Hungary.

In October, what was left of Company 101/35 was transported by train back to Hungary. (21 p. 656) After a delay of several weeks in Mohács, the train arrived to Budapest where the tired MUSZ were turned over to Germany for more slave labor.

---

17   Laci's claim for German reparations #703916 BV, 1/30/1971.

1968–1970: The War of Attrition

The euphoria that touched Israel in the months after the Six-Day War nourished itself from many sources: the magnitude and speed of the victory, relief from an imminent threat, the capture of new territories and the liberation of Jerusalem. But at the heart of that euphoria was the genuine belief that peace with the Arab neighboring states was finally at hand.

To most Israelis, peace was not just the opposite of war. Peace meant that our existence as a nation was no longer in question, that we were truly a "nation like all other nations" as we often used to say. Peace meant that our neighbors no longer wished to eradicate us. Peace to us was secondary only to our independence. When we greeted each other saying "Shalom," we truly meant "Peace" and not just "Hello" or "Goodbye".

I grew up hearing my parents predict that by the time I turned eighteen, the military draft age, there would be peace, and that my military service would no longer be necessary. It was a common hope. I am not sure if they truly believed the prophecy or just wished it. But in the summer of 1967 it felt as if it was becoming a reality. Peace was almost inevitable.

For a few months after the war, even the West Bank was negotiable, though King Hussein had yet to agree to hold such negotiations. Dayan was famously quoted that he was "waiting for the phone to ring." (15 p. 315) Those Israelis who viewed the West Bank and Jerusalem as essential to our security or who believed it was part of our historic land were not yet vocal. The settlements that they would build in the following decades had not even been planned. Everything involving peace was possible and nothing was unimaginable.

Of all the war and victory songs written in that time, the *Song for Peace*[1] still touches the hearts of Israelis. Its beautiful melody starts as a lament, a quiet mourning of the dead:

> ....He whose candle was extinguished
> and was buried in the soil,
> a bitter sob won't wake him...

---

1   Lyrics: Yaakov Rotblit, melody: Yair Rosenblum.

and then its pace picks up, culminating with a shout calling for peace.

It is quite telling that the desire for peace expressed in this song was written for an army entertainment troop[2] that was part of a combat infantry unit that took part in some of the hardest battles of the war.

The *Song for Peace* became the marching song of the Israeli peace movement. A blood-stained copy of its lyrics was found in Prime Minister Rabin's pockets after he was assassinated on November 4, 1995 at a peace rally in Tel Aviv. (15 p. 313)

There were no songs for peace written on the other side of the border. Barely three months after the Israeli cabinet made its offer; the Arab League Summit responded by announcing in Khartoum the famous "Three No's" resolution.

Shocked by this hostile response, the political and public opinions in Israel shifted. The territories that were first seen as pawns to be traded for peace turned into assets that were essential for national security. Although a new war still was regarded as a distant threat, Israel began developing the political state of mind and military infrastructure for long-term occupation of Sinai, the West Bank and the Golan Heights.

Meanwhile, the Soviet Union who saw the Arab defeat as a failure of its own weapons technology, strategy and military training, began rearming Egypt and Syria at a rapid pace, hoping for a quick "re-match." Within months the Egyptian and Syrian air forces and ground-based weapons systems with artillery in the lead were restored to their original strength. More importantly, the most advanced ground-to-air missile systems were installed along the borders with Israel and around airfields to protect the restored air forces from another surprise air attack. And in case the new missiles systems failed, all military planes were hidden in newly built deep bunkers under bomb-proof layers of reinforced concrete. The first of the lessons the Arabs learned was already implemented.

The war that could have produce peace instead spawned even deadlier wars.

On July 1, 1967, while Israelis were still basking in the limelight of their victory, an Israeli patrol encountered an Egyptian army unit just south of Port Fuad at the northern end of the Suez Canal (27). The battle that developed drove the Egyptians off with casualties on both sides. What seemed to be a small border skirmish was in fact the first shot in a new and lengthy war.

A series of scuffles that followed on land, air, and sea reached a new height on October 20 when the Egyptian navy fired an anti-ship missile toward the

---

2 Lehakat Ha'Nachal.

Israeli destroyer INS Eilat that was patrolling the Sinai shores near Port Said. Eilat was hit and sank taking with it forty-seven of its sailors, among them my high school friend Haim Segal. Israel retaliated by shelling Egypt's principal oil refineries near the city of Suez and setting ablaze large storage tanks. Hitting the storage tanks with artillery fire was no small feat. Three years later I would learn in artillery school how that was done. Six years later I would see the damage with my own eyes.

Skirmishes continued on and off for months. To most Israelis they represented nothing more than the day-battles of previous years with the Syrian army, except that the new battles were far away from population centers. To many, these skirmishes provided proof that the new territories were the buffer zones that Israel needed for its own security. They labeled them "strategic depth." Headlines reminded the public of the vulnerabilities prior to the Six-Day War. They claimed that the skirmishes along the Suez Canal, hundreds of miles from Tel Aviv were nothing more than a nuisance.

On March 8, 1968 when Nasser announced that the scuffles of the last few months were in fact a new war, Israel finally realized that the state of active war with Egypt and Jordan did not end with the Six-Day War. The name Nasser chose, the "War of Attrition," reflected his strategy of forcing Israel out of the Sinai Peninsula, and possibly other newly captured territories, by inflicting casualties over an extended period of time. Israelis, unlike the Arabs, could not tolerate loss of life when inflicted continuously over an extended time, he argued. Unlike Israel, the Arabs have plenty men and time; they could stand such losses and in the end would be able to push Israel out of the occupied territories without actually going to a full-scale war.

King Hussein of Jordan joined Nasser in this effort. Rather than negotiate the fate of the West Bank he chose the militarily option by turning a blind eye when PLO terrorist squads began infiltrating across the Jordan River into the Israeli controlled territories. Ambushes on IDF patrols and attacks on isolated new Israeli settlements that popped up along the Jordan River led to pursuits by helicopters and on foot. A secondary war that became known as the *Mirdafim*, the "Pursuits," was underway.

A year after Israeli forces reached the Suez Canal and the Jordan River along the West Bank the Attrition War and the *Mirdafim* were in full force. Artillery attacks along the Canal and daily ambushes on patrols both in Sinai and the Jordan valley began taking their toll on Israeli morale: exactly as Nasser and Hussein intended.

1968-1970: The War of Attrition | 185

Ironically, Israel found itself defending a line along the Suez Canal that it never intended to capture. When Israeli forces were rushing through Sinai during the Six-Day War, anxious to destroy the retreating Egyptian army, Defense Minister Dayan ordered them to stop and establish a defensive line twenty miles short of the canal. But by the time his order reached the lead forces they were already bathing in the canal. In deference to the facts, Dayan declared the canal "one of the best tank ditches in the world." Soon after, that line was named after the new Army Chief of Staff, Haim Bar Lev. (28)

Dayan had a point. The canal in most locations was approximately 325 ft wide at the surface. A tall sand wall along the eastern, or Israeli, bank made it an even more formidable barrier.

The wall was originally built in the mid-nineteenth century using the Canal's excavated sand. The French engineers who designed the canal determined that the prevailing winds in that area were blowing mostly from west to east and therefore if the dug-out sand was deposited on the east bank of the canal it would be blown towards the desert and away from the canal. Subsequent dredging added more sand to the wall, turning it into a steep rampart that was believed to be nearly impossible to scale even by foot and as a bonus, provided an excellent cover for Israeli forces behind it.

The natural reaction in Israel to the early casualties of the War of Attrition was, as Nasser hoped, distress and a demand for action. Israel could not tolerate human casualties, partly because of its small population but mostly because of its cultural bias sanctifying life. Israel needed to act and it had two options to consider.

The first, the easiest and the one that best matched Israeli military tactics, was to move most troops away from the canal, out of artillery range, just like Dayan intended during the Six-Day War, and leave behind only skeletal observation outposts. The rest of the forces were to be kept inland to enjoy the strategic depth and natural barriers that the vast desert and its geography offered. The thinking of the advocates of that option was that as long as the Egyptian army was prevented from crossing the Canal in full force, incursions by small units would be easily contained with the air force or by the highly mobile ground forces that would be permanently stationed at a safe distance, outside artillery range. Even if the line along the canal were to be breached by a major Egyptian force, the depth of the peninsula, the scarcity of roads that were available to cross through the easily defensible mountain passes, and sand dunes would allow Israeli forces to reorganize and respond effectively, well before the invading forces presented any danger to the Israeli heartland.

But Israeli culture and tradition could not tolerate the loss of land, no matter how useless or remote. Twenty years after the establishment of the state, land was viewed as sacred.

That mentality drove the second alternative that was adopted after bitter debates between the two schools of thought. (29) Rather than watch the line from a safe distance, Israel would build permanent posts along the canal and defend them with elite units who would be protected against artillery and aerial attack by massive bunkers. The IDF, under the command of its new chief of staff, General Haim Bar Lev, chose to hold a line that it did not wish to capture in the first place.

Barely a year after demonstrating the astonishing virtues of an agile army supported by a superior air force, the Israeli command played into the hands of the Egyptian army (29 p. 57) by committing to a static war and constructing one of the longest and strongest forward defense lines in history. Instead of electing where to attack and dealing the enemy blows where it least expected, the IDF moored its best forces in forts where they, rather than the enemy, were subject to constant commando attacks and artillery barrages. The political and military establishments committed Israel to defending worthless desert territory while forsaking its true values of strategic depth and a potential pawn for peace negotiations. The new Israeli strategy for the upcoming war, and ultimately the outcome of the Yom Kippur war that followed in 1973 were set in stone, or rather in concrete and steel.

The Bar-Lev line was built into the sand wall along the east bank of the canal. The French engineers who chose to locate it there could not imagine its strategic value in the eyes of Israeli generals a hundred years later. The height of the wall was augmented to more than sixty feet and at its base widened to more than a hundred and twenty feet. Its slope facing the canal was made even steeper to further deter armored vehicles, or even commando units, from climbing it.

The strongpoints along the line, or *Maozim* in Hebrew, were built into the rampart. Digging trenches and bunkers into the sand was easy and quick and the soft sand proved an ideal absorber of bomb shrapnel and bullets. The distance between neighboring *Maozim* provided direct lines of sight and overlapping fire-power coverage. A road, code-named "Lexicon," was paved behind the sand wall to provide shielded vehicle travel. The Bar-Lev line was to become unbreakable.

Construction of the Bar-Lev line was popular in Israel at first. It projected strength, determination, and above all it promised to keep all threats away from the heart of the country. Its cost of five hundred million dollars enriched many contractors and created an economic boom that was a welcome relief after years of deep recession. Although the number of casualties was growing, the trickle was slow, a mortar attack on one *Maoz* along the canal took the lives of two paratroopers and another the next day took the life of an artillery officer; while wounded soldiers were flown almost daily by helicopters to hospitals in Tel Aviv. But life in Tel Aviv, Haifa or Jerusalem remained carefree.

But as the war extended into 1969 and then 1970, its real cost began to sink in. Front pages of major paper carried almost daily pictures of young soldiers killed in a *Mirdaf* or "Pursuit" in the West Bank or in a *Maoz* along the Bar-Lev line. Uncharacteristically, the Syrian border remained quiet. Morbid jokes began circulating among military age men such as *"If we don't meet beforehand, we will meet on the front page news."* The compulsory military service that before the Attrition War was for men two and a half years was extended to three years. But even that extension was insufficient to reduce the burden carried by the regular army. Reserve units had to be called in to hold the line along two fronts and help build and fortify them.

My turn to serve in a *Maoz* came in January 1970. My entire AR unit was called up. My order arrived on the first anniversary of my first date with Liora, the love of my life. The promise of the AR system not to call on cadets during their school year was broken again. Just like before the Six-Day War, the growing stress of the Attrition War spread into every layer of the Israeli society and economy. This was no longer a war carried out by a handful of soldiers and paid contractors in remote locations. Everyone was called to pitch in.

On our last date before my departure, Liora and I went to see an old movie. It was a poor choice. The protagonist, a young journalist, was heading out to cover a war in a remote location. An emotional scene just before his departure showed him and his girlfriend kissing a passionate and tearful goodbye. In the next scene the journalist was killed by a stray bullet. Liora could not bear the similarity with our situation and burst into tears. Her tears were still welling and her face wet when we kissed our own final goodbye.

I met the 40 ARs that were called up for this round at the Technion, at the same location where our Six-Day War deployment began. But the anxiety that dominated the last deployment was replaced with excitement and anticipation for the adventures ahead. Despite the known dangers I doubt that anyone there worried harm might come our way.

Our bus ride to Rephidim in central Sinai took us through the entire length of the Gaza Strip, El Arish, and large swaths of the vast Sinai desert. It is hard to imagine today that an unaccompanied civilian bus, filled with unarmed soldiers, could pass through these territories without an incident.

It was my first visit to Gaza and Sinai. Once we entered the Strip through the military check point at its north end I watched out the window as the bus drove along the two-lane highway on the Mediterranean coastline. We entered Gaza City and passed through its main square full with street merchants, continued along the coastal road that was dotted with poor villages and small towns until reaching the Rafah military check post at the southern end of the strip. Arabs, the same people whom today we recognize as Palestinians, looked at the passing bus with vacant stares, neither hatred nor affection. They knew where we were headed but I could not tell if they cared or not.

The bus stopped outside El Arish, the "Capital" of Sinai, in a vast parking lot in front of a large warehouse marked prominently by the word SHEKEM—military canteen. The parking lot was filled with Israeli buses, military supply trucks, tank carriers, some Jeeps and a few civilian vehicles. Hundreds of soldiers were walking about, to and away from the SHEKEM. We later called it the largest IDF canteen in the Middle East. It was the last outpost of civilization for those heading south and the first for those returning home. Here, one could stock up on cigarettes, shoe polish, candies, soda, anything that a soldier serving in the Wild West may need—even condoms. None of us heading to a *Maoz* on the Canal could hope for opportunities to use condoms in the weeks ahead. But if the SHEKEM carried them, there had to be buyers.

The El Arish SHEKEM also served fast food. To meet kosher laws, the hamburgers were vegetarian, made from soy based imitation meat. I do not believe that even one such hamburger would sell in Tel Aviv, but in El Arish they were selling like hot dogs. A full meal package also included an ice cream, made of course from imitation cream. Only the French fries we called "chips" were real.

We headed out of the SHEKEM into the peninsula. Dark granite mountain ranges, as far as fifty miles away, framed the vast yellow-white plains that were dotted with greyish-green dry shrubs. There was not a single settlement or even a tent in sight and yet, occasionally, we saw one or two men in black robes and white keffiyehs walk purposefully. We could not tell where they came from, where they were going, or how they could survive in the desert without carrying any supplies or water.

We reached Rephidim after dark.

Rephidim was the biblical Hebrew name given after the Six-Day War to the Egyptian air base Bir Gifgafa. It was located approximately fifty miles east of the Canal's central section. The name Rephidim suggested that this might be the site where Moses got water out of the rock. (30) Without a doubt, it was the site where Nasser met his air force pilots just before the Six-Day War, challenging Israel to come and fight them.

Rephidim served as the Sinai division's central command and a forward air force base. Although it was a major military base, it had the feel and look of a Wild West town. Only a few one-story permanent brick and concrete buildings remained from the Egyptian air base. The rest of the vast base consisted of caravans, prefabricated buildings and large tent compounds that were clustered in sub-camps belonging to the various military corps.

We arrived in the early evening hours. The streets of this mostly transient city were filled with male and female soldiers walking to and from the mess halls. Military dress codes did not seem to apply to Rephidim. Some soldiers wore military shirts hanging loosely over their jeans, others walked about in sandals and shorts. Female soldiers walked about in tight shorts and sandals. Military contractors who mixed with the regular army servicemen and reservists wore shorts and cowboy hats. Some carried side arms, some did not.

"*So this is where the condoms from the El Arish SHEKEM are being used,*" blurted one of the ARs when our bus passed by a group of female soldiers. The laughter was mostly nervous.

For fear of ambushes, the roads along the Suez Canal were closed after dark and reopened after the morning patrol. Like most travelers to the Bar-Lev line, we had to stay for the night in Rephidim. Our bus was directed to the "hotel" section of the base, a complex of vacant tents furnished only with cots. The "guests" had to provide their own blankets. The mess hall near the "hotel" stayed open late. Surprisingly, the food was excellent. And it was about to get even better. The food in the *Maozim* was the best the IDF served, barring, of course, the pilot-grade menu.

A helicopter landing in the nearby airbase woke me at night. It could have brought in a casualty from a *Maoz* under attack. But it could also be a general returning to his office.

The early desert sun rising above a mountain range in the distance woke us up. After breakfast, we were divided into groups of ten and assigned to four *Maozim*. Two military trucks came to ferry us to the Canal.

We headed west through the desert plain and then through long rows of yellow sand dunes stretching north to south as far as the eye could see. The softly curved dunes, illuminated by the bright sun, reminded me of the beach. I could see myself relaxing on one of these dunes, enjoying the sun. But unlike the beach, each row of dunes was followed by another and then another without ever yielding to the blue sea. The black asphalt road shimmered in the hot sun as if it were wet, playing tricks on our eyes. It was *fata morgana*, a desert mirage.

Past the last dune the road turned south on road Lexicon along the shores of the Great Bitter Lake, a shallow salt valley that together with the Small Bitter Lake to its south was flooded when the canal was dug. Several small ships were anchored in the lake.

Just south of the Small Bitter Lake the road took us behind a tall sand wall. We reached the Canal. I was excited knowing that I reached the farthest extent of Israel's vast new territory, though the wall blocked the view of the canal itself. I was also anxious knowing that we were within the Egyptian artillery reach and possibly even an Egyptian commando ambush. But then the sense of pride of being among the few chosen to serve in this historic location more than compensated for these feelings.

Moments later the truck turned right into a narrow driveway marked by a small military sign reading "*Maoz Lituf,*" my home for the next twenty days.

Several parallel rows of barbed wire entanglements marked the *Maoz* boundaries and the edges of the driveway. Small red sheet metal triangles and signs in Hebrew, Arabic and English warned of land mines. After passing through an opening in the sand walls, the truck stopped in a courtyard the size of a football field, surrounded like a crater by sand levees on all sides.

Ten of us got off the truck. The driver was visibly in a hurry to leave.

"*I don't mind driving along the Canal,*" he apologized while rushing us to unload our gear, "but I hate being inside a Maoz. Those Egyptians can shell us at any moment. I bet they can hear my engine running and are loading their cannons as we speak."

A young, disheveled, and unshaven man emerged from a narrow opening in one of the levees carrying a helmet in his hand and an Uzi on his shoulder. "*Welcome to Maoz Lituf, my name is Yuval,*" he greeted us. His unbuttoned fatigue shirt carried the insignia of a lieutenant. His exposed bare chest was well-tanned as was his face that was framed with hair stubble that had not been shaved in days. Whatever his role, military standards of dress and grooming were clearly not part of the routine in Lituf. I liked him immediately.

Standing with my back to the gate, I heard the truck rushing out, not even slowing to make the turn into Lexicon. In front of me was the canal levee, a tall sand wall, at least five or six stories high. Several soldiers standing in a trench on its top, only their helmeted heads visible, measured us up with curiosity. The sand walls surrounding the *Maoz*'s courtyard to my right and to my left had door-sized openings that must have been entrances to the bunkers. Each of those bunkers was covered by several layers of steel bars. The bars in each layer were densely packed to form continuous armor-like sheets. The edges of the rails terminated in an irregular pattern, lending the bunker roofs a haphazard appearance. To my right was a mortar launcher along with numerous mortar shells standing on their tails.

Two soldiers in their underwear and wearing unlaced boots and buttoned up flak jackets, their helmets by their feet, were sitting near the launcher on a bench by a folding table busy preparing lunch. The open shed behind them had stacks of vegetable crates, an icebox, and two gas burners. This was clearly the kitchen. A smell of grilled meat filled the courtyard. I could not tell if the two scantily clad men were the cooks, the mortar launcher operators, or just two hungry soldiers preparing a late breakfast.

Yuval interrupted my thoughts. He was the commander of Lituf, he told us. His only job, he declared, was to return us to our mothers and girlfriends alive and in one piece. This was not a new claim to me. I heard it in boot training from the most brutal commander just before ordering us to do fifty seat-ups. It sounded hollow then but had a ring of truth now.

I found it harder to believe that the IDF trusted this young and disheveled officer to defend a thirty mile segment of the canal and an entire *Maoz* with all its inhabitants. The Egyptians must be truly a sorry bunch, I thought, if this officer along with forty of his men, some still in underwear, and ten newly arrived AR's could hold them off.

The *Maoz* safety rules were simple. We could be bombarded at any moment, he warned. Lituf had already been shelled twice that day and Yuval guaranteed we would be shelled again at least once before nightfall and then plenty during the night.

"*I don't care what you wear while you're here, I don't care if you shave or polish your boots,*" he announced. "*But if I catch one of you outside the bunker without your flak jacket on, fully buttoned and helmet in your hand or on your head, I will* send you to the brig for thirty-five days. And your time will start only after you completed your tour here."

I looked back at the two cooks by the kitchen. Yuval noticed and laughed. The two cooks did meet Lituf's dress code, he confirmed, and then he ordered us to put on our own flak jackets and helmets, so we met dress code too. Before continuing, he pointed out the entrance to the nearest bunker.

Of course, Yuval did not have his flak jacket but then he was the *Maoz* commander. Who could fault him?

The *Maoz* used whistles as an alarm system. Everyone carried one. Whoever heard a cannon or a mortar launcher, "exits" as they called them, had to blow his whistle. Everyone had to run to the nearest bunker when a whistle sounded. We had 60 to 80 seconds to reach the bunker if it was a mortar "exit" and only 15 seconds if it was a cannon's.

I recalled Kobi's lecture in Sha'ar HaGolan about mortars flying along a steeper and longer trajectory than cannon shells. I felt like an experienced veteran. Though I still had to hear a mortar "exit" to truly distinguish it from cannon.

"How do we know if it's safe to leave the bunker?" asked one AR.

"*Good question, wait a few moments after the last landing, step to the entrance and wait 80 seconds. If you don't hear a new exit or whistle you should be safe. And by the way, each bunker has two exits. Use the other one if the exit you used is blocked. Don't worry if both are blocked. You're probably dead anyway.*" Yuval laughed at his own joke.

"When's lunch?" someone asked.

"*It's always lunch or dinner here. You cook your own meals. There is no cook, but we have excellent supplies; the refrigerator, or rather the icebox, is in the shed behind you. Take what you want, spend all the time you want preparing it. A supply truck delivers water every day and food and mail every other day—if it can make it.*"

A faint thud followed by a whistle blow interrupted Yuval. "*Leave your bags on the ground and follow me,*" he yelled running towards an opening of a bunker. We barely entered the dark corridor when a loud explosion shook the walls.

It was a direct hit. Most likely, a 155 mm shell, Yuval declared.

"Welcome to Lituf," someone said. A few AR's laughed nervously.

It took my eyes a few minutes to adjust to the darkness of the barely lit bunker. We were inside a tube-shaped corridor lined with corrugated sheet metal. A row of bunk beds on both sides of the tube nearly filled the entire space, like the crew quarters in a submarine, leaving just enough space for one man to pass. Some beds were vacant, others were covered with blankets and haphazardly scattered personal items, in sharp contrast to the meticulous order I got used to during military training. Two soldiers were asleep, oblivious to the explosion outside or to our presence. Dim sickly yellow light from two or three bulbs hanging from the ceiling barely illuminated the space. The sound of a blowing fan suggested that air was being circulated. Although not air conditioned, the bunker felt pleasantly cool.

We sat on two of the vacant beds and Yuval coolly continued his instructions. As we just witnessed, he bragged, the bunkers could easily hold off explosions of 80-pound cannon shells. But the objective of the central command was to upgrade the bunkers to provide protection against heavy aerial bombs. Our job was to help build up this new protective layer.

Most of the reinforcement work had to be done on the bunkers' roofs where Egyptian snipers could see us. Therefore, we could only work after dark. In fact, most of the *Maoz* people worked at night, either in construction or on watch. Like owls, they slept during the day.

We walked out of the bunker, collected our belongings that were covered with sand raised by the explosion, and walked to our bunker on the opposite side of the *Maoz*.

"Be sure to put anything you don't use under the bottom bed," Yuval instructed. "Keep the path between the beds clear so people can run in and out even if the light is out. Go out and start exploring the *Maoz*," he advised and left.

Eager to see the *Maoz*, I dropped my unpacked bag on one of the beds, buttoned up my flak jacket, took my helmet and Uzi, and walked out.

I memorized my way out, thinking that I should be able to get in or out in a hurry even with the lights out. After walking three bed lengths, I reached the end of the corridor where I had to make two sharp left turns. Outside light was visible only after the second turn. Old military tactics never die, I thought. This was exactly how the Ottoman Turks built the gates in the walls of Acre or Jerusalem. They had two sharp turns to slow invaders even if they successfully rammed the gate doors open. Some walled city gates even provided ports from above to pour boiling oil on the invaders. The sharp turns at the bunker ends were actually intended to prevent shrapnel from flying in, though they would also slow Egyptian commandos down if they ever succeeded crossing the canal and penetrate the *Maoz*.

A steep row of stairs opposite the bunker's exit was carved into the slope of the canal rampart that was one of Lituf's walls. I climbed these stairs and found myself in a deep trench lined with corrugated sheet metal. The trench wall facing the canal was topped by several layers of sand bags that shielded my view of the canal and, of course, me from the snipers. I started walking along the trench towards a bay facing the canal. A soldier standing there on a platform that elevated him above the sand bags watched the opposite side intently through a telescopic binocular mounted on a stand. To his right a machine gun was also mounted on a stand.

I covered my head with the helmet and stepped up on the platform to take my first close glimpse of the Suez Canal. I could smell salty seawater that could be from either the Mediterranean or the Red Sea. It didn't matter to me, it was equally blue.[3]

The view of the straight ribbon of blue water lined with concrete banks was tantalizing. The opposite side was a surprisingly idyllic lush tropical green. Little farm mud huts peeked from behind the trees and bushes in a complete contrast to Lituf's desert and war environment. Several Egyptian soldiers, dressed in desert yellow uniforms, were strolling along the opposite banks, carefree as if on a vacation. One soldier sat on the concrete bank dangling his feet above the water, smoking a cigarette.

The soldier to my side finally noticed me, took his eyes off the telescope and greeted me cheerfully and introduced himself as Shay.

Shay, a year younger than me, still had a year to go in his regular service. In his three months in Lituf he saw friends hurt by Egyptian snipers and shelling. He was counting the remaining days of his tour, anxious to leave Lituf for good.

I pointed out the Egyptian soldier dangling his feet over the canal to Shay. Wasn't he worried about Israeli snipers? *"Not really,"* Shay explained. The Egyptians learned they were usually the ones who started skirmishes. And we learned, Shay added smugly, that before they start one, they call back those who stray along the canal. So for now we're safe.

As a good tour guide, Shay offered a visual tour of the canal, pointing out a sniper on the opposite side. He swung his telescope towards a grove of tall palm trees.

"*Yup, I found a monkey,*" he exclaimed while locking the telescope in position. He moved away, instructing me to look slightly below the top of the palm tree, right of the cross-hair.

I could almost touch the few yellow coconuts hanging in the sharp image under the canopy of the tree. In its shadow, almost behind the coconuts

---

[3] Joining of the two seas with the Canal had an interesting environmental consequence, the Lessepsian Migration, named after Lesseps, the developer of the Suez Canal. Marine species migrated from the Red Sea and colonized some of the Mediterranean southeastern portion.

I saw the sniper crouching on a platform like a monkey on a tree. But unlike a monkey, he had a rifle on his lap.

"Monkeys," the *Maozim* lingo for snipers, posed little threat during the day. Soldiers in the *Maozim* learned to keep their heads down. But at night, when construction work on bunker roofs was done, the "monkeys" illuminated the entire *Maoz* with powerful infrared projectors and with infrared sights on their rifles sniped at their targets.

But we too had infrared sights, Shay reassured me. As soon as an infrared projector was turned on, our sniper on watch took it out, often with a single bullet. It did not require much skill to hit such a large and bright target. Therefore most of their sniping at us was against faint, dark moving shadows. It was mostly ineffective, but still dangerous.

In Lituf we also had an advanced American technology that the Russians, and therefore the Egyptian, still didn't have, the Star Light Systems or SLS. The SLSs were electronic telescopes equipped with image intensifiers. Like radio amplifiers that boost faint radio signals and produce sound, the image intensifiers could enhance images illuminated by the faint light arriving from stars in the sky to produce bright black and white (actually green and white) images on a fluorescent screen just behind the eye piece. It was a true marvel to see bright detailed images at night, as if it were daylight. During clear nights, which in the desert were almost every night, we could watch through the SLS the Egyptians across the canal without revealing ourselves with infrared projectors.

A commotion on the opposite side drew our attention. A colorful bus arrived blowing a musical tune and stopped near the palm grove. The "monkey" I saw in the shadow of the tree canopy climbed down like a monkey along the tall trunk. Soldiers jumped out of trenches that I had not noticed until then. Others emerged from the farm huts. All were running towards the bus and lining up at its front door. Some in the line began pushing each other trying to improve their position. Soon, the front of the line became wider and its tail narrow, very much like the line in the El Arish SHEKEM. But the action in front of the bus was far more animated. With that level of excitement, I concluded, the bus must have been dispensing something far more valuable than vegetarian hamburgers or condoms.

"It is the second Thursday of the month," Shay cried out, "this is their SHABAZAN day!"

I did not need to have the term SHABAZAN explained, everyone in the IDF knew the Hebrew acronym for "Mobile Brothel Services."

However preposterous this may sound, SHABAZAN existed on the Egyptian side of the canal. And even more astounding, the Egyptians weren't the only ones who enjoyed it. Israeli soldiers, across from a 325 foot-wide canal enjoyed it too. The war stopped with its arrival and did not resume until it left, and often for hours afterwards. A Freudian psychologist might have concluded by this evidence that the War of Attrition was nothing more than the expression of frustrated sex drives.

The calm brought to this section by the SHABAZAN gave time for the denizens of Lituf to take a relaxed shower, cook a gourmet meal and even eat it, play volleyball in the courtyard or sun bathe under the beautiful February desert sun.

"*The IDF should have sponsored SHABAZAN visits,*" I suggested to Shay. "*Even better,*" he retorted, "*send one to Lituf too.*"

With the "monkey" gone, I continued exploring the opposite side with Shay without having to crouch in the trench. A tall watchtower stood directly across. It was higher than our ramp, Shay explained to allow them to peek into the *Maoz*. Checking it through the telescope, I saw that it was occupied by a soldier who was watching me through his own telescope. I waved at him. He did not respond. He was probably upset at missing out on the SHABAZAN.

I rested my elbows on the sand bags and leaned my head on my arms admiring the lush green of the opposite side. It was a two or three mile deep strip running along the canal. Desert plains, just like on our side, extended beyond that strip. I could not take my eyes off the combination of the canal's blue waters, the palm trees, and lush green of mango and citrus trees and the yellow desert beyond. So much contrast in such a narrow width: blue, green, yellow; canal, farmland, desert. And when put together, a deadly battlefield.

"*Before the canal could be dug,*" Shay continued his narration, "*a water supply had to be brought to the thousands of manual laborers who would dig it in the desert. The solution was a fresh water canal running from the Nile Delta to Lake Timsah, north of us and then along the Suez Canal.*"

That network of fresh water canals still carried Nile water a century later. Plenty of fresh water combined with warm weather created a true paradise. "*This must look like the Nile Delta,*" Shay suggested, "*only smaller.*"

I continued watching the paradise across the canal with the telescope. On closer inspection I noticed it was an abandoned paradise. It had no farmers. They had been driven out by the Egyptian army and their farmland was designated a military area. The trees had not been pruned for years and their fruits were rotting on the branches. Fields were overgrown by weeds, and stray farm animals wandered about aimlessly.

Shay's day-watch ended. We climbed down to the courtyard to find several ARs preparing a meal. One was peeling and cutting potatoes into strips for French fries. Another was cutting fresh vegetables into fine cubes and adding them into a large salad bowl. Thick heavily seasoned steaks were already waiting on a board in the hot sun to be grilled. They invited us to join them.

The supplies were superb. The icebox was filled with cold cuts, blocks of cheese, frozen meats, even sweet chocolate milk. Crates of fresh vegetables, fruits, snacks, and canned food were stacked in the corner. Anything a young and hungry soldier could desire. Even sodas labeled as SHEKEM property were in the icebox. They were not free, however. A coin box next to the cooler filled with coins and bills indicated that the honor system was alive and well in the *Maoz*.[4]

Shay finished his meal quickly and asked me to help prepare the mortar launcher for the evening artillery duel that would come when the SHABAZAN departed.

We walked to the ammunition dump outside the courtyard and brought back several heavy wooden crates containing mortar bombs. While Shay re-adjusted the launcher's azimuth and elevation using data he read from an often-engaged-targets list, I started pulling the bombs out of the crates and their tubular cardboard containers and set them standing on their tails. Each bomb carried several rings of different colors on its waist-like tail section. They were removable extra propellants. Their number and color combination could be adjusted depending on the target's range. The large pile of discarded rings behind the mortar launcher was proof that many of our targets were not fully in range.

Our preparations were interrupted by the dull thud that sounded like an exit.

"*Mortar*," shouted Shay and blew his whistle.

All of us except Shay ran to the nearest bunker. Shay remained standing behind his mortar launcher ready to fire back when ordered.

We waited for a minute, then two and then three. Nothing happened. The mortar bomb that was to follow the "exit" we heard never arrived. Puzzled by a bomb that remained suspended in midair we walked out of the bunker. Shay

---

4   I did not see any alcohol in the *Maoz*. Though military regulations have most likely regulated it, drinking at that time among my age group was rare.

and Yuval were already standing near the kitchen surrounded by a group of Lituf soldiers trying hard to appear angry. A few started teasing us. We knew we needed to be embarrassed but couldn't figure out why.

"*Watch,*" said Yuval, approaching the upright icebox. He lifted the door, held it for a moment, building up our anticipation and curiosity and then let it drop. The door swung and hit the icebox in a dull thud. It sounded just like a mortar exit.

"*The whole Maoz stopped everything it was doing because one of you dropped this door. Next one to drop it gets an extra night of watch duty,*" he concluded the demo.

Shay told me later that Yuval himself caused an "icebox alarm" the day before.

A real "exit" came minutes after the departing SHABAZAN blew its musical horns.

We rushed back to the bunker in time for the first round's explosion. It was distant, obviously missing the *Maoz* by a wide margin.

"*Their artillery officer must have had a premature ejaculation,*" someone in the bunker joked.

But the next ten rounds fell well inside the *Maoz*. They were loud and shook the ground. The bunker linings rattled when hit directly. The lamps hanging from the ceiling on thin cords swung and our shadows danced in an erratic rhythm.

It felt safe inside the bunker. And yet, it was eerie to hide inside our holes like mice, unable to look out and hoping that the bunker was well-engineered and built to withstand what was coming.

Then came several loud mortar exits. They were nearby and the explosions of their bombs came from afar. Shay was retaliating on our behalf.

The duel lasted more than an hour. I lay on the top bunk bed and closed my eyes. It was a lot like lying in my own bed at home and listening to a thunderstorm outside. But this storm rained iron shrapnel instead of raindrops.

When we emerged from the bunker, Shay was sitting on an empty crate, smoking a cigarette and drinking a soda. The row of mortar bombs we prepared was nearly gone and the pile of colored rings had grown.

I was working with Shay preparing new bombs when I was called to join the AR's to meet Sergeant Gaddy, our construction commander.

Two bottom beds in our bunker, facing each other, were our conference room. Gaddy, a tall skinny unshaved man wearing military boots, shorts, and a flak jacket over a T-shirt, fit the mold of Lituf soldiers. Like Yuval and Shay, he was informal, relaxed, and friendly.

Gaddy started by explaining the objectives of the new construction. Our bunkers were already protected by several layers of railroad rails, stacked side by side to provide continuous sheets of steel. The layers were called SHACHPATZ; the Hebrew acronym for "Explosion Layer." Each SHACHPATZ was held together by its own weight and the weight of the SHACHPATZs above

The flak jackets that were then a new addition to the IDF protective gear were also dubbed SHACHPATZ. That term is still being used by present day IDF soldiers who may not know its origin.

The SHACHPATZ, Gaddy continued, proved to be excellent protection against artillery fire. But it cannot hold out aerial bombs. It had to be augmented by layers of gabions.

The gabions were metallic cubical wire cages filled with rocks. Gaddy led us outside and pointed at a completed gabion on the roof of our bunker. It was a three-foot-tall cube of rocks, most the size of a watermelon. They were held together by chicken wire mesh.

Our job was to fill such cages with rocks that were stacked in a pile behind the bunker. It was simple; we could even use a hoist to lift the rocks to the roof. But it was dangerous, even on dark nights, Gaddy admitted.

Shay was still sitting on the crate by his launcher when our briefing was over, smoking another cigarette. He stood up when he saw me and invited me to join him in closing Lituf's gate for the night.

We walked out along the driveway to the point where it met Lexicon road. Next to the fence's outer ring was a free section of barbed wire spiral. We picked up one end and pulled it until it blocked the driveway. After tying both ends to the fixed fence, Shay set up the first booby trap, a Carl Gustav submachine gun attached to a metal rod planted in the ground. The gun's barrel pointed across the driveway. He then picked up a thin steel wire attached to another rod across the road and tied it carefully to the gun's trigger that would be activated when the wire was tripped. It was a primitive trap. I was not convinced that this booby trap could hold anyone off, let alone stop an invasion. It was probably no more than a fancy doorbell intended to draw our attention that guests have arrived. We carried several landmines from the ammunition dump, scattered them on the driveway and Shay armed them. Then we closed two more barbed wire gates before setting up one last booby trap.

We were locked in our own prison; fifty men, alone in the desert, facing a hostile army across the waterway. Even with the all-powerful IDF behind us, we were still alone. No one could enter and we could not leave without setting off the traps and mines that we just laid down.

The sun went down behind the Egyptian desert plains. A half-moon illuminated the silvery waters of the canal and our bunkers. We could not start our work while it was up. Despite its bright light, we could not light any outdoor fire or smoke outside the bunkers. Any heat source, such as an open fire or a lit cigarette produced infrared radiation that could be easily picked up by the "monkeys'" infrared sights.

I returned to the lookout on the Canal rampart. Another Lituf soldier manned it. Shay was resting ahead of what could be an active night. The SLS telescope was already in place on a tripod. The moon at mid-sky was reflected from the canal and illuminated the palm trees. I could easily make out their contours even with a naked eye. A careless Egyptian soldier sitting on the banks lit a cigarette. The bright match flame illuminated his face. He would be dead, I thought, if we too had "monkeys."

I asked to check out the SLS.

After pressing the "On" button, a green screen lit up inside the binoculars and a clear image of the opposite side came into view. The person who just lit his cigarette was sitting at the edge of the canal, his feet dangling over the concrete wall that sloped down towards the water line. His cigarette tip turned bright each time he drew smoke. I panned the binoculars and found the palm grove. A "monkey" was climbing up a tree. I could see his telescoped rifle hanging on his shoulder.

Further north I could see the mouth of the Small Bitter Lake and the ships in its middle. They were kept darkened, just like us.

I asked the guard about these ships. They were grounded by the Egyptian army after the Six-Day War, he explained, to prevent shipping in the canal while we held the east bank. They also sank several additional ships in the Great Bitter Lake further north and in the Canal itself.

It didn't make any sense to me, or to him, that they would choose to forego the income the canal generated; unless, of course, they had planned all along to turn the canal into a war zone. Nothing made sense: destroying the farmers and their farms on the opposite side, destroying ships to block the canal. But war was not supposed to make sense.

At 10 pm, after taking a nap in the bunker, I climbed to the emplacement on the rear rampart facing east and announced on the radio that I was in position for my watch. A regular telescope on a tripod, not an SLS, pointed at the gate.

With the bright moon setting behind me the view through the telescope was nearly as vivid and bright as through the SLS. I could see the outline of the landmines on the driveway, read the sign at the entrance and see a few lights on the slopes of the mountain ridge twenty to thirty miles to the east.

If the "monkeys" have similar telescopes, I thought, then working on the bunker when the moon was up was just as dangerous as in broad daylight.

Shelling began just as my shift was nearing its end. Most people were deep asleep in the bunkers. The few outside were in their trenches. Only a direct hit could hurt us. The message the Egyptian artillery officer sent was clear, there was no reason why we should sleep while he was awake and he would try again once we started working on the roof. Shay did not fire back. He had no message to send and he certainly did not want to start up a duel just as we were to begin construction.

It took half an hour for this one-sided shelling to cool off. It caused no casualties or damage. We assembled near a large pile of rocks behind the bunker; our flak jackets buttoned up and helmets secured on our heads. Three of the *Maoz* staff joined us. The shift boss introduced himself as Yigal. I had not seen him during the day and I could not quite see him in the dark, but I was certain that he was deeply tanned, unkempt, unshaved, and with his hair overgrown. By then I already understood, Lituf's staff soldiers looked identical. Their sloppy dress code and grooming had a uniform pattern.

We set up a "bucket brigade" between the rock pile and the manual hoist that was operated by two men. Another two unloaded the rocks on the roof into a pile. Once the pile grew sufficiently, the bucket brigade climbed to the roof and started passing the rocks from the pile to the gabion. We tried to minimize "roof-top-time."

When I reached the top of our bunker, I could see the outline of the palm trees across the Canal. The night was dark but their silhouettes were well defined against the star-studded sky. We were in the "monkeys'" line of sight.

The bunker rooftop was dark and flat. The rails that made up the top SHACHPATZ layer were barely distinguishable from each other. I bent down to feel them. There was barely a crack between any two rails. The SHACHPATZ was a perfect armor.

Then I heard several "whooshing" sounds followed by light crackles.

"*On your bellies,*" shouted Yigal, "*snipers!*"

A few more rounds were fired. I could not tell if they were aimed at us or merely in the direction of the *Maoz*. Whatever the intent, the "monkey" succeeded in disrupting our work. There were more volleys of sniper fire through the night, but thankfully no shelling. No one was hurt. The morning news in Tel Aviv would not even mention that Egyptian fire was directed at an Israeli outpost.

I woke up at noon. Yigal was already in the kitchen preparing a late breakfast. I joined him and prepared a large omelet for both of us. When we sat down I asked him about the SHACHPATZ rails.

"*They came from the El Arish train,*" he said, surprising me.

I remembered vaguely that there used to be a train line between El Arish and El Kantara, a small town on our side of the Suez Canal.

Indeed, Yigal confirmed. During World War I, the British army built a railroad from the Suez Canal through El-Arish to Jaffa, and later extended it to Haifa. It was hard to believe that the SHACHPATZ rails were historic relics.

The Haifa port was not completed until 1933, Yigal continued. Before the port, Haifa was a small fishing village. The only deep-water port in the region was in Port Said, north of Kantara, and the train running along the coastline was the only mode of shipping available to Palestine and the British army stationed there. In the 1920's, one could take a luxury train from Haifa, through Jaffa, Gaza City and El Arish to Kantara, cross the canal by boat and then continue by train to Alexandria or Cairo.

The SHACHPATZ rails in Lituf and most of the Bar-Lev line *Maozim*, Yigal concluded, came from the El Arish train tracks. They were dismantled by Israeli contractors and carried by trucks to the new *Maozim*. It seemed like an elegant and clever solution to me. The train was not running anyway; why not use its tracks?[5]

Later that afternoon I joined Yigal to patrol Lexicon.

We hopped on a half-track, Yigal at the driver seat and I next to him behind the machine gun facing forward. On the way out we attached a barbed

---

5 Turns out I was wrong. And so were the generals who conceived and designed the Bar-Lev line. Only three roads in Sinai ran from the Israeli border to the canal. They were narrow and their shoulders soft. A single bus or a truck could block the road for hours if it had to stop.

Three years later I discovered, along with the rest of the IDF, that when tanks had to be transported on wide-body carriers during a real war, even a minor breakdown or accident turned into a gigantic traffic jam that blocked traffic for days and becoming an inviting target for enemy air raids.

Whereas the British army had the insight to build a railroad to ferry goods, weapons and personnel from one end of their territory to the other, the IDF, after committing the mistake of building the Bar-Lev fortifications, committed even a graver mistake by dismantling the most effective route to rush supplies and reinforcements to these fortifications.

wire spiral to its back so that it would drag behind us raking the road like a fine tooth comb. Three other Lituf soldiers joined us in the back, one of them standing behind a second machine gun mounted on a massive stand and facing sideways. We turned north onto a dirt road that ran parallel to Lexicon. The barbed wire spiral behind us raised a huge dust cloud that followed us like a long dragon's tail.

The dirt road was patrolled and raked with the barbed wire every morning and at dusk, erasing all marks that might have been left behind by animals or humans since the previous patrol. I asked Yigal to stop and walked a few steps on the soft dust layer to test it. My footprints were deep and easily detectable. No one could sneak through our lines without leaving clear footprints on this dirt rood.

Within a few miles we reached the end of our section. The next section to our north was the responsibility of our neighboring *Maoz*.

The drive along this empty road illustrated how thin our line was. Although the *Maozim* were originally intended to be the watchful eyes of the IDF, in 1970 they were believed to be the line that could not be breached. In truth, they were supported by the canal itself that was expected to hold off a massive invasion and by additional forces further away behind the line. Yet twenty or thirty *Maozim*, each with only fifty men, were all that held the one-hundred-mile-long front.

I did not dare think about a full-scale invasion across the entire length of the canal. Or, more precisely, like most Israelis, I did not think that such a possibility even existed. The Egyptians, in our eyes, were too timid, weak and disorganized to mount such a broad-scale attack. Unfortunately, the IDF command thought so too.

For the next few nights the bright moon rose later but also set later, leaving no dark hours to safely work on the bunker's rooftop. That did not prevent us from hoisting rocks to the roof and stacking them in large piles, ready to be distributed into the gabions when darkness returned.

The Egyptian did not sit idle either. They continued shelling us randomly, making certain that we didn't adjust to a regular schedule, shelling intensity, or pattern. Newspapers that were delivered a day or two late reported casualties in other *Maozim*. So far, we were spared. Yuval was keeping his promise of returning us home safe. But luck played a role too. It was only matter of time before it showed its other face.

A week after our arrival moonrise was sufficiently late to leave some early evening hours for work. We started transferring the rocks from the roof top piles into the gabions that filled up quickly. Almost every night "monkeys" sniped at us and missed. This was a deadly game, a true Russian roulette. But since none of us was hit, we believed our odds were too low to be concerned. We just laughed at the clumsy "monkeys."

By the third week, boredom replaced the initial excitement. My mentality and appearance caught up with the *Maoz* permanent staff; I was tanned from waist up, unshaven, hair overgrown, and my dress sloppy. I learned to distinguish between mortar and cannon "exit" sounds and count the time to a "hit." I cooked enough gourmet meals to make any chef proud, built numerous gabions, dodged hundreds of sniper bullets and artillery shells, and read all the cheap novels in the *Maoz* "library." I was looking for new excitement.

The pile of discarded color rings that Shay was collecting behind his mortar launcher was calling me. The rings were filled with rocket propellants and I was studying to become a rocket scientist. This was a match made in heaven. Unfortunately, the *Maoz* was not prepared for rocket scientists, nor were the Egyptians.

Every rocket needs a fuselage, the cylindrical body that contains its fuel. The cardboard cylinders, the mortar bombs shipping containers, were barely suitable, I observed, but they were worth a try. Although they could hold the rings that would be the rocket fuel, they could not withstand high pressure. Their performance as rockets would be inherently limited.

I picked a cardboard cylinder, filled it with propellant rings and crimped its open end to form a rudimentary rocket nozzle. I carried my creation outside the *Maoz* under the rear emplacement where I stood watch the other night. I positioned the "rocket" on a few blocks that served as the launch pad, tied several rings together to form a fuse and attached one end to the nozzle and ignited the other. The flame propagated slowly along the fuse and reached the nozzle. Suddenly, the entire volume inside the cylinder caught fire. The rocket rose from the blocks and flew up, high above the ramparts, high above the levees. I howled with glee, not bad for a homemade cardboard rocket. Within seconds the Egyptians retaliated against the introduction of new weaponry with intense shelling. Yuval did not think it was funny.

A few days later, the truck and the driver that dropped us off came to pick us up. The following day I was home. I took my first afternoon nap when a loud "boom" woke me up. I jumped off my bed looking for my flak jacket and helmet when I realized I was safe at home. I didn't know what that loud noise had been and wondered about it. I found out that evening news that a Syrian

MiG 21 successfully penetrated Israel's air space and rattled Haifa's inhabitants with a supersonic flyover and a sonic boom. A smaller headline in the following morning's paper reported that Shay from *Maoz* Lituf on the Canal was killed by an Egyptian artillery shell while returning fire.

That summer I graduated from the Technion as an Aeronautical Engineer and reported for my mandatory three years' military service. Six months later I was commissioned as an artillery lieutenant. The Israeli borders remained mostly calm during my three-year service as the commander of surveyors' units.

The War of Attrition ended in August 1970 as part of a ceasefire agreement between Israel, Egypt and Jordan.

October 1973: The Yom Kippur War

December 1971 was a quiet month along the Israeli borders. Since the end of the War of Attrition, the Egyptian, Jordanian and Syrian armies had not challenged the IDF. Israelis felt invincible, convinced that the hard hits suffered by the Arab armies during the Attrition and Six-Day wars convinced them to leave Israel alone.

December 1971 also marked the mid-point of my military service. After a year and a half in service, most of it as an artillery officer, I was an experienced commander of an artillery surveying unit, one of only two such units in the standing army. Our primary role in peace time was to scout future locations for artillery positions along the borders, measure their coordinates using precise surveying techniques, mark the locations, document and publish internally our results. The precise coordinates we generated could improve the accuracy of our artillery when fired from those positions. To further improve accuracy, we also measured the coordinates of potential enemy targets that were visible from our side of the border.

This was a fascinating and gratifying assignment. We were independent and mobile. We traveled extensively along the various front lines; a few months along the Suez Canal, then a few months along the Lebanon border, followed by time on the Golan Heights. My orders came directly from division headquarters or the Artillery Corps Headquarters. I was responsible for the timely completion of my mission, but otherwise I was free. We prepared our own meals, took our own breaks and leaves, went on side trips if we so desired. It was a magnificent time to be in the service.

The extended ceasefire along our borders dulled the IDF preparedness. By December 1971, half of the *Maozim* along the Bar-Lev line were abandoned to save costs and manpower. Maintenance of the abandoned and even the inhabited *Maozim* was neglected. The strongholds that were built at a high human and material cost were forsaken to the desert sands and winds.

Life in the still populated *Maozim* had grown easy and relaxed. The "monkeys" were gone from the treetops across the Canal and their artillery turned quiet. The elite IDF units that held the line were replaced by third tier reserve units.

I spent many months in 1971 visiting the *Maozim* to measure the coordinates of their main bunkers and the coordinates of prominent Egyptian features on the opposite side. We walked freely on the ramparts facing the canals and carried our instruments to the bunker rooftops. We worked unperturbed in broad daylight, often with Egyptian soldiers watching us from the distance, only mildly curious about what we were doing.

Peering through my theodolite telescope and binoculars, I saw that farmers had returned to the green belt. They were tending to their lush gardens using farm animals and ancient farming techniques.

I visited *Maoz* Lituf. The gabions we built nearly two years earlier were topped by more layers. The bunkers looked as if they could now hold off the explosion of an atomic bomb. Three middle-aged reservist men wearing only shorts were standing in the kitchen cutting potatoes for French fries and vegetables for salad. Heavily seasoned steaks were waiting on a board under the hot sun to be grilled. Nothing changed. Even the flies hovering over the steaks seemed the same. Except that Shay's mortar launcher was gone along with Shay. The three middle-aged men did not wear flak jackets and their helmets were nowhere to be seen.

The defense of Sinai against what seemed to be an unlikely Egyptian invasion relied on three lines that ran parallel to the canal. Each of these lines was served by its own road running north to south. Lexicon road that I remembered well from the Attrition War served the *Maozim* along the canal.

Six miles to its east ran the Artillery Road. As its name suggests, the road was designed to serve artillery units who could engage Egyptian targets from positions along both of its sides. But at the same time, they were within range of Egyptian artillery units. To avoid being hit, Israeli batteries were trained to set up, fire a few rounds quickly and then "leap" to a new position. The Artillery road was designed to facilitate agile "leaps."

The road also served a series of unmanned forts called *Taozim* located along a ridge overlooking the canal. The *Taozims* were well stocked with supplies and ammunition for reserve units that were to be deployed as part of an emergency defense plan code named "Dovecot" (*Shovach Yonim*).

We worked for weeks selecting potential positions along the Artillery Road and measuring their coordinates. Often, while preparing such a site, we found partially exposed remains of Egyptian soldiers who had been buried by the shifting dunes and then exposed when the dunes shifted again. They died on the last day of the Six-Day War fleeing the IDF, within sight of the Canal and the safety beyond it.

Further to the east, well outside the range of Egyptian artillery, was the Lateral Road. It ran from Baloza in the north, passing through Tasa and west of the Gidi Pass in the central section, to the western end of the Mitla Pass in the south. The road was planned to allow units to move quickly and safely from one section of the Canal to another.

My surveyor unit and I also spent months along the borders with Lebanon and Syria. With the exception of a few penetrations by terrorists and localized flare-ups, these borders were quiet too.

One winter, after completing a job in the balmy resort town Eilat and swimming in the Red Sea, we were ordered to travel to the snow-covered slopes of Mount Hermon to measure the coordinates of the northernmost Israeli stronghold at one of its peaks. Within less than a week, we swam in a tropical sea and built a snowman.

Only one little dark cloud tarnished the peaceful days of 1971. Egypt's President Anwar Sadat, who succeeded President Nasser after his death in 1970, declared 1971 as the "Decisive Year." After demanding several times the full withdrawal of Israel from the Sinai Peninsula and offering in return peace, Sadat announced that if his proposal was rejected, or ignored, he would resort by the end of that year to military solutions.

Israel's government rejected his proposal outright. It had already rejected a far more modest proposal by the Defense Minister Dayan a year earlier. (31) Soon after the Attrition War, Dayan concluded that holding the Bar-Lev line was untenable and unnecessary. He repeated his earlier idea that flexible positions, further back in the desert, combined with an operational Suez Canal and fully populated Egyptian cities, functioning factories and refineries along the canal would provide far better security for Israel than a fortified line. A few months after Dayan floated his idea, Sadat "recycled" it and presented it as his own. In 1971 he expanded it even further.[1]

With December 1971 coming to a close and the "decisive year" to an end, the IDF command worried that Sadat might make good on his threat

---

[1] I cannot escape my own deep sense of missed opportunities. In hindsight, knowing that Sadat proved to be an honest and reliable peace partner, I can only imagine all the "what ifs": "What if" we accepted his offer to withdraw only twenty miles from the Canal? "What if" we withdrew from Sinai and signed a peace agreement? But in 1970 and 1971 we did not trust Sadat or any Arab leader. Giving up the Sinai Peninsula or just a twenty-mile strip of desert land along the Canal seemed too steep a price for a questionable state of peace.

and launch a surprise attack. The Army was put on high alert. My unit, along with most of the standing army, was kept on base for several weeks expecting hostilities to resume along the Egyptian border, the Syrian, or both.

When December 31 arrived and passed without an incident, Sadat and his empty threat became the target of Israeli jokes and scorn. Hubris reached new heights. Israelis on the street and their leadership were convinced that the successes of the Six-Day War and the War of Attrition clearly provided sufficient deterrence. The Arabs would not dare to attack. There was no need to make territorial concessions.

On May 1, 1973 Liora and I were married in a military ceremony at the Artillery Corps headquarters. Our *Chuppa* was placed under the crossed barrels of two long-range cannons that were captured from the Jordanian army in 1967. Two large army projectors illuminated the stars above us.

A few weeks later, I completed my mandatory active military duty, proud that not a single one of my soldiers was hurt under my command: not in accidents, not in training, not in skirmishes, and not in wars.

Two weeks after our honeymoon I got a call from my battalion commander. My replacement officer ran his soldiers through a minefield. One command car in his convoy hit a mine. Two soldiers bled to death while waiting for a rescue team to clear a path through the mines. I remembered that minefield. I drove by it several times. It was fenced and well-marked. The battalion commander asked if I would agree to return to service. But I already was enrolled as a graduate student at the Technion.

On Yom Kippur, even secular Jews try to reconnect with their religion. They fill their neighborhood synagogues to capacity, do not operate their vehicles, and many of them fast. All public transportation is stopped. Only emergency vehicles may travel, and even they respect the holy day and refrain from blowing their sirens. All stores, places of entertainment, and restaurants close. Radio and television stations stop broadcasting from sunset to sunset.

Yom Kippur that year started as any Yom Kippur before, or after. Only a shofar blowing in a neighborhood synagogue and birds chirping broke the silence.

Liora and I were sitting on the balcony of our third floor apartment in mid-town Haifa, enjoying the silence and the view of the Haifa Bay and the Galilee mountains beyond when we were startled by two Phantom jet fighters flying overhead towards the mountains up north. Their loud after-burners shook our windows. Minutes later, two navy missile boats emerged from the harbor also heading north. It was impossible to believe that military exercises would take place on that day.

I turned on the radio and tuned it to GALATZ, expecting it to be quiet. Instead it came with an announcement:

"*Moments ago, an IDF spokesman announced that around 2 pm, Egyptian and Syrian forces launched a coordinated attack in Sinai and the Golan heights. Our forces are responding to these attacks and are pushing the enemy back. Due to activities by Syrian planes above the Golan Heights, air raid sirens were sounded in Israel. These are real sirens.*"

As if to further confirm that this was a real emergency the announcer continues:

"*The reservist soldiers that belong to the following units are required to report immediately to their mobilization centers:*

Bright Day,

Colorful Rainbow,

Good Times."

Liora and I listened in disbelief. A few years earlier, the open mobilization system was tested without prior warning and created a national panic and an international crisis. Thousands of callers flooded the telephone systems of their military units and headquarters. Even worse, the exercise nearly ignited a regional war when neighboring Arab states interpreted these exercises as preparation for an Israeli surprise attack and responded by mobilizing their own armies.

The IDF learned its lesson and pledged not to test this mobilization system without an advanced warning. A surprise mobilization on Yom Kippur could not possibly be a test.

The announcer barely finished reading the list when the first car on our street started its engines and drove away. We looked out. Men still wrapped in their prayer shawls, the Talith, were running out of the street corner synagogue heading back home. Moments later they transformed from worshipers into soldiers in uniforms. Carrying a small backpack and still fasting they rushed to the nearest bus station to catch the first bus to the main bus terminal.

The phone rang; Laci was on the line worried that I had already been called up. "*I wish I were,*" I told him. I could hear his sigh of relief on the other side. Because I was so recently discharged, I hadn't been assigned to a reserve unit yet. He hoped that the army would "forget" me.

I did not share his hope. I was certain that if I did not reach the front within a day I would miss the war. I had no doubt that we would defeat the Arabs quickly and I wanted to be part of that victory. I hung up the phone and started packing my backpack. I did not have a plan but wanted to be ready just in case.

I agreed with Liora that if I were mobilized, she would move back with her parents. Why stay alone in an empty apartment?

At 4 o'clock, the phone rang. The army didn't forget me after all. I was ordered to report immediately to a mobilization center south of Tel Aviv. I didn't need the caller to tell me that from there I was surely heading to Sinai.[2]

I called Laci, cheerfully breaking the news to him and asked for a ride to the central bus terminal. While waiting for him, the phone rang again. Liora had been mobilized too. This was our first signal that something was amiss. Though eligible for reserve duties, married women were never called up. Not even during the Six-Day War. She was ordered to report to a mobilization center north of Haifa to process reservists reporting to service, track issued equipment and the whereabouts of recruits.

The Haifa central bus terminal was chaotic. Thousands of reservists and regular servicemen were anxiously looking for transportation. Military police officers, strained to maintaining order, directed soldiers to buses that were heading to other major bus terminals in the country and large deployment centers. I was directed to a line of hundreds of men and a few women, all waiting to board buses to Tel Aviv. But the line moved fast. Buses were departing as soon as they were filled, replaced by new ones almost instantaneously.

I was too busy trying to board a bus to notice how amazingly well the transportation system operated. Only three hours earlier it was no more than a paper plan labeled "Activate in Emergency." Not a single bus driver or MP was in the terminal, yet in less than three hours drivers were summoned from their synagogues or homes, found their buses and received their orders. The MPs, most of whom were certainly on leave were called in, briefed and put in place.

But most astonishing were the thousands of reservists who were anxiously pushing to board a bus that would carry them closer to a war they knew nothing about. Many left behind children, wives, parents, jobs and businesses,

---

2   When I look back through the perspective of decades at that phone call, the only emotion I can recall is relief that I was included. I do not remember joy nor fear or concern. I am certain that Liora did not cry when we said our goodbyes like she did when I departed for my service in the *Maoz*. We were sure that our separation would be short. Unlike the Six-Day War, we didn't even need to be concerned with a long waiting period. The war had already started. The Arabs must have already been routed. The Phantoms that flew overhead were our proof. And the lack of reports from the front must have again been the "fog of war." It worked so well in 1967, it must be working again—in our favor—so we thought.

not knowing how long they would be gone. Many I saw in the terminal did not return or if they did, were changed forever.

Israelis are social animals. In any large gathering they try to find old acquaintances, be it a friend from high school, military training, military unit, or a friend of a friend of a friend. And if no one is found they strike conversation with the next person. Conversations along the line to Tel Aviv turned into an active rumor mill.

Rumors about the Egyptians crossing the Canal were circulated and amplified as they were passed from mouth to ear. By the time I reached the front of the line, stories that the Egyptian army was already trapped on the Israeli side by the Air Force who destroyed their bridges became accepted facts. Some along the line quoted sources stating that the IDF would not be satisfied this time by merely pushing the invaders back to where they came from. This time the IDF should and would reach Cairo and Damascus to finally force the Arab governments to sign peace treaties with Israel.

It was standing room only when I boarded the bus. At least twenty men were squeezed in the aisle with their bags at their feet. The radio speakers in the ceiling repeated the message I had already heard at 2 pm. Nothing in these messages could possibly feed the rumors we heard in line, and yet we all believed that the war had already been decided. All we needed were the details.

The highway to Tel Aviv was busy with buses, some heading north carrying soldiers from central Israel and the south to fight on the Golan Heights and others heading south carrying soldiers like me to fight in Sinai. Several transporters, all heading north were carrying tanks or heavy artillery pieces. They could reach the front by midnight. Some on the bus counted the tanks heading north and concluded that the situation on the Golan Heights might be more serious than in Sinai. In that they were right.

The central bus station in Tel Aviv was also chaotic. The frenzy was further heightened by the darkness of the blacked-out station and surrounding streets. Finding the right bus was a challenge.

The bus ride to the base at the northern edge of the Negev Desert was long. Hundreds of vehicles traveled on a dark two-lane road with only their parking lights on. The heavy, mostly south-bound traffic slowed to a snail's pace. After midnight, I stood at the gates of the base looking for the headquarters of my new field artillery brigade.

The huge base hummed with activity. The rollup doors of huge storage hangars were wide open, revealing mothballed tanks and self-propelled cannons parked side by side with barely enough room for a person to walk between them. Men, some still in civilian clothing, were climbing on these weapons like Lilliputians on giant Gullivers, laboring to wake them up. The bright lights from the hangars rendered the night into day. Black-out was clearly not on the minds of the commanders of this strategic base. That could mean only one thing, that like in 1967, the Arab air forces were no longer a threat.

I found the headquarters of the artillery brigade. It was located in a typical military building the IDF inherited in 1948 from the British army. The caller who deployed me, a young, tired-looking corporal, still in regular service, was sitting by a metal desk with three telephones in front of him, still calling recruits from a long list. He checked me off his list and sent me to the assembly point for the brigade's surveyors' unit. I was to become their commander. My new unit included fifty surveyors and we were part of General Adan's division. We needed to reach the northern section of the Suez Canal as quickly as we could. That was my only briefing for the night.

I had never prepared a reserve unit for departure to war. I suppose no one in this base had done so in such urgency. For better or worse, I had to rely on my instincts.

While walking to our assembly point I tried to think of the tasks ahead: find my unit, introduce myself, determine who had already reported, receive personal equipment and arms, collect our vehicles from the artillery hangar, top off their fuel tanks and their reserve tanks, collect our professional equipment that should be arranged in sealed metal boxes, confirm that the sealed boxes contained what they should, get topographic maps of the entire canal region and if available also of the opposite side, get rations and water for at least three days, find the transporters that would carry our vehicles and the bus that would carry the personnel. When done, load the vehicles on the transporters and be prepared for departure by noon along with the entire brigade. I assumed that we would head towards Baloza, just east of Port Said at the northern tip of the Canal. If roads were open, we could reach our positions, and have the brigade ready to fire no later than midnight, Sunday; thirty-two hours after receiving my call. Not bad!

By this plan, a long night awaited me followed by a long day on the road and then another night setting up in Baloza. And that would be even before firing our first artillery shell. But of course by then, I thought, the war could be over anyway.

I found my unit near the storeroom. Almost all were present and many already fully equipped. A short, chubby guy in battle fatigues, probably in his forties, was barking orders. Though there were no rank insignia on his uniform the others obeyed him nevertheless. I stood on the side for a few moments watching the dynamics. The short guy knew his men by name and role. He was efficient and knowledgeable. This was not a new unit. In fact, I appeared to be the only newcomer and most likely the youngest. My success as the new commander would depend on this man that the others kept calling Kupy.

Kupy noticed me and introduced himself. He was the unit's master sergeant. I was right. He was more important than I would ever be, despite my senior rank. The Master Sergeant was the one who made sure our equipment was in order, our vehicles were running, our soldiers were fed and above all, that they were content.

Under the light of the wide-open hangar I noticed his graying hair and a large moustache. He had been with this same unit for more than twenty years. I was barely five years old when Kupy was already a reservist. Many of the men were his age. They had served together in the Sinai Campaign in 1956, in the Six-Day War in 1967, and countless other deployments. The youngest was three years my senior. Kupy and many others were professional surveyors. I was their junior in age and professional experience and yet the Army made me their commander. The best I could do was to let Kupy do his work and learn everything I could from him, and fast.

Before sunrise, our ten half-tracks were loaded with theodolites, telerometers (distance measurement equipment), radios, camouflage nets, Jerry cans filled with water, rations and personal equipment. Machine guns were in short supply, each half-track had only one. Without taking off their shoes, some of the men found a corner on their vehicles and curled up for a quick nap.

Kupy was too energetic for a nap. Sitting on a crate behind his half-track he set up a small camp-site gas stove and started boiling water in a small brass pot with a long handle and a long curved spout. This was not a standard issue coffee pot. I saw similar pots in Arab markets in Jerusalem and Acre. It was Kupy's first demonstration of his uncanny ability to turn any hardship into an exciting experience. He added several heaping teaspoons of finely ground coffee to the cold water and allowed the grounds to float to the top. The wonderful smell of cardamom and coffee overcame the military smells of fuel, grease, vehicle exhaust, and sweating men. The boiling water underneath the floating grounds started bubbling up. When the boiling coffee started rising, Kupy lifted the pot from the fire, waited for it to subside and then put it back down until it boiled again.

He repeated the process seven times, a Bedouin recipe for perfect Turkish coffee.

When it was ready, like a magician pulling out a rabbit from his hat, Kupy pulled out two small rounded cups, approximately the size of shot glasses and poured coffee for both of us.

The crate, he later explained, served him since 1958. Like Mary Poppins' bag, it was full of surprise rabbits—far too many for its size or weight.

I was preoccupied with my coffee when another small miracle formed in plain view. It was not nearly as audacious as the Israeli air attack in the early hours of the Six-Day War, but no less important. Early in the morning, gigantic transporters started streaming into the base, too numerous to count. They arrived to transport to the front our cannons, half-tracks, and tanks of the armored units.

These gigantic flatbed trucks were wider than a typical highway lane. They were difficult to maneuver. Only well-trained drivers were licensed to operate them. They were critical for the delivery of heavy weapons to the front. Tanks could not travel long-distance on their tracks and still be battle-ready. But if not driven properly, even a single transporter could cause a serious accident or clog a critical road. Many of the transporters that arrived had already completed one round trip, delivering tanks to the northern frontier. Like the rest of us, their exhausted drivers were operating on sheer adrenaline and a lot of coffee. Hundreds of transporters were needed to carry just one division to the front.

If the availability of buses in the central station the day before was admirable, the arrival of tens of transporters to my base, all with trained drivers, all on time, all in working condition ready to make the trip to the canal was nothing short of a miracle.

MPs scrambled to direct the transporters to the few loading ramps where tanks waited to be loaded and then lined up the loaded transporters in convoys along the main road leading out of the base. The MPs had to be trained for that role. If even one transporter was forced to U-turn, it would delay the entire operation by hours. Not one transporter had to U-Turn.

The primary weapon for my brigade was the 155 mm self-propelled Howitzer cannon. It was made in Israel and mounted on an old Sherman tank chassis: a unique Israeli design that recycled WWII surplus tanks. They were unsightly; elegance was not a design priority. But they were ideal for modern artillery duels and desert operation. Thanks to their agility, relative to the traditional towed guns, they could be repositioned quickly to evade anti-artillery fire. They could travel off road, on dunes or behind them, while providing armored protection to their crews. They were cheap, and most importantly, made-in-Israel and thus not subject to embargo by suppliers like France, who in 1967 changed their policy when Israel needed them most. I trained on these cannons and respected their resilience, range and accuracy.

Our cannons started lining up behind the loading ramps. This was a massive operation. I witnessed such loadings before, but never at such large scale. Our brigade alone, I figured, would need at least sixty transporters to carry the cannons and half-tracks. More would be needed to transport many tons of heavy cannon shells, fuel trucks to feed the large tank engines, spare parts, and, of course, buses to carry the crews. The tank brigade of our division would need even more transporters and trucks. I was witnessing the wake-up of a giant. I don't believe any army has ever deployed such a large force in such a short time and so effectively.

We were ready for departure slightly before noon, right on schedule. Cannons and halftracks were checked, equipped and loaded on transporters, supply trucks loaded, ammunition trucks ready and twenty or thirty buses in place to carry the troops.

The "fog of war" persisted. Radio announcements remained vague. They reported of incursions by the Egyptian army into the Sinai and of the Syrian army into the Golan Heights. They reported that the air force destroyed bridges the Egyptians built on the Canal and that Israeli forces were repelling the Syrians, but no details. This was an ideal breeding ground for rumors: hundreds of idle soldiers interacting with each other in an information vacuum. Speculations already put IDF forces in Cairo and Damascus. At the very minimum, these rumors suggested, the invading armies were already destroyed. In our confidence, not one of us imagined that the "fog of war" was hiding the facts that the fighting was not going in our favor and that an existential threat was hanging over our heads.

Our long convoy left the gate and headed south towards the Gaza Strip with most of my surveyors' unit in one bus. Five Jeeps of the scout unit led the way. As we neared major intersections, they sped up to alert the Military Police of our arrival. Traffic had to be stopped to let our convoy through. It was a national security priority; it could not be delayed or broken up by ordinary traffic rules.

We reach El Arish after dark. The huge canteen was dark and its parking lot empty. No one heading to Sinai would stop for a hamburger, and certainly not for condoms. There was hardly anyone traveling in the opposite direction.

We turned west into a narrow two-lane coastal road marked by a road sign reading "Baloza 114 km, Kantara 154 km."[3] The drivers kept their headlights

---

3   71 and 96 miles, respectively.

off, relying on the nearly full moon to illuminate the road as it passed between soft dunes. Sand blown from the dunes covered segments of the road, but their shoulders were marked by the scouts using tiny flashlights, or even by their own Jeeps to assure the drivers did not miss the road. Hitting a soft shoulder with even one wheel of a heavy vehicle could cause it to stop or even roll over and bog down the entire convoy. Traffic slowed considerably.

On the bus, we were oblivious to these difficulties. Exhausted from a sleepless night and two stressful days, we dosed on and off in our seats. Sitting by the window, I occasionally woke up to notice our location. Patriotic music from the bus radio provided some background noise.

A news brief at midnight recycled the old news:

"*The Egyptian army continues its attacks on several sectors along the Suez Canal but our forces are pushing them back. The Air Force destroyed most of the bridges built across the Canal. On the Golan Heights, Syrian troops broke the line but Israeli forces are pushing them back.*" I dozed off again.

The news brief did not tell us that the Bar-Lev line was no more. The most fortified line in history, the line built to hold off any Egyptian crossing, collapsed within a few hours. Half of its *Maozim* already fell or were evacuated, most of their men killed, wounded or taken prisoners. (27 p. 45) Lituf, the *Maoz* I helped build, was the first to fall. On Sunday afternoon, as we were leaving the gates of our base, secure in our belief of the invincible might of the IDF, Lituf had been overrun.

The brief did not mention that the air force had lost dozens of its planes; that the Egyptian surface to air missile (SAM) system along the Canal prevented the air force from attacking the Egyptian bridges; that a new generation of portable anti-tank guided missiles, Saggers, had already destroyed or damaged tens of Israeli tanks; that the Egyptians had developed an ingenious method to cross the canal and had more than a dozen replaceable bridges. (31 p. 223) The news did not mention that the Syrians breached the line on the Golan Heights and that several Syrian tanks were already at the edge of the Golan Heights looking down at the Sea of Galilee. The "fog of war" was dense indeed.

MONDAY, OCTOBER 8, 1973

Monday morning's rising sun woke me up. We were standing still in a traffic jam, miles from Baloza. Kupy and two others crouched in the aisle over three campsite gas stoves preparing Turkish-Bedouin coffee and cracking off color jokes. Behind him I saw the bus driver lying on the floor, sound asleep.

One of my soldiers, whose name I had yet to learn, was sitting on the driver's seat, engine cut, waiting for the convoy to start moving. The first news brief of the morning repeated the news of last night.

When he saw I was awake, Kupy handed me a cup of fresh brewed coffee. It was strong and sweet. It remained thick even after the grounds settled to the bottom. He had made enough for everyone. Despite his large moustache and manly behavior, I started to see him as our doting mother.

After clearing out the coffee operation, Kupy took control of the intercom microphone and announced that he would begin taking wagers, one Israeli pound per person, predicting the last day of our deployment. Winner takes all. If there was no winner, then the pot would remain in his hands for communal benefit. Most wagers favored the fifth day of the Sukkot holiday, six days from now. Only two thought that by Simchat Torah, 11 days away, we would be home. Not even one of us considered betting on a later date.

I got off the bus to stretch. Beautiful dunes lay on both sides of the road. The early morning sun painted their soft curves in reddish colors. I walked behind one of them. The silence and stillness of the desert enveloped me. The soft dunes absorbed the sounds of the men waking up. I sat down and closed my eyes. The warmth and the stillness among the softly curved mounds of sand made me feel like I was back in the womb.

I returned to the still-idle convoy. The road ahead and behind us was filled with buses and transporters standing bumper-to-bumper, one behind the other.

It suddenly occurred to me that a single Egyptian MiG could destroy this entire convoy in a single flyover. To reinforce my grim thoughts I noticed a short convoy of five civilian pickup trucks heading east, back to Israel, weaving their way among the stranded vehicles. They were driven by bearded men wearing black yarmulkes and white shirts. They were Rabbis, recruited just like us from their synagogues on Yom Kippur to give final rites to the fallen. They passed by us slowly, almost at walking speed. The drivers kept to themselves and did not respond to questions. But the tarp at the back of one of the trucks was not fully closed. I peeked in. The floor was covered with dead bodies covered by military blankets. Their feet still wore IDF issued black boots showing through the blankets. The revolting sweet stench of decaying bodies was a clear sign that they were a day or two old, the very first casualties of the war. There were at least fifty dead in this convoy. Apart from Liora's unusual mobilization, it was the first sign I had that this was not like the Six-Day War.

Were they from one sector along the Canal or all three sectors? There had to be casualties along the Syrian front too. Could our casualties already be in the hundreds? The news briefs had not mentioned casualties. If they had been low, the news would have mentioned it. The omission suddenly seemed ominous. The "fog of war" that only moments ago seemed like a promising sign turned into a concern.

More convoys carrying additional fallen soldiers passed us throughout the day. Still miles away from Baloza, a platoon of Israeli Centurion tanks passed on the dunes near us heading east. The tank commanders stood exposed in their turret as they normally do, even during battle. Their faces were covered with goggles, sand and soot. Their torsos were bent and their shoulders sagged. They did not flash the customary V sign when they saw us. They did not cheer. A few of the tanks carried their dead, limp bodies covered with military blankets, tied on stretchers to the side panels.

Our second day on the bus ended with the Chief of Staff Lieutenant General Dado Elazar speaking to the nation for the first time since the war started. "We will break their bones," he promised when speaking about the enemy.

Moments after that fateful broadcast, aides would put on his desk reports of the day's battles. They would translate into terrible statistics; two days into the war our casualties were already in the hundreds.

An hour later Dado would receive another report describing how the first tank battalions of our division to reach the canal were mauled by the Egyptian infantry. Not by tanks. The Soviet made anti-tank portable Saggers were missiles that the Israeli intelligence dismissed as just another run-of-the-mill anti-tank weapon. (31 p. 35) One entire battalion was destroyed and its commander, Lt. Col. Yaguri, taken prisoner. (31 pp. 246-248) The other units retreated after suffering heavy losses and without scoring any gains. The platoon I saw that morning was all that remained of those battalions. No wonder they didn't cheer.

At the end of the second day the Egyptian Army Chief of Staff, Lieutenant General Shazly, noted in his diary the wide gap between the quality and fighting spirit of the Israeli units in the field and the senior command in headquarters: "They are evidently made of better stuff than their senior commanders." (32)

By the time we reached Baloza late at night, reality had already caught up with Elazar. The new order he issued to the Israeli armored divisions in Sinai commanded them to minimize direct contact with the two Egyptian armies that crossed the canal and to minimize casualties. It would take more than a week before Israeli forces took another initiative in Sinai. It was mostly left to us, the artillery, to continue the fighting in the south while the northern divisions on the Golan Heights, with heavy air force support, pushed back the invading Syrian army and then moved across the ceasefire line to within twenty miles of the outskirts of Damascus.

OCTOBER 9, 1973

After more than thirty hours on the road in interminable traffic jams, our brigade reached its first position, a few miles west of the Lateral Road, just past Baloza. The Artillery Road that was built specifically for times like this was ten miles further west, in enemy hands. The Lateral Road that was designed to provide secure passage outside the Egyptian artillery range became the new Artillery Road. We only had a few artillery positions designated there under just-in-case scenario. Instead of guiding the brigade's cannons into prepared positions, we had to scout and find new ones and survey their coordinates while the cannons were unloaded.

Shortly after, our brigade was finally an active fighting unit. Heavy cannon fire began landing on positions of the Egyptian Second Army, mostly east of the Canal, on what only days earlier was Israeli territory.

It did not take long for the Egyptian artillery to retaliate. Using advanced radar systems, they tracked the trajectories of incoming shells and successfully located their origin, often after only one or two shells were fired. Their response was swift and mostly accurate.

These capabilities may not seem too radical four decades later where field computers can analyze the trajectory of a rocket while in flight and guide a missile to intercept it. But in 1973, even the largest computers had less computing power than a twenty-first-century cell phone. All our calculations, by the surveyors or the artillery officers, were performed manually or graphically on large charts. The IDF was still testing experimental field artillery computers. But the Egyptians, or rather the Soviets, already had computers capable of analyzing radar data and control their cannons.

To minimize losses, our cannons had to "leap" frequently and fast. Each such leap required my surveyors' unit to locate a new position and measure its coordinates. The precisely measured coordinates allowed the artillery officers to re-engage previous targets quickly and accurately. We were busy traveling along and off the Lateral Road, scouting new positions for batteries and battalions and surveying them.

Our job required cool nerves to stand on a dune, leveling theodolites, measuring angles at precisions of arc-seconds, and then sit with trigonometric and logarithmic tables on our laps and compute coordinates without errors, at precisions of centimeters, while a war was raging around us. At night we had to use light sparingly not to disclose our positions to enemy commandos who might have been scouting. The surveyors did not fire a single shot throughout the entire war and yet thousands of artillery shells reached their targets thanks to our work.

We were surprised during our first days at the front by the lack of air force presence, neither Israeli nor Egyptian. We expected the air force to make up for our relatively smaller artillery force. But like many other puzzling observations those days, we discovered the true reasons months or even years later. We assumed that the Israeli air force was preoccupied in the north and once the war on the Golan Heights was decided it would be freed up to support us. But in reality, the SAM systems along the canal kept Israeli planes off a strip stretching fifteen miles east of the canal. The air force suffered terrifying losses during the first day and night of the war trying to demolish the Egyptian bridges. In the following days it avoided entering those missiles' range. On the other hand, outside that dangerous strip, Israeli planes enjoyed overwhelming superiority that deterred Egyptian planes from bothering us. This invisible umbrella protected us in our positions throughout the war; it protected our convoy when it was stuck for more than a day in traffic jams; it protected our deployment base during the first night, the bus terminals in Haifa and Tel Aviv, and the entire State of Israel.

For days we engaged in artillery duels with the Egyptian's Second Army. Our battalions would go into a position we selected, fire a few shells from each cannon and when anti-artillery came in they would "leap" to a new position that we prepared while they had set up and fired in the previous position. Some of their fire was intended to support the armored unit holding the line, some to make enemy artillery batteries uncomfortable and some to engage targets that our division selected. But at sunset, the front calmed down. It was as if both armies were operating on an 8 to 6 schedule. Our units switched positions one last time for the day but held fire to keep their locations undetected, thereby having some advantage should fire resume at night. Thankfully, the Egyptian artillery chose to keep the same schedule. At least we got some rest at night.

Our first night along the Lateral Road we bivouacked[4] with the brigade headquarters in a flat area protected by dunes all around.

---

4   Bivouac—a French-origin term describing a temporary and unsheltered camp.

We parked our half-tracks in a rectangle, dug foxholes in the sand that looked like shallow graves and set our sleeping bags inside. Each squad lit up a small campsite gas burner at the foot of their half-track and warmed up their rations. I joined forces with Kupy who, once again, demonstrated his cooking skills converting Luf[5] and bully beef into edible substances.

We sat in the dark, whispering quietly, smoking and listening to small transistor radios playing patriotic music and news at low volume. The nearly full moon rose later than the previous night and the darkness that is unique to the desert brought the stars closer. The Milky Way was strikingly visible and the constellations easily identifiable. Despite the day's events, the night was quiet and calm.

Then the commander of our scout unit came by and asked to talk to me. Our headquarters had received intelligence reports that Egyptian commando units were prowling in the area. The beautiful serene night turned into a frightening jungle teeming with danger. Our soldiers were not trained in close range combat. The thought of facing commando units was daunting. The dunes surrounding us that only a moment ago we saw as secure and cozy turned into monstrous traps.

I moved our lead half-track near the top of the dune with only its machine gun visible from the other side and posted a guard. The scouts and the headquarters covered the other dunes. We had machine guns facing outwards in all directions.

The bivouac turned dark and quiet, gas stoves were turned off, cigarettes extinguished and radios silenced. We tried to blend with the dark and quiet desert.

Lying in my foxhole and watching the skies, I wondered if other intelligent species who must be living on one of the planets that orbited the stars above were also busy killing members of their own species. Was our civilized life condemned to destroy itself?

A bright dot travelling slowly across the dark sky grabbed my attention. It was neither a star nor a satellite. The next day, news briefs reported that an Egyptian FROG[6] ground-to-ground rocket hit Rephidim, our main base in Sinai, killing several soldiers.

The night was quiet. Although commandos were dropped by helicopters inside our territory, our brigade did not encounter any. Not yet. Egyptian artillery remained quiet as well, and so did we. Until Kupy started setting up his

---

5   Luf was the IDF version of Spam. It was kosher but looked and tasted just like Spam.
6   FROG—a NATO acronym—Free Rocket Over Ground.

morning coffee-brewing operation, that is. Muffled explosion, "exits," from the west marked the start of a new "business day."

The first shell landed within seconds behind one of the dunes surrounding us. A mushroom cloud of smoke and sand marked its impact.

We rolled up our sleeping bags in record time as the drivers who slept inside their half-tracks revved their engines. A second shell landed in the valley just short of our bivouac. One shell long, the second short, the third I knew would be a direct hit. We scrambled to move. Thirty seconds later, a shell hit our previous position.

There had to be a spotter watching us from behind one of these dunes, I thought. We were the headquarters unit, not a firing battery. We did not generate cannon flares or fly-in-the-air shells that would betray our location. Their artillery could use radio signals to locate us, but we were not the only ones using radio. Someone was watching and "walking" the fire towards us.

The scouts broke up into three units and went out to look for those spotters. Moments later, almost drowned by the loud explosions of the barrage landing on our old bivouac, we heard a few bursts of machine guns firing about a mile away. A brief radio message from the scouts' commanders confirmed in code language that two Egyptian commandos were eliminated.

Leaping from position to position along the Lateral Road became a routine. Avoiding anti-artillery fire became second nature. We learned to eat our meals while on the move, sleeping on the ground with no tent, fully dressed, in our shoes, ready to move on thirty seconds' notice. Any delay could cost lives.

After a few days we ran out of new firing positions along the Lateral Road and two miles to its east and west. Old positions had to be recycled.

Radio news briefs began dispersing the "fog of war." Instead of claims of quick and decisive victories, reports described losses and setbacks. A new reality of a war of survival settled in the minds of the Israeli public, soldiers in the field, and even more so in the minds of the military and political leadership. Moshe Dayan was overheard saying to Prime Minister Golda Meir that the Third Temple was about to fall. (31 p. 231) After the fall of Solomon's Temple in the hands of the Babylonians and Herod's Temple in the hands of the Romans, the State of Israel was about to fall too. The illusion that the enemy would be easily repelled burst like a bubble.

Newspapers painted a sad picture of an army caught unprepared. Maps outlined the territories lost to Egypt and Syria. The situation to the north was far more critical than in Sinai. The Golan Heights did not have the same strategic depth. If the Syrians had not been pushed back within the first day, they might have threatened northern Israel. Pundits suggested that for the time being, Israel should put all its efforts into winning the war on the Golan Heights and just holding the line in Sinai.

This analysis partly explained why Israeli planes were hardly visible in Sinai. Fortunately, even the little air cover that was available was sufficient to prevent Egyptian planes from attacking Israeli ground troops.

But simply holding the line meant that the Egyptians east of the Canal were now digging in. As the days passed, Elazar's promise to "break their bones" was almost comical, had it not affected us so tragically.

Even before the first day of the week-long Sukkot holiday, we all understood that there would be no winner in the wager that Kupy arranged during our bus ride. But for sure, we thought, we would be home by Hanukkah. That was two months away. No one wants to fight in the winter, we argued, and released the wager pot to Kupy's management.

Desert combat might be ideal for military maneuvers but it is far from ideal for human comfort. Water was delivered in small tankers towed in from a distant base. It was precious and the delivery unpredictable. We were permitted to approach the tanker only with canteens in hand that could be refilled as often as desired. We were forbidden from drinking or washing directly from the tanker. The long lines discouraged us from refilling the canteens for purposes other than drinking. We did not shower, shave, or even brush our teeth. Hygiene took a back seat, far in the back. After a few days, bearded smelly men in dirty uniforms became the new normal.

Just before we ran out of rations a new delivery arrived: bully beef, Luf, sardines, canned corn and beans, no fresh fruits or vegetables. But to our relief, reserves of the standard rations ran out and the next delivery brought surprises. The five-man or ten-man ration boxes were filled with cans that were clearly pulled off supermarket shelves, still carrying the original manufacturer's labels. Sardines were replaced with tuna cans, Luf with chicken goulash, and salted peanuts with roasted almonds. Even desserts were augmented by canned exotic fruits. I could almost see supply officers in uniform running down supermarket aisles, pushing carts and emptying shelves of canned food.

Man can get used to anything. Playing artillery duels with the Egyptian artillery turned into a routine, we did not even wait for their "exits" to order a new "leap." "Business hours" were from sunrise to sunset and if they disturbed our sleep one night, we disturbed theirs the following night. The unshaved stubble of our beards stopped itching and the smell of men who had not showered or washed in more than a week blended into the sharp smell of fuel exhaust and exploding fire powder.

After our second night on the Lateral Road the threat of commandos dissipated and we felt confident enough to resume warming our rations on open fires. Kupy's crate became our social center. He turned sliced Luf into hamburgers, sardines and tuna into fish fry, and canned corn and beans into soup garnished with croutons made of dried biscuits and ancient bread. From sources that he kept to himself he "commandeered" a bag of military coffee that with his Bedouin brewing technique became almost tolerable. There was even schnapps in the crate that he generously shared when we lit our cigarettes after dinner. Kupy enjoyed life to its fullest and would not let a war stand in his way. But he did not let his guard down; he cooked and we ate and socialized with flak jackets on, weapon and helmet at our side and sentries watching from all the dunes around us.

After dinner we rolled out our sleeping bags, placed them in our personal fox holes, crawled in and listened to radio reports of the day's events. The updates remained vague, no mention of losses of lives or territories. Analysis and projections of the future course of the war that followed the briefs reminded the weather forecast of an approaching storm. Like the weatherman, commentators did not really knew where would it hit, they just knew it was coming. Between such reports, the radio carried music and messages from home to soldiers in the front.

One evening, laying in my foxhole by my half-track, smoking and watching the starry sky I caught the message: *"To my beloved husband, Gaby, serving somewhere in Sinai, with love from your wife Liora from Haifa who misses you so much."* I wished I could send her my love too. Not knowing where I was, or even if I was alive, Liora needed my message more than I did.

Rumors of IDF forces crossing the canal had swirled from the first moments of the war. By the end of the first week they were all discredited. But then new rumors of an upcoming crossing began circulating. The rumor machine speculated that a unit from General Ariel Sharon's division was already scouting the opposite side. Briefings of the artillery brigade command that I attended daily could not confirm any of these. However, the impressive improvement on the Syrian front, with IDF forces already moving into Syrian territory and possibly threatening the outskirts of Damascus, suggested that the standoff in the southern front might break soon.

I didn't believe crossing the canal was likely. Before any crossing could take place, we had to reach the Canal through the well-fortified positions of two Egyptian armies. But the rumors persisted.

During one of our artillery duels, a Jeep stopped by our headquarters, just off the Lateral Road. The driver handed out army-issue postcards and promised to mail them that day. We swarmed him, dropping everything we were doing. In the week since leaving home we had not received or sent any mail. We couldn't make telephone calls either. Though the brigade had a radiotelephone antenna that could carry telephone conversations, it was fully dedicated to military communication. I was sure that Liora, Zsuzsi, and Laci were frazzled. Each night that passed without a military officer knocking on their door to deliver a death notice meant only that the day before I had still been alive. They, along with the entire population, must have been demoralized.

The green postcards were small, with barely enough room for addresses. But there was little to write anyway. The military censors destroyed cards that carried classified military information that was probably everything other than our military address. Writing that I was not in any danger would be interpreted by Laci or Liora as a lie, a cover-up of the real truth.

The first postcard I wrote home read: "10/11/73. Lovely Liora! Everything is OK. I am rushing because mail is about to be picked up. Don't worry about me and please send my love to my parents. Kisses, Gaby."

That's all!

But the card still carried a little bit of me; a stain that could be grease from my Uzi or my thumb print, my own handwriting and the sense that Liora was touching the same postcard I touched. That was as close as we could get to physical intimacy. I took several cards, sent one and kept the rest in my pocket, ready to send at a moment's notice. All started with, "Everything is fine with me, I am doing well." I only had to add the date and number them serially in the order sent.

I received a letter from Laci three days later. "Dear Gaby, we still have no news from you. We are nervous but we hope that with God's help you are well… We are stuck at home, not daring to leave the phone, and besides, there is nowhere to go…"

MONDAY MORNING, OCTOBER 15

On the tenth day of the war, the brigade got orders to relocate to the central section, just off Tasa. We could not tell if the entire division was moving with us or whether this move was in advance of the next phase of the war. If our brigade commander knew the answers he kept them to himself.

My surveyors' unit and the scouting unit went ahead, traveling south on the Lateral Road to Tasa, a small military base, home of the central section's headquarters and a field hospital. At Tasa we turned west on Akavish, "Spider" in Hebrew, the code name for the "longitudinal" road to the Great Bitter Lake.

Traffic on Akavish was nearly at a standstill. A long row of half-tracks and armored personnel carriers (APC's) filled with soldiers, Jeeps with large antennae and machine guns on their hoods, command cars and trucks, all heading towards the Canal. Only a few vehicles, all with blaring sirens and flashing headlights carrying casualties, were going back to Tasa.

Two idle tanks just off the road were attached with heavy towlines to a gigantic metal box, mounted on large drums that most likely were its rollers. We moved slowly with the traffic past that strange structure. I could only speculate that it was a floatation device, a raft or possibly a link for a floating bridge.[7] (31 p. 359)

If I needed any confirmation that the convoy, the strange device towed by the tanks, and most likely our own brigade were heading to the canal, several half-tracks we passed were decorated with signs "Cairo Express" or "Sadat, we are coming for you."

The mood in Sinai was changing from somber and confused to excited and confident. Nothing happened yet, no one crossed yet. But the passive, stationary phase was coming to an end. We were taking an initiative. Maybe we were finally going to "break their bones."

A few miles further on Akavish road and a few hours after idling in traffic, we turned towards the dunes south of the road to a spot selected by the brigade commander for our command post. It was on the slope of a ridge facing the canal. It was visible from the Canal, hardly an ideal place for the command post of a primary artillery unit. But at least the cannons would be hidden behind the ridge, I thought. And if anything would happen in this "theatre," we would have a front row seat.

Traveling on their tracks, the cannons could move across the dunes and avoid the Akavish traffic. They reached their positions moments after we completed measuring their coordinates, positioned themselves with barrels

---

7   Rabinovich also described them as British-made Unifloat pontoons consisting of iron cubes linked together. The Army Engineering Corps filled the cubes with polystyrene foam (Styrofoam) to ensure their floatation even if their skin is punctured.

pointing towards the northern end of the Great Bitter Lake and waited for new orders.

In the afternoon, we saw for the first time in this war, Israeli planes providing ground support. One Skyhawk at a time arrived from the east and while still far from the Artillery Road pulled steeply upward in a tight arch ending with the inverted plane facing back east, away from the canal. But midway through that arch, it released all its bombs.

Watching from below, I was horrified. The bombs at first appeared to be flying at us. Then they passed us overhead and continued flying west, hitting Egyptian forces well beyond the Artillery Road that marked their line. I realized that the centrifugal force that helped eject the bombs also accelerated them towards the Egyptian positions.

This was a maneuver designed to drop a nuclear bomb from high altitude. Once the bomb was released, it flew in one direction, while the plane flew in the opposite direction, away from the nuclear blast and radioactive radiation. In Sinai, the bombs were traveling to their targets while the Skyhawks were flying away from the SAMs and the anti-aircraft fire directed at them.

Despite the clever technique, I saw one plane being hit. A long and slender cigar-like missile rose from the dunes behind the Egyptian lines aiming at the approaching Skyhawk; the pilot noticed it and released flares that exploded midair. But they did not fool the missile.

We watched the explosion with anguish, the plane caught fire and then two objects ejected from the burning plane. They fell side by side for a short while, and then a white and orange parachute opened above one of them. A light westerly wind carried the pilot eastward, towards our lines. The other piece, the canopy, reached ground on the Egyptian side.

Soon after the last plane disappeared, our brigade started heavy shelling. From the ridge we could see our shells exploding north of the Great Bitter Lake.

"*I think they're firing at the 'Chinese Farm,'*" Kupy explained. He knew the place from the Six-Day War and from his contractor work during the Attrition War.

The Chinese Farm was an experimental desert farm developed for Egypt before the Six-Day War by Japanese contractors. It included several buildings and numerous irrigation canals. When Israeli soldiers captured it in 1967, they found equipment with labels in Japanese. Confusing the Japanese characters with Chinese, they named the location "The Chinese Farm." The name stuck in the Israeli terminology.

The farm, abandoned since 1967, was recaptured by the Egyptian army on the afternoon of Yom Kippur. The dried-out irrigation canals made excellent trenches to accommodate and protect an entire infantry division of the Second Army charged with holding the northern section of the canal.

From the southern end of the Chinese Farm that division controlled a five-mile stretch of a dirt road named Tirtur that ran nearly parallel to Akavish, from the Artillery Road to Lexicon. It ended at the gate of *Maoz* Matsmed, a Bar-Lev line fort on the northern shore of the Great Bitter Lake.

Two years earlier, while still the commander of the Southern Command, General Sharon observed that Matsmed was an ideal site for a bridgehead in the event that Israeli forces chose to cross the canal. With the Great Bitter Lake providing a natural obstacle, he reasoned, the southern flanks of the Israeli forces would be well-protected while crossing.

Unaware that Matsmed would provide another significant advantage during the Yom Kippur War, Sharon ordered it to be prepared for its role as a bridgehead by building a yard the size of several football fields that was protected by tall ramparts. The yard was planned as the staging area for bridge assembly, the crossing forces, forces that protect the bridge and to manage the crossing. The walls would provide cover from direct fire and hide activities from the Egyptians. Furthermore, a section of the wall facing the canal was thinned relative to the rest, allowing it to be knocked down to pass the bridge.

The plan, that at times seemed unlikely, also considered various bridging techniques. Irrespective of the technique, it acknowledged that a straight road, passing through a flat area, and aligned with the openings of the yard would be needed to deliver the bridging equipment. Typical of his aggressive nature, Sharon ordered Tirtur Road to be built.

Now, ten days into this new war, *Maoz* Matsmed and Tirtur Road sprang from obscurity as the chosen site for the upcoming crossing. Whether it was the insight of a genius, luck, or divine intervention, Sharon could not have picked a better location for the crossing for reasons even he could not have foreseen.

The final decision to cross the Canal was made by the Israeli cabinet early that day. (31 p. 358) A few days earlier, a unit from General Sharon's division discovered that most of the eastern shores of the Great Bitter Lake and a mile long section of the Israeli side of the Canal north of it remained mostly unoccupied by Egyptian forces. It was a no-man's-land.

The Egyptian Third Army holding the southern section of the canal assumed that Israeli forces were unlikely to attempt crossing through the Great

Bitter Lake and thus preferred to concentrate its forces along the canal itself south of the lake, thereby leaving its shores exposed.

The Second Army, tasked with holding the east bank of the canal north of the lake saw the Chinese Farm, with its complex structure of dried-out irrigation canals, as a perfect site for an infantry division. From that location they controlled Tirtur Road and had oversight of Akavish Road. But by pure lapse of judgment, they left Akavish Road unoccupied, the section of the canal north of the lake and most importantly, Fort Matsmed and the bridgehead yard.

This little keyhole, through which Israeli forces could slip into Egyptian territory on the other side of the Canal, was right under the nose of Sharon, who, from the first day of the war was obsessed with crossing and who intimately knew the virtues of Matsmed as the chosen crossing site.

Although Matsmed, the yard and most of Akavish were mostly clear of Egyptian forces, the southern end of the Chinese Farm controlled Tirtur as well as the last section of Akavish before reaching Lexicon—the Canal road. If Israel was to establish a secure bridgehead, the Chinese Farm had to be cleared. The aerial attack we witnessed that afternoon and our heavy artillery shelling that followed were the prelude to the battle for the Chinese Farm. Many of the vehicles that filled Akavish Road that Monday morning were part of the paratroopers' brigade heading to the Chinese Farm and towards one of the deadliest battles in Israeli history.

But even before the paratroopers attacked the Chinese Farm, several rubber boats and inflatable rafts were smuggled during the night between Monday and Tuesday to Matsmed and by Tuesday morning a paratrooper brigade and a tank battalion were operating on the Egyptian side of the canal. When the battle on the Chinese Farm ended, the road to the Canal and in effect the road to Cairo was open. In slightly more than a week, the war had turned dramatically in Israel's favor.

It was now our turn to provide a surprise. The Egyptians did not expect to encounter Israeli units on their side of the Canal. The few reserves they kept back were concentrated around Cairo to protect the regime. Finding no resistance after landing in Egypt, the Israeli tank battalion began moving freely within a radius of twenty miles of the bridgehead, clearing SAM missile batteries and removing the obstacles to the operation of the Israeli air force in that area. Quite uniquely in military history, ground forces were providing support to the air force.

TUESDAY, OCTOBER 16, 1973

On Tuesday morning, we returned to Akavish Road to scout and prepare new positions for the brigade's batteries that supported the paratroopers fighting in the Chinese Farm throughout the night in what was expected to be a quick and decisive clash with inferior forces. Instead the paratroopers were vastly outnumbered by an Egyptian division dug into the dried-out canals. Although the Egyptians incorrectly read the true intent of this battle and its critical importance to Israel's plans, they fought bitterly, motivated by the ambition to protect the territory east of the Canal that they viewed as a sign of their victory.

After surveying the new positions along Akavish road we returned to "our" dune to watch the Canal area. The Canal itself was barely visible but the Great Bitter Lake stood out through the mid-day desert haze like a turquoise gemstone in the parched yellow desert. From a distance it looked like a fresh water lake, an exotic vacation spot.

Israeli planes, Skyhawks and Phantoms, appeared occasionally from the east to bomb the Chinese Farm area using the "Back Flip" maneuver.

By midday, the fight at the Chinese Farm slowed. It would resume at full intensity after sunset. Meanwhile, the Egyptian artillery that was freed from supporting its own fighting units turned its attention to us. Their shelling was directed mostly towards the batteries that in response began "leaping" between the alternative positions we prepared. But they also targeted us. Several shells exploded on the dunes near us, two of them only feet away from where I sat.

The explosions, almost simultaneous with the sickening whistle of the incoming shell, were deafening. A huge sand cloud rose and showered me and the three men sitting next to me with hot sand filling our eyes and nostrils. But amazingly not one of us was hurt. As we later figured out, the deep sand protected us by absorbing the shrapnel of the shells that got buried in the deep sand by the strength of their own impact. Had the shells explode on hard rocky surfaces, where shrapnel is not absorbed, and with exploding rock fragments added to the mayhem, the outcome would have been vastly different.

The Egyptian shelling stopped as abruptly as it had begun.

The close call rattled me. It was the first time in my entire military service that I reflected on my own mortality. Despite the close call that suggested we had been spotted by the Egyptian artillery, we were ordered to remain in place, exposed to another possibly deadly round of shelling.

A new, sobering thought came to my mind: an aide to a general in Tasa's command bunker must have estimated that morning the number of casualties that the command would be willing to sacrifice to achieve the day's objectives. I, like anyone else in my unit, the brigade or the division was nothing more than a statistic in his projections. The aide and his general who were safely protected in their bunker did not care who the day's casualties were as long as the objectives were met and the numbers did not significantly exceed their projections. To them, I was not a person with a name, life, and family. I was simply a pawn on their chessboard that had to be sacrificed to play the game.

Until that moment that was a foreign thought to me. But when the order to stay put came, despite the almost certain upcoming shelling, I wondered if that morning's sunrise was my last. The feeling that each new sunrise could be my last did not leave me until weeks after the war ended.[8]

An hour later we were ordered to leave that targeted spot.

That night, Prime Minister Golda Meir announced to the Knesset that "at this moment, while we are convening in a Knesset meeting, an IDF force is operating on the west side of the Canal." (33) Crossing the Canal was no longer a rumor, it was happening, and we were part of the effort. Finally the war in Sinai reached its turning point.

It was, however, an unfortunate and poorly thought-out announcement. The Egyptian army had not yet realized that Israeli forces were operating on their side of the canal. And even if they had, they assumed it was a small and irrelevant effort. Fortunately, their leadership dismissed that announcement as nothing more than bragging. (31 p. 393)

Under the cover of darkness, while the battle for the Chinese Farm was still raging, Israeli tanks towed the pontoon bridge sections I saw on Akavish the day before to the yard. The Egyptian infantrymen fighting for their lives in the Chinese Farm didn't notice the tanks or the massive structures they were towing and let them pass without harm. The sections were assembled at first light and by midday they became the first Israeli bridge spanning the Canal. The bridge was completed before the Chinese Farm, Akavish Road, or the bridgehead on the opposite side were fully secure.

---

8 When I think today of Laci's endurance during his labor service in Hungary and in a German concentration camp I cannot help wondering if he too looked at each sunrise as possibly being his last. If so, what gave him the fierce determination to continue fighting, suffering another day and another day, hoping that one day in the distant future his suffering would end?

WEDNESDAY, OCTOBER 17, 1973

On Wednesday morning, our brigade slowed its fire. But soon explosions of our shells in the Chinese Farm area were replaced by much larger explosions. We could not see the Israeli planes, but they had to be the source of those massive explosions. We did not realize it then, but finally the shield of SAM missiles that protected the Egyptian forces was gone. Israeli planes could provide our ground forces close support.

Late in the morning, a convoy of military Jeeps, their canopies removed, passed by our position rushing effortlessly on the dunes leaving behind a trail of sand clouds. They were equipped with multiple radio antennae, evidence that they served high-level commanders who were listening to multiple bands. Two colonels rode in the lead Jeep. In the Jeep behind them, sitting in the front, to the right of the driver, was the Defense Minister, General Moshe Dayan. Though dressed in standard battle uniform without rank insignia he was easily recognized by his black eye patch. A true politician, he waved at our cheers and applause.

After arriving from Tel Aviv by helicopter, Dayan was heading to Adan's headquarters less than a mile from our position for a conference with Adan, Sharon, Bar Lev, and Chief of Staff Elazar to finalize plans for the crossing of Adan's division, our division.

Sharon, who envisioned the crossing years earlier, designed and built the bridgehead area near Matsmed, discovered the breach between the two enemy armies, fought to secure the Sinai side of the bridgehead and even suffered an injury at the yard the day before from an Egyptian air attack, was ordered to stay behind.[9] (31 p. 408)

From our perch on the dune that afternoon we noted a new battle erupting along the southern shores of the Great Bitter Lake. Our dune was as close as one could get to battlefield stadium seating. Except that we were not mere spectators, we were actors in the following scene.

The small distant explosions we saw along the shores were accompanied by occasional fires that released tall black smoke plumes. Soon an entire section of the shore was dotted with dozens of black plumes reaching up like thin curly fingers.

---

[9] Sharon was denied the right to cross the canal because of earlier incidents in which he was accused of being insubordinate. Elazar ruled against him during that meeting in Adan's headquarter, out of fear that he might lose control of Sharon once on the other side.

I pulled out one of our theodolites, set it up on a tripod and pointed the telescope towards one of the smoke plumes. The theodolites telescope image was inverted, the smoke plume in the eyepiece was pointing down. But with the high magnification I could tell that it was attached to a burning tank. The desert haze and the blinding afternoon sun low in the western skies prevented me from telling if the burning tanks were Israeli or Egyptian. But I knew that in each of those far away, toy-like vehicles were two or three men who were alive and healthy in the morning and were now dead or badly burned. This was not a soccer game where a hurt player jumps to his feet after the referee blows his whistle. In this game the fallen would never rise. This game was played without referees.

The evening radio news briefed that an armored brigade from our own division ambushed the Egyptian Twenty-Fifth Brigade near the Great Bitter Lake and destroyed it while suffering only minimal losses.[10] (31 p. 412) The "fog of war" was lifting. I was relieved to hear the news mention that Israeli casualties were low. But it was still sad that so many died in front of my eyes, whether friends or enemies.

With this victory, the strength of the Egyptian Army on our side of the Canal was diminished significantly. The destruction of this Egyptian brigade was necessary for the success of our full-scale crossing. Egyptian tanks that could be deployed back across the Canal to foil our incursion were destroyed. The Egyptian generals, once they realized that we were at their backs, had to make a painful choice: protect their gains in this war on the east side of the Canal and abandon their rear, or protect their rear but abandon their gains.

Later that day the Chinese Farm was finally cleared and Tirtur Road opened. Our division along with our artillery brigade could cross the Canal with confidence.

THURSDAY, OCTOBER 18, 1973

Simchat Torah is the last day of the Sukkot holiday. Even the most pessimistic wager taken by Kupy on the bus ride was officially lost. By the end of that day I would be the farthest away from home in my life. The next holiday on the horizon was Hanukkah, two months away.

Back home, in a normal year, Simchat Torah was a joyful holiday. Stores and businesses close like on the Sabbath. Many Israelis hit the road heading to

---

10   Abraham Rabinovich, p. 412.

picnics or to the beaches. Observant Jews in synagogues celebrate the end of the annual cycle of Torah reading and the start of the new one by dancing in the streets with Torah scrolls in their arms.

But in 1973, Simchat Torah at home was a somber holiday. The war that was closing in on its second week was far from over, victory was not at hand, the list of fallen was growing daily, and many more were recovering in hospital from horrific injuries, mostly burns, sustained in burning tanks. Hundreds were missing: never before had so many Israeli soldiers gone missing. Almost every household had at least one member serving somewhere on the front. Many families had not heard a word since their soldier left in a hurry on Yom Kippur. There was little to celebrate that day.

In Sinai, Simchat Torah was another day of war, like any day for nearly two weeks. Some would lose their lives that day, some would be injured and maimed for life, and many who escaped physical injury would be emotionally scarred.

Israeli planes, free to fly in a twenty or thirty mile radius around the bridgehead, provided consistent ground support. An occasional Egyptian plane that tried to challenge their superiority was promptly shot down.

Early in the morning our brigade received exciting news. In an hour we were to be ready to move west on Akavish Road towards the Canal. Although the range of our cannons could easily reach almost any target on the opposite side, we were slated to cross. It could mean only one thing: the list of our targets would reach farther into Egyptian territory, much farther than any Israeli cannon shell had ever reached.

Some of us speculated that we might end up shelling Cairo. Others joked that if we did, it would be the Eleventh Plague; we could make it into the next edition of the Bible.

Most of the brigade cannons and half-tracks lined up in a long convoy on the dunes off Akavish. A few batteries, true to the "One Foot on the Ground" approach, were left behind as backup. They would join us once we were established on the opposite side.

With the scouts in the lead, we started west. Traffic was heavy, but it moved smoothly. I had traveled this road many times since my first time during the Attrition War, but never with so much anticipation mixed with anxiety.

It was certainly dangerous because stray Egyptian soldiers could still dot the dunes around us. Our cannons moving on their tracks in a long convoy were an inviting target to air attacks, Egyptian artillery, or even a small tank company that could slip through our lines. But it was a historic event. I always dreamed of being part of one. Finally the war was turning in our favor and I was there.

We were leaving one continent and entering another, Israel was in Asia and Egypt was part of Africa. Many see the Canal as the boundary between the two continents, like the Bosporus Straits in Turkey that separate Europe and Asia,

Just before reaching the intersection with Artillery Road we were stopped at a Military Police checkpoint and ordered to wait.

I ordered our half-tracks to spread out on the dunes and got off my vehicle to get my instructions. All traffic to the bridgehead was controlled from that checkpoint, the MP explained. It was released in batches of five vehicles by radio command from the yard after the previous batch was on the bridge. "*The Egyptians were shelling the yard and the bridge and their planes are bombing it fiercely,*" the MP continued. "*You want to get through it and to the opposite side as fast as you can. When you reach Lexicon, you'll be stopped again and cleared to cross. When you reach the bridge, you'll see it is made of floating segments, be sure to have only one vehicle on each segment.*"

We waited nearly half an hour before my batch of four half-tracks and a command car was released. We continued traveling on Akavish towards the intersection with Lexicon, careful not to get off the road where land mines or unexploded ordnance could be waiting. We reached the intersection with Lexicon within minutes and were stopped again by a MP.

A few burned Israeli tanks near the road facing in close range several destroyed Egyptian tanks were silent witnesses to the hard battles that raged there last night or the night before. These were only a small fraction of the price paid by the IDF to make our crossing possible.

The Great Bitter Lake glistened a short distance away. The few ships trapped in the lake since the Canal was closed in 1967 were still there, just as I remembered them. I wondered if they were still manned to guarantee that the ships are not considered abandoned and if so, how did the crews feel, sandwiched between two huge fighting armies. It could be scary, I thought, but exciting too. War was different for spectators.

A wide flat plain stretched to our left. Through the hot shimmering air rising from the surface, the white salty crust looked outlandish and hostile. It reminded me of the moonscape image that Neil Armstrong sent back after landing on the moon.

Three or four miles to my right I could see the outlines of *Maoz* Matsmed that overlooked the bridge. I tried to recall if I visited it during my regular service. But the images of all the *Maozim* I visited blurred together. They all looked like Lituf, my first *Maoz*.

Several planes circled the sky above Matsmed like angry wasps. They were too far away to identify.

"Those are Egyptian MiGs," said the MP who was watching them with me. "Just watch! In a minute, two or three Israeli Mirages will show up out of nowhere and shoot down a couple of the MiGs. The rest will flee."

He barely finished his sentence when two Israeli planes that looked like another pair of dots in the clear blue sky, dove from above and with no visible resistance from the MiGs set three on fire. The rest scattered away. The burned MiGs crashed into the lake in front of us.

As soon as the MiGs disappeared the MP cleared us to cross, "Over there is Hatzar-Mavet,"[11] he said pointing towards Matsmed. "*Go three miles on Lexicon, the opening to the court yard will be on your left, turn in and someone will give you instructions. It's quiet now. Race as fast as you can before new MiGs show up or artillery comes down. Hurry and you'll cross before the new round.*"

We drove on Lexicon, running for our lives, passing several burned Egyptian tanks with the dead bodies of their crew lying nearby. I was standing on my seat next to the driver, exposed to get a better view, looking left and right for any motion or threat, my cocked Uzi pointing outward. Another surveyor stood on the front center seat behind the loaded machine gun. But the desert was motionless and quiet.

We passed Matsmed and found the opening to the courtyard, a wide gap in a tall sand embankment. A soldier wearing a helmet and a flak jacket stood at the entrance guiding us to the bridge. The yard was just how I imagined it, a large area fully enclosed by sand walls with only two openings, the one we just entered and another across on the opposite wall. Several bulldozers and tanks were parked near the ramparts. Two military ambulances were parked to my right next to a row of ten or twenty bodies fully covered with military blankets.

The MP at the gate noticed my glance and explained they had died in Hatzar-Mavet and the bridgehead on the other side. The name of this place was not a grim joke after all; it had earned its title. "*Go fast,*" he ordered, "*You don't want to join them.*" We needed to move fast on the bridge while being mindful

---

11   "The Courtyard of Death" in Hebrew; it was the unofficial name of this site.

of the distance between vehicles so that each floating segment carried only one vehicle. "*Last night two tanks got too close to each other and sank the segment they were on,*" he added. "*It held up the crossing for a couple of hours.*"

We drove across *Hatzar-Mavet* and through the opposite opening. We were on the bridge. There were no MiGs in the sky and no shelling. I was fully immersed in my emotions: a mixture of joy, excitement, anxiety, but mostly pride. To my left a short section of the canal ended at the Great Bitter Lake. To my right, a straight blue ribbon stretched to infinity. Another bridge barely a hundred yards from ours was already spanning the canal. I did not know how many crossed the bridge before us, but without a doubt, we were the first artillery unit.

Our half-track barely landed on the opposite side when an enemy MiG started diving towards the bridge. I looked up in horror, but an Israeli Mirage was already chasing it. The pilot noticed the threat and aborted his dive. It was too late for him. A short burst from the Mirage guns ended the brief fight. The MiG exploded over the lake.

From the bridge we continued on a dirt road that was cleared the day before. There were no more checkpoints. The road was lined on both sides by abandoned mud huts surrounded by lush tropical vegetation, fruit trees, and flowering bushes. Next to some of the huts stood cone-shaped mud towers covered with fist-sized holes. Doves, the symbol of peace, flew in and out of those holes. Farm animals, donkeys, geese, chicken were roaming loose. They looked healthy even though the farmers were gone.

We moved slowly, no longer feeling the urgency of getting in and out of *Hatzar-Mavet*, but fully aware of the dangers of small squads, or even individuals, hiding behind the bushes. The paratrooper and tank units that passed before us rushed forward to head off Egyptian reinforcements as far out west as possible. Other units were destroying as many SAM batteries as they could. They could not possibly conduct a thorough search to clear the green strip we were crossing.

Above and behind us another aerial dogfight between MiGs and Mirages took place. It ended with the loss of more MiGs.

I was amazed at the tenacity of the Egyptian air force and the willingness of its pilots to go on what seemed to be suicide missions. It was also reassuring that we were watched and protected from above. We witnessed three attempts to destroy our bridges. Not one MiG had the opportunity to fire its guns. They were all destroyed or fled before firing a single shot and not one of our planes was lost. The enormous advantage of an effective aerial umbrella was evident.

We emerged from the green strip back into the desert and reached a paved road. We turned north and after about a mile reached the gates of an Egyptian military base. A sign in Arabic welcomed us to Deversoir Airbase. We turned into the base when an unarmed Egyptian soldier, wearing a sand-colored uniform, emerged from the field adjacent to the gate with his arms raised. He was the first Egyptian we encountered.

We stopped, and one of the surveyors in the back got off and searched him for weapons or hand grenades while we covered him with our Uzis. After finding him clear, we offered him water that he accepted while blessing us in Allah's name.

We could not keep the prisoner. We had no personnel to guard him and there was no prisoner collection center nearby. To mark him as a prisoner, I ordered him to remove his shoelaces and belt and hand them over to me. That's how our soldiers were treated when sent to the brig. I had an empty bottle filled with water, handed it to him, pointed him in the general direction of the Egyptian line and shooed him away. He started walking slowly, looking back in disbelief. Once he was certain that we would not shoot him in the back, he took off his shoes and began running barefoot towards Egypt. The line could not have been too far and with some water in hand he had a fair chance.

We entered the base, a small airfield next to a cluster of military-style buildings. It reminded me of some of the older Israeli bases that dated back to the British rule in Palestine. The British rule and its architects left their mark on Egypt too.

We selected an open area near the gate for the brigade's headquarters. It had numerous deep trenches that could accommodate almost all our vehicles. At the end of the open field was a deeper trench protected along its sides by two 20 ft high sandbag walls, several layers thick. We assigned that protected space to the brigade's ambulance and a supply truck. My driver selected one trench for us and drove our half-track on an inclined ramp to the bottom. Other than the tall antennae, the entire vehicle was hidden below the surface. I was pleased with the work of the Egyptian Corps of Engineers. In the distance I could hear the rumblings of Egyptian artillery pounding *Hatzar-Mavet*. I felt for the soldiers of the IDF Engineering Corps who had to stand there exposed, directing traffic and repairing the bridge that must have suffered damage from the endless bombardment.

After leaving a squad behind to direct the new arrivals, we headed out with the scouts to prepare positions for the brigade cannons.

An Israeli tank company was parked outside the gate, their crews resting by their treads. We started passing them when two large Egyptian helicopters appeared behind us flying slowly at low altitude along the parked convoy with their rear doors open. They looked like two giant khaki dragonflies. Two soldiers stood by each of the open doors with a barrel between them. It was a surreal sight.

We began firing at the helicopters with our Uzis and machine guns. The tank crews jumped back into their vehicles and joined us with their machine guns. One of the tanks fired its cannon at one of the helicopters. It missed. We witnessed what was possibly the first attempt in military history to use a tank gun as an antiaircraft weapon. The operators of the SAM missile batteries that were destroyed by Israeli tanks tried similarly to mark their place in history by using their missiles as antitank weapons. They too failed. (31 p. 421)

But then a Mirage appeared, and with a short burst of cannon fire blew up one of the two helicopters. The second helicopter managed to drop its barrel in front of the leading tank before it too was hit by the Mirage's cannon fire. The barrel exploded simultaneously with the helicopter. It was a napalm bomb.

This might be a very technical comment, but my surveyors and I were facing a professional challenge. Determining precise coordinates in enemy territory is quite difficult. Normally, surveyors determine new coordinates by measuring distance and azimuth from points whose coordinates they already know. We had no access to the Egyptian list of trigonometrical points. We had to generate our own grid.

We selected two points near Deversoir and used precise observations of the sun and almanacs to determine their coordinates. All calculations were done manually. These two points became the basis for a new grid that we stretched as we moved south all the way to Suez City at the southern end of the canal. Weeks later we connected our Egyptian-side grid with the Israeli grid. We were off by only a few meters, an extraordinary result for artillery applications.[12]

We turned back to Deversoir after establishing the first Israeli coordinate grid in Egypt and marking new artillery battery sites. The vast desert plain was painted red by the setting sun. Behind me a long tail of dust was raised

---

[12] I find it amusing that today even a very simple GPS device can provide far better results in an instant.

by our half-tracks. It must have looked like the dust cloud raised by Pharaoh's chariots and horses chasing the Israelites fleeing Egypt three thousand years earlier, (34) possibly in the same desert plain.

The evening started quietly. To avoid unwanted attention we kept silent and had a full blackout. Thankfully, the Egyptian artillery and air force had not noticed us yet and left us alone. Other than the sounds of muffled explosions from *Hatzar-Mavet* that continued earning its deadly reputation, there was no sound or light to disturb the stillness of the desert.

The third day after the incursion by the paratroopers into the African side of the Canal was coming to an end. Battles between brigades of Adan's division and Egyptian tanks, now west of the Canal, supported by our brigade in the wide plain west of Deversoir must have convinced the Egyptian army command that this was not a localized infiltration. It was only a matter of time before Deversoir registered on their maps as a relevant target for their artillery and air force.

We parked our vehicles in their assigned trenches. Only one command car was left standing in the open field. We set our sleeping bags in the trenches next to our vehicles and divided the night among us, one third remaining awake at all times.

I joined Kupy in his trench to prepare our ration dinners when our medic asked to see me. He was visibly in distress. Embarrassed and fidgety, he told me that he was terrified of being in enemy territory. He was scared of shelling, air attacks, commando raids and even attacks by stray Egyptian soldiers. He understood that others had families too, but he could not get out of his mind the thought of his young children left without a father. He was afraid of sleeping in any of the ditches. He begged to be sent back across the Canal.

I could not do that. Sending a vehicle back at night and passing through *Hatzar-Mavet* once again would be far more dangerous than staying put, and the effort would also put a driver in danger. The medic understood the logic of this argument, and yet his fear was overwhelming. He could not shake it off. I felt for him and wanted to help. And then I looked at the ambulance's ditch, protected by two walls of sandbags and suggested that he sleep there. Nothing could penetrate these walls with direct fire, I explained and it would be nearly impossible for an artillery shell to go over a wall and straight into the ditch in between. It was the safest place in the entire area. I took him off the night watch list and he went to sleep feeling much better.

I went to sleep wearing boots and my flak jacket, my helmet and Uzi at my side. The radio in my half-track kept bringing in conversations from our units and others who shared our frequency. Occasionally it caught a conversation in Arabic.

After midnight, just when I was getting up to attend my shift on the brigade's radio, an artillery barrage landed around us. I never experienced such intensity. The bombs were coming in as if fired by a machine gun. An eerie whistle, sounding like a note from an organ pipe announced the arrival of each one. That whistle didn't sound like any of the cannon or mortar shells aimed at me before. These were Russian-made Katyusha rockets. The Katyushas were 40-year-old technology, a World War II weapon. The Germans called them "Stalin's Organ." With the exception of minor changes, the Russians and all their client nations still used them. Even the IDF established several Katyusha battalions using launchers and rockets seized from Egypt and Syria during the Six-Day War.

Katyusha rockets were typically launched by arrays of launchers mounted on Russian-made trucks. A launcher consisted of a pipe to accommodate the rocket and electrodes to ignite its propellant on command. After being loaded, as many as forty-eight rockets could be fired in a rapid sequence. The recoil of the departing rockets caused the launcher array to sway ever so slightly side to side, causing the stream of rockets to spread out into a narrow fan covering a large area.

Once exploded, the Katyusha rockets sprayed their targets with thousands of razor-sharp shrapnel. Katyushas were not accurate, but deadly when hitting large targets of "soft" objects such as infantry encampment, civilians, or "soft-skinned" vehicles. They were and still are the weapon of choice of terrorists. Their organ-like whistles and their rapid sequence of impact could terrify anyone. The Egyptian artillery wisely selected this weapon against our brigade. The medic was right to be afraid.

Although the rest of the night was quiet, I could not sleep.

FRIDAY, OCTOBER 19, 1973

All my surveyors with the exception of the medic were present for the morning roll call. No one was hurt. The ditches prepared by the Egyptian Corps of Engineers protected well their new owners. The tops of several half-tracks that had remained exposed were scratched by shrapnel, the tires and windshield of the command car that had been parked outside were blown. Only the large craters scattered around the field and several rocket tail sections—still intact—proved that the base had been heavily bombarded.

I sent a soldier to check on our medic. He returned pale and rattled. The medic, the brigade doctor and two other medics were all dead.

One Katyusha rocket, descending towards the ground at a steep trajectory passed above one of the sandbag walls, barely clearing its top. The driver of the supply truck who chose, of all places, to sleep on top of that wall, escaped miraculously injury. The rocket landed between the walls, hitting the ambulance directly and killing everyone sleeping in the safest place in our camp.

The medic and the other three men were the only casualties suffered by my unit and the brigade command unit in the Yom Kippur War.

Two surveyors collected the remains of the fallen, confirmed that they had their dog tags and carried them back across the bridge to the regional collection center at *Hatzar-Mavet*, adding them to the growing rows resting under military blankets.

We were still waiting for our next orders when several MiGs appeared in the sky heading to the Yard. The first MiG started diving when three Mirages materialized out of nowhere. One Mirage locked onto the tail of the diving MiG and shot it down. The remaining MiGs turned around trying to fire on the Mirages. From the ground, the maneuver truly looked like a "dog fight": three pairs of planes chasing each other in one large circle like dogs trying to catch each other's tail. It was not clear to me how it happened, but within seconds three MiGs were in flames spiraling down towards the Great Bitter Lake and three Mirages broke away, unharmed.

The dog fight was hardly over when someone shouted "MiG!" A lone MiG was diving towards an adjacent unit camped behind a sand rampart separating them from our brigade's vehicles.

I ran toward the rampart to take cover when the diving MiG fired its cannons, strafing the soldiers a hundred yards away. A Mirage then arrived firing its cannons and setting the MiG on fire just as the pilot released one of its bombs. I could see the MiG's pilot helmet and his face covered by the visor as he passed by, flames bursting from the fuselage of his plane. His plane crashed and exploded outside the Deversoir base. The bomb he released as the final act of his life exploded, injuring several soldiers. A distinct hiss followed the explosion and a large piece of iron landed on the sand in front of my face. When I reached to touch the still hot shrapnel, the one-inch-long steel fragment burned my fingers. I kept that piece of iron as a souvenir from a courageous Egyptian fighter pilot and the close call I survived.

Deversoir had become too dangerous. It was only a matter of time before another artillery attack or an air raid claimed an even heavier toll. We were ordered to move out of the base quickly and head west towards the open desert plateau. The vast space and our mobility were far better protection than any of the trenches of Deversoir.

More than one hundred thousand rounds of cannon, mortar and Katyusha rockets were fired by the Egyptians at the bridge area and Deversoir throughout the war. Hundreds of MiGs and helicopters raided the area. As I could see for myself, most of them were lost. This small area was one of the deadliest spots of the war. (31 p. 458) More than seven hundred Israelis were wounded or killed securing the bridgehead, assembling and maintaining the bridge or crossing the Canal. The Egyptian toll was even higher.

We returned to the plain behind Deversoir heading west. Taking advantage of the vast flat topography, we spread out trying to avoid the dust plume raised by the vehicle ahead and making it harder for a MiG pilot to hit more than one vehicle in a single dive. From space, our force must have looked like an armada crossing an ocean. The Nile Delta was ahead of us, barely thirty miles away. To our south, the plain was bordered by a low range of hills. To the north was Ismailia, a small town built for the workers of the Suez Canal, though after seven years of conflict along the canal, the town was ruined and abandoned. Behind us, in the distance, another mountain range was part of Israeli territory. That is where we had waited the day before for our turn to cross the canal.

After heading a few miles west we turned south, toward the hills, moving parallel to the Canal. I could see no one ahead or behind us. I could not tell if any Israeli forces had ever passed there, but I would have seen a plume of dust raised by anyone else moving on that plane. Though some enemy tanks or infantry armed with anti-tank weapons could still be loitering, it was sufficiently safe for the cannons to move forward without immediate protection from their division tanks. We were now in a race against time. With the war turning in our favor, Egypt with the support of the Soviet Union was surely going to request a ceasefire that would deny us a clear victory. Only six days earlier, with the initiative still theirs, Egypt and Syria rejected an Israeli proposal for a ceasefire. We could not waste the opportunity we had created to bargain from a position of power.

I was surprised by how excited I was to see the dozens of vehicles speeding through the desert. Despite the unknown dangers in enemy territory and the fresh memories of the recent events, my heart was pounding with exhilaration. I felt trapped in Deversoir. I felt free in the open. There was no threat in sight, not even from the Egyptian artillery and MiGs. They were occupied with *Hatzar-Mavet* and Deversoir.

I was not the only one thinking of the historic significance of our incursion. The news on the radio already mentioned that we were in the Land of Goshen, the biblical land given by Pharaoh to Jacob and his family when they settled in Egypt. (35) I didn't need the radio commentator to see that we were completing a three-thousand-year old circle. We were tracing the Exodus story backward: yesterday we crossed a waterway into the land of Egypt and today in a role reversal we, the Israelis, were galloping through the desert on our own chariots of iron to chase the Egyptians in their own land.

We reached the hills south of the plain and climbed a narrow winding dirt road that goat or camel herders must have trampled over for millennia. By my map, we were heading up the Geneifa Hills. The topography slowed us and forced us to converge the widely spread vehicles into a narrow convoy. Our view was limited by the hills surrounding us, the vehicles ahead and behind me, and the dust we were raising. My driver strained to avoid the ravines just off the road. The considerations of the goat herders did not include the needs of military vehicles when they designed the curves in that road.

My half-track was about to reach the top when I heard a few bursts of machine gun fire from the hill ahead. It was followed by an urgent call on my radio from the scouts' leader just ahead of me for everyone to stop and remain below the top. And then came his report; they had encountered an Egyptian supply convoy a mile to their west. The scouts shot at one of the trucks and hit it, and then took cover behind a fold. The convoy stopped but did not return fire.

I was now in the lead and started slowly moving up until I could see a plateau at the end of the road. An Israeli APC was rushing from the convoy towards us. Its commander stood in his open hatch half-exposed and waving a flag. I checked it out with my binoculars. It was without a doubt an Israeli APC. I could even see its IDF registration number. When it was a short distance away I could hear the commander yelling in Hebrew *"Hold your fire. Hold."* An orange plastic panel tied to its top identified it to Israeli pilots from above as a friendly vehicle. Tragically, the panel was not visible from the ground.

I was horrified. The scouts just hit an Israeli vehicle. I checked the convoy through my binoculars. It included Russian-made ZiL trucks. Hundreds of them were captured from Egypt during the Six-Day War and put to good use. The ZiLs of the convoy were certainly marked with orange panels. But through the blowing desert dust the trucks looked yellow, just like Egyptian vehicles. One reservist was killed.

I found the commander of the scout unit sitting on the ground by his idle Jeep, crying. I sat next to him, put my arms around his shoulder and said nothing. There was nothing I could say that would have made a difference. A moment later we got off the ground and moved on.

Geneifa Hills were actually a plateau. The most prominent topographic feature visible from our position was Mount Ataqa, a giant dark tabletop to our south, near Suez City. It was easy to see that the Egyptian Third Army would be trapped if we could reach the foot of this giant tabletop before a ceasefire took effect. It would no longer matter if they were destroyed or surrendered, half of the Egyptian force that crossed the canal would no longer be able to fight. This would mark a clear victory for us. The possibility was distinct and tantalizing.

The entire convoy reached the plateau and we continued our mad rush south. With Mount Ataqa in sight, our strategy became obvious: get our cannons as far south as we could. Even if we didn't reach the mountain, our shells would.

A few miles further south my driver pointed out a perfectly symmetric conical hill on our right. It was too small to be a volcano and too perfect to be natural. The only feature on my map that could match it was a strange symbol that I did not recognize. It was a SAM missile battery; most likely one of those destroyed by the first tanks to cross the canal.

We stopped with only moments of daylight left to prepare positions for the brigade's cannons. The wide-open plateau was far from ideal for artillery batteries. Flares of firing cannons could be seen by the Third Army in the east, remaining Egyptian forces in the west, and without a doubt, by spotters on Mount Ataqa. But this was not the time to be too orthodox about artillery tactics. We had to expand our territorial bulge as far south as we could while racing against a ticking clock. A ceasefire could be announced at any moment.

We established our new bivouac after sunset, north of a dirt road leading to the Cairo-Suez Highway. At this rate we could reach that highway within a day or two and cut off the main supply route to the Third Army.

Dusk in the desert lingers for a long time, as if the hot sun refuses to go to sleep. When dark finally settled in, our cannons were ready to engage targets in three directions. I never saw such an unusual formation, some cannons pointing south, others to the east, and still others west. The Third Army cannons were probably pointing both east and west as well. But very soon, even if their crews survived, they would be left with no ammunition or fuel.

We arranged our vehicles in a circle, machine guns facing out, and dug foxholes in the rocky desert soil. Remembering the previous night's ordeal, we dug them deeper than usual. After a dinner of cold rations was washed down by a shot of brandy from Kupy's stash we settled down for the night, posting large shifts of guards to watch for stray enemy soldiers who were certainly lurking in the dark looking for water and food.

When the camp turned quiet, I climbed to the back of my half-track, pulled out my map and under the cover of a blanket turned on a small flashlight. I drew on its protective plastic sheet what I estimated to be the boundaries of our new territory. It was a peanut-shaped bulge west of the canal, stretching twenty or thirty miles south from the northern end of the Great Bitter Lake and approximately ten or twenty miles wide. The bulge was surrounded by enemy territory on all sides. Only a thin strip, thinner than my marker's tip, connected us to Sinai. It was the line passing from Deversoir to a floating bridge, possibly two by now, that Egyptian planes and cannons were trying desperately to sink, to the deadly *Hatzar-Mavet* near Matsmed and then along the section of Akavish south of the Chinese Farm and north of the Third Army. It was a very precarious link.

I looked at the map in disbelief. We were planning to trap the Third Army, but on my map we were the ones who were walking into a trap. We were much too far to hear the explosions from *Hatzar-Mavet*, but I had no doubt that the shelling there continued and that at first light the MiGs would show up again. I looked out of my half-track and saw the black shadow of Mount Ataqa covering much of the star-studded sky. It had to be swarming with artillery spotters watching and wishing us ill.

But the map did not tell the real story, nor did the intimidating Mount Ataqa. The real story was that after two weeks of a difficult war, momentum was on our side. The real story was that the Third Army, the spotters on Mount Ataqa, the few enemy infantry still left in the Chinese Farm, and the Egyptian army left to our west were no longer protected by SAM missiles. Our formidable air force was watching and protecting us from above and a huge reserve army that was caught by surprise on Yom Kippur was finally catching its stride. We were heading south to close up the only opening still available to the Third Army. No matter what the map showed, the bulge I drew on the plastic sheet was not our trap, it was the Third Army's trap door.

Saturday morning, the first day of our third week at war brought news that only a week ago would have been welcome. Henry Kissinger, the US Secretary of State, was en route to Moscow to negotiate with Brezhnev terms for a ceasefire in the Middle East. We could not tell why Kissinger would be interested in pushing a ceasefire that would seal the Arabs' achievements and deny us a clear victory. Was the US worried about Soviet intervention?

We were still thirty or forty miles north of the Cairo-Suez Highway. It could still take us two, maybe three days, to reach it. And if we didn't, we would be committed to protecting a bulge with long borders and no depth. I was certain Israel would never agree to those terms.

We continued surveying the plateau of Geneifa Hills while our cannons exchanged fire with the Third Army cannons and "softened up" the enemy positions south of us.

In the evening, a supply truck arrived with new food rations and for the first time since the start of the war, a change of fatigues. After two weeks in the desert dust, surrounded by greasy equipment, we still wore the same set of uniforms. We had not showered or shaved either. Water that was precious in Sinai was even more so in the Land of Goshen. Although water was plentiful in the fresh water canals it could not be trusted as potable. Every drop we used had to be brought in by tankers from the other side of the Canal.

Even without showering, changing into new uniforms was wonderful. We stripped at the back of the truck down to our filthy underwear, threw our old clothing to the quartermaster and got the new ones. And the new ones were truly new, still folded and tied with straps. They were dark green. Not the IDF standard issue olive green. Their style and fabric were different, too. Only when I unfolded the shirt I saw on the left pocket the marking "U.S. Army." Another truck that arrived the following day delivered yet another surprise, clean underwear marked "Fruit of the Loom." Israeli stores didn't carry that brand. The underwear and the green uniforms were part of an American emergency airlift code named "Nickel Grass."[13] In the following days, I saw our artillery batteries receiving green shells with American markings and trucks, still painted in American colors, but already carrying IDF license numbers.

MONDAY, OCTOBER 22, 1973

The UN Security Council passed a resolution calling on Israel, Egypt and Syria to cease hostilities that day at 6:52 pm local time. We were still at the same

---

13   Nickel Grass was an extensive airlift that started on the fourth day of the war. It relied initially on El Al planes but when they proved inadequate for the scale required, President Nixon authorized the use of American C-5 Galaxy and C-141 Starlifter air transport planes. The planes stopped for refueling in the Portuguese Azores Islands, the only European country that permitted such landings. The airlift included in addition to our underwear, tanks, Phantom and Skyhawk planes, artillery and tank ammunition, replacement parts and more.

place on the plateau of Geneifa Hills. But the range of our targets extended further south.

I don't know if it was just my perception, but our cannons' fire seemed to intensify. It was certainly not my imagination when Egyptian artillery, for the first time since we left Deversoir, directed fire at us. More Israeli planes flew along the canal, while they still could, hitting Third Army positions. It was strange to stand on the Egyptian side of the canal and watch Israeli planes hit Egyptian targets on the Israeli side of the canal. Two Egyptian planes, trying to interfere with the Israeli planes, were shot down. The noon radio news brief acknowledged what we all understood: Israel was making a last ditch effort to encircle the Third Army. The race against time was reaching the finish line.

The sun was setting. The ceasefire was approaching fast. We were still in our old position. It did not mean that the tank units had not made progress. We were well within range of all necessary targets.

We huddled in a group around our small transistor radios looking at our watches, 6:50, 6:51, 6:52. *"The war is over!"* we screamed in unison. A bottle of wine that had been delivered with the Friday supply for the Shabbat Eve blessing materialized. We poured it into our plastic mess cups and toasted our own survival and the survival of Israel.

And we placed bets again: how soon would Israel declare that Egypt had violated the ceasefire and hostilities would resume.

We cheered again when the 7:00 pm evening news brief confirmed that a cease fire between Israel, Egypt and Syria went into effect eight minutes earlier and that all fronts were quiet.

For the first time in two weeks the desert was truly quiet. The stars in the moonless skies looked brighter. But the threat of a nighttime raid had not dissipated. Isolated Egyptian troops were still wandering, thirsty, hungry, disoriented and probably unaware that a ceasefire went into effect.

The sound of Israeli planes bombing Third Army targets woke me up just after dawn. The early morning news brief acknowledged what we guessed: overnight IDF forces west of the Suez Canal encountered enemy fire. Israel considered it a violation of the conditions of the ceasefire and as a consequence, the IDF resumed its activities in that area. Only one soldier bet that the violation would be declared within ten hours. The rest of us bet on five hours or less. I was certain that we would be back at war in less than an hour.

The drive to cut off the Third Army was on again.

We were back on the road to scout new artillery positions along the highway to Suez City that ran along the fresh-water canal.

The devastation of war that was barely noticeable on the plateau of Geneifa Hills was visible along this road. Hundreds of burned trucks, tanks, APVs and cannons, mostly Egyptian, littered both its sides. Some vehicles were undamaged, abandoned by soldiers running for their lives. Corpses of Egyptian soldiers still lying next to their burned vehicles were already bloating in the heat. Hungry stray dogs feasted on corpses that were once their masters. The smell of war permeated the air: a sickening mixture of decaying human and animal cadavers combined with the still-persistent smell of gunpowder and smoke from burning rubber, plastic and fuel.

We stopped at the gates of an abandoned Egyptian base to measure its coordinates. It looked similar to Deversoir: single story buildings, a few bunkers and ditches for vehicles. An Arabic sign declared: Geneifa Camp. (31 p. 456)

While we were working, several groups, each with more than fifty Egyptian soldiers, appeared along the road marching south in formation, hands raised over their heads to signal surrender. An Egyptian officer led each group shouting orders as if they were on parade. Their faces showed defeat, fear, desperation, apathy and simple exhaustion. There was not a single Israeli guard accompanying the hundreds of prisoners of war.

Someone must have assembled them, collected their weapons, shoelaces and belts, like I had done to our single prisoner and sent them on towards the nearest Egyptian line. The IDF still did not have a facility in the Land of Goshen to handle prisoners of war. The urgency to close the noose around the Third Army was higher than managing prisoners of war. Fortunately, the Egyptians were more eager to become prisoners than the Israelis were to keep them. If they ever made an attempt to return to the war I never knew about it.

Drivers of supply and ammunition trucks heading south jeered and blew their horns when passing the surrendered soldiers. I watched the prisoners with sadness. They were trying to march proudly, hoping to preserve a bit of their shattered pride. But they must have understood how vulnerable they had become. Just a day earlier they were fighting soldiers, part of the army that for the first time in history dealt defeat to Israel, but now they were helpless creatures at the mercy of their enemy.

But I also found watching them satisfying. This was how victory looked in the field. It was ugly. There were no trumpets or waving flags to celebrate it, no crowds to cheer. Victory was the stench of decaying bodies, destruction of weapons and property, and the humiliation, fear, and desperation of the defeated. It could have been us. But instead, it was them.

Then again, I could also hear Laci's voice reminding me that God created all humans in his own image. Even the Arab enemy was created in God's image, he said. Only the Nazis forgot this. I could hear him warning me to always be careful not to lose God's image. *"The temptations of power are high,"* he once told me; *"one moment you are still in God's image and the next you are the devil. Be sure to behave in a manner that will not cause your conscience to haunt you to your last day."*

As if to demonstrate what he meant, a supply truck stopped next to one of the marching units, the driver jumped out of the cabin leaving the engine running; he approached the soldiers and started searching them for valuables. Two of my surveyors started walking towards the group, also hoping to get some loot. I stopped all three of them and ordered the driver back to his truck.

The surveyors returned to their work grumbling. The driver moved his truck half a mile further south and stopped by another Egyptian unit to continue his pillaging.

This Israeli driver might have flashed his finger at me, but my attention was already drawn to another event: several gunshots and an explosion coming from the direction of Geneifa Camp. Two Israeli soldiers ran out of a bunker near the gate yelling in panic and reached my half-track breathless. They were drivers of a supply unit. They had arrived from Sinai with supplies and entered the bunker looking for souvenirs. Instead they found two armed Egyptian soldiers who fired and threw a grenade at them. Their friend, a driver too, was hit. He could be dead, they told me. They were too scared to get him out or return fire.

I alerted the scout unit on my radio. Within minutes they found the third driver dead at the entrance clutching his spoils of war—a can of Egyptian fava beans. They tossed hand grenades inside the bunker, killing the two Egyptians. My surveyors did not try to loot again.

Soon they would not need to. The Egyptian army was collapsing. Thousands of soldiers fled west towards Cairo or the Nile Delta, dropping along the way anything that would slow them down. Roads and trails were littered with helmets, bayonets, personal items, shoes and even personal arms. Within days, almost all of us had Kalashnikov (AK-47) submachine guns, matching bayonets, Egyptian hand grenades, explosives, anti-tank grenades, helmets, even a silk Egyptian flag trimmed with gold fringes.

Egyptian vehicles were abandoned too, some in excellent condition, gas tanks full. But driving them while fighting was still ongoing was asking for death. Israeli tanks shot any moving Egyptian vehicle without warning. The hundreds of burned vehicles along the Suez road were proof that they rarely missed.

But Kupy, who fancied a shiny Egyptian command car he found off the road, had his own plan. He moved the vehicle behind one of the dunes, crawled under the vehicle and removed the gas tank plug. While the gas poured through the open drain, wetting the desert sand, he opened the hood and pulled out a black electrical wire. *"This vehicle is not moving until I say so,"* he chuckled smugly and hid the gas tank plug and the coil wire in his trunk.

Progress was swift. Egypt, Syria, and their patron, the Soviet Union, filed angry protests with the UN that the Israeli aggression was in violation of the ceasefire agreement. We did not need international protests to confirm that the war was no longer following their script. By Tuesday at midnight, forces of our division reached Adabiya, a small Egyptian port city on the west side of the Gulf of Suez, south of Suez City. The Third Army, one-third of the entire Egyptian military strength, was trapped. Sharon's division was on its way to surround the Second Army as well. The ceasefire would stop him in his tracks. Israel now had it within its power the ability to destroy the entire Egyptian armed forces and reach Cairo within days. Egypt was on its knees. (36)

But the two superpowers, America and the Soviet Union, decided that the war that had been started by Egypt and Syria with the intent to destroy an unprepared Israel had to be stopped before they were defeated and humiliated again. In truth, Israel was exhausted too. A ceasefire was desired by all parties.

WEDNESDAY, OCTOBER 24, 1973

The Syrian and Egyptian fronts turned quiet at 7 am. But barely forty-eight hours after the fragile cease-fire took place, the Third Army tried to break the blockade by putting a bridge in the water. Israel responded with heavy shelling. From Geneifa Hills I could see Israeli Skyhawk jets diving unopposed towards targets along the Canal. Skirmishes on the Golan Heights and along the Suez Canal continued for months.

The ceasefire did not bring me any euphoria. I was happy to be alive. But like all Israelis, my thoughts were with those who were not: the medic who had been killed in Deversoir, the rows of men covered by military blankets in *Hatzar-Mavet*, the pickup trucks we met along the Baluza road carrying back the dead of the first day, the reservist killed by our friendly fire, even the poor supply truck driver who lost his life in Camp Geneifa for a can of Egyptian fava beans. That morning Israel was not celebrating a victory, it was licking its wounds: 2,687 soldiers dead and 7,251 wounded; (36 p. 91) more than the casualties of the Six-Day War and the 1956 Sinai Campaign combined.[14]

The statistics of 7,251 wounded and 2,687 dead did not count the wives of these men or the women who would have married them but could not, the children raised by fathers who could not play soccer or teach them to swim, and the children who were never born, the parents who lost their sons, some of the Holocaust survivors who were visited by yet another tragedy.

Technically, the war ended in a stunning victory, even more so than the Six-Day War when taking into account the starting conditions: Israel gained more territory then its enemies, destroyed more tanks, cannons and airplanes and inflicted more casualties. But despite these gains, Israel was not truly in a better position. Just the opposite: the war exposed troubling vulnerabilities and it had nearly ended in a defeat. The feelings of a looming Holocaust that dissipated even before the Six-Day War ended were back. They would continue traumatizing Israelis for decades. Israelis no longer felt that their security was guaranteed. Some even began asking if there was a victory at all.

As if that was not enough, Israel's positions on both fronts, particularly facing Egypt, were not defensible. Although the IDF artillery was within range of Damascus suburbs, its tanks on the road to Cairo and the Egyptian Third Army surrounded, neither Syria nor Egypt were defeated. Their armies were positioned within a stone's throw from Israeli positions and were rearming faster than the IDF. A new war could erupt without any warning. Israel had to remain on full alert, its reserves fully mobilized and its economy put on hold indefinitely. The first signs of runaway inflation that would plague the country for more than a decade were already visible.

To resolve that untenable situation, the Israeli cabinet offered passage to the Egyptian Third Army soldiers through its lines without their weapons. Their officers would need to turn themselves in as prisoners of wars (POWs) and be exchanged, together with the other eight thousand three hundred Egyptian POWs, against the 230 Israeli POWs. Alternatively, Israel offered to exchange territories. Its forces would leave the Canal's west bank in return for

---

14 Long after the war, I stayed in a Dead Sea resort. That resort was also a retreat for handicapped war veterans. Men my age rolled in wheelchairs along the corridors; some were disfigured by burns, some were missing limbs and some blind. Most were casualties of the Yom Kippur War. They might have been wounded in places where I myself served, possibly not far from where I was. They were still paying the war's price, every day, every moment.

Egyptian retreat from its east bank. Egypt turned both offers down. To them, the achievements of the first day of the war were trophies that symbolized a national victory. (31 p. 485) They would not part with them.

Kissinger was the first to recognize the opportunity that this logjam presented. It could force Israel and the Arab nations into face-to-face peace negotiations. By keeping the Third Army on the Israeli side of the Canal, Sadat would preserve his national pride, while Israel could claim victory as well by keeping it trapped. But for the 30,000 men of the Third Army to survive in the desert, Israel had to permit passage of water, food and medical supplies.

The challenge for this master diplomat was to convince Israel that its interests were best served by keeping the Third Army alive. It was a counter-intuitive idea for a nation that fought a bitter war to win this position. But if successful, so Kissinger's thinking went, he would appear as an honest broker with power to exert pressure on all parties. He could then be able to pull Egypt away from the Soviet sphere of influence and bring peace to the Middle East.

Two days after the cessation of hostilities Kissinger presented a proposal to Israel accompanied by an ultimatum from Nixon: Israel was not to destroy the Third Army; instead it would allow it to receive humanitarian supplies. He demanded an answer within a day. (31 p. 487)

In retrospect, this was a scheme dreamed up by a genius. It spawned the peace treaty with Egypt that was followed by a peace agreement with Jordan. Kissinger was unpopular in Israel in those days. Being a Jew, some even viewed him as a traitor. I wish, however, that Kissinger's genius had been available in the days following the Six-Day War. He might have helped Israel recognize that giving up territories that were heavily populated by Palestinians would have served its own interest. History might have looked very different if the West Bank and Gaza strip had not remained under Israeli control.

In reply to Nixon's ultimatum, Israel proposed that the terms of supplying the Third Army be negotiated directly by Israeli and Egyptian representatives at a location, time and representation level to be determined by Egypt.

It was a gamble. Since the negotiations of the armistice in 1949 that followed the War of Independence, there had not been any direct high-level discussions between Israel and Egypt, or with any Arab nation. All previous invitations by Israel for direct negotiations were rejected outright. The Arab nations did not recognize Israel and refused to meet any of its officials. But this time, quite surprisingly, Egypt accepted the invitation. It had only one condition: that humanitarian, non-military supply would be immediately delivered to the Third Army. Israel accepted.

I was disappointed, and so were most Israelis, to hear that the Third Army would be resupplied. Commentators criticized the government. What was the point, they argued, of holding a siege when supplies were allowed through? The reward, the right to speak directly with an Egyptian general, seemed trivial. The American pressure to accept this deal reminded me of a similar American ultimatum in 1956: the retreat from Sinai that I believed produced the wars of 1967 and 1973. It was clearly a bad deal. The leadership that allowed Israel to be surprised, commentators added, was now squandering the results of the war.

The direct negotiations between Israeli and Egyptian generals started in the wee hours of October 30 in a tent near the 101st kilometer milestone on the Suez-Cairo road.[15] Foreign correspondents who drove from Cairo with the Egyptian general noted with irony that the Israeli general had to fly from Tel Aviv. (33 p. 112) More than anything, this comment represented the asymmetry of these discussions: Cairo was under the gun, not Tel Aviv. But the obvious winner would still have to make concessions to appease the loser.

Negotiations between the generals in the tent at milepost 101 and between Kissinger, the Israeli Prime Minister Golda Meir and Sadat in Washington and various capitals continued at a fast pace. The first tangible results came within two weeks: a formal cease-fire agreement that included exchange of POWs and a process for the delivery of Egyptian supply convoys to the Third Army through IDF controlled territory and UN checkpoints to drop-off points on the canal where the supplies were ferried over by amphibian vehicles. The content of the convoys was inspected at the UN checkpoints by both UN and Israeli officers.

Despite the ceasefire agreement and the goodwill that developed between the negotiating generals, Israeli positions west of the canal remained vulnerable. Our division could easily be trapped if Egypt broke our only link to Sinai, the bridge or the road out from *Hatzar-Mavet*. The deployment of our entire division was extended indefinitely. It was still early November but we already understood that we would be celebrating Hanukkah on Egyptian land.

This was hard on most reservists. I finally realized that I would likely lose at least one semester of graduate studies. To mitigate that, I asked my professors at the Technion to mail me course material. I might be able to study independently, I thought, turn in homework and exam work and hopefully gain back some lost time.

Others in my unit were not as lucky. Owners of small businesses agonized that competitors would swallow up their customers. Salaried employees had their

---

15   It was the furthest reach of Israeli territory, 101 kilometers (approximately 65 miles) from Cairo.

salaries guaranteed during their time in service, but they worried their jobs would be lost as their employers lost business. And then there were the families left at home.

Kupy was the first to recognize that although we could not control the cards we were dealt, we could still control how they were played. Having only a few assignments to keep us busy and with plenty of free time, he declared we could turn our camp into a vacation site. One morning, he asked for my permission to take our command car with a driver on an unspecified mission. He was back at dusk, his driver at the wheel of our command car and Kupy at the wheel of an Egyptian command car, the car he left behind the dune near Camp Geneifa. After a victory lap around our campsite he stopped in front of me and got out smiling smugly. Kupy had already registered his vehicle as an IDF vehicle and got himself assigned as its authorized driver.

Kupy got his own car, just like he promised.

The two command cars were packed to the brim.

"*Geneifa was an Egyptian supply base,*" Kupy explained while we watched two soldiers unloading cooking equipment, three large tents, tarps, armchairs, Egyptian canned hummus, fava beans, cracked olives and candy. "*An IDF quartermaster has gone through most of the stuff and units were invited to come by and take their pick. We arrived just in time. We're going to have fun.*"

Kupy returned to Camp Geneifa the following day and the day after, until he was satisfied that our camp had turned into a desert resort.

One large yellow Egyptian tent became our dining hall, complete with tables and benches. Another, with a large tarp covering the floor, became our club. In one corner Kupy placed four leather armchairs around an elegant coffee table decorated with mother of pearl artwork. The set must have served a high-ranking officer. A large radio that probably came from the same officer was tuned to GALATZ. In another corner he placed a rectangular table with multiple chairs. It became our arena for Shesh-Besh (Backgammon) tournaments, with room for players and kibitzers. A bookshelf by one of the tent's walls was soon filled with books and became our exchange library. The silk Egyptian flag was hung from the roof as the club's primary decoration. The dining room and the club were electrically wired to a "Pak Pak," the nickname for a small gasoline-powered generator. Dining, Shesh-Besh, reading, or music continued into the wee hours.

A third, smaller tent was our kitchen. It was fully equipped, stocked heavily with Israeli and Egyptian rations, fresh supplies, and private provisions from home. Kupy turned us gastronomically independent. Three "volunteers" were assigned daily to produce dinner for our unit. The meals were surprisingly excellent and the menus imaginative. We rated them daily. Topping the previous day's rating became a challenge.

Our only real assignment was to systematically map the new territory. The results would serve our artillery brigade should war resume, and if the IDF did eventually retreat, we would have enemy territory well-mapped and surveyed. To me it was a license to thoroughly tour an exotic and historic land. For several weeks we left our "resort" in the morning, explored a new area and returned in time for a gourmet dinner and an evening of entertainment in the club.

We started at the outskirts of Suez City, the Canal's southern port. The city center remained in Egyptian hands. We chose the roof of an abandoned school building, off the Cairo-Suez highway, as our first landmark. The mouth of the Suez Canal as it opens into the Red Sea was visible from the rooftop. In the distance I could make out the outlines of several collapsed oil tanks. They were remnants of an Egyptian oil farm that suffered direct hits by Israeli artillery during the War of Attrition.

We continued north along the agricultural strip, measuring the coordinates of prominent landmarks on and off the canal's banks.

One of our stops was a UN post on the canal that monitored the transfer of supplies to the Third Army. Before the war it had been an Egyptian stronghold and on the first day of the war it served as the launching pad for one of the many bridges that carried Egyptian troops to Sinai.

Four UN soldiers greeted us at the gate. Their dress code was even more relaxed than ours; two of them were dressed only in shorts, sandals and blue UN berets. No shirts! Only the armed guard at the gate was in full military outfit, including a blue helmet. Eager for company, they invited us for a cold beer. With a cold Dutch beer in hand, I climbed the post's emplacement to watch the arrival of an Egyptian convoy to supply the Third Army.

The blue ribbon of the canal stretched before me. I looked in admiration at the tall rampart on the opposite bank. This was the first time I saw it as it was seen by the Egyptians. Its steep slope was perfectly shaped to prevent tanks and even infantry from climbing it. It had been shaped that way in the earlier days of the War of Attrition. No one could survive working on the face exposed to the "monkeys" during the heydays of the war. Rectangular structures placed at regular intervals along the top marked the positions of tank ramps. Almost directly opposite from my position was an opening in the rampart, wide enough to allow a vehicle, possibly a tank to pass through. It looked as if a slice of the rampart was cut out perfectly by a giant knife. The UN officer standing next to me explained in broken English that the Egyptians cut this opening in the first hours of the war using water cannons, and then they put in the bridge. It was hard to believe, but I knew it was true.

At least one hundred Egyptian soldiers were clustered at and near the opening, unloading large bags from a barge tied to the bank. Like khaki ants hauling grains to their nest, they were hauling bags on their backs to a waiting truck.

Below, on our side of the canal, another group of Egyptian soldiers were loading another barge. I wondered about Egyptian soldiers on our side. "*I am sure you don't want your soldiers to unload food for the Egyptians,*" my UN friend explained. "*I wouldn't want to do it either,*" he chuckled, "*so we had to let them through across the canal unarmed. They will be sent back when the convoy leaves,*" he promised.

We headed north towards the suburbs of Ismailia, the last stop in our assignment. On the way we stopped at Deversoir and visited the two bridges. Times had changed. Signs in Hebrew and English designated one of the two bridges carrying traffic to Asia. The other must have had signs on the opposite side marking it as the way to Africa. Two military policemen, their white helmets shading their eyes from the bright sun, were catching a nap on two armchairs someone must have hauled out of an office in Deversoir. They seemed to be the only military force holding that strategic point.

That evening on the way back to our "resort" we found a lone goose trotting along the main road. One of the surveyors recognized its culinary value and suggested we adopt it. I agreed. It might lay fresh eggs, I thought, not knowing if it were a male or a female. And if it didn't, it could be groomed to be the centerpiece for our final dinner—a feast we were certain would take place on our last night of deployment. We named the goose Avi, short for Avaz, goose in Hebrew.

Generations of IDF soldiers learned to expect short but frequent leaves. Owing to the country's small size, they could leave base at noon on Friday and be back on Sunday morning, the start of the new workweek. Weekend leaves were sacrosanct. Only on rare occasions would a soldier go for more than three weeks without at least one leave. When the Sinai became an Israeli territory, leave cycles of four or even seven days were established to account for the longer travel time. "Two weeks in, one week out" cycles were not unusual. After more than a month since the start of the war, the IDF began authorizing leave rotations in frontline field units.

To help soldiers leaving for only four days' break from the Land of Goshen, the most distant territory, the IDF started running direct flights to and from Fayed, a previously Egyptian airbase on the western shore of the Great Bitter Lake.

The first flights from Fayed were operated by Hercules (C-130) cargo planes that were delivered to Israel by the Nickel Grass operation, the US-led airlift. Later, an Air Force Boeing 707 was also introduced.

When I boarded the Hercules on my first flight home from Fayed, I expected a routine flight, just like the flights I took from Sinai. I soon found out that flights from Fayed could not possibly be routine.

The only flight path in and out of Fayed passed over the bridge area and then along the narrow corridor held by the IDF between the Second and Third Egyptian Armies. Climbing on takeoff from Fayed put airplanes in the line of sight of Egyptian soldiers on either side of the corridor and within range of their shoulder-held surface-to-air Strela missiles. To remain out of sight, planes had to thread their way across the canal at low altitude, grazing the dune tops on take-off and approach. Every flight in and out of Fayed challenged even the best pilots and the nerves of their passengers.

I was among the first to board the cavernous plane. We were herded on board by two ground crewmen through its gangplank door at the rear even before the last arriving passengers got off. The pilots, anxious to turn around quickly, did not even turn off the engines; the propellers were still spinning and blowing desert sand. Inside, the plane was rudimentary; no paneling, fuselage ribs and the cabling were exposed. The metal floor with anchoring eyes at regular intervals was clearly meant to support large pallets or vehicles, not a hundred or more passengers. Two canvas benches along the sides were the only concession made by the plane's designers for the occasional human cargo. The flow of soldiers boarding the plane had not slowed even after all the seats were taken. I could hear the crewmen outside urging the last passengers to run aboard even as the gangplank door was already closing.

It was a "standing room only" flight. We were at least a hundred passengers still trying to position themselves when the plane started rolling forward. Those without a seat simply crouched on the floor leaning against each other. No one could be bothered with niceties such as safety instructions or seat belts.

I watched the take-off through a small round window on my right. We were airborne after a short run, but the plane did not gain any altitude. It leveled off barely above the tree tops, banked sharply and headed towards the bridges on the canal. I watched in horror as dunes passed my window at eye level. I heard about planes flying between mountain peaks in the Alps. But these were not the Alps. I could only hope that the pilots and the plane controls could react fast enough to clear the next dune. Twenty minutes into this roller-coaster ride, the plane pitched sharply. The dense mass of screaming passengers on the metal floor shifted backwards, crushing those in the rear against a net stretched across the back.

We landed in Tel Aviv and stopped next to two gigantic American C-5 Galaxy planes. New, freshly painted tanks were rolling off the gangplanks at their rear and lining up in two long rows. They were the Israeli side of the new Middle Eastern arms race.

I sat on the bus heading up Haifa's hills of Mount Carmel, to Liora, my heart thumping. I looked out the window in disbelief. Stores were open as usual. People on the street were walking about doing their business, mothers were pushing their baby strollers and a young couple was kissing passionately behind a tree. *Hatzar-Mavet*, our division still in the Land of Goshen, or the trapped Third Army belonged to another world, only one hour's flight away.

The bright smiling fall sunshine made the bus ride on a dark night a month earlier seem like a bad dream. On the bus's radio the Beatles were singing:

> And when the night is cloudy
> There is still a light that shines on me
> Shine on until tomorrow, let it be….

I stood at the door of Liora's parents' house in my stained, green US Army fatigues, unshaven, hair overgrown, tanned and smelly. I had not showered in weeks. Liora didn't know I was coming. The small bag I packed a month earlier was filled with dirty Fruit of the Loom underwear and an almost clean army issued towel I only used twice. After five weeks "on the road" I had no gifts for my sweetheart, other than myself. I felt exhausted when I knocked on the door. The Land of Goshen and Israel were in the same time zone, but nevertheless I suffered from jet lag, I had just arrived from another world.

The door opened and there she was, exactly as I saw her in every dream, every night. She stood there looking at the bearded man in the door. Then she jumped into my arms screaming in joy. And at that moment I had nothing to say. I only wanted to hold her in my arms, smell her hair and wipe her tears that mingled with mine.

After four days of blessed clean sheets and restorative company of my family I returned to the Land of Goshen.

Hanukkah found me still in the desert camp. The nights on the elevated Geneifa Hills plateau turned cold and windy, the sand raised by the blowing wind became a constant nuisance, penetrating our tents, coats, nostrils and eyes.

The "resort," despite its many comforts, grew to feel like a Siberian penitentiary camp. But Kupy, determined to celebrate the first of the eight days of Hanukkah properly, arranged for yeast to be brought from home and late that afternoon supervised a small crew as it fried fresh jelly doughnuts.

I was walking from our club tent to the dining room to join the celebration when I noticed a flame burning on top of Mount Ataqa. It was the first light I ever saw on the mountain; I knew this was unusual but I didn't assign any importance to it.

The following night, the second night of Hanukkah, there were two flames on the mountain. I checked through my binoculars: they were burning in two large barrels, most likely filled with kerosene-soaked sand. On the third night of Hanukkah there were three lights, then four and on the last day, eight flames were burning on top of the dark land mass. They burned for hours after sunset. They were visible from the positions of the Third Army east of the Canal, the Egyptian posts to the west and maybe even from Cairo. To us at the foot of the mountain, they were a reminder that the miracle of the victory of the Maccabees over the Greeks had been repeated in the land of Egypt. I never found out who placed the barrels on Mount Ataqa. Or was it just another Hanukkah miracle?

On January 18, 1974, Israel and Egypt signed a disengagement agreement in which Israel agreed to withdraw from both banks of the Suez Canal to a line west of the Sinai Passes. (33 p. 175) The Egyptian army was allowed to keep its positions on the East bank of the Canal. A UN force was assigned to keep a buffer zone between the two armies.

In return, Egypt agreed to reopen the Canal for shipping, including Israeli and Israel-bound ships and repopulate the cities along the Canal. This became the first step towards normalization of relations between the two nations. The operating canal and its rebuilt cities were expected to provide sufficient incentive for Egypt to keep the peace. In return for its concessions, Israel had for the first time in its history a genuine hope for peace and security along one of its borders. That, more than anything else, was worth the high price we all paid.

This agreement was nearly identical to a proposal made by General Dayan in December 1970 calling for a unilateral Israeli withdrawal from the banks of the Suez Canal. In return, Egypt was to reopen it for shipping. (31 pp. 11, 493) Dayan's proposal was never rejected by the Israeli cabinet but it was not approved either. It was entered into the minutes and ignored.

Two months later Sadat presented a similar idea as his own. (33 p. 146) But President Sadat's proposal, unlike Dayan's, was rejected by Prime Minister Golda Meir in an address to the Knesset, suggesting in a dismissive tone that Sadat might re-open the Canal anytime he so wished without the need for any Israeli concessions or approval.

Thousands paid with their lives, broken bodies and souls for that mistake.

We bid farewell to our camp on the African side of the canal a month after the disengagement agreement and repositioned to a site along the new line, west of the Mitla Pass. From our new camp we could see Geneifa Hills that were in Egyptian hands again.

Days before leaving that exotic land we paid a visit to the grave of a fallen Jewish soldier buried in a British World War II military cemetery in Fayed. At the foot of his tombstone we buried a sealed bottle with our names, the date and occasion of our visit for a future archeologist to discover.

It was also time to prepare for our parting feast and for Avi, the goose we fed and readied for that day, to become the centerpiece of our table.

But someone had to separate Avi from his soul.

Battle-hardened soldiers drew straws to select the one for the task. An ax was procured from an Egyptian tank where it was installed by the Russian manufacturer as standard equipment to break ice or clear trees along its path in the Sinai desert.

Tough men, one by one, raised the ax over Avi's neck, but not one could lower it. When it appeared that Avi's life would be spared, a squad of military engineers drove by and happily adopted him. That night Avi was served as dinner to their officer, my good friend from the Technion.

We crossed the Canal eastward for the last time. *Hatzar-Mavet* was quiet. The signs directing traffic to Asia or Africa were gone. Both bridges carried Asia-Only traffic. I looked around with teary eyes. I knew I would never miss that place. But how could I not miss those who did not return with us?

Many Israelis saw the surrender of the enclave in the land of Goshen as a loss. But for the first time since October, we could breathe easily. Our front line was straight, backed by the vast Sinai desert, all of it Israeli territory. We didn't realize it at the time, but giving up the Land of Goshen bought us peace with our largest adversary. That war was our last engagement with the Egyptian army.

We were still in Sinai on Passover observing the festive meal, the Seder, marking the Exodus in military style. The Mitla Pass behind us, still littered with destroyed Egyptian vehicles reminded us of the victories of our times in 1956 and 1967. The army rabbi was chanting "If he passed us through [the sea] on dry land and did not sink our oppressors in it—it would be sufficient."[16] A passing wind blew open a flap in our tent and exposed the vast desert

---

16 The *Dayenu* hymn from the Passover Haggadah.

View of the levee on the Israeli side of the Suez Canal from the rampart of the UN post on the Egyptian side. Note the opening that was cut by the Egyptian army during the first hours of the Yom Kippur War using powerful water cannons. Multiple openings like this one allowed infantry and vehicle access to the Israeli side.

Seen through the UN post's telescope: Soldiers of the trapped Egyptian Third Army unload their supplies.

landscape that was illuminated by the full moon, the Red Sea beyond it and the Land of Goshen on the opposite shore.

The same full moon illuminated the way for our ancestors on the same night three thousand years earlier when they fled the Land of Goshen. It was the same desert landscape and the same shimmering silvery water they saw when they turned around to watch the Red Sea close on Pharaoh's chariots of iron.

November 1944-May 1945: Dachau and Mühldorf, Germany

It was a mild, clear December afternoon in Mühldorf, a quaint German town, fifty miles east of Munich. I was there in 1984 with Liora and now in 2001 with her and our three children, Aharon, Tammar, and Dan.

We stood in a clearing in a vast pine forest outside the town, looking at a large concrete arch. One could mistake it for a bridge, but there was no river or railroad track passing underneath. I tried to gauge its size; at least ten times taller than me, spanning nearly the full length of a football field. The most striking feature was the thickness of the arch, about twice my own height, much thicker than needed to support its own weight or anything else that it might have carried. Large chunks of concrete debris scattered over a large area alluded to the fact that the standing arch was a remnant of a larger structure.

The forest was quiet; I listened carefully trying to hear birds sing. Nothing. Even birds knew better than to sing in this place that was both hallowed and evil.

I remembered this place from my previous visit. The arch still looked immortal, indestructible and enigmatic. But there were changes. Signs in German along the dirt road from the highway through the forest discouraged visitors from going any further, warning of an unspecified deadly danger. And a large swastika, spray painted at the top of the arch, reminded us that Nazism was not dead and that the Neo-Nazis also considered the arch historically significant.

The five of us stood holding hands, watching the massive structure silently. Like the birds, we kept the silence, whispering, as if loud words would disturb the many dead whose remains were undoubtedly scattered in that area. The arch, with the swastika on top, projected evil. It was built with blood, tears and the lives of thousands of slaves. My father was one of those slaves.

We walked around the open field and into the forest to look for clues to the secrets of this arch. I inspected a few pieces of concrete wondering who

Liora and Tammar under the remaining arch of the Mühldorf bunker, 2001

carried the cement they were made from, the gravel, who mixed them and poured the mixture into molds? I discovered a well-defined footprint, impressed fifty-seven years earlier in wet concrete by a prisoner. Like the Tomb of the Unknown Soldier, a place of mourning for all soldiers missing in action, the imprint could belong to any of the slaves who worked and died here. It could memorialize anyone, known or unknown. I placed my foot next to the mark. The footprint was two sizes smaller. It could be Laci's.

I joined my children and closed my eyes. The light breeze ruffling through the pine needles sounded like the prayers of thousands of desperate slaves still echoing in the forest.

Before we left, each of my children took a chunk of concrete, a reminder of their grandfather's struggle to survive, physical evidence of family history.

Several years after that visit, Holocaust-era German archives were declassified.[1] A few weeks after requesting any documents the archive might have about his imprisonment, I received copies of his registration form as a Dachau prisoner and his worker's card from Mühldorf, issued only days after his arrival at Dachau. They were dry legal documents, but they linked me to one

---

[1] email@its-arolsen.org.

of his darkest moments. I recognized his hand-written signature at the bottom of the registration form. I remember as a child watching him sign documents. I could see him in my mind bending over this form and signing it. The signature brought him back to life.

Liora, a trained graphologist, explained to me when she saw it that a signature projects how a person wants to be perceived by the world and reflects his emotions at the moment of signing.

"A slave would have a small diminutive signature written by the trembling hand of a frightened man. Instead, Laci's signature had flair; a tall 'L' and a tall 'F' in his last name 'Laufer' and even a taller 'L' in his first name 'László.' Even at the gates of the oldest German concentration camp," she commented, "Laci was still a proud man, tall, like the 'Ls' in his first and last names."

Laci's 101/35 MUSZ Company reached Dachau's train station on November 11, 1944.[2] The Hungarian men, no longer MUSZ but slaves nevertheless, jumped off their cattle car[3] (37) and were immediately surrounded by yelling Kapos,[4] SS officers and barking dogs.

Dazed after traveling for days from Budakalász near Budapest, (9 p. 1188 (II)) without food or water and with barely any sleep, they would have had no illusions about this place. After years in the Hungarian Labor Service they must have known that the system was designed to kill its subjects quickly while sapping their strength.

But they also had hope. The Red Army was progressing quickly on the Eastern Front. The Allies had landed in Normandy. But it could be months before Germany collapsed, and another winter was coming. They were in a race for survival.

From the station, they were marched to the camp and through the iron-gate made famous by the motto *Arbeit macht frei*—"work will make you free"—emblazoned at its center. They must have scoffed. After two years of hard forced labor, they were still not free.

---

2   Ironically, his granddaughter, Tammar, was born on the same date, thirty-three years later.
3   Moshe Sandberg was also a slave in Mühldorf. After the war he immigrated to Israel and described his experiences in a book. Sandberg's prisoner number 124753 was only 221 prisoners behind Laci's number of 124532. This unusual coincidence suggests that the two arrived on the same day, possibly on the same train. Sandberg actually mentions having seen upon arrival Labor Service units who arrived "straight from the Russian front." Based on that, I am following almost exactly his description of the arrival process and the first few days.
4   Kapo—prisoner functionary. Kapos, selected from among the prisoners, helped the SS to manage the inmates and in return enjoyed a lighter workload, more food and other benefits.

From the gate they reached a large open square, the camp's parade square. Several groups dressed in ragged striped prisoners' uniform marched from another gate across the square to their long barracks at the opposite end. They were singing a joyless song in step with the rhythm of their brisk march. Many were pitiful, no more than walking skeletons. Some who were barely able to march were supported by a friend who hardly seemed fitter.

The 101/35 Company stopped near a large building and was ordered to wait. Hundreds of new prisoners were already standing in groups of fifty or sixty, waiting for their turn. They too were dressed in civilian clothing. Some, like the 101/35, wore Hungarian military caps that marked them as Hungarian Labor Servicemen.

When the last group from their train arrived, two prisoners dressed in striped uniforms walked out of the building; one carried a stool and the other a large truncheon that he swung like a cheerleader's baton. The stool was placed in front of the group and the prisoner with the truncheon stepped on it and in perfect Hungarian asked for their attention and ordered them into formation. He then introduced himself as the Camp Elder and explained the registration process. They would be ordered to surrender their personal belongings and valuables. These would be returned to them on their departure, he promised and urged them to keep the receipts they would receive. Laci had heard that ruse before. But it did not matter. He no longer had any valuables.

The wait was long. The sun had set and a cold fall wind was blowing. The prisoners in the barracks at the opposite side of the square lined up for a muster call that lasted an hour and then lined up again for dinner. There was no dinner or drink for the hungry, thirsty, and tired new prisoners.

Finally, Laci's group was ordered to march in. A functionary prisoner ordered them to undress, put their clothes and anything they carried into individual piles, but keep their shoes on.

Laci stood naked, waiting in a long line for his turn to register. At the head of the line was a long table covered with a military blanket. Naked prisoners stood at attention in front of clerks sitting behind the table. The clerks were prisoners, too. But their uniforms, Laci observed, were tailored to fit. They were lined to protect them from the cold, spotlessly clean, and pressed with sharp creases. These were clearly privileged prisoners.

At the corner of the room stood an SS officer, dressed in a black uniform and wearing a peaked cap marked with a skull, armed with a revolver in his holster and a whip in his right hand.

The officer looked disinterested. He inspected the prisoners visually as they approached the table, his eyes scanning each naked man from head to toe, and when a prisoner finished registering, he directed him by motioning his whip to a door on the left or to the right. After watching a few such selections, Laci noted that the weak-looking, limping or visibly sick prisoners were sent to the left.

Were the weak sent to a sick bay, easy office work, or life of privilege like these clerks? Laci asked himself. The clerks behind the registration table looked healthy, strong, and fit. A weakness or handicap could not be the ticket to an advantaged life in Dachau. It had to be like Ukraine, Laci concluded; one had to be strong, and even more importantly, appear strong, to survive. Despite shivering from fear and the cold, tired, hungry, and fatigued, Laci mustered his will, controlled his shivers, pulled back his shoulders and stepped resolutely towards the clerk in front of him.

The clerk behind the table glanced indifferently at Laci, pulled out a blank, legal size, yellow form and wrote on the top line "Dachau" and in the adjacent box, "*Sch.U.Jude*," and then he ordered Laci to turn in his valuables, his Hungarian military ID card and all his pictures. Laci had only one picture left from home, Lili holding the one-year-old Judit. The picture accompanied him to the front near Stalingrad, the retreat through Ukraine and the train ride to Dachau. It warmed his heart when he stood outside in the cold blizzards of the Ukrainian steppes. It stayed with him through Kiev and now it had been taken, for no reason, it had no value to anyone other than Laci himself. He knew he would never see it again. From that moment on, Judit and Lili would reside only in his memory.

While the clerk wrote on the form a number, 124532,[5] Laci tried to read the abbreviations "*Sch.U.Jude*." He spoke German fluently, but I doubt he knew that it meant "Schutzhäftling Ungarische Jude" or "Hungarian Jewish prisoner on protective custody." (38) Had he known, he would have wondered who was protected from whom: him from Germany or Germany

---

5 I was surprised to see that Laci's serial number did not include a letter, such as A-124532. There were several classes of prisoners in Dachau, German criminals at the top echelon, then German political prisoners, prisoners of war, Roma, and at the very bottom, Jews. I expected prisoners would be sorted into their classes by letters in their serial numbers. Otherwise, Laci's serial number seemed too low. Dachau must have seen more than 124,531 prisoners in its eleven years of operation prior to Laci's arrival; unless, of course, if the numbering system, like in Auschwitz, did not assign numbers to those who were murdered upon arrival. They disappeared while in German "Protective Custody."

from him. Or was it just a euphemism. True to the German motto *Ordnung muss sein*—"there must be order"—even Jews in Nazi Germany could not be imprisoned without a court order, unless, of course, the arrest was for security purposes.

"Name," the clerk yelled impatiently at Laci, pulling him out of his thoughts.

"Laufer László;"

"Date of Birth?"

"29 June 1914;"

"Occupation?"

Laci hesitated. He was a lawyer. Germans respected titles. In the outside world they would have addressed him as "Herr Dr. Laufer" or simply "Herr Doctor." But he was a Jew in Dachau, standing naked in front of a prisoner clerk. Titles and education could not possibly matter.

His registration form declares him as an *"Angestellte in Holzindustrie,"* an "Employee in the timber industry." Laci must have understood that a manual skill, not his law degree, would save his life. He chose to state the only skill he could perform somewhat professionally, either because he learned from Sándor who owned a lumberyard or because he felled trees during his years in the Hungarian forced labor. His body looked strong and his hands bore calluses. The SS officer watching had to be pleased to get another lumberjack for the Third Reich.

Not surprisingly, the box "educational background" was left blank. Lumberjacks did not have university degrees. What a brave and clever choice Laci made!

The next box "Languages" includes "Hungarian and German." Speaking both languages was not unusual for Hungarians, former members of the Austro-Hungarian Empire. Laci spoke German well. He must have calculated that acknowledging it would be advantageous. Other survivors of concentration camps realized that "Knowing German meant life." (39)

When asked if he was married Laci gave Lili's full name and maiden name:

"Liliá Rozenzweig."

Ironically this was the first legal document I saw spelling out both her first and maiden names. In other records, as it was the custom in Hungary, she was listed by her husband's name as "Dr. Laufer Lászlóne," Mrs. Dr. Laufer László, even on the memorial plaque in the Budapest Holocaust Museum and the marble memorial in Gyula's Jewish cemetery.

He then stated that he had one child. Obviously he did not know then that Judit and Liliá were deported to Auschwitz on June 26, 1944 and murdered within hours of their arrival on his thirtieth birthday, June 29, 1944.[6] (40)

The form ends with two statements:

"I have been informed that I will be prosecuted for documented misrepresentation, if any of the information stated above is found to be incorrect. "

"Read aloud to the prisoner, approved, and signed."

Laci signed the form. He must have chuckled bitterly when he read the threat of prosecution.

"*Prisoner 124532,*" yelled the clerk in Hungarian, "*remember this number. It is your only identification. You no longer have a name, and now move on.*"

The new prisoners were pushed by a functionary prisoner into the next room where they were deloused, and their head and entire body hair crudely shaved by a prisoner using dull shears.

Imre Csengeri was standing next to Laci when he saw his bald head and laughed. I don't think Laci found it funny, but he must have been happy to be near his friend from home and from the long service together in Ukraine.

We know the two stood together in the registration line because they had consecutive serial numbers 124531 for Csengeri and 124532 for Laci. Next to them stood Imre Friedländer with serial number 124533[7] (41) and Theodor Neumann with serial number 124534.[8]

After their hair was sheared, they were pushed into a room with 30 or 40 shower heads installed in the ceiling. They were handed bars of soap and warned not to drink the water from the shower heads as it carried disease.

Someone outside turned a valve on and a strong stream of hot water came down simultaneously from every shower head. Some of the thirsty men could not control themselves after not having had water for more than two days and drank the malodorous water. Most of them died within days from dysentery. The water was turned off before many had time to rinse the soap off.

---

6   Mrs. Diósy was also on that train and confirmed the dates in her memoirs. Her husband, Imre, also a MUSZ, was captured by the Soviets and released from the POW camp on May 1948, three years after the war.

7   Both Csengeri and Friedländer were listed in a detailed list of Mühldorf camp's dead. It covers the camp's short history from its opening in June 1944, to its last full day of operation on April 28, 1945.

8   Confirmed by a letter from Andre Scharf, KZ-Gedenkstätte Dachau, April 22, 2014.

Still wet, they were herded to the next room and issued striped pants and shirts made of a coarse fabric, a pullover, prisoner's jacket, cap, and an overcoat. Some of the clothing items were too large, some too small. The functionary who threw the items at them did not even try to match them to fit. Finally, they were handed a strip with their prisoner numbers and ordered to sew them onto their shirts. They did not get any shoes. They would need to depend on their own shoes, and if they failed, the Third Reich would rather lose a slave than provide a new pair.

The MUSZs of the defunct 101/35 Company became German slaves. Some of them rode together from Püspökladány to Gomel. They had known each other for at least a year. About half would not survive to see the collapse of Nazi Germany. Many more would die soon after liberation from diseases and injuries suffered while in camp. But those who survived would thank the friendships and trust they developed during the many months of Labor Service. Hardly anyone could survive life in a concentration camp for more than three months without a friend to lean on.

They were marched across the dimly lit parade square by a veteran prisoner to their "block," as the long barracks were called in Dachau. When they crossed one of the cross streets, they could see a tall fence topped with barbed wires. It was electrified, designed to kill anyone who touched it. Bright white beams circling from the top of watchtowers searched for prisoners attempting escape.

Very few prisoners ever escaped a German concentration camp.[9] The challenge was not only scaling or crawling under the elaborate fences and evading the guards and their dogs, but also to survive outside. Even sympathetic locals declined hiding runaway prisoners. Anyone caught harboring escaped prisoners, particularly Jews, was executed along with his family and often with other randomly caught neighbors. Surviving outside the concentration camp was often harder than inside. Yet, the SS spared no effort to prevent escape.

The quickest way out, prisoners used to joke, was through the crematorium chimneys.

A prisoner functionary met them at the door. Like other functionaries he looked healthy, well-dressed and confident. He was the "Block Elder." Even those who did not speak German must have already understood that the title "Elder" signified power, not necessarily age.

---

9 Analysis by the State Museum Auschwitz-Birkenau in Oświęcim shows that 802 prisoners attempted escape from Auschwitz and only 144 were successful. According to the Dachau camp memorial site (http://www.kz-gedenkstaette-dachau.de), 582 prisoners attempted escape. There was no record of how many remained free.

The Block Elder led them in. A long narrow alley separated between two rows of bunk beds, or rather three levels of wooden shelves padded with thin straw sacks. The shelves appeared fully occupied to the last available inch with prisoners lying on their backs or sitting at the edge with their legs dangling into the alley. They turned quiet when the Elder entered, leading the new inmates. To anyone but the Elder, fitting in even one additional prisoner would be impossible. But by moving one veteran inmate to the right, another to the left, he cleared enough space for all his new charges. This narrow strip of territory was to become the prisoner's bed, home and the storage space for his few earthly belongings.

Even the restricted life in Dachau left a few remaining choices that inmates tried to use to optimize their condition. For example, which was better: the top shelf, the middle or the bottom? At first glance, the top would be the best. It provided slightly more privacy, less interruption from upper bunk mates climbing up and down; it could even be a better hiding place from the wrath of the Block Elder. But climbing to the top became painfully hard after many days of hard labor and malnutrition. It could sap the little energy still left at the end of the day. In a life where every calorie mattered, selecting the wrong shelf could prove deadly.

Or, which was better, sleeping with one's head facing his neighbor's head or his feet? At this high density sleeping arrangement, the intimacy between two neighbors was closer than between husband and wife. Every sound, smell and movement coming from the left and the right was amplified.

How to face the alley, head first or feet first? It mattered when trying at night to slide out between two sleeping prisoners to use the bucket at the end of the block, without disturbing their sleep.

A critical issue was protecting from thieves the few possessions a prisoner had, particularly while sleeping. Every item was critical for survival. There were active black markets in the camps where everything could be traded: spoons for cigarettes, cigarettes for a portion of bread, even gold teeth for a few daily rations of bread. Everyone could trade. But thieves supplied most of the available goods. They stole from inmates in their own block or other blocks, from functionaries, guards, the kitchen, warehouses, parked trucks, and even civilians, if their work assignments permitted some contact.

With no safe place to keep their possessions, prisoners slept fully dressed, their shoes under their heads, their tin cups tied to their pants and their spoons in the pocket along with a slice of bread they might have saved from dinner. Those who did not learn by the first night how to protect their possessions started their first full day in camp without their shoes, coat or eating utensils: an almost certain death sentence, often within a day or two.

After giving each of the new prisoners a slice of bread and a slice of sausage, the Elder called it a night. No one was allowed to leave the block until the morning call. A bucket at the end of the block was the communal chamber pot. The unlucky prisoner who reached the bucket when full had to haul it out to the main latrine a few blocks away, an unpleasant chore even on a mild night.

For the next two days the entire block had no assignments other than the morning and evening *Appells*.[10] Two full days without work, chores or endless parades were an unusual gift. A full day without any duties was granted only once a year—on Christmas.

Other camp survivors (42) describe the enormous shock of their first days in camp. Nothing in their previous life could prepare them for this experience. They landed on a different planet (43) with inhabitants, rules, and language that could not be imagined, let alone comprehended, by members of "Planet Earth."

Even survivors of the harsh Hungarian Forced Labor had to learn quickly these new rules and language—or die.

They had to learn that their food rations were insufficient to sustain their lives. They might have not known the exact calorie count. But if received at all, the daily rations would provide only 1,400 calories while work outside in the cold would consume at least 4,500. Unless they found food supplements, this calorie deficit would consume their body fat and muscles in less than three months, unless, of course, death struck sooner.

Hunger in the camp was the most effective killer, even if not the primary cause. Hunger accelerated the path to death from other causes. It opened up the body to diseases and made disease or injury more persistent. It made the weakened prisoners careless at work, more susceptible to beating, punishments, and accidents. Even the slightest loss of mobility could spell death in the hands of Kapos, OT supervisors, or in an accident. And hunger made the body thin and sickly. Sickly looking prisoners failed the weekly selections and were sent to Auschwitz or Dachau to be disposed of in the gas chambers. It did not matter which tentacle of hunger seized the victim, the end result was always the same.

They had to learn how the camp hierarchy operated. They must have recognized quickly the immense power vested in the hands of the Block

---

10   Appell—"roll call" in German.

Elder and his functionaries. They could injure or kill any of their prisoners, anytime and for any reason. But they must have also noticed that all functionaries looked well-fed, obviously by having better access to food. They could only guess whether they earned, traded, or stole it from other prisoners or from the camp supply.

Standing for hours in the morning and evening Appells, they must have noticed that the Block Elder was fearful of the SS officers who watched the proceedings closely. The Elder and his functionaries were like lapdogs, eager to please their patrons by torturing and injuring their subjects. The power granted to any of them could be withdrawn by an SS officer instantaneously. Their status was guaranteed for only twelve hours: from morning Appell to evening and from evening Appell to morning. To survive, almost all camp functionaries subjugated their souls to the devil. Only a handful kept both their jobs and dignity successfully.

Laci was lucky to speak German. Although he was in a "Hungarian" block and his Block Elder was Hungarian, Dachau was a German camp. Orders were given mostly in German. In the words of Primo Levi: "The greater part of the prisoners who did not understand German died during the first ten or fifteen days after their arrival: at first glance, from hunger, cold, fatigue, and disease; but after a more attentive examination, due to insufficient information." (39 p. 93)

In two days, the "Earthling" Laci became a KZ.[11]

On the third day, after the morning Appell, the entire block was marched back to the train station along with hundreds of prisoners from other blocks and loaded into boxcars. A few hours later they were in Ampfing. Laci's group and KZs from three boxcars were ordered off the train and lined up on the ramp by yelling Kapos. Several SS officers holding angry barking dogs on their leashes stood behind and watched. Most of the train cars remained locked and the train departed carrying its cargo to the next unknown destination.[12]

---

11 KZ—acronym for *Konzentrationslager*—"concentration camp" in German. Prisoners were often called KZ.

12 I saw Ampfing's new train station on my drive to Mühldorf, off the Munich highway exit. The old station was destroyed by British Liberator bombers less than two months before the camp was liberated.

   Laci told me that he watched these bombings, lying under a tree while the SS officers were hiding in nearby bomb shelters. He must have been euphoric to see his tormentors running for their lives and their facilities destroyed.

   The station I saw from the road projected none of the terror of SS officers, vicious barking dogs and Kapos with truncheons herding confused prisoners out of the boxcars.

The camp, located deep in the forest, away from prying eyes, was the construction site of a massive bunker that was part of a network of bunkers scattered around Dachau. Construction began in June 1944. It was part of Germany's last-ditch effort to win the war. The Red Army was steadily progressing from the east, recapturing territories occupied by Germany in 1941, and was already going beyond. They were now nearing Hungary's eastern border. Germany had been defeated in North Africa and the Allies were progressing from the south through Italy. Regular aerial bombings mostly by American and British bombers inflicted heavy damage on the German industry, transportation, military installations and civilian centers. And the Allied had just landed in Normandy opening a new front in the west. To win the war Germany had to have a new weapon with overwhelming capabilities unmatched by the Allies.

One of these potential superweapons was the Messerschmitt Me-262, the first operational jet-engine-powered fighter airplane. (44) It was the fastest and most agile plane in the skies and was believed by the Luftwaffe, the German air force, capable of stopping the massive bombing missions launched from Britain by outmaneuvering the fighter planes that accompanied the bombers, and then destroying the bombers themselves. Although its initial role was as a defensive weapon, once Germany regained its air superiority, it could become an offensive weapon as well.

A few prototypes of the Me-262 had already flown combat missions. But to have any effect, Germany had to build hundreds of these planes each month. To scale up the manufacturing of this critical weapon, while avoiding continuous Allied aerial attacks, factories had to be moved below ground or into massive bunkers. Furthermore, with the front converging on Germany from all sides, such critical facilities had to be located in the heart of Germany, as far as possible from any front line.

In March 1944, the German high command considered converting mine-shafts, caves, and tunnels into critical industrial facilities. (44 p. 99) Hundreds were identified, but only a few qualified. (45) Consequently, Hitler and Göring ordered the construction of immense bunkers, between six hundred and eight

---

A commuter train stopped and unloaded two young women with their baby strollers. Even the parents of these women, I thought, might not have been born when Laci's train stopped there.

But the grandparents of these women were there. They must have seen the prisoners. Were they glad to see Jews marched like slaves to what was likely to be their end? Were they repulsed by the inhumane cruelty they witnessed? It was probably both.

hundred thousand square feet each, six to eight stories below ground, with only the top exposed. (46) Six of these bunkers were to be built within seven months: two near Mühldorf to manufacture parts for the Me-262 (47) and four in Kaufering near Landsberg, west of Munich to assemble the planes. (48)

Both sites, at Kaufering and Mühldorf, were ideally located for the construction of these bunkers. They were in the heart of Germany, at that time still far from any front, near rivers that could provide water and gravel to mix concrete, near forests to hide the construction and to camouflage the bunkers and near existing railroads along which supplies could be delivered and manufactured parts could be shuttled. The plants housed in these gigantic bunkers were projected to produce four hundred planes per month. (44 p. 100) They were to become the core of the entire German airplane manufacturing effort. Germany's military might was going to reemerge there.

There remained only one problem: manpower. Most able-bodied German men were already serving, many had died, injured, or imprisoned in POW camps. Women, teenagers and older men were operating critical services such as power stations, hospitals, bakeries, food distribution, sanitation and burying the dead. They could not be diverted without collapsing what remained of the German economy and social structure. But Jewish men from recently occupied Hungary were available; or more precisely, those who were not yet deported to Auschwitz or if deported, not gassed. They remained as almost the only available source of labor, other than Russian POWs.

The proximity of Dachau to Kaufering and Mühldorf made it the perfect processing center for the new slave labor. Trains carrying Jewish men started rolling in from Hungary and Auschwitz.

Extraordinary construction projects, like these nationally critical bunkers, require extraordinary engineering. Franz Dischinger, a prominent German engineer and a Hitler sympathizer, was selected to design the Mühldorf and Kaufering bunkers. (49)

One of my engineering professors told in class that he once assigned his students a project: to design a pipeline that would carry blood from the north of Israel to the south. Not one of his students asked why blood needed to be carried in pipelines across the country. They were only concerned with the technicalities. *"Those engineers had no heart,"* the professor lamented, *"like Dischinger."*

Dischinger achieved fame by inventing advanced techniques for the construction of concrete domes. He also held patents on bridge construction and pre-stressed concrete. Hitler himself reviewed Dischinger's plans for the bunkers and initially rejected the use of concrete because the reinforcement steel might rust and not survive the Thousand-Year Reich. Hitler wanted the bunkers built with stone. On the verge of the collapse of the Third Reich, Hitler and his regime were still obsessed with their grandiose illusions and with their hatred of the Jews. Eventually, he conceded to the plans.

Dischinger's design called for a catenary-shaped arch, a natural shape that uniform cables hanging between two poles take due to their own weight. (50) Of course, the bunker arch was an inverted (or concave) catenary. A catenary is best suited to carry its own weight under the force of gravity and therefore an inverted catenary is the most likely to withstand force from above, like the impact of large aerial bombs.

The arch, spanning 260 feet and rising 50 feet above ground, was made of a nine-foot-thick concrete that was to be augmented to fifteen feet by a second layer to be added after the first layer was set. That thickness alone was nearly the height of a two-story building.

To support the arch while the concrete was poured and until it hardened, KZs amassed a gravel mound and covered it with thin concrete slabs to shape its precise contour. When the nine-foot thick concrete arch that was poured on this contour was set, the gravel was drained through openings in its base into a trolley that ran in a pre-built tunnel below the mound.

A British intelligence committee determined after the war that only an engineer with access to an "abundance of cheap labor" but suffering from "the dearth of good construction equipment, lack of basic construction material such as cement and form lumber" would choose this as a construction method.[13] (46 p. 2)

The construction of the Mühldorf bunkers was managed by three organizations, each with its own responsibilities. The design and primary management were in the hands of Organisation Todt (OT), a government branch named after its founder Fritz Todt. (51) Before the war, OT was a civil engineering group within the Inspector of German Roadways. One of its major tasks was construction of the German Autobahn (highway) system. But later in the war it was absorbed by the Ministry of Armament and War Production

---

[13] After the war, the US Army demolished six of the seven arches of the Mühldorf bunkers. It was its largest demolition project in Germany. The arches were overdesigned. Calculated to withstand one-ton bombs, they required a hundred and twenty-five, well-placed, tons for demolition.

and charged with constructing major military installations such as the launch pads for the V-1 and V-2 rockets or the Atlantic Sea Wall—a massive array of coastline fortifications.

The actual construction was contracted to Polensky and Zöllner, an old, well-established German construction firm.

P&Z recalled two hundred of its workers and necessary equipment for this project from other projects in Europe. (47 p. 2) But in addition to its engineers, managers and foremen, it needed at least eight thousand manual laborers to clear the forest, pile the gravel into mounds, carry steel bars for reinforcement and cement bags to the concrete mixers, build wooden forms to hold the liquid concrete and help drain the gravel.

I remember seeing a painting of slaves building the Egyptian pyramids, thousands of men climbing like ants the steep slopes of the pyramid carrying on their backs square stones. In the forefront of the painting stands a half-naked Egyptian slave master cracking a long whip over the bent backs of the slaves. In Mühldorf, P&Z foremen played that role.

The third organization, the SS, procured the slaves from among prisoners of war and Jews from occupied territories, mostly Hungary. They owned the KZs and sold their labor. They were responsible for housing and guarding them after hours in their barracks and delivering them daily to the work site and back. Organisation Todt, through their contractor P&Z, were responsible for assigning the *Hilfsarbeiter*, or "helper workers" as the KZs were classified, their work, guarding, managing, and feeding them lunch while on site.

Some of those civilians P&Z personnel treated their KZ slaves with compassion. Some shared with them their own lunch, others tried to reduce their work load. But most were brutal and uncaring, just like the SS.[14]

As law and order required, all workers were paid for their labor. Legally, the KZs were not slaves. Their pay scale was determined by their country of origin and race rather than skill or ability, German prisoners at the top of the pay scale. Jews, at the bottom, were paid one-third that of a German prisoner, 60 pfennigs per hour. The SS, acting as the trustee of these "non-slave" slaves, collected their earnings on their behalf and, of course, neglected to pass it on.

---

14 I cannot imagine a professional returning from work in the evening, eating a warm dinner, enjoying pleasant music, playing with his children and sleeping peacefully in his clean, warm bed, after overseeing slaves dressed in tattered clothes plodding in the snow, seeing them fall from unsafe scaffoldings to their deaths or simply being beaten to death by their Kapos. And yet, there were hundreds of these professionals in Mühldorf and Kaufering.

At the end of the war, P&Z sent OT a bill of 25,867,592 reichsmarks, partly to cover the cost of 1,699,184.40 reichsmarks for the 2,831,974 hours of the Jewish *Hilfsarbeiter*. (47 p. 3) That bill was never paid. Nor did the SS, P&Z, and OT compensate the 3,076 KZs who died out of the 8,300 deported to Mühldorf, or the emotional and health consequences of the enslavement of those who survived. (47 p. 10)

Seventy years after World War II, P&Z has a live website. It is an active concern with projects in Saudi Arabia, Iraq, Oman, Libya, Brazil, and Abu Dhabi that include a major highway, bridges and palaces. The company was founded in 1880 and until World War II it built bridges, tunnels, a mountain pass in Austria, and a shipyard in Holland. Today's website is mute about P&Z's activities during WWII. Like Dischinger, they wish the world would forget about this part of their past business. The present-day P&Z is distancing itself from its criminal use of slave labor and its close association with the Nazi regime. But this is a modern sentiment. In 1955, during its 75th jubilee celebrations, P&Z proudly displayed the plans of the Mühldorf bunker as an example of its capabilities. In Germany, as late as 1955, Nazi involvement did not carry a negative stigma. The success of a unique engineering project mattered more than its purpose.

Walking together, Laci, Csengeri, Neumann and Friedländer marched through the streets of Ampfing, open farmlands and forest roads. Angry Kapos and barking SS dogs kept the KZs in line. After a few miles they reached *Waldlager 5* ("Forest Camp 5"), as the sign on the gate indicated.

The idyllic name did not conceal its true nature. It was one of several KZ camps surrounding the construction site. Tall double electrified fences topped with barbed wire surrounded the camp. Signs marked the area between the fences as a "free shooting" zone, anyone inside that space could be shot without warning, as if warnings were given anywhere else. Engineers of the US Army discovered after the war that the fences reached below ground to prevent escape by tunneling. The Germans spared no cost or effort to prevent the escape of the slaves whom they intended to kill when their usefulness was at an end.

Compared to Dachau, Waldlager 5 was small and at first sight it might have seemed an improvement to the MUSZ who had endured the conditions of the Hungarian Forced Labor. Unlike the Hungarian Army, the SS provided housing, tent-like huts made of cardboard or plywood painted dark green. The huts, called *Finnenzelte* ("Finnish tents"), (47 p. 9) looked much friendlier than the Blocks in Dachau.

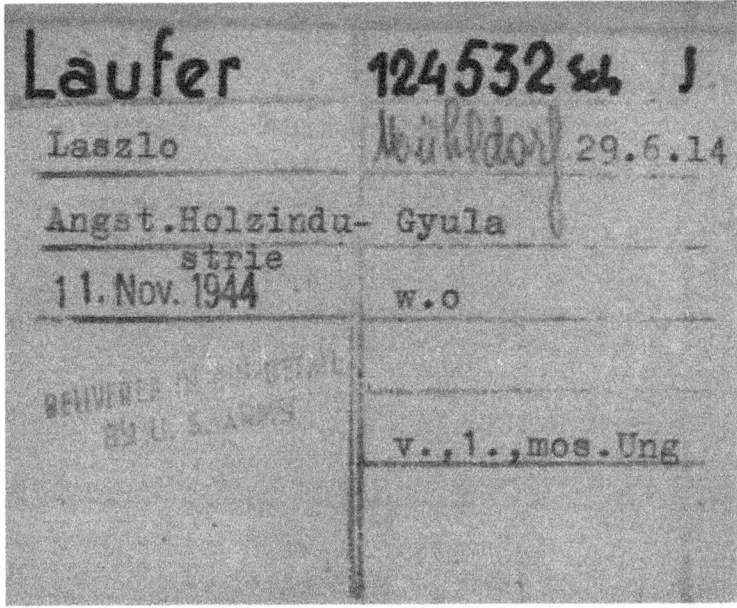

Laci's Mühldorf registration card. The date shown, November 11, 1944, is of his arrival to Dachau. The reverse side of this card shows the date of his arrival in Mühldorf, November 14, 1944

A wide dirt road divided the camp into two areas: on one side the green Finnenzeltes and on the other side, smaller huts still under construction. Several prisoners were carrying timber from a pile near the construction site to a spot where one of the new huts was being built.

Registration in Waldlager 5 was similar to Dachau. Laci's registration card still showed him as prisoner number 124532 in "Protective Custody" and marked as "Angestellte Holzindustrie"—employee in the timber industry.

After registration they were deloused and a camp elder assigned Laci and Csengeri to their Finnenzelte.

Csengeri opened the small front door, lowering his head to enter and held it open for Laci to join him. The Finnenzelte that looked so promising from the outside was dreadful. An overwhelming stench filled the closed and crowded space. Although most of the Finnenzelte's occupants were away at work, the smell of their unwashed bodies permeated the filthy straw covering the ground and lingered in the air, mixing with the smell of excrement rising from a bucket at the far end. Two rats ran away when the two humans invaded their territories, squealing in excitement. Hiding behind the bucket, they eyed their new prey that they would savor at night along with the lice crawling in the straw.

For the first time since entering the German KZ system, Laci and Csengeri were left alone, free to move around the camp. About half of the Finnenzeltes were empty. But the rest were occupied by sleeping KZs. They were the night shift crew. Construction in Mühldorf continued around the clock, six days a week.

They went from Finnenzelte to Finnenzelte to look for KZs from Gyula or Békéscsaba, for someone who might bring news from home. They had not seen or heard from anyone from home in more than a year. But they did not find anyone.

In the last Finnenzelte they found two men, or rather two living skeletons, lying on the floor. One was asleep and the other was looking at the yellow glow of the light bulb with glassy eyes. His slightly open mouth was gasping for air with slight short breaths. Csengeri lowered himself next to the man to ask if he knew anyone from Békéscsaba.

"*Is that you, Imre?*" whispered the man in a barely audible voice when he saw Csengeri.

Imre watched him startled, unable to respond. He now recognized him. It was Farkas Lipòt.

"*Don't you recognize your uncle anymore? I am Lipòt.*"

Csengeri was speechless.

Lipòt's eyes filled with tears. "*I thought no one would recognize me. Look what happened to me,*" Lipòt said.

"*Lipòt Bácsi,*[15] *of course I recognize you,*" Csengeri said finally, trying but failing to hide his horror. Lipòt became a *Muselmann*.[16] (37 p. 61)

Csengeri lifted him in his arms like a baby. Lipòt's flesh has dissipated. Only bones were left, held together by sagging skin. He had been consumed by hard labor and a starvation diet. His spirit was broken by the brutality surrounding him and by the loss of any hope. Lipòt expected death with apathy or maybe with anticipation and gratitude.

Csengeri laid him down on his mat.

"*Please tell everyone at home that you saw me here and that I thought of them,*" Lipòt whispered. "*But please don't tell them how I looked.*"

---

15 *Bácsi*—"uncle" in Hungarian (pronounced "Baachi"). It may also be used by a young person to address respectfully an older man.

16 *Muselmann*—a German KZ term of unclear origin describing an inmate that has been reduced by hunger, exhaustion and disease to near death and has already given up on life.

There was nothing that Laci or Imre could do to help him. Three days later, Lipòt's body was carried out during the morning Appell and thrown like a log on a cart with other dead bodies. His block elder crossed him off his list. His cause of death was recorded as *Herzschwäche*, or heart failure.[17]

Laci and Csengeri were so preoccupied with their search for acquaintances and their own thoughts that they barely noticed that the camp turned dark and that the day shift slaves were back. Shouts of "Appell," "Everyone to the Appellplatz," brought them back to reality. Prisoners of both day and night shifts rushed to the parade place for the evening roll call.

After lining up by their blocks, the Block Elders counted the KZs of each block and reported their number to the Camp Elder. Two KZs were missing.

"*Two 'degenerates' are missing,*" he began to yell as two SS officers arrived for the final roll.

The SS ordered a recount and threatened the Camp Elder loudly that he would pay with his life if the two were not found. The Camp Elder knew the threat was real. He was visibly agitated, yelling obscenities as he swung his truncheon at the Block Elders who in turn yelled and threatened their Kapos.

All the while, the prisoners stood at attention. The new prisoners who had nothing to eat since a breakfast of ersatz coffee and a slice of bread in Dachau were thirsty and hungry. The fall evening was turning cold. After repeated counts the two KZs remained missing.

Hurriedly, the Kapos and block elders were sent to search the camp. Within minutes two of them returned dragging a skeleton-like inmate. His naked upper body was covered with mud.

"*We found him dead, face down in a puddle near the latrine,*" one of them announced to the SS officers. "*Must have croaked on his way here.*"

"*One less pig to worry about,*" one of the Germans shrugged.

The KZs remained standing for hours. The second inmate was not found. Some of the standing inmates fainted and were left lying at the feet of the others. No one moved. Occasional shouts of the Camp Elder and threats of the SS officers broke the quiet. Finally, triumphant shouts came from the far end of the camp, near the latrines.

Two Block Elders showed up announcing they found the missing KZ, dragging him under his arms while the terrified man pleaded for mercy.

"*We found him hiding in a bush near the latrine,*" one of the Elders declared.

"*You were trying to escape,*" snarled one of the SS.

---

17   Farkas Lipòt, prisoner 83433, was listed on the Mühldorf list of dead. He died on November 17, 1944.

"I was in the latrine when the Appell was called," pleaded the prisoner. "I do not want to escape, I did not want to do anything wrong. I had diarrhea and by the time I could run to the Appellplatz the camp turned quiet and I knew I was late. I was afraid to come."

"Beat him," ordered one officer pointing towards the Camp Elder.

Two Block Elders lifted the man from his knees and held him tight against a pole that was standing at the center of the Appellplatz for that purpose. Using his truncheon the Camp Elder beat the inmate until his cries faded away.

"Leave him there," ordered the SS when he saw the man was dead.

The two victims were left in the Appellplatz until the next morning, waiting for the morning collection of the night's dead.

Laci and Csengeri spent their first night on the Finnenzelte's floor squeezed between their new mates. They were woken up before dawn by the Kapos cursing and yelling and rushed to the morning line-up in the Appellplatz. While being counted, two Kapo aides hauled a large kettle filled with steaming liquid and a cart filled with bread loaves.

This was the breakfast. Every four prisoners were given one loaf of bread, to split among themselves. This was their bread ration for the day.[18] Whoever had a cup also got coffee. No cup, no coffee.

A line of a hundred prisoners formed in front of the food. When Laci reached the head of the line his tin cup was filled with a brownish warm liquid. Together with Csengeri, Neumann, and Friedländer, they got one loaf.

Like other inmates, they moved to a corner near their Finnenzelte to figure out how to divide their bread. They had no knife, of course. Laci sipped the brown liquid. It had a foul bitter taste. It was made of ground acorns.[19]

After four days in the KZ system, the permanent, deep hunger that would accompany them until they died or were liberated was already dominating. Hunger would squeeze their stomachs in a knot, consume their thoughts

---

18 In addition to the morning ration, KZs received lunch at their work site. The quality of that lunch was usually consistent with the camp's starvation diet. But in a few work sites, it was nutritious and helped extending the lives of the KZs employed there.

19 Acorns fill my yard every fall. I once read that acorns are edible and nourishing and that American Indians used them to make flour. I tasted a raw acorn. It was horribly bitter, hardly the substance to use for flour. To eliminate their foul taste, I tried to soak and boil a batch of peeled acorns multiple times: they turned yellowish and soft, but their bitterness hardly dissipated. I doubt the Waldlager 5's kitchen made any effort to wash out the bitterness of their acorns before brewing the ersatz coffee. It must have tasted terrible. But at least it was warm, and some vitamins, minerals, and calories must have leaked into the liquid, making it a worthwhile drink.

and take over their dreams. (42 pp. 74-75) Their eyes would constantly scan for anything that could fill their empty stomach: weeds, potato peels, even sawdust.

Dividing a loaf of bread required elaborate strategies that would assure that the four shares were precisely equal, or at least that the distribution felt fair. Once the bread was divided, each KZ had to decide for himself whether to eat it at once, enjoy a brief moment of satiety but then suffer a punishing hunger until the next distribution, keep the ration and eat it in small chunks throughout the day but risk it being lost or stolen, or trade it.

"*I have an idea,*" started Csengeri after the four thought for a few minutes how to divide the bread. "*Laci and I will be one team, and the two of you will be the other. I will break the bread in two as fairly as I can, and you two will choose which piece you want. Tomorrow we will switch roles, you will break the bread and we will get to choose. Once the bread is split, Laci and I will do the same with our share.*"

Friedländer already anticipated that he would need a knife and sharpened the handle of his spoon on a rock. He turned the knife to Csengeri who cut the bread into two pieces. He collected the crumbs and distributed them among the four people.

The bread was at least a day old and very coarse. It probably contained sawdust. They had eaten sawdust bread in the Hungarian Force Labor system and easily recognized it. Like the coffee, the bread provided only marginal nutritional value.

A veteran KZ passed by the four and advised not to eat their portion all at once. Their suffering until their next portion would be enormous, he warned.

Laci shrugged and did not reply. Trust was a rare commodity in the Waldlager. That KZ might have had good intentions, but nothing could be more devastating than losing a daily ration. He preferred to suffer until the next day's distribution, but be certain that the few calories he received remained his. Laci ate his entire portion. At least his pocket was empty, he thought, and therefore ready to accommodate other food items should he come across one.

The Appell was at seven. If they wished to wash, they had to do so beforehand. There were only two faucets of running cold water to serve the hundreds of KZs and one latrine with multiple holes in the ground with no partitions. Relieving oneself was difficult, washing in the morning was nearly impossible.

Primo Levi discusses the importance of washing daily, even in the middle of the winter in freezing water and in filthy washbasins. (42 p. 40) It was not just about hygiene. It was part of the fight of the KZ to maintain his human dignity: a "moral survival."

The morning roll call was shorter than the evening. The SS were more interested in getting the slaves to work than in torturing them. And that morning the count matched.

"*Is there anyone here with experience in construction?*" asked the SS officer when the count was completed.

Prisoners hesitated to respond. Often these were trick questions intended to find victims for an atrocity or degrading chores. But five prisoners stepped forward. They were assigned to a Kapo wearing a blue armband who marched them away.

"*Is there anyone who worked with timber before?*"

Laci stepped forward. It was a risky decision. But from the Appellplatz he could see the construction site of the new wooden huts. A job there could be relatively easy and safe, he thought. It was a risk worth taking.

Three other KZs stepped forward. The SS waved with his switch towards a Kapo standing by who jumped to attention shouting "*Jawohl*" and then motioned to the KZs to follow him. As Laci hoped, the Kapo led them to the hut construction site across the wide dirt road.

Several triangular-shaped, low-lying huts, no more than three or four feet tall, were already completed in what was, as the Kapo explained, the winter camp. Short ditches dug parallel to the standing huts filled the remaining space of the new site. They were approximately three feet deep and thirty feet long. (52)

"*Work here is much easier than at the bunker site,*" said the Kapo when they stopped next to one of the ditches. "*These are the Erdhütte.*[20] (47 p. 9) *We're all moving here in a month and we need to build them fast.*"

The ditch they were looking at was to become the corridor that runs along the Erdhütte. The Erdhütte itself was made of two wood plates attached together lengthwise to form a triangular prism, or a tent, supported by logs and anchored to the ground above the ditch. Ten "beds," or more accurately placements for straw sacks, were dug into the flat ground on each side of the ditch. The Erdhütten were covered with dirt for insulation and camouflage.

"*We need logs,*" the Kapo explained. "*We'll go to the forest and cut down some pine trees and bring them back. You may even be able to organize*[21] (37 p. 72)

---

20   Erdhütte—"Mud huts" in German.
21   "Organize" in the KZ language meant to get something in a semi legal or even illegal way. It could simply mean "stealing" from Germans or farmers. Stealing from another inmate

some extra food along the way," the Kapo concluded magnanimously. *"I won't stop you."*[22]

The Kapo led them and ten other earlier recruited KZs through the gate into the forest. Some of them carried crosscut saws, long enough to cut thick logs. Laci remembered seeing workers in Sándor's lumberyard working in pairs using similar saws, one man held one handle of the saw on one side of the log and the other the handle on the opposite side. Other KZs carried axes. Two KZs pulled an empty cart. An armed SS officer riding on his horse followed the procession.

Along the way Laci noticed stumps of freshly cut trees. They were only two or three inches in diameter, about the size of the logs he saw in the pile. The uncut trees were mostly thicker and taller.

The Kapo was right, Laci thought. This was not dangerous and the weather was rather comfortable. He had done similar work before, and he might even find some food in the forest: winter mushrooms, like Endre used to find, edible leaves, even acorns or chestnuts.

They reached their work site. At least ten slim trees were standing there.

They started cutting them down and removed their branches. The group was ordered to have twenty trees cut and stripped of their branches, loaded on the cart, and returned to camp before lunch. If they were late, the Kapo warned, they would not have lunch.

"Schnell, arbeit," snarled the SS in German.

Laci and his saw-mate began cutting a pine. The wood was soft but the saw was dull. But in less than an hour their tree was cut, stripped of its branches and added to the logs piling on the cart. They only needed to cut two more logs to meet their quota.

"We just may make it to lunch," Laci's teammate said while wandering off their immediate area to find their next log.

They were out of sight of the SS and the Kapo. It was an opportunity to scavenge. The forest was preparing for winter. The leaves of the deciduous trees had already fallen, their acorns and nuts buried under the dead leaves waiting to sprout in the spring. Only the pines remained green. Winter mushrooms could hide under layers of dead needles. Laci and his mate did not have much time, they could not remain out of sight for too long and they had a quota to meet. Almost immediately, Laci found winter mushrooms under one

---

could still be expressed as "organizing," but not always. The word was later adopted in the Hebrew language and often used in the IDF with a nearly identical meaning.

22 Though extremely rare, there were kind Kapos.

of the trees and following his lead, the other KZ found a few for himself. They ate them raw.

Digging under a barren deciduous tree, they found a handful of chestnuts still enclosed inside their thorny cupules. They quickly pocketed several as the SS officer appeared behind them on his horse yelling obscenities.

It was a close call. Laci already knew that finding "illegal" food could be punishable by death.

With fresh food in their stomachs and chestnuts in their pockets, the next two trees came down easily.

They returned to their "golden patch" before returning to camp to get more mushrooms and chestnuts.

Close to noon, twenty logs were piled on the cart and the KZs began pushing it back to camp. When they arrived, a line of prisoners was already standing in front of a large kettle with steaming fluid. They unloaded their logs on a pile next to a timber-peeling machine and joined the line.

Lunch, like breakfast, was meager, a cupful of vegetable soup. The Camp Elder's functionary used his ladle to fill the KZ's cups. Laci noticed that the ladle skimmed the thin liquid at the surface barely capturing any vegetables that sank to the bottom. Those were waiting to be scooped out when the *Prominenten*[23] (42 p. 90) and other privileged were served their lunch. When Laci was served, the ladle was not even full.

Laci sat down to eat his soup alone, facing the functionary and watching him distribute the soup. The Camp Elder stood behind him watching the process like a hawk. Occasionally he uttered a word and the functionary reached to the bottom of the pot bringing up rich soup, loaded with vegetables and even scraps of meat, giving it to the lucky KZ in line.

On one occasion, the Camp Elder ordered a KZ to return his portion and get a refill from the top of the pot.

The Camp Elder was obviously controlling the distribution. He must be selling the privilege of soup from the bottom of the pot, Laci concluded, and chestnuts might be the right currency. If that was true, then they were like gold coins: they did not spoil and they fit in his pocket.

After lunch they returned to the forest for another load of logs and reached a new spot.

---

23 The *Prominenten* ("Prominents" in German) were the KZ functionaries. They included the Lagerältester (Camp Elder) at the top, Kapos, cooks, down to the Scheissminister (Latrine Superintendent) at the bottom. Prominents were rewarded for their services and stood a better chance of survival then their peer KZs.

Laci and his mate began cutting. Winter mushrooms were abundant. They ate while cutting, chipping at the hunger that would not be satiated with mushrooms. They needed proteins and they needed fat.

With night coming early—their workday was mercifully short. It was dark when they returned. The logs they brought at noon were already peeled and moved to the construction site. Laci watched that progress with dismay. Two new Erdhütten were completed since morning. He counted the ditches; at this rate the construction would be completed in a month.

After unloading the logs they were marched back to their side of the camp in time for the evening Appell. It was getting cold. Heavy storm clouds were coming in from the west.

Roll call was quick. The SS officers were anxious to return to their well-heated barracks to warm up with a cognac or schnapps.

It was Laci's second night in Waldlager and he already had business to conduct: trading his chestnuts for soup or sausage. He had no idea how trades were conducted. He knew they had to be illegal but certainly existed. Was the Camp Elder the trader? He might be too important to trade in chestnuts. But trading his chestnuts tonight would make sense because then he could free his pockets for a new supply the next day.

Dinner was carried in by functionaries of the Block Elder. It was soup again and Laci's portion was once again drawn from the top, watery and nearly empty of any substance. But as the functionary was pouring the soup into Laci's cup, Laci handed him one chestnut. The functionary took it and handed it to the Block Elder.

Laci walked away from the line and sat down watching the distribution. Again, some KZs got their soup from the bottom of the pot. Most others had to be satisfied with a watery meal.

But when the line was thinning, the functionary simply nodded towards Laci. It was nearly imperceptible but Laci saw it. He approached the pot with another chestnut in hand.

"*You're a smart guy,*" the functionary whispered as he filled Laci's cup with another portion of the soup, this time from the bottom. "*But learn how to trade. People are watching.*"

Laci returned to his corner and continued watching. When distribution was over, two functionaries carried the cauldron to a small Finnenzelte. The Block Elder followed them moments later.

Half an hour later, the empty kettle was carried out and placed outside. Hungry KZs swarmed around the pot fighting each other for their turn to lick the bottom of the empty container.

In the morning, when breakfast was brought in, the last night's functionary was serving it again. Laci approached him with two chestnuts in hand. The functionary took them without a word. Laci wondered if this was considered payment for last night's extra portion of soup or down payment for dinner. He would have to wait and see. But at least he knew chestnuts were an acceptable currency.

After morning roll call, they headed out to the forest. On his walk, Laci tried to tally up the calories he consumed and those he burned. He knew the calorie content of bread, hot water, and fat. He assumed that chestnuts had at least as many calories as a small potato. Yesterday his calorie balance did not quite break even. But it was close: his body could tolerate a small deficit for a very long time. Although still hungry, Laci knew that for the time being, starvation or overwork were averted. He was one day closer to seeing Judit.

But Csengeri, Imre Friedländer, and Theodore Neumann were not that lucky. They were sent to the *Baustelle*, the bunker construction site. At the end of their first day, only Csengeri was back to their Finnenzelte, exhausted. His face, clothing, and hands were covered with grey dust and his shoes muddy. He lay on his mat on the floor barely able to speak or keep his swollen eyes open. Laci had to help him out to the Appell and supported him while standing.

"*Where are Imre and Theodor?*" Laci asked him.

"*I have no idea. We got separated once we got to the site. I think that there is another KZ camp around here. Maybe they were sent there.*"

Lying after dinner on the mat next to Laci, Csengeri told him that they were building a gigantic concrete structure, like a giant bunker.[24] (52 p. 174), (37 p. 96) Though the need to build bunkers in Germany's heartland was a wonderful sign that the German army was retreating, Csengeri was troubled that he was helping the enemy build its military strength. It was like rubbing salt on his many wounds.

Of the various construction assignments, Csengeri got the worst. He was assigned to carry 100 pound cement bags up a ramp to a tall concrete mixing machine, three or four stories high, where he dumped its contents and returned to carry up another one. Cement dust leaked through cracks in the bags and

---

24 Charmatz claims that they were building a launch site for the V-1 and V-2 rockets. Sandberg even described the rockets as V-3 that was believed to be more advanced than the V-2. Evidently many inmates, including Laci, could only guess what they were building.

filled his eyes, nose, and throat. (52 p. 175) Not only were the bags heavy, but he could barely breathe. It was like a madhouse scene. There were civilian supervisors, dressed in mustard yellow uniforms. They yelled at the Kapos and the Kapos beat the KZs for good reason or not. Some Kapos were armed, with sticks, others used whips. Almost every KZ was hit at least once. "*Good thing our striped shirts and jackets are made of some hard canvas,*" Csengeri added with his cynical humor, "*I could hardly feel the whip hitting me.*"

Laci pulled mushrooms from his pocket and handed them to Csengeri.

Work at the Baustelle was not only exhausting but deadly. In addition to cement bags, KZs carried large iron rods to the top of the structure, inserted them into wooden forms that were filled with concrete mix by cranes swinging from above. Carrying iron rods was somewhat easier than cement bags because they did not generate cement dust. But they were heavy, bulky, rough, and ice cold, causing many hand injuries. Lack of attention to safety caused numerous accidents by falls from the top of the arch or ramps and by falling objects. And what accidents did not do, savage beating did. Even a light or moderate injury, such as a deep cut or a broken leg was deadly for the lack of treatment.

Construction of the winter camp progressed fast. By mid-December forty Erdhütten were completed and the entire camp moved from the Finnenzeltes to the Erdhütten.

Entrance to an Erdhütte was through a small door at the triangle-shaped front. Even the shortest KZ had to bend to get through the low door, as if crawling into an animal den. Surprisingly, the Germans provided small wood stoves that were placed at the far end and kept the well-insulated huts warm. But this comfort was hardly sufficient to make up for the daytime exposure, loss of calories, and frostbites.

The huts were arranged along little alleys, five huts on each side. Each group of ten huts was considered a "block." The Block Elder and his handful of functionaries kept one hut for themselves that was comfortably furnished with armchairs and a table. The remaining two hundred KZs squeezed into the remaining nine huts.

The provisions Laci "organized" in the forest enhanced his diet with supplements of bread, soup and even sausages he bartered with the Block Elder's functionaries and other inmates. Laci learned that trading took place after work near the latrines. Everything was for sale and surprisingly, prices were consistent. An economist would have labeled it an efficient market. One could trade a pair of shoes for sausages or sausages for cigarettes and cigarettes for gloves. Even dentists were available to extract a gold tooth if needed for a trade.[25]

After one full month in Mühldorf, Laci was still strong and healthy, unlike most of his comrades from the 101/35 unit. Almost everyone suffered injuries: sprained ankles from the daily marches to their work site and back; infected cuts and scrapes that their starved bodies could not heal; broken bones from falls and beatings; infected eyes and persistent coughs from continuous exposure to cement dust; and not the least, frostbites. But worst of all was their diminishing strength. After a month of severe calorie deficit their body fat was mostly consumed. All that was left were their muscles. Their sunken eyes, hollow cheeks, and thin limbs revealed how quickly hunger, hard work, and cold were eating them away. Two of the older members of his group, who survived two years of Hungarian Forced Labor, died before the first month was out.

Laci watched with anguish how quickly they and many of the construction workers were declining. Within a month they were showing worrisome signs. Not *Muselmann* yet, but the spark in their eyes was fading. Their eagerness to survive was gone. Laci knew that if the Americans did not arrive by January, Csengeri, Friedländer, Neumann and many of his Forced Labor friends would not return home.

Laci's luck seemed to run out when the timber harvesting crew returned from its last expedition in the forest. The next day, during the morning Appell, he received his next assignment. The previous day Csengeri was picked for a new assignment. He did not return. There were rumors that a new camp was being built at the opposite side of the construction site and most of the construction workers lived there. Laci hoped that Csengeri, Friedländer and Neumann were there.

At the end of the roll call, after the Block Elder and the SS officer completed their counts and recounts and every one, the living, the sick and the dead were accounted for, the SS officer gave a note to the Block Elder to read aloud. The camp needed wood workers. Laci and three other KZs from his previous team stepped forward. Once again, Laci bet on his life. A short man with an angry face met them. He was their new Kapo.

---

25   Laci was a heavy smoker. He must have craved cigarettes. But if he traded food for cigarettes he would not have survived. Cigarettes provided comfort, but no calories. And yet, many KZs preferred cigarettes over food.

November 1944-May 1945: Dachau and Mühldorf, Germany

The Kapo walked them across the Appellplatz where another group of KZs was already waiting. With an SS officer riding on a horse behind them they headed out of the Waldlager towards the Baustelle. Laci's heart sank. From the distance Laci could hear the sounds of heavy machinery, jackhammers, even shouts, probably Kapos yelling at their slaves.

The sky was gray and the air was damp and cold. It smelled as if a snowstorm was coming. The dirt road was muddy and slippery. Walking fast, with an armed SS officer on a horse behind them and an angry Kapo with a lash at their sides, made it nearly impossible to avoid potholes, ice-cold puddles, or tripping over randomly scattered rocks. Laci's shoes quickly filled with water and he could feel his feet sloshing inside.

After about two miles, the road emerged from the forest into the bunker construction site. It was a vast clearing dominated by an enormous concrete structure shaped as a half-cylinder, like a giant barrel cut in half lengthwise. Cranes on both sides of the half-cylinder were swinging large buckets towards the top and then releasing their grey liquid content as directed by a supervisor.

Hundreds of KZs in striped uniforms hurried on the structure and around the locations where the liquid concrete was released by the cranes. It was an unbelievable sight. To Laci it seemed as though it had been drawn out of a Jules Verne novel. The scene of a mysterious gray concrete structure, under gray sky, in the depth of a vast forest, surrounded by hundreds of people dressed in gray performing a mysterious choreographed dance could not be real. Only a novelist describing life at the bottom of Earth or on another planet could dream up the construction of this edifice of an evil empire.

The half-cylinder stretched at least two hundred yards, taller than a four-story building. Standing at its foot, Laci could see hundreds of short iron rods, protruding from the concrete like the beard of an unshaved giant.

They turned left and started walking with the half-cylinder to their right. The Kapo and the SS kept urging them to move faster, obviously not wanting them to absorb what they saw. Almost running along the structure they reached a new section: the curved surface was covered with large wooden boxes, rather than concrete. KZs were climbing on the structure carrying iron bars, similar to those Laci saw protruding from the concrete, but much longer. Others, standing inside the boxes took the bars and arranged them inside the boxes, tying them together to keep them standing vertically and to form lattice-like structures that were only partly visible to Laci at ground level.

They passed next to one of the giant cranes as it started lifting a large bucket taller than a standing man.[26] (46) One end of the hose that was used to fill it with concrete was pushed aside by a KZ, keeping the other attached to a tall concrete mixer at the crane's base. When freed, the bucket was lifted by the crane. When it reached the top of the mound, a supervisor signaled the operator to align it with a wooden box and then pulled a cord to release its content. When the bucket emptied, several KZs holding rakes jumped into the molasses and spread it around to even its surface.

As Laci passed near the concrete mixing machine he saw a line of KZs marching up on a long ramp from a stack of cement bags at the bottom to the opening of the mixing bowl at the top. Each KZ carried a bag, emptied it at the top into the mixing bowl and turned back down for another bag. Kapos at both ends and along the ramp shouted and beat the helpless KZs with truncheons. Almost no one was spared. The cold drizzle did not slow the KZs or their tormentors.

They continued to run on the dirt road along rails that served as tracks for the cranes to roll freely along the construction site. When they reached the end of this section, they saw what was to become its extension, a gravel mound shaped like the previous sections. Tens of KZs hauling thin concrete slabs climbed on the mound and placed them carefully on the gravel following instructions from German engineers in mustard-yellow overalls, standing on the mound and monitoring the position of the slab through telescopes mounted on tripods.

"Those are theodolites," commented one of the KZs in Laci's group. "*They are using them to accurately define the shape of this structure.*"

Others KZs carried wooden boxes up the mound and laid them on slabs that had already been aligned by the engineers.

A tourist would have admired this large, complex, and well-organized operation if only he could ignore the immense suffering and loss of life of the hundreds of KZs. Even a layman could tell that this was to become a giant bunker for an important war machine.

Walking along the length of this half-cylinder, Laci could see the stages of this construction process, from a nearly completed structure to the precisely shaped gravel mound that would support the concrete when it was poured and until set. It was also a preview of the various jobs he might get, their risks and

---

26 Figure 32A of the Joint Intelligence Objectives Agency report provides many of the details described here.

merits. Although he was not free to choose one, he could at least make a wise decision if asked again to volunteer: which one would expose him to the least to the Kapos' truncheons, which would burn the fewest calories, or be least dangerous.

All the tasks were deadly. They were hard, outside in the cold drizzle, snow, and Arctic blizzards, under the eyes of angry Kapos, and unsafe. There were no good options.

"You there, stop gawking and walk," came a yell from the SS officer on the horse behind Laci, followed by a loud crack of the whip. The whip missed, but there would be other blows that didn't.

They briefly stopped near a group of KZs building one of the wooden boxes.

"Look at these boxes," their Kapo spoke to them for the first time since they left Waldlager. Like many other Kapos in the camp, he spoke Hungarian. *"These are molds for the concrete, we call them forms. We are now going to the joinery where your job will be preparing wooden boards and fasteners for these forms. You will work hard. But if you are careful, follow orders and keep your heads down, you will be much better off there then here outside."*

The angry-looking Kapo was a decent man after all. No wonder he spoke in Hungarian, the SS would not have liked what he said. And once again, Laci chose well by becoming a timber worker.

They entered the joinery, a large wooden building at the edge of the clearing. Like everything in Mühldorf, it was built in a hurry. But unlike the bunker, the large industrial facility was not expected to survive the Thousand-Year-Reich. It was filled with noisy machines and many KZs running about to service them. The place was pleasantly warm, an enormous relief from the cold wind and the icy drizzle in the Baustelle.

Laci no longer needed to worry about the cold, slipping on ice, falling off tall structures, being crushed by falling objects, and not the least, losing precious calories to the cold weather. The only dangers were the Kapos and possibly the machines. He knew he could handle both.

Looking from the entrance at one end of the joinery, Laci saw two columns of large machines arranged in rows. Most of the machines were large circular saws manned by KZs cutting large boards. Several drill presses were used to drill holes in the fasteners that held the boards together into forms. Most of the boards were recycled, gray and dirty.

Sawdust rising from the machines filled the air. With hardly any ventilation, everyone: KZs, Kapos, civilian P&Z supervisors, and the SS officer watching them all from the opposite end had to breath the same dirty air that made them choke and cough.

Beams from large floodlights in the ceiling broke through the dusty cloud and illuminated the space brightly. The scant daylight that entered through the small windows was barely noticeable.

Many KZs ran in pairs along the corridor between the two columns of machinery carrying boards to the saws from a pile at one end of the joinery and cut boards from the saws to other piles at the opposite end.

Four or five P&Z supervisors dressed in yellow overalls, similar to those on the bunker site, monitored the KZs. They were agitated and anxious, yelling at the Kapos and the slaves indiscriminately. The Kapos, in turn, were yelling at the KZs and beating them. The KZs were anxious, too. But they had no one to yell at or beat. They were just running as fast as they could, looking left and right trying to avoid the Kapos. The KZs at the saw pushed the boards into the saw blades as fast as they could. But unfortunately for them, the saws could not be prodded by yells or beatings. Instead, the operators had to absorb the punishments.

The joinery was a bad place too, not far removed from hell. But at least it was warm. For Laci that was a miracle. His striped uniforms and shoes started to dry and his muscles, tight from the cold, relaxed.

"*You two come here,*" yelled one of the civilians in yellow overalls in German, pointing at Laci and the KZ next to him.

They ran to him, removed their caps and stood in attention.

"*You see this board being cut there,*" he pointed at the saw next to him. "*Pick it up and carry it to the pile over there,*" pointing to the pile at the far end of the hall.

The board was large, bulky, and heavy. Laci and his partner picked it up. It was cheap wood that splintered easily.

Following the lead of other prisoners, they ran with the board and laid it on a pile of boards matching theirs in size.

Suddenly, Laci felt a sharp blow of a whip on his back.

"*You idiots,*" came the shout along with another blow. "*Lay the board like everyone else did!*"

Laci and his partner now noticed that their board was not aligned squarely with the rest of the pile. Slightly rotated, the corners were sticking out by an inch. They corrected its position and ran back to "their" saw while the supervisor behind them continued cursing them and the entire Jewish race.

Running along the corridor between the saws Laci noted that all the supervisors' overalls were marked with a company logo Polenski und Zöllner.

They did not work for the SS or the German army, Laci realized. The KZs were slaves, or possibly employees, of a commercial company.

Lunch was at 12:30 sharp. The SS officer blew his whistle and two KZs entered from the door behind him carrying down the main aisle a large steaming cauldron. Another pair followed with a crate of bread loaves. The smell permeating the space was heavenly. All machines stopped. The joinery turned quiet, the sawdust settled down, the few KZs still carrying wooden boards finished their round and joined the line that formed in front of the food. The P&Z supervisors disappeared, leaving only the SS officer to watch the KZs and their Kapos, who, in turn, monitored the food distribution. For a brief moment life felt normal again: no threats, no yells, pleasant warmth, clean air to breathe, and the intoxicating smell of wonderful food.

When Laci reached the front of the line, he saw a soup unlike any since he arrived at Dachau. It was rich, large chunks of vegetables floated in the broth along with fatty animal organs and chunks of potato. The KZ filled Laci's cup to the rim and the other KZ next to him handed him a quarter of a loaf of bread and a slice of sausage. It was the best meal he had eaten in months.

The KZs often wondered if the rich lunches were an act of kindness by the manager of the joinery or a cold business calculation intended to preserve the strength and extend the useful life of the valuable labor force. Whatever the reason, each lunch and each day in the joinery brought Laci one day closer to the finish line.[27]

A heavy snow blizzard started to fall outside while Laci was eating his soup. Through the small dusty windows he saw a thick white blanket coming down, covering the ground and trees. The hot soup and the warm air caused him to sweat but he shivered as he thought of the KZs outside hauling the cement bags to the mixing machine and the ice-cold iron bars to the top of the bunker.

The *Mittagspause*—lunch break lasted exactly thirty minutes. It ended just as abruptly it began, with an ear-piercing whistle blast.

Unbeknownst to Laci, that same day an historic event started running its course nearly four hundred miles to the northwest. It would significantly affect his odds of winning his race with time and the fate of many KZs in the Nazi concentration camps system.

---

27   P&Z was responsible for feeding its workers lunch at food quality that was consistent with the camp's starvation diet. However, several small work sites fed their workers a nutritious lunch. Although one good meal a day was not sufficient to fully compensate for the overall calorie deficit, it did reduce it and therefore extended the lives of its beneficiaries. With only months left to the end of the war, delaying death even by one day could mean survival.

After landing in Normandy in June, the Allied armies progressed rapidly through Western Europe, pushing the crumbling German army back behind Germany's pre-war borders. But the fast progress had consequences: many of the units were exhausted after months of continuous battles and needed a respite, supply lines became too long, deep-water harbors were mostly unavailable and the few that were did not have the capacity to service all the necessary supply ships. By late November 1944, progress on the western front was nearly stopped.

Sensing an opportunity, Hitler decided to secretly assemble a large force in the Ardennes where his intelligence suggested the Allied forces were the weakest. It was also the location where he scored one of his greatest victories in May and June 1940 when against all odds and contrary to predictions of the French army command, he chose to break through the hilly and forested Ardennes that were considered "impenetrable" by tank forces. Catching the French, Belgian, and Dutch armies and the British Expeditionary Force by surprise, he captured, with hardly any resistance, Belgium, Luxemburg, and the Netherlands, forcing the harried retreat of the British forces at Dunkirk, and by bypassing the French Maginot Line, occupied northern France and Paris.

Just like in 1940, Hitler hoped to use a well-timed surprise attack to push through the thinly protected line. This time, however, he only wished to insert a wedge between the British Army in the north and the US army to the south to provoke a political split between the two allies that would then allow him to negotiate separate peace treaties. With the western front stabilized, he believed he could deal more effectively with the Red Army in the east and at the same time continue developing his new radical weapons such as the Me-262.

Although the Allied armies in the Western front significantly out-numbered the Germans, the secretly built-up German forces in the Ardennes were far more powerful than the forces holding the line there. Hitler hoped the imbalance might be sufficient to give him the local victory he needed.

On a dreary morning of December 16, 1944, under the cover of fog and low clouds, the German infantry and armored troops moved across the US lines outside Luxemburg. To preserve ammunition and to further heighten the effect of surprise, they held back their artillery until their ground troops met the first resistance. This was unusual. Attacks of this scale normally started with a heavy artillery barrage aiming at "softening" the resistance. The surprise was complete. For two days, the Allied forces did not comprehend the true nature of the attack and attributed it to a local initiative and refrained from sending reinforcements. Furthermore, selecting foggy and cloudy weather to initiate the attack precluded any ground support by the British and US air forces. The German planning and timing were perfect. By the time their progress was stopped a few days later, the Germans had created a fifty-mile-deep pocket, or a "bulge", inside Allied territory. The battle, now remembered as the Battle of the Bulge, would last more than a month[28] and cost the lives of nearly a hundred thousand US, British and German soldiers. (53) Despite the disastrous outcome to the German Army, it would delay the arrival of the US Army to the gates of Mühldorf. Laci's race with time was extended by at least a month.[29]

The 99th Infantry Division that would liberate Mühldorf in May was among the first units to face the German attack in the Battle of the Bulge. Having landed in Normandy only two months earlier, they were still inexperienced. Despite being outnumbered and surrounded, the division held back German progress for days until reinforcement arrived.[30]

On a late January afternoon a P&Z supervisor selected randomly twenty KZs in the joinery, including Laci, and ordered them to follow him to the construction site. The cranes had already been rolled along their tracks to the side of the gravel mound that will support the construction of a new arch. It was already covered with thin concrete slabs and wooden molds and buckets of concrete were being hoisted by the cranes and emptied into the molds. The desperate KZs reached the foot of one of the cranes and were turned over to the site Kapo.

"*Is anyone here from Waldlager?*" the Kapo asked them.

---

28 Battle of the Bulge, December 16, 1944–January 25, 1945.
29 Many elements of the battle: the well-disguised buildup of German forces, the negligent complacency of the Allied armies in the face of convincing intelligence predicting an upcoming attack, the huge local disparity between the attacking and defending forces, and the unavailability of air support during the initial phases of the battle brought back to me memories of the Yom Kippur War. It is surprising how quickly history repeats itself. Less than thirty-two years after the Battle of the Bulge, the Egyptian army concealed a massive buildup across the Suez Canal despite obvious visual and even audible signs detected by Israeli forces and overwhelming intelligence. They created an enormous disparity between the attacking and defending forces at the start of the war. In the absence of fog, clouds, and snow in the Sinai desert, they relied on well-placed ground-to-air missile systems to neutralize the superiority of the Israeli air force. And just like the Battle of the Bulge, the initial Egyptian success was later reversed resulting in their near defeat. This was an eerie replay of an old story.
30 To the nineteen thousand American soldiers who lost their lives in that battle we can add at least three hundred Mühldorf KZs who would have survived, had the 99th Infantry Division arrived one month sooner.

Laci and five other raised their hands.

"*You will be transferred to Mettenheim. It's a shorter walk from here. You will join the night shift*[31] *(47 p. 16) of the cement team. It's too late now to send you to the camp and then bring you back for your shift, so I will put you to work right away. It's good because you will learn what to do while there is still light,*" he added, chuckling.

Laci's heart sank. His fears had just materialized. He was now assigned to the worst job at the worst shift. The wonderful soups at lunch, the reassuring warmth at the joinery were no longer his. He would have no opportunity to find food supplements and he had nothing left to trade. He was now condemned to live on starvation food rations while subjected to the harshest possible conditions. Very soon he would look like Csengeri: thin, weak, covered with infected wounds that would not heal.

After nearly a full day in the joinery, Laci started carrying bags to the mixer: fifty steps from the stack to the ramp, turn slightly right and start climbing the ramp; a hundred and two steps to the top; turn around with the back to the machine; lay the bag on the ledge; wait for the Kapo to cut it open; turn the bag upside down and shake to fully empty it; take the empty bag and run down the wet slippery ramp back to the stack; drop the empty bag in a pile; turn around with your back to the functionary who will load the next bag on you; run out as fast as you can to avoid the Kapo's truncheon hitting your head. Total steps in a round trip: three hundred and ten, to be completed in six minutes to meet the hourly quota of ten bags or daily quota of one hundred.[32]

Five tons of cement were carried by each of the sick and starving KZs every day.[33] Every day they had to rise from their bunks and decide once again

---

31 When I once asked Laci what did he do in Mühldorf, all he told me was that every evening he and his unit walked about two miles from their camp to their work site, crossing a creek along their way. Once on site, they worked through the night hauling hundred-pound cement bags up a ramp, emptied them at the top and returning to the bottom to pick up another bag. I asked if he knew what they were building. He did not.

32 It is hard to think of working a cement mixer as heroism. Heroism conjures up monumental acts of courage such as jumping into a gushing river to save a drowning child. But deciding to survive one freezing night after the other, suffering indescribable hunger and pain, carrying innumerable cement bags and enduring the beatings of callous Kapos is courage that only very few have. It is the courage to survive. Only three-and-a-half months separated Laci from freedom. But he could not know that. His decision to survive the worst was open-ended.

33 To visualize the enormity of the task accomplished by these unknown heroes, I looked up the dimensions of the seven arches in Mühldorf and estimated that three million cement bags were needed to build them. To mix these bags into concrete, a hundred and twenty

to subject themselves to this inhumane task in the hope of seeing their little sons and daughters again. Had they known that their children were already murdered in the gas chambers along with their mothers, they might have chosen death too.

Laci completed his first ten rounds before dark. Large floodlights came on and illuminated the work site brightly. Wet surfaces began freezing under the ice-cold air. KZs carrying steel bars, cement bags and wooden molds started slipping. Each one who fell was rewarded by a heavy beating, yelling, and cursing.

A loud siren signaled the end of the day shift. The day shift KZs were lined up by their Kapos to return to Mettenheim, Laci's future camp, north of the construction site across the Isen, a small tributary of the Inn River that flows at the edge of Mühldorf.

The night shift marched in as the day shift marched out to their warm Erdhütten. Laci remained standing near the mixing machine catching his breath. The parade was pitiful. The KZs were dressed in torn rags, baggy pants tied with strings to their dreadfully thin waists, many without coats or with coats missing sleeves, some wearing only wooden clogs padded with old wrapping paper. A few lucky KZs had rags, instead of paper, wrapped around their feet for warmth and cushioning. Many walked awkwardly, trying to hide a limp or other injury from the examining eyes of the SS officer riding behind. The group sang in a hoarse voice a Hungarian marching song ordered by their Kapo. Laci never understood why their tormentors, in Mühldorf and Ukraine, insisted their victims sing. They certainly did not try to boost their morale nor could they possibly enjoy the forced out-of-tune singing. It had to be one additional form of torture.

The P&Z supervisors of the day shift left as soon as the siren sounded. Just like their slaves, they were eager to see the day end. But, unlike the slaves, they returned to comfortable barracks to enjoy an excellent meal, accompanied by drinks, music, and often, women, who were KZs like the men, only with different duties.

---

slaves had to work the day shifts and another hundred and twenty in the night shifts, each carrying a hundred bags in each shift, every day except Sunday for twenty-one weeks, or nearly five months.

Indeed, pouring concrete for the arches could not start before October, after the site was cleared, leveled, roads and rail tracks built, foundations dug, machinery brought in and placed on rails, gravel mounds built and tunnels dug underneath to carry the gravel away once the concrete arches solidified. And then in March, when British planes began bombing the area, construction nearly stopped.

The night shift supervisors arrived in time to receive their KZs. Their faces and behavior expressed anger that they were ready to mete out on the KZS. They were unhappy being out in the cold, unhappy to have the night shift, unhappy about the high quota they had to meet, and above all, unhappy to miss the evening activities.

Transition between the shifts only took moments. Construction of this nationally high-priority project could not suffer any delay; the Führer was monitoring it personally. The Kapo arriving with the new KZs stopped them near Laci and ordered him and the other five to join the group. His orders for the night were brief; they all knew their roles.

Laci looked, trying to recognize old comrades. Many, like him, were transferred from Waldlager. But none of them looked like any he remembered from the 101/35 unit in Ukraine or even from his first days in Waldlager. They all looked alike with sunken faces and indifferent expressions.

The siren announced the midnight break. A steaming large cauldron was brought to the foot of the concrete mixer. The light wind carried the smell of imitation coffee. It was not soup. Even the diluted soup that the day shift workers got had more calories than coffee.

A slight tap on his shoulder interrupted his bitter thoughts. A living skeleton smiling a toothless smile stood behind him. Laci looked at him in disbelief, barely recognizing his old friend Ludusk Woldermann. There was nothing left of the Ludusk he had seen barely two months earlier in Waldlager. His thin neck barely carried his heavy head. Only his voice remained unchanged. Ludusk was crying. His weeping reminded him of Lipót Bácsi, the Muselmann he saw on his first day in Waldlager. Ludusk was almost a Muselmann.

"You do not recognize me, Laci?" Ludusk wept while hugging Laci. "Look what they did to me. Even my friend cannot recognize me anymore. Do you remember, Laci, how we used to celebrate our birthdays together?"

Laci hugged him, holding him for a while, "Nonsense, Ludusk, you look fine. You will be dancing on the graves of these monsters. The war is almost over."

Laci kept hugging him as they reached the front of the line.

"Take my coffee, my friend," Ludusk offered. "I'm sure I no longer need it."

That night while carrying a cement bag, Ludusk tripped on the slippery ice just in front of a Kapo. The Kapo beat him to death.[34] Two KZs dragged his body off the ramp and placed it next to two other corpses. In the morning the

---

34 Ludosk Woldermann, prisoner number 124529, died on January 30, 1945. His cause of death was stated as "Acute Heart Weakness."

bodies were collected, placed in a large pit at the edge of the site and sprinkled with lime.[35]

The sun was rising when they crossed the frozen Isen on their way to camp. Laci, tired, hungry, his eyes burning from cement dust and his nose and throat choked, barely noticed the creek that was hidden below a layer of snow. Béla Klein, another member of 101/35 MUSZ Company, who looked only slightly better than Ludusk, was walking next to Laci. His face, lit by the red rising sun, looked like a mask under the gray layer of cement dust.

"We're lucky the creek is frozen," Béla whispered. "It's not deep but ice cold. When it wasn't frozen, my shoes filled up with water and my feet stayed cold for hours."

A tall water tower that appeared beyond a curve in the road was the first sign of the camp.

They passed through Mettenheim's gate in time for breakfast that was followed by the morning Appell. Laci was assigned to Béla's block. It must also have been Ludusk's.

The block was similar to that in Dachau, bunk beds, three decks of wood planks covered with straw. It housed one hundred fifty KZs.

Laci got Ludusk's bunk. It did not matter. His bunk was just like any other. All Laci wanted when he saw it was to lie down. More than twenty-four hours passed since he woke up in his Erdhütte in Waldlager. When his eyes closed, he did not feel the lice feasting on his blood, he did not hear the other KZs getting ready for their daytime rest. His dreams carried him to the soup at the joinery, his last proper meal for a long time.

He woke up in the evening in time for dinner. While in line, he saw Theodore Neumann and Imre Csengeri. They lived in the adjacent block. Csengeri was not a Muselmann yet, but working the day shift at the construction site since they arrived had completely reduced him. His days were numbered. Without Laci's mushroom supply, his decline progressed just like the other KZs, only delayed by a couple of weeks.

But Theodore looked healthy. He did not tell Laci where he worked. But he could not have possibly worked at the construction site.

Béla Klein, prisoner number 124537, died two weeks later. His cause of death was declared as "Enterocolitis," an inflammation of the digestive tract.[36]

---

35 Lime—white corrosive powder of calcium oxide.
36 It is more likely that Béla died of typhus. Concentration camps were chronically infested with lice. The SS tried to fight the infestations by delousing all new arrivals and the KZs in camp regularly with DDT. But the poor hygiene and dense living quarters rendered their efforts useless. Despite the cold winter, typhus spread rapidly. Sooner or later, nearly all the

The first Allied bombings of the Mühldorf area began late morning on March 19. (54) It was a sunny spring day and British Liberator bombers (not Americans as Laci thought) targeted the Ampfing train station. Several bombs missed their targets and hit nearby private homes. Mettenheim camp was the closest to that train station, and as a night shift worker, Laci was free to lie under a tree and watch the show. The explosions of the large aerial bombs were deafening. And the smell of the smoke rising from the explosions and the ensuing fires was intoxicating.[37]

In the course of a month, aerial bombs destroyed the train station, many of the tracks, other facilities nearby and much of the city of Mühldorf. Oddly, not even one bomb fell on the bunker site or the camps surrounding it. Aerial photos of the bunker taken by Allied reconnaissance planes show the large clearing in the forest and the massive construction site. It is unclear why the analysts did not assign to the site the priority it deserved. But what could have become a critical Nazi manufacturing facility was never bombed.[38] (46 p. 27)

Although the bunkers were not bombed, their progress was profoundly affected by the month-long bombing. Roads and railroads were damaged and critical supplies such as fuel, cement, iron bars, and food could no longer be delivered. The food shortage that had already affected the KZs intensified and

---

KZs contracted it. Most did not survive, having already been weakened by starvation and overwork and without any treatment. Béla was no exception. Listing "Enterocolitis" as his cause of death might have been an attempt to whitewash the sad reality that typhus was rampant.

37 Laci once told me that he knew the war was coming to an end when bombers started bombing Mühldorf. I asked him if he was hiding in a bunker. He did not! Bunkers were available only to the Germans. KZs were expendable. But Laci added that he was happy to lie under a tree and watch the attack, seeing the Germans being beaten and the all-powerful SS run for their lives.

I knew that was a true statement because during the Sinai Campaign in 1956, on the night of October 31, the Egyptian destroyer Ibrahim el Awal entered the Haifa Bay to shell the industrial complex and the refineries along the coast. Sirens were sounded and Zsuzsi, Noemi who was five and me, an eight year old, ran in our pajamas to the ground floor of our three-story apartment building. Laci, instead, climbed to the roof to watch. He later explained that being on the ground floor was no safer than on the roof if the building were hit and collapsed.

In hindsight, he was right. The Ibrahim el Awal bombarded Haifa without scoring a hit. Israeli Navy ships and the air force challenged her, hit her turbo-generator and rudder, rendering her motionless. The Egyptian ship surrendered the following morning and was later repaired and introduced into service in the Israeli fleet as INS Haifa.

38 After the war a joint US-British intelligence unit reviewed the site along with other German underground sites and recommended that the Air Force "test the resistance" of the concrete arches by practicing aerial bombings. Such tests were never conducted.

even Germans in the neighboring towns and in the camps started to experience food rationing.

Ironically, while supply transports were reduced, transports of new KZs were accelerated. This was another sign that the war was turning against Germany. Anxious to erase all evidence of their atrocities, the SS began evacuating prisoners from concentration camps along the path of the rapidly advancing Red Army. (52 p. 174), (37 p. 104) KZs that could still walk were marched out of the camps in Poland towards Germany and at some point along their march were loaded on trains to Dachau. Those who could not walk were murdered. Facilities and documents were destroyed. Auschwitz's gas chambers were blown up in November and the camp was evacuated on January 16, 1945.

Sándor was among the KZs in Auschwitz who survived to the last day of the camp's operation and who were ordered to march in what was later known as the "death march." He refused and was shot dead at the gate with the *Arbeit macht frei* sign above his head still promising false hope.

With more KZs arriving daily, living conditions in Mettenheim became more difficult and food rations, as small as they already were, were reduced even further.

The KZs transferred from Auschwitz, Treblinka, and other camps in the east confirmed dreadful rumors of mass deportations of Jews from rural Hungary to Auschwitz; the existence of industrialized murder machines that included large gas chambers and crematoria that could liquidate entire train loads of thousands of Jews within hours; a selection process that kept alive only a small minority of the deportees, but never a mother with her small child.

Laci's hope of seeing Judit and Lili must have diminished but had not disappeared. There could still be a miracle; they could still escape deportation by hiding, by finding their way to Budapest from where Jews were not deported, by escaping to Verebély, Lili's home town, by forging documents; so many possibilities for one little miracle.

By early April, work at the bunker site came to a near halt. Many days, the KZs remained in their barracks. One morning, the KZs in Laci's barrack were marched out of the camp, through the forest, and past the bombed-out Ampfing station where they were loaded on a waiting train and dispatched to clear rubble from Munich's main train station. (37 p. 107)

The station had been bombed the day before. Overturned and burned train cars were on nearly every track. Rescue workers were still pulling injured and dead passengers out of the wreckage and loading them into waiting ambulances. Most buildings outside the station collapsed due to direct hits and their surviving inhabitants were searching desperately in the rubble for their missing relatives.

Next to one of the overturned train cars were piles of bags of sugar, flour and potatoes. To their delight, the KZs were ordered to collect the bags and haul them to a nearby collection point. Like the others, Laci ate as much sugar as he could while filling his pockets with potatoes.

When one of the tracks was cleared from overturned cars and the rails were repaired, a long ambulance train marked with large red crosses pulled in, carrying hundreds of wounded German soldiers. They were offloaded to waiting ambulance trucks.

The sight of German casualties, desperation, and the destruction of a major German city did not bring joy to the KZs. They were apathetic, desensitized by their own misery, physical weakness and diseases, and preoccupied with their own survival and hunger. But it did remind Laci of Shylock, Shakespeare's character from the Merchant of Venice, saying "If you prick us, do we not bleed?" Except that for once, the blood he saw was not Jewish.

Many SS guards began to recognize that Germany's defeat was inevitable and started to befriend the KZs, hoping that at a last moment kindness might provide some reprieve if they were captured and accused of war crimes. Others, seeing the same writing on the wall, chose instead to intensify the torture of the KZs, blaming them for the aerial attacks and for Germany's losses.

Despite the slackening of the workload, death rates remained high. Eleven KZs died on April 22, fourteen on April 27, and eight on April 28, the last day of record keeping. (41)

On the night of April 26, 1945, Laci and the KZs in his barrack heard the rumble of American cannons firing along the approaching front. No one cheered. The Block Elder and the SS guard patrolling outside would not have taken kindly to those cheers.

Rumors, true and false, kept spreading. Scraps of old newspapers, sometimes used as wrapping paper and tossed away by a careless civilian worker or a page left for the KZs to see, told a sketchy story of the progressing war. Nazi Germany papers never admitted setbacks. But headlines such as "The Wehrmacht is pushing the enemy back across the Saar" were sufficient to understand that Allied forces had already crossed the Saar; that the war was already waged on traditionally German soil. But the rumbling sound of approaching cannons did not need an interpretation by a newspaper.

On April 28, a wild rumor spread rapidly: a group of German officers had revolted against Hitler. Hitler was dead. One prisoner claimed overhearing an SS guard confirming the news.[39] (55)

But the cheers, even by some SS officers, were short-lived. The evening Appell was as rigorous as ever. The KZs stood for hours in the windy Appellplatz enduring another confusing roll call. Records of the dead that day were no longer complete, records of the sick were absent and the counts by the Block Elders did not match the records of the SS officer. If there was any revolt in Munich, its consequences had not reached Mühldorf.

The war was coming to an end, but so were Laci's strength and the remainder of his health. He could barely walk; he could hardly stand through the endless Appells. Thankfully, night shifts ended weeks before. Building at night under the bright projectors would have attracted the British and American bombers like bees to honey. But his days were numbered. After nearly two months of night shifts at the cement mixer and ever-diminishing food, his body could no longer fend off disease. For days he suffered abdominal pain, during the last two nights he felt slight chills, he was becoming feverish. Small rose-colored spots appeared on his abdomen and spread to his back. Laci saw too many victims of typhus to ignore the signs. During more than five months in the Mühldorf camps he had out-lived many of his old friends. Csengeri, his closest friend whom he remembered from back home, from the 101/35 in Ukraine, the friend he helped while working in the forest, died less than two weeks earlier. Zoltan Friedman died a week before him. Imre Friedländer died in February. So many were gone and now, when American cannons arrived at the gate, the disease was claiming him too. Only his spirit, still feeding on his promise to return to Judit and Lili kept him from becoming a Muselmann.[40]

Appell ended. Laci could hardly walk. Two KZs carried him back to his straw mat where he dropped unconscious.

Through a thick lethargy Laci felt someone put a hand under his head and raise it.

---

39 This was mostly an unknown but true fact. A revolt, in Munich, by a group of German officers was announced that day by Munich Radio. The revolt was suppressed quickly and fifty-seven of its organizers executed.

40 Laci knew exactly how he would die when he got the typhus. He described to me the progression and stages of the disease. In the coming days his fever would rise significantly. He would become delirious, unable to move. Once delirious, his body had to survive for ten days. If it did, the fever would break and he would recover. But how to survive ten days of delirium in that hellhole without water, food or sanitation and without being able to control any of his bodily functions?

"*Laci, please drink this. You need to drink now; you need all your strength.*"

Laci opened his eyes. In the faint light of the block's sole light bulb he recognized Theodor. He had barely talked to him since coming to the barracks in January. They were in different blocks, different shifts.

"*Please drink this. It's soup, from the bottom of the pot. It will make you strong.*"

Laci could not open his eyes. He could not eat anything.

"*Please my friend, you must eat. You need this liquid, my friend,*" Theodor whispered. "*I know the Americans are coming. I can already hear their cannons. By the time you wake up they will be here. Just think of the American cigarettes you will be smoking. Take just one sip, just one, for me. You need every drop.*"

Laci struggled to drink but the world went dark.

Next morning Appell was called unusually late. The Block Elder walked by Laci who was lying motionless, his eyes closed. He touched his forehead and announced to his record keeper,

"*He is sick, typhus. He will not make it. We are leaving him here.*"

Delirious, Laci heard this as if this voice was coming through layers of cotton. The block turned quiet.

Laci tried to lift his body, to join the Appell. He had to. Even through his delirium he remembered his first Appell in Waldlager. Images of the KZ being held to the pole and beaten to death by the Block Elder were vivid. He could hear the KZ screaming and then his body turning limp. But all Laci could do was raise his head and then drop back on his mat.

"*Laci, my friend,*" he heard Theodor whispering. "*We are leaving the camp. All the sick are staying behind. I left some bread under your head. Take care, my old friend. I am sure we will meet soon in Budapest.*"

Theodor put a blanket over Laci but Laci continued shivering.

Hours passed. Laci lost count of time. The block was quiet, there was no sound outside.

A KZ entered the abandoned block and announced loudly to someone who remained outside, "*There are three sick here. They are all unconscious.*"

A second KZ entered to check on the three. When he reached Laci he pulled his eyelids open, touched his forehead to check his fever, checked his pulse and then looked under his shirt. His chest and abdomen were covered with rose-colored spots.

"*He is alive but very weak, it's Fleckfieber (Spotted Typhus),*" he muttered. "*Let's take him to the medical hut and give him something to drink.*"

Laci could hear the rattle of a cart rolling in. He heard this rattle many times when dead KZs were carried away from the Appellplatz to their mass grave outside the camp. He now had the opportunity to ride it while still alive. The two picked him up carefully, one holding him in his arms and the other by his legs, and laid him on a hard board. He was aware that the other two sick KZs were laid beside him.

The cart was pushed out of the hut. Bright sun flooded his face, penetrated through his closed eyelids as deep red light illuminating a beautiful scene in his hallucinating mind. Judit was playing in a wide field of red poppy flowers and white daffodils. He remembered that field from Gyula. He could smell the daffodils.

Dressed in her white holiday dress, she was running towards him, waving a bouquet of flowers. The bright sunlight reflecting from her long black hair scattered into a golden halo. He could hear her laughing and calling, *"Daddy, look at these flowers that I picked for Mama."*

Laci smiled as the spring sun warmed his pale face. He could see himself bending towards Judit with his arms spread wide open, ready to pick her up.

The cart passed through a deserted camp.

Some of the SS fled the previous night wearing civilian clothes. The remaining SS loaded those KZs still capable of walking onto a train. They ordered a few civilians to lock the blocks containing sick KZs from the outside and set them afire.[41] It was a perfect plan; all eye-witnesses to the atrocities that took place were either taken away or burned.

The destination of the train was less obvious. Both the Nazis and Allied military intelligence believed that Hitler was building a "Nazi National Redoubt" where all elite Nazis, including Hitler, Göring and Goebbels would congregate and fight a desperate last battle.[42] The train was headed to that "Redoubt." The Mühldorf KZs were to become the construction workers and slaves of the remaining masters of the master race.

According to the Mühldorf list of dead (41) "only" 2,074 KZs died there. "Only" because a separate report puts the number of Mühldorf deaths at 3,076. (47 p. 10) But both reports ignore those who died weeks, months, and even

---

41 According to Sandberg, this plan did exist. However, after the camp was evacuated, the SS commandant, fearing the approaching Americans, chose to flee without burning the sick KZs.

42 Nazi National Redoubt—rumors circulated that the leaders of the Nazi party built a hiding place in the mountains south of Bavaria to which they and 100,000 elite troops were to retreat and continue their struggle until final victory was reached. The rumors of the existence of such an Alpenfestung or Alpine Redoubt were so convincing that even the British and US intelligence believed that it existed.

years after liberation, some from diseases incurred in camp and some from emotional devastation.

The list was compiled by cold-hearted bureaucrats. It must have served the purposes of Nazi accountants who had to write off the dead like any property owner would amortize an asset. It included the names, prisoner numbers, dates of birth and death, country of origin of the dead, and often the cause of their death. But behind these lines there are thousands of human tragedies, brides who would wait years for their husbands' return never knowing their fate, or mothers standing by a window for the rest of their lives, looking out in the hope that their lost son would walk up from the street corner, knock on the door and walk in. It tells the stories of slow deaths and infinite agonies, stories of sudden and untimely deaths.

One day before all able prisoners were loaded on a train to be taken to the fictional Nazi hiding place in the Alps, the killing machine was still operating at full steam; clerks in the record office were still busy entering new names. It seems that the camp doctors were the first to flee because the last two weeks of records did not show causes of the victims' deaths. The clerks missed the names of the hundreds of sick prisoners that were left behind to die when the camp was evacuated. Like Laci, they must be listed in the German archives as "Liberated," because no one was left to record their actual fate.

The unaccounted dead from Mühldorf are a miniscule fraction of the millions who disappeared in the Holocaust without a trace. The names of some of these victims were lost forever because their entire families and previous communities were also erased. Not even one person was left alive to remember their names and remind the world that they ever lived. The list of Mühldorf camp's dead at least reminds us and the world that once there were 2,074 men who lived and fought like lions to survive and that they almost made it, they came within weeks or days of winning, surviving to tell their own stories and the stories of their lost families and communities.

The first KZ to die in the camp was the 51-year-old Ernö Kalman, who died on July 28. His cause of death was recorded as "bad heart." Ernö was among the first slaves brought to the area to start building the camp for the thousands of slaves that followed. Ernö was not there long enough to die from starvation or exhaustion. Was he murdered as an example to the others? Or could he really have died from a "bad heart" as the record shows?

In the following two months twenty-seven additional KZs died. Such a mortality rate would be considered devastating by the managers of any construction site. But for Nazi concentration camp operators that rate was low.

Indeed, by October, the death rate rose significantly, to sixty deaths that month. The men who arrived with Ernö in July were starting to fail from malnutrition, overwork, terrible hygiene, and constant torment. They lasted three months.[43]

By November, the death rate reached ten to fifteen per day, all reported as suffering from various heart ailments. After a slow start, the death factory was gaining speed. The camp was achieving one of its primary objectives, killing Jews efficiently while extracting every bit of value from their bodies.

But with the ranks depleting rapidly and the old slaves growing feebler by the day, the Germans had to bring in new blood. Literally. Laci's group arrived in November. The members of his group could be identified by the first three digits of their KZ numbers. They all started with "123" or "124".

To confirm my assumption, I wrote to the Dachau archive and requested the records of ten KZs whose numbers were in sequence with that of Laci's. Within days I got their names: Alexander Spitzer (Prisoner number 124528), Ludusk Woldermann (Prisoner number 124529), Zoltan Friedman (Prisoner number 124530), Imre Csengeri (Prisoner number 124531), Imre Friedländer (prisoner number 124533), Theodor Neumann (Prisoner number 124534), Revi Ladislaus (Prisoner number 124535), György Rubinstein (Prisoner number 124536 (he was transferred to Buchenwald less than a month later), Béla Klein (Prisoner number 124537), and Salamon Spitzer (Prisoner number 124538), who survived. All ten, like Laci, arrived from Budapest on November 11, 1944. Only three of the ten, Laci, Neumann and Spitzer were alive on liberation day less than six months later.

Two members of the "124" cohort, the 34-year-old Imre Müller and the 47-year-old Jenö Schwarz, were the first to die, within two weeks of arrival: one from stomach perforation and the other from pneumonia. Did Laci know them?

Nearly all of the 230 deaths of the "124" cohort and 200 of the "123" cohort occurred in February and March. Evidently, the strength of the KZs diminished within three months. Every day consumed a little bit of body fat. Every day of beatings, cruelty, and desperation broke another invisible fiber in their souls. Their life in camp was a race between time and their internal

---

43   It is hard to understand why laborers so critical for the survival of the Third Reich were pushed to their deaths through starvation, disease, cold, beating, hanging and gunfire. Was the hatred of Jews so intense that it overcame the Germans' survival instinct? Did the "Final Solution," the plan to exterminate all Jews in Europe, take precedence over Germany's self-interest? A sane mind cannot comprehend how reducing the life expectancy of Germany's last remaining source of critical labor to three months was more critical than building the new superweapon, the Me-262.

hourglass. For most of the "123" and "124" cohorts the hourglasses were drained by March. Surviving his first month in Mühldorf without significant loss of body weight and in good health meant for Laci that his internal hourglass was reset, that the remaining sand was nearly sufficient to carry him across the finish line.

The list also tells that during two days in mid-March, the Mühldorf camps were struck by an epidemic of "heart failure." The hearts of seventeen KZs failed in those two days, nearly one heart every three hours. There were twenty-nine additional deaths in those two days, but apparently, the good doctors at Mühldorf were overwhelmed by this sudden outbreak of "heart failures" and were unable to attend to the other twenty-nine dying KZs, let alone diagnose their cause of death.

The last victim on this list was the 45-year-old Moses Seidenfeld, prisoner number 46911 from Poland. He died one day before the camp was evacuated and four days before the first American soldier stood at the gate.

I could not fail to notice that his prisoner number was much lower than Laci's. Only 15 other prisoners on the list had a lower number. This low number signifies that Moses arrived to Dachau well before Laci and his "123" and "124" cohorts, well before Ernö, the first victim on the list and his "83" cohort. Moses might have been in Dachau and then in Mühldorf for an entire year. He survived while the internal hourglasses of 3,075 KZs ran out. Somehow Moses found more food than the others; somehow he cheated death every day for hundreds of days while others could last only sixty to ninety days. And then only four days before his dreams became true, the last grain of sand slipped through his hourglass. For Moses, time won the race.

Yehi zichro baruch—may his memory be blessed.

May 1945: Liberation

Mühldorf camps were liberated by the US 99th Infantry Division, one of the forty-two divisions of General George S. Patton's Third Army. It is ironic that Patton, who was not known as sympathetic to Jews and certainly not to Holocaust victims and survivors, was the General who liberated Buchenwald, Mauthausen-Gusen, Dachau, and its satellites.

Many survivors, like Laci, who were clinging to life by its last thin threads, owe their lives to Patton's disciplined units and hard drive that resulted in the fastest and deepest penetration of any previous army in history. It brought his army to Munich and the gates of Mühldorf before more KZs lost their lives. To those whose race against time was almost lost, Patton was the miracle they prayed for.[1]

The 99th division originated from Pittsburgh and was initially nicknamed "the checkerboard" for its shoulder patch that consisted of three blue-and-white checkerboard rows taken from the Coat of Arms of the city's namesake William Pitt.

A more apt nickname, "Battle Babies," was coined after the Battle of the Bulge. Barely two months after landing in Europe, with hardly any battle experience, one of the 99th platoons defended tenaciously a road near Losheim Gap thereby preventing the German Army from progressing to Antwerp. In recognition, that platoon became one of the most decorated of World War II. (56)

On March 11 the division crossed the Rhine River near Linz. Their headquarters reached its final stop near Geisenhausen on May 1. On May 2, or the day after, a unit of the division discovered one of Mühldorf's camps,

---

1 Laci told me that the end of the war found him in an American hospital recovering from typhus. He had no idea how he got to that hospital or even where it was. He did not even tell me where he went after recovering. The answers I found were surprising. As many times before, chance, timing and coincidence played important roles in the last stage of his fight to survive. His survival was out of his control, he was hallucinating.

possibly Waldlager. However, only on May 4 they reported liberating three labor camps and a concentration camp named "Forest Camp" (Waldlager). (57) The Division, along with other thirty-four US Army divisions, was recognized by the United States Holocaust Memorial Museum in Washington, DC as a Liberator and their flag is displayed at the museum's lobby.

But it was the commander of a four-person public health team from another unit who set up the ad hoc hospital where Laci along with nearly 200 KZs from the Mühldorf camps recovered.

On May 3, Dr. Michael Shimkin, the commander of Public Health Team 2 of the Third Corps of Patton's Third Army, returned to his base in Dorfen, a little town twenty miles west of Mühldorf, after traveling for the previous ten days through occupied German towns, reorganizing public health departments and hospitals and delousing thousands of people in POW camps.[2] (58)

That evening at Headquarters, the Chief of Preventive Medicine greeted Shimkin with a report from his units that they liberated several concentration camps that day and found the conditions there even more horrifying than Buchenwald.

After seeing Buchenwald three weeks earlier, Shimkin dismissed the report as an exaggeration. He could not believe that atrocities such as "incinerators, torture chambers, lampshades made of tanned human skin, emaciated corpses stacked like cordwood, and the starved, diseased, still-living specimens of human degradation" could be topped.

The next morning he headed with his team in their command car to Ampfing, towing a trailer filled with half a ton of DDT. They carried no weapon other than Shimkin's riding crop that, in his words, he "inherited" from a Nazi official.

It was a clear sunny spring morning. Everything along the way stood in sharp contrast to what they saw in the destroyed cities. Orchards were in full bloom, white snow-covered peaks of the Alps in the distance and open fields blazing with colorful wild flowers.

They arrived at Ampfing to discover, surprisingly, that it was largely intact. Most buildings, even warehouses, remained undamaged. When they reached the center of the town they stopped a civilian to ask for the military governor

---

2   After the war Dr. Shimkin developed a successful career in medical research including pioneering cancer research. He was among those who discovered the link between smoking and cancer. (http://libraries.ucsd.edu/speccoll/testing/html/mss0104a.html)

or the mayor. There was no military government yet in Ampfing and the town's baker was the Mayor.

Finding the baker was easy. Two men dressed in striped uniforms and wearing striped caps were hauling out large loaves of bread and stacking them into a horse-drawn wagon parked outside. The KZ uniforms were familiar, but the sight of two KZs hauling bread out of a German bakery was new.

Shimkin pulled up next to the wagon and asked if any of the KZs spoke English. When the two saw the US officers, they jumped to attention and removed their caps. Shimkin found it amusing that the prisoners saluted him the way they saluted SS officers. One of the two, while still standing in attention, introduced himself in broken English with heavy French accent as Andre Israel, a French prisoner. Assuming that he needed to enhance his credibility as a legitimate KZ, Andre added that he was transferred from Auschwitz and showed the number tattooed on his wrist.

Shimkin was hardly aware of the varying brutalities of the Nazi camps or the unique place that Auschwitz had in such ranking. He was just eager to find the nearby camp where prisoners were reported to be dying. He cleared room on his seat for Andre to join him and asked him to lead the way to his camp.

They started out of town towards the forest. On their way, Andre briefed Shimkin that the SS had already taken the healthy prisoners, leaving behind approximately two hundred sick and dying. Their camp was only one of several others that surrounded a large bunker construction site that he thought was designed to host a V-2 factory. Andre and several of his friends had already transferred the sick from the other camps to their camp.

When asked, Andre told Shimkin that a US Army officer and two soldiers arrived at the camp the day before. They left with Andre an official-looking note stating: "This authorizes the bearer to obtain all necessary supplies for his camp." It impressed the Germans, Andre said with a smile. It even convinced the baker to give them the bread he and his friend were hauling away.

The road ended at a gate in a tall fence capped with barbed wires and dominated by watch towers equipped with searchlights. They reached the camp. Little huts covered with mud and several wooden barracks were visible from the gate.

"We lived in these huts, we called them Erdhütte," Andre explained as they drove through the gate that was opened by one of the inmates. "The SS used to live in the barracks there," he pointed to the other direction toward a row of solidly built wooden buildings.

They entered one of the barracks. It looked like an infirmary. An examination table stood in the front room, surrounded by shelves filled with jars, possibly some ointments and medications.

"Is there a doctor here?" Shimkin asked loudly as he entered the building.

A thin man with an expressionless face, dressed in the standard KZ uniform, stepped forward. There was nothing to show that he was indeed a doctor but he did know that there were nearly two hundred sick men in the camp, most of them with typhus, some with pneumonia, some with infections and broken bones, and all of them severely malnourished.

They entered the adjacent room. A heavy stench of human excrement filled the large space. It was unlike any infirmary or hospital Shimkin had ever seen. Two rows of two-story bunk beds lined the walls on both sides. All the "beds," or rather wooden shelves padded with filthy straw, were occupied with partially clothed skeletal men, their bones visible through their thin skins and their shaved heads looking large relative to their decimated bodies. They looked more dead than alive. Those still awake were mostly indifferent, their faces expressionless, their eyes fixed at a point in space as though peering into this room from another world. Many suffered from ulcerated wounds that Shimkin diagnosed visually as unable to heal due to protein deficiency.[3]

Lying on the narrow slab of space allocated to him, squeezed between two other dying KZs, through the haze of his unconsciousness, Laci heard men speaking English. Even his hallucinating mind understood that the Nazis were defeated, but he had not won yet, he still had a mortal disease to defeat.

When Shimkin walked out of the barracks, a prisoner arrived, reporting that there were one hundred and fifty sick KZs and ten prisoner doctors still alive. There used to be many more doctors but most died, along with lawyers, actors, professors, most of them Hungarian.

The number of the sick was in Shimkin's opinion too low to justify an army evacuation hospital, but too large for his team to treat without assistance.

---

3   Laci was among those dying men. It is hard for me to imagine him as one of the skeletal, faceless Holocaust survivors I saw in pictures and documentary movies. But my logical reasoning tells me that after months of starvation, hard physical work in unbearable cold, physical abuse and weeks of lingering disease he could not have looked any different.

   The true question for me is not how Laci looked when Dr. Shimkin found him, but rather how could he return from this unimaginable state of an "otherworldly creature" to our world and become a fully functioning man? How could he bring himself to become a husband, father, lawyer and a friend once again? How could he remain emotionally stable and limit the effects of these horrors to his regular nightmares?

He decided to improvise a field hospital near the camp and appropriate German labor as his help.

He left two of his team members in the camp to begin delousing everyone and to prepare the sick for evacuation while he, the driver, and Andre headed back to town to requisition space, beds, food, and personnel for his provisional hospital.

Ampfing or Mühldorf were unlikely to have their own hospital, Shimkin thought, so his best options were either a large school or office building.

The OT had a big office building in Ampfing, Andre suggested during their drive. He did not know of any hospital but he knew that the Wehrmacht took over the school in Mühldorf.

They found the OT building at the edge of Ampfing, an abandoned one-story office building with two wings. Behind the front door was a large lobby with a receptionist desk. Two corridors led out of the lobby to the offices in both wings. The offices were still furnished with desks, chairs, filing cabinets, and even several phones. Electricity was off and water only trickled from faucets in the few lavatories at the end of the corridors.

A small building in the back had a large kitchen where a man, still wearing a mustard-yellow OT overall was busy preparing lunch for himself. He was the only OT employee on site, or at least the only one who still did not mind being identified as such. He introduced himself as the building caretaker.

It was convenient to find a large vacant building with its caretaker still in place. All that Shimkin had to do was order him to remove all furniture from the rooms by the end of the day, leaving only one chair in each and promise to send him help.

They left the building and returned to the bakery. Wonderful aromas of freshly baked bread greeted them. The baker was pulling large round loaves of dark German rye bread and several housewives were waiting for their turn to buy.

Hardship skipped this place, Shimkin thought comparing this idyllic image with the chaos and destruction he saw in Munich and the death and desperation in the concentration camp only miles out of town. He stepped into the bakery, ahead of the line of waiting women, and ordered the baker to stop his work immediately and ordered him to find within two hours fifty strong men capable of hauling furniture and fifty women with cleaning supplies ready to set up a field hospital for sick people from the concentration camps.

The baker tried to protest that if he closed the bakery, the women waiting outside and other households would not have bread that day.

Shimkin did not reply, he just cracked the riding crop he held in his hand. The loud crack provided all the authority he needed.

"And where will I find fifty men and women?" the baker continued.

Shimkin just snapped his crop again. The baker nodded his head obediently.

"Wonderful," Shimkin spoke. "Do you know where the OT Bureau is? Take them there. The building's caretaker will order them to clean it up. All furniture should go outside, and all floors should be washed and cleaned. Two hours! You have two hours."

"Oh, and also be sure to bring enough food for a hundred and fifty people: bread, mashed potatoes and a little boiled meat. And before I forget, I need power and water turned back on for that building."

They left Andre behind to monitor the preparations.[4]

Shimkin and his driver returned to Dorfen to find the Chief of Preventive Medicine and request a medical unit with ambulances to transfer the sick and several trucks to transfer beds from a Wehrmacht barracks in Mühldorf that Shimkin hoped was not yet looted.

The Chief, moved by Shimkin's report, assigned six ambulances, two trucks and allocated large quantities of blood plasma, sulfa medications, and other medical supplies. In less than half an hour the convoy was ready to depart.[5]

The OT building was humming with activity when Shimkin's convoy arrived. Men were hauling furniture out of the offices and piling them in the yard in large stacks of desks and chairs. Inside, women on their knees were scrubbing the floors with rags that they were rinsing in buckets filled with fresh water. In one of the rooms, a light bulb was on. Evidently, power and water were turned back on.

"The nice thing about Germans," Shimkin commented in his essay, "is that they follow orders well."

---

4 I could not avoid thinking of the rapid role reversal for the KZs and the Germans. Within days the OT caretaker and the Ampfing baker were turned from members of the Master Race into obedient servants of a Jewish US officer and a KZ, still in his striped uniform. And the KZ, from a disposable *Untermensch*, or subhuman, became the master of hundred Germans working to assemble a field hospital for dying KZs.

5 I learned in my military service that wartime logistics can be fast and generous, even wasteful. Allocation of a truck that might require in peacetime days of paper work and approval at multiple levels can happen during war in minutes. Food rations and gasoline that were ordinarily counted meticulously were dispensed almost without limit during Israel's Yom Kippur War. Even arms were handed out with few controls. Judging from Shimkin's account, the US Army at the end of World War II was no different.

The building caretaker stood at the door, proud of his accomplishment. He jumped to attention when he saw Shimkin. He was a man programmed to please, even if his new superior was the enemy.

When Shimkin confirmed that the OT building was nearly ready for its first patients he ordered his driver to begin transporting the sick, while Andre with the trucks and five of the strongest men were sent to the Wehrmacht barracks in Mühldorf to get beds.

Mühldorf, unlike Ampfing, was heavily damaged. But the school, a two-building complex, remained undamaged. Scattered uniforms, abandoned boots and opened military ration cans were silent witnesses to its recent use and more importantly, that its last occupants changed their uniforms into civilian outfits in an attempt to escape an unpleasant stay in a POW camp.

Andre and his men entered the classrooms that had been transformed into military dormitories with two-story bunk beds and small crates that served as cabinets. Surprisingly, there were no signs of looting, possibly, because the citizens of Mühldorf still feared reprisals from the Nazi regime.

The two-story bunk beds could not serve as hospital beds but the mattresses were good. They loaded the cleanest two hundred mattresses onto the trucks. To accelerate the loading, Andre picked on the street a few more men.

With the trucks loaded they returned to the OT building in time for the arrival of the first ambulances with patients. In less than half a day the OT office building became the active hospital where Laci was saved.

Hardly conscious, Laci felt two strong pairs of hands lifting him off the filthy straw and placing him on a stretcher. Unable to open his eyes, he heard English being spoken. He felt his stretcher being carried out of the barrack; once again, bright sunlight touched his face and then his stretcher was loaded onto a vehicle. He heard other stretchers being placed next to him. Then the engine started and soon they were moving on a bumpy road. Laci lost consciousness.

He came to lying on a mattress, on his back, naked. A middle-aged woman knelt on the floor next to him, gently washing his body with a wet lukewarm sponge. He opened his eyes and saw her face and her covered head. She was not a nurse, just an ordinary woman. She was murmuring in German: *"We did not know anything about it. I am so sorry."*

The touch of lukewarm water on his naked body felt so good; the soft sponge was gentle. Lying helplessly in the care of this German woman he felt like a baby again. It had been years since he had been touched by a woman. But he was emotionless. He was not happy to be free. He did not feel triumphant.

He did not feel anger or hate. He was just terribly tired. There still was one enemy to conquer, only one victory to score before he could see Judit.

The woman finished. She dried him with a towel and dressed him in pajamas. Still striped but with no number sewn on it. She covered him with a soft blanket and placed a pillow under his head. He passed out again, overcome by his fever.

A male nurse in military uniform was holding his wrist measuring his pulse when he woke up. The room was dimly lit by a light bulb casting long shadows. The nurse pricked his arm with a needle. "*Plasma and sulfa,*" he said. "You've got spotted typhus. Try to eat, but be careful in the beginning; your stomach cannot digest too much food at once. You will be OK. Just hang on."

The middle-aged woman reappeared with a bowl of steaming broth and a slice of white bread. Another woman joined her and lifted Laci's head and leaned it against the wall. Gently, they started feeding him as if he were their own baby. Spoonful after spoonful, he could feel how the warm broth entered his blood stream giving him strength.

He fell asleep for the first time in nearly three years on a clean mattress, a pillow under his head and only one threat to worry about, the spotted typhus. Only nine days to go before the fever broke, and now, with sulfa and food fighting for him, he would win.

On the fifth day, able to eat boiled meat, Laci felt his strength returning. The fever was still high. He was still mostly delirious, but more and more sounds of the outside world were penetrating his consciousness.

At noon, while the German woman was feeding him lunch, as he lay on the mattress, his head propped against the wall and his eyes closed, two male nurses in uniform ran into the room shouting that Germany surrendered. The war was over. Laci could hear them running to the adjacent room and then to the next announcing the victory. He opened his eyes; the German woman was still feeding him, with tears rolling down her cheeks. For the second time in her life, her nation was defeated. But this time she knew she would carry shame and guilt forever.

She noticed Laci looking at her. "*My son was killed in Russia, in Stalingrad. My husband was killed in Africa. My house was destroyed. When I look at you I know that we did terrible things. And now we lost the war. I wish you a fast recovery. I hope you return to your family soon,*" she whispered. "*We have suffered too.*"

Laci closed his eyes. The gentle touch of this defeated enemy woman felt good. The food she fed him was bringing him back to life. He had won. He just needed to get stronger. Judit and Lili were waiting for him. He was not sorry for this woman nor was he happy for her losses.

On the tenth day the fever broke. Sweating profusely, Laci felt that he was waking up. The window was open and a breeze carrying fresh spring air and the smell of new blossoms came in, the same fragrances as in Gyula, cherry and peach blossoms. He could hear birds singing.

He looked around the room. There were ten mattresses on the floor but half of them were vacant. He did not know if their occupants had died or recovered. Several sick men were still lying unconscious. Laci looked at their shaved heads, sunken cheeks, pale skins and bony arms resting over their blankets. They looked like dead, but they were still breathing.

Laci tried to stand up but his legs buckled under the weight of his thin body. He fell back on his mattress breathing heavily, fully exhausted.

A middle-aged woman wearing an apron and a headdress walked in. She was cheerful. Laci thought he remembered her taking care of him while he had drifted in and out of consciousness.

She introduced herself cheerfully as she knelt down by his mattress on the floor and tucked in his sheet. *"We counted the days since you arrived and today is the tenth. We knew you would wake up this morning."*

"I am Dr. Laufer," Laci introduced himself. For the first time in months he was not a number. He was again a man with a name and a title.

"May I call you by your first name?" the woman offered.

"No," he shot back.[6]

The woman left and returned with a set of civilian clothes, a neatly folded, starched, white cotton shirt, gray pants, underwear, and wool socks. She left them by his bed, allowing him to dress privately. She promised to be back with a pair of shoes.[7]

Another woman came in carrying a tray and put it down next to him. Dreams are made of simple things: two slices of white bread, a small bowl with two soft boiled eggs, still warm, a small container with strawberry jam, and a

---

[6] Of course I was not there to hear that conversation. But I know that Laci would not have had it any other way. He was "Dr. Laufer" to the car mechanic and his clients alike. He was "Laci" only to his family and close friends, not even to his children. To us he was and remains *Apuka*, "Dad" in Hungarian. That German woman had not earned the right to call him Laci.

[7] I can see in my mind Laci staring at his new clothes. These were not just garments. They were powerful symbols of freedom. Wearing a white shirt and gray pants meant that he could go anywhere he wished. Wearing a shirt without a number sewed to it meant that he was a person with a name. These clothes, provided to him by a German woman, meant that he was readmitted to civilization, no longer marked as a slave by tattered clothing, Hungarian military cap and yellow arm band or striped KZ uniform. He was back from hell.

thin sausage. It was a simple meal, but it had the luxuries of home. Laci did not know it then, but freed prisoners died when their first meal was too large or heavy. Their fragile stomachs could not handle it. His meal had to be simple. Dr. Shimkin must have supervised even that basic step.

Laci finished his meal and lay back, resting his head on his pillow, enjoying the luxury of leisure and a full stomach. He felt a strange lump under his pillow. Careful not to topple his tray, he reached under it and found chocolate bars and packs of cigarette. He counted them there were five chocolate bars and five cigarette packs.[8]

Laci's body was quickly gaining strength. It was fascinating to observe how quickly a young body could recover, even from the most devastating blows. A day after his fever broke he could get off his mattress and walk slowly along the corridors, leaning occasionally on one of the walls and needing rest after each short walk. By the third day, he could go out to the yard without help. Recovering patients were sitting outside on armchairs that once served the directors of the OT building, some smoking, some eating, and some just basking in the spring sun with their eyes closed. They were enjoying luxuries that were now denied to most Germans: plentiful food, cigarettes, and rest. But there was no joy in the yard. The patients sat quietly immersed in their thoughts and fears of the unknowns of their new lives.

A German woman wearing a white apron approached Laci and asked if he wished to eat. Yes, he did. He was insatiably hungry. He still needed to be careful with his diet, but like a growing teenager he constantly craved food.

She returned a few moments later carrying a plate with a thick slice of white bread spread thinly with butter and strawberry jam.

Laci sat in the sun and closed his eyes while holding his plate, savoring the smell of fresh bread and the feeling that he could take his time eating it. Possessing food was a simple joy all by itself. His mind was still blank. He could not think of the present or the future. He tried to think of Judit, Lili, his mother, his father. He tried to recreate Judit's image, her voice, her smell, or her little hands. But none came to him. He could see her so vividly when he was hallucinating but when fully awake his mind could only remember the horrors. He could hear the Kapos yelling, their voices clear. He could see Zsoldos, the sadistic Hungarian sergeant, forcing him to run barefoot in the snow. He could

---

8   In one of his few accounts of his liberation, Laci told me that he found five bars of chocolate and five packs of cigarette under his pillow. He was amazed that even though he was not an American soldier he earned the right to these rations by simply being in an American hospital. But even more amazing to him was that none of these luxury items was stolen.

see his face and his callous smile when one of MUSZ drowned in the frozen creek. But he could not see Judit.

An American soldier pulled up a chair next to him and asked if he could speak English.

"No, I am sorry; I speak Hungarian, German and Latin."

That was good enough for the soldier who spoke fluent German. The doctor was pleased with his recovery, he explained. In a few days, after he fully recovered and gained some strength, he would be transferred to another camp because the hospital would be closed as soon as the last patient recovered. He would be sent to a newly established camp for Displaced Persons near Munich. Until the previous month, that place had been a boarding school for children of elite Nazis. It was quite comfortable and Laci could recover there until he was ready to travel back home.

As much as the Allied armies were anxious to clear their hospitals and camps from liberated KZs, Soviet POWs, refugees, and migrant workers that had been trapped away from home, they had to restrict travel through Europe for at least two or three months. Many of the roads and railroads were damaged by the war or sabotaged by the retreating Nazis. The few available roads were jammed by military traffic carrying supplies and fresh troops in one direction and captured German weapons, prisoners of war or troops in the opposite direction. Roads were also dangerous, Nazi soldiers returning home from the war, in uniform or without, could still be hostile, and ordinary criminals were looking for easy prey.

Soon after regaining his consciousness Laci asked to track down his family through the newly established Red Cross Family Tracing Service and submitted his own name to the database. He also mailed a post card home to Gyula. It was brief and simple. Military censors would have held it up otherwise. It must have read:

> Mrs. Dr. László Laufer and Judit Laufer
> 37 Béke sugárút
> Gyula
> Hungary
> Mühldorf, May 16, 1945
> My Dear Treasures. I am alive. Your Laci.

The card was never delivered. There was not a single Laufer left at that address to receive it.

With Laci's body recovering, his mind was awakening too. No longer focused on day-to-day survival and no longer cut off from sources of information he would learn that Hitler was dead; that after the occupation by the Nazis more than a year earlier Hungary was liberated by the Soviets; that Budapest was heavily damaged by one of the longest and most violent sieges of the war; that the Jews of Europe were nearly completely wiped out; and most important of all, that the vast majority of rural Hungarian Jews, more than 420,000 people, were deported to Auschwitz in a brief period of fifty-seven days where most of them were murdered in the gas chambers. The deportation was so fast and the killing so efficient that even the Jews of Budapest did not fully appreciate its extent until it was too late.

A few days later Laci was transferred to the Feldafing Displaced Persons Camp near Munich. It was the first of many DP camps established in Europe by the Western Allies, mostly the Americans, to care for the liberated KZs and the millions of other refugees in their territories. The camps were a temporary solution to the immense human catastrophe. They were intended to provide shelter, medical care, and food to their occupants and a mechanism to verify their identity and confirm that they were not wanted war criminals, German soldiers in civilian clothing, or escaped German prisoners of war.

As often happens, what started as a temporary solution evolved into a nearly permanent fixture. Shifting political trends in Europe and the massive destruction everywhere created a mass migration, mostly from the east to the west. The number of displaced persons and the extent of their needs had grown beyond any earlier projections. By some estimates, at the end of the war there were between 11 and 20 million displaced people. The last DP camps closed more than a decade after the war. (59)

Feldafing was a story of compassion and demonstrated the sense of responsibility the American army felt towards the KZs, even before the war was officially over.

On May 1, 1945 an American unit captured a German cattle car train parked on a railroad siding in a small station near Tutzing, twenty miles south of Munich. The train left Ampfing on April 26 carrying approximately four thousand KZs from the Mühldorf camps. Although the KZs were deemed by the SS to be capable of walking, many were emaciated and sick, but not as sick as Laci who was left behind to die. Two days later, and after having traveled only 20 or 30 miles, the train was bombed by Allied bombers who mistook it for a German troop transport train, killing several KZs and wounding others. (47 p. 18) When the train was discovered, most of the SS soldiers who guarded it had already fled and the American unit was left with an unexpected human disaster that required a quick solution.

Fortunately, a German hospital train was parked on the adjacent track and many of the sick and the injured could be hospitalized there. But even more fortunately, an abandoned elite school[9] for Hitler Youth (Hitlerjugend) was found near the railroad track, three miles north of Tutzing and was taken over to house those who did not require immediate treatment.

The school with its multiple barrack-like buildings, many facilities, and fenced grounds was an ideal place to accommodate a large group of mostly sick men. In addition, being on the shore of a lake, Starnberger Lake rendered it an almost idyllic site, in sharp contrast to the harsh environment of Waldlager. Thus the Feldafing DP camp was born. In time, Feldafing would become the first all-Jewish DP camp. (60) It would remain in service for nearly eight years.

Ironically, a boarding school that was built to indoctrinate the next generation of Nazi leaders was converted into a camp for victims of that regime where they could convalesce, regain their physical and emotional strength, and train themselves for their new lives. Hitler could not imagine even in his worst nightmares that after making Germany Judenfrei, Jewish religious schools would be established in the same school that was intended for his beloved Hitlerjugend.

The camp consisted of two-story stone buildings, wooden barracks, and individual homes, or villas. (61) It was run by the American army and the United Nations Relief and Rehabilitation Administration (UNRRA) until self-governance could be established.

I tried to visualize the camp and its inhabitants by inspecting grainy black-and-white archival pictures. Many are undated and are likely from a time long after Laci left, but they all show the spirit of the survivors who, like Laci, had lost everything but were eager nevertheless to build a new life. I examined their faces; some of them might have known Laci. I tried to engage my imagination to pierce through the two-dimensional pictures and enter into the other dimensions that only real life or imagination can create, sound, color, smell. I tried to go back in time, penetrate the minds of these people; feel the deep sadness hidden behind their smiles, their determination and hopes.

One of the pictures shows a dozen smiling men and women and two little children, all lined up in front of two Nissen huts. (62) The children stand in front of one couple who might be their parents. One child might be two years

---

9 Reichsschule Feldafing.

old and the other a year old, a happy young family. A teenage boy standing next to the group is looking away from the camera with the obvious expression of "I am minding my own business," just like any teenager would do.

Without any captions, the picture could be interpreted as a group of friends vacationing in a rural campsite. One of the participants, wearing knee-high boots, a newsboy hat and a heavy coat, looks as if he just returned from a hike in the woods that appear in the background. The rest, some wearing overcoats and some jackets, appear as if they are heading out for dinner. Women's underwear drying on two laundry lines stretching between the two huts in the background suggest that at least some of the members of this group are staying in these huts.

The year is 1947, the place is Papendorf, Germany, and the subjects of this picture are former residents of Feldafing and passengers on the ship *Exodus*.

And those facts tell a much different story: these are not ordinary people. They are symbols of the determination of the remnants of the Jewish people to return to their homeland and rebuild it from its ashes. They could be the protagonists of a bestselling novel by Leon Uris, (63) later made into an epic movie starring Paul Newman. They were the catalyst that led to the establishment of the State of Israel.

I remember the filming of the movie *Exodus* in Haifa. It was quite an event in that sleepy city where the standing joke was that "the sidewalks were rolled up every night at 8 pm."

For about a month, celebrities like Paul Newman, Eva Marie Saint, and Sal Mineo decorated Haifa's streets. A small crowd of fans, including myself, occupied the sidewalk in front of Hotel Zion where they stayed to catch a glimpse and possibly an autograph.

But the true story of the ship Exodus was more dramatic than the movie and had far more historic impact than a box office hit. The ship that became known as Exodus was built in 1927 to carry passengers and freight in the Chesapeake Bay, and was named the President Warfield. (64) In World War II she served as a British transport ship, was attacked by a German submarine but managed to evade the only torpedo launched at it.

After the war she was purchased by the Haganah, the Jewish paramilitary organization, for a one-time mission: to transport illegal immigrants to British-controlled Palestine by breaking the British-imposed blockade and beaching itself, with its passengers onboard, on the shores of Tel Aviv. Once removed from the ship, the passengers were supposed to be whisked away to the Kibbutzim in the area and disguised as local settlers.

The effort was more symbolic than strategic. Even the ship's new name, *Yetziat Europa* (the "Flight from Europe"—or "Exodus"), alluded to the flight of the Israelites from bondage in Egypt and the chase by Pharaoh's iron chariots to the Red Sea.

On July 11, 1947 Yetziat Europa was loaded with 4,515 passengers—mostly Holocaust survivors—and headed from the small port of Sète west of Marseille, toward Palestine.

From the moment of its departure the ship was shadowed by British destroyers and a cruiser. Approximately twenty miles from Palestine's shores, British troops boarded Yetziat Europa and towed it to the port of Haifa. Despite the international public outcry, the passengers were not allowed to set foot in Palestine. Instead, they were transferred to three British ships and after a circuitous journey, were deported to Germany. The symbolism of deporting Holocaust survivors back to Germany was overwhelming. Some of the passengers on the Exodus, including the unnamed subjects of the picture, were interned in Papendorf.

Now that I know their story, I look at these Holocaust survivors in admiration. Despite what some might call them, they were not "lambs led to the slaughter." Within months of their liberation, at least one of the couples in the picture chose to bring new life to the world. Within two years of their liberation, the subjects of this picture chose to challenge Britain, one of the world's superpowers. They lost the battle, but they won the war. Their ordeal on the Yetziat Europa was one of the reasons the UN agreed on November 29, 1947 to the partition of the British-controlled Palestine and establishment of the independent State of Israel. The smiling people in this picture were not "lambs." They were lions.

Another picture caught my eyes. It shows twenty or thirty children, aged six or seven, in a classroom facing the camera. (65) They are all bright-eyed, looking at their teacher who stands with his back to the camera raising his arms like a conductor leading a chorus. In the background there is a large banner in Hebrew that reads: "We are singing for you, Homeland and Mother." To the left of the banner hangs a picture of Theodor Herzl, the visionary who established Zionism as a political movement, and to the right is a picture of Chaim Weitzman, Israel's first president.

That classroom could be the one where I spent my own childhood years. I have an almost identical picture of myself at age six. But the captions show that this classroom is in Feldafing. The picture is undated, but with Weitzman's portrait in the picture, it was likely taken after the State of Israel was established.

I could not tell if these children were born after the Holocaust or survived it miraculously. Some of them could be orphans. But without a doubt, they came from many different backgrounds, cultures and languages and were readying themselves for a life in Israel. They had already learned to identify with the leaders of the new nation, Hebrew was their new language, and the songs they were singing to their new and common motherland was their new culture. One may cringe today in the belief that this was brainwashing. But replacing old cultures that failed them with a new culture, filled with purpose and hope was the right thing to do.

These children were part of the huge immigration wave that came to Israel in its first years of independence. In four years the country's population doubled. I cannot imagine how America, the richest country on earth, could cope with an equivalent wave of three hundred million impoverished and traumatized immigrants who landed on its shores in a span of four years. Feldafing and other DP camps like it made a difference in Israel's ability to respond to this challenge and turn it into a blessing.

Other pictures from Feldafing show that preparation for a new life was not limited to children. There were vocational schools training adults to become tailors, (66) printers, (67) car mechanics, (68) shoemakers, (69) metal workers, (70) carpenters, (71) and hairdressers. (72)

There was even an amusing picture showing the training of future lumberjacks. (73) Four shirtless men and one woman (she does wear a shirt) are standing side by side carrying heavy logs on their shoulders in a pose that broadcasts "look how strong and muscular we are. We are the 'New Jews'". But if these people were preparing for logging careers in Israel, they were in for a disappointment. Israel in those days was busy planting new trees, not chopping them down.

Although the camp was self-governed, it did not have an independent economy. All provisions, housing or health care were provided either by the US Army or the UN. Yet, the Jewish Community Treasurer issued its own currency in denominations of 10 cents, 25 cents, 50 cents, 1 dollar, 5 dollars, and ten dollars. (74) The bills looked like Monopoly money. I do not understand the economic basis for these notes; did a Feldafing dollar have the same value as a US dollar? What provided the intrinsic value to these dollars and why was there a need to print them?

I also found a picture that seems to represent the camp in its early days, probably as Laci found it. (75) It shows a group of men standing in a yard behind two barracks-like brick two-story buildings. Seven military trucks are parked at the edge of the yard. The men are standing idly and chatting with each other. They are relaxed. No one seems to be in any hurry. Some are dressed in civilian pants and undershirts. Obviously, it was a warm day. Several men are still wearing the KZ striped uniforms. They were probably recent arrivals. Many liberated prisoners thought that KZ uniforms would protect them from the suspicion of being collaborators or escaped German POWs and chose to continue wearing them for some time.

Like all new arrivals to Feldafing, Laci had to register as a Displaced Person and obtain a gray identification card issued by the UNRRA. The card, bearing his picture, certified his Hungarian nationality and stated that he "has been until his liberation by the US Army imprisoned under the Nazi rule as a political prisoner in the following concentration camps: Dachau, Mühldorf. His KZ Prisoner number was 124352." The document was necessary to travel home and to re-establish his citizenship there.

Laci remained in Feldafing less than two months.

July 1945: Home at Last

Traveling after the war through Europe was difficult and dangerous. Survivors and migrants often spent weeks on the road hitching rides on horse-drawn wagons, farmers' trucks, and trains. But two pictures from Feldafing tell a different story. (76) Both are captioned: "A group of survivors repatriating to Romania, at the train station." The first shows a large group of men and women standing or sitting in a grassy field next to a railroad track facing a train station. Many of the men are shirtless and the women are dressed lightly. The year is not stated, but it was certainly a hot summer day. The second picture, (77) undated as well, shows men and women boarding a train, all wearing overcoats, obviously a fall or winter day.

At least on two separate occasions, one in the summer and one in the fall or winter, transportation was arranged to repatriate camp inmates. Laci might have taken the summer train to Romania and disembarked when it stopped in Budapest.

I carefully checked the first picture, trying to identify Laci among the waiting passengers. I could not find him, but I could sense the anticipation among the passengers.[1] Many of them would have already known that some of their loved ones would not be waiting for them. But the sunny grassy field projected only a sense of a happy picnic, lacking any anxiety. It was in sharp contrast to many Holocaust pictures showing SS soldiers loading children, women, and the elderly into cattle cars.

The crowded train carrying concentration camp survivors from Feldafing approached the Budapest Keleti pályaudvar (Eastern train station). The exhausted passengers shook off the fatigue of a long ride in a hot train, endless stops and delays. Those sitting by a window craned their necks to see

---

1   I had a similar feeling myself, waiting at Fayed military airport on the Egyptian side of the Suez Canal for the plane that would take me home for my first leave after the Yom Kippur War. I felt a joyful anticipation to see Liora and my family mixed with anxiety to find out who among my friends would not return.

the landscape passing by. Those in the aisles stood leaning on the benches facing the windows.

Moving through the industrialized suburbs of Budapest they saw the astonishing depth of destruction left by the Nazi's last-ditch effort to hold off the Red Army from capturing the city. Although not a German city, Budapest had been declared by Hitler as a "Fortress City," meaning that it was to be defended to the last man. (8 p. 349)

The siege of Budapest lasted one hundred and two days, longer than the siege of any European city other than Stalingrad. Even the battle for Berlin lasted just two weeks and for Vienna just one week. (6 pp. 36-37) It left more than eighty percent of its apartment houses destroyed or damaged.

Although the war in Budapest ended five months earlier, much of the destruction was still untouched. It would remain that way for years. Most of the buildings along the track were in ruins. The few still standing were scarred. Mercifully, the dead corpses, humans and animals, were already removed, but the roads visible from the train were still littered with burned vehicles, blown-up tanks, and burned cannons, German and Soviet.

But the destruction in the suburbs paled relative to what the passengers saw when the train crossed the Danube over the railroad bridge. The magnificent bridges that once connected Buda with Pest were gone, blown up by the retreating Germans, ostensibly to slow the advancing Soviet Army. Only the two supporting columns of the Lánchíd (Chain Bridge) remained standing in the water like sentries on the two opposite banks of the Danube, their limp chains dangling into the water. (6 p. 37)

The train pulled into the station slowly as if mourning the destruction. The doors opened and the Budapest passengers stepped off silently. There were no ecstatic reunions.

Laci was among the last to emerge. No one waited for him. He was not even sure he wanted to be back in Budapest. But he had returned to look for his Judit and Lili.

He stood on the ramp looking around, trying to absorb the moment. Severe destruction was not new to him, but this was different, he knew this place and not long ago he had loved it. The grandiose station he remembered was shattered. Laci walked along the ramp into the main hall. A Russian soldier armed with a semi-automatic weapon at the entrance demanded to see his ID. He grunted when he saw the Displaced Person's card written in English but waived him through.

The typical hustle and bustle of this major station was gone. The shoeshine man that Judit admired was no longer there. Gone were the flower and gift shops. No one sold food. Only a few vendors at the corner sold the still available goods: cheap cigarettes, probably made of weeds, and matches. The few passengers passing through were destitute. No one could afford even the cheap cigarettes.

Carrying a small bag with the few belongings he received in Feldafing, Laci stepped out of the station towards the Danube along Rákóczi út. Évi lived at the foot of Gellért Hill across the river. Her postcard bearing her return address reached him in Feldafing. She and her son András were the only living persons in this world waiting for him. Böske, their mother, was dead; Sándor, Judit, and Lili were still missing.

When he left Budapest three years earlier, Rákóczi út was one of the most vibrant streets of Budapest. Now it was deserted. The only traffic along its four lanes, scarred by heavy tank tracks, was military vehicles marked with a red star and an occasional overcrowded bus that meandered among the many potholes. Hardly any building remained undamaged. The few stores in the buildings still standing were empty and deserted; their glass windows shattered. Few people walked on the street.

Laci reached the Danube. He looked across the river in disbelief. The magnificent castle on the hill and the King's Palace were damaged, the green dome crowning it partially destroyed, the walls facing the river blackened by fire that had consumed its interior. Buildings at the foot of the hill were reduced to rubble. Budapest's most glorious symbol was terribly defaced.

A small ferry carried him across the river. Évi was home when he knocked on her door. She hugged him without saying a word. He crossed his arms around her shoulders feeling them shaking as she sobbed.

Only 82,000 deportees returned to Hungary after the war, most of them by July. (78) Évi heard from her husband, who was still in a hospital in Germany but would be back soon. The hope that Judit, Lili and Sándor would return was diminishing fast. Like more than 420,000 other Hungarian Jews, they had disappeared without a trace. They were last seen in Gyula and that's where Laci planned to go.

Fast forward 66 years to summer 2011. Liora, our son Dan and his wife Molly, and I visited my cousins Tomi and Zsóka in Hungary. We met them on an unseasonably cold July afternoon at Tomi's wife's, Erika's, country home, a few miles outside Budapest.

We were sitting on the patio surrounded by lush farmland stretching beyond her meticulously kept yard. A vast stretch of sunflowers in full bloom painted the land in bright yellow. The soothing sound of the small water fountain in the little waterlily pond provided a surrealistic background sound to the solemn work we were conducting.

Before her death, my aunt Évi left Zsóka a shoebox full of old family photos, letters and documents, mostly from the darkest days of our family's history. Dreading the stories she might discover, Zsóka never opened the box. For nearly thirty years the box remained untouched in the back of her closet.

With my encouragement, Zsóka agreed to bring the box to our reunion. It was years since we were all in one place and I worried that we might never assemble again. This might have been my only opportunity to discover untold stories of our family.

A stack of old photos greeted us at the top; some showing our parents, Laci and Évi as children together with our common grandparents Sándor and Böske. Others showed our great-grandparents and some showed me, Noemi, and my cousins as children. I recognized many of the pictures that my parents mailed.

But soon we were through the photos and reached a new layer, letters, postcards, and receipts. The first document was an envelope. The return address showed that the letter had been written by Laufer Sándorné, our grandmother.

I never saw Böske's handwriting, but any graphologist can tell you that seeing the handwriting of a person is like having a dog sniff a scent. It is a living trace of the writer. It can show if the writer was under stress, in a hurry, even some of the writer's characteristic traits. This envelope was touched by Grandma Böske. It was the closest I would ever get to feel her presence. It was almost as if I made a direct contact with the grandmother I never knew.

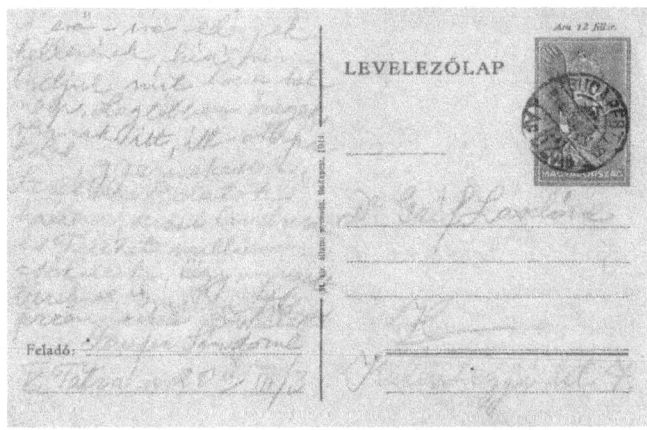

Böske's last postcard to my aunt Évi dated December 1, 1944. Böske was murdered by Arrow Cross thugs the following night.

I asked Zsóka if she recognized the return address, Pozsonyi utca 39, Apartment V/3. She did. This was one of the Swiss protected houses. (79) A "safe" house established by the Swiss legation to provide refuge to Jews from the Arrow Cross gangs who were rampaging through the streets of Budapest, killing them randomly by the thousands.

We knew that Böske received protection from Raul Wallenberg.[2] We were surprised that she also received help from the Swiss. The undated letter was addressed to Mrs. Igriczi, Böske's housemaid, who was asked to bring some provisions to the safe house. From the letter it was clear that Böske either could not or would not leave the safe house, not even for minor shopping. She and thousands of Jews like her were trapped in safe houses, squeezed four, five or even more in one room with little food, water, or heat, a self-imposed prison sentence.

Beneath the envelope was a postcard. I already recognized Böske's handwriting. It was addressed to Évi. But when I picked it up, my heart skipped a beat. The postcard was dated December 1, 1944. Böske was murdered by Arrow Cross gangs on December 2. That date was indicated in her death record in Gyula's archives. The return address was Tátra utca 20/a, Apartment III/3. Evidently, she left the Swiss house and moved to this address.

Records in the Budapest Holocaust Memorial Center confirm that this house was a Swedish safe house and was raided by the Arrow Cross, the Hungarian Fascist Party, on the night of December 2. All its inhabitants were forced at gunpoint out of their beds, marched three blocks to the Danube, ordered to undress and then shot dead. Their bodies, some still alive, were thrown into the frozen Danube. We will never know why she left the Swiss house.

Tomi began reading aloud from the postcard Böske wrote in her last hours:

> My Dear Treasures, Bpest, 1944. XII/1 (Budapest, 12/1/1944)
> We are still here with no change waiting to see what will happen. Until now, I have had a bed, have not suffered cold and eaten partly from my own supply, partly thanks to others' mercy. God will continue to protect us. Do not worry, my dearest, all bad things will end at some point.
> I really miss you but I give thanks to the Good Lord that at least you chose a different path—many people would trade places with you. I do not

---

2 Raoul Wallenberg and Carl Lutz, Swedish and Swiss diplomats respectively, saved tens of thousands Budapest Jews during the Nazi occupation and the rule of the Arrow Cross government by issuing them diplomatic documents and hosting them in "safe houses" that were declared as diplomatic immune facilities.

understand why I cannot get from Mrs. Wagner the things I requested from her, blankets, socks, underpants [long johns], tea, sugar, potatoes, since we do not know what the next day will bring us. Most of us here are old, and some of us have children too.

    I would like to get news from you. Lots of kisses to you and Andris. Be calm and patient. Keep me informed through Gyuri.

Your Böske

Mrs. Sándor Laufer

Tátra St. 20/a III/3

We remained silent, immersed in our emotions. Unlike Böske's previous letter, this card read like a farewell, her last message. Liora and Molly had tears in their eyes. I hugged Liora and then reached across the table to hug Zsóka.

Later during our visit to Budapest we went to see the house on Pozsonyi utca. It was a plain looking urban apartment building in the Újlipótváros neighborhood. It was a block away from the Danube and within an easy stroll from the Hungarian Parliament. Embroidered curtains decorated the windows of many of the apartments and pots with blooming geranium flowers hung from balcony rails. Two real estate agencies occupied the street level floors. There was nothing to mark it or to remind its inhabitants or a passerby of its remarkable history.

From that house we walked a few blocks to the house on Tátra utca 20/a, a red brick building, the façade decorated with bronze trimming. There was no marking on this house either to indicate that more than a hundred Jews lived there for weeks, hiding from the wrath of Hungarian gangs, before being found and murdered, staining the Danube red.

But there were two signs on the walls of the adjacent house. They commemorated two dignitaries who lived there; a Hungarian parliament member, who served until the Nazi invasion of Hungary, deported to Mauthausen, survived and then forced into exile by the Hungarian Stalinist regime. The other sign carried the bust of the founder of the Hungarian Ballet Institute.

We stood silently facing the locked front door of Böske's last home. I looked up to the third floor trying to guess behind which of the five windows facing the street she lived. Could she hear the shouting gangs as they were approaching the house in the middle of the night and breaking down that door with their rifle-butts?

The next document was an old receipt dated April 28, 1944, six weeks after the Nazi occupation of Hungary, issued by the Hungarian Commerce

Bank of Pest to my uncle Laci Gróf. The bank acknowledged the "receipt of an envelope (or package) sealed by [his] handwritten signature that contains a gold bracelet pendant, a gold bracelet, a gold watch, and two gold wedding rings. Received under Decree 1600/1944."[3] (9 p. 1190)

It is safe to conclude that if the receipt remained in the family's possession for nearly seventy years the envelope and its contents were never returned. The envelope, along with many other great Jewish fortunes, was stored in the bank's basement and became part of one of World War II legendary treasure heists—the Hungarian Gold Train. (80) (81)

The next item in Zsóka's shoebox was a five-page letter from Laci to Évi. The well-preserved, still-white pages were densely covered with handwriting that I easily recognized as Laci's. He had much to say; the lines were long, running from edge to edge leaving no margins. I had difficulties reading his handwriting in Hungarian but I noticed the date at the bottom of the last page, next to his signature. The letter was written in Gyula on August 11, 1945. In less than three months Laci recovered from a deadly disease, regained his strength and found his way back home from Feldafing.

I handed the letter to Tomi.

> I am already writing this letter in our old house at the address: Béke sugárút 3 (today's address is Béke sugárút 37),

Tomi read aloud.

The first sentence already answers a nagging question I had for years, did Laci and Évi get possession of the house after the war. They did.

I closed my eyes as Tomi continued reading trying to imagine the world that Laci found. Budapest was in ruins, but a sense of a new beginning that comes with the destruction of evil provided an air of optimism. Évi and András, her firstborn, were alive. My father Laci survived and was on his way back from Mauthausen. But Böske was dead, and Sándor's brother who returned from Auschwitz reported that Sándor was shot on January 17, 1945, the day the SS abandoned the camp. There was no word from Judit and Lili. They were deported with Sándor to Auschwitz and almost certainly murdered upon arrival.

To be sure, Laci himself changed. When the Biblical Jacob wrestled an angel, his hip was put out of joint. (35 pp. 35:1-7) Laci had wrestled with Satan.

Tomi's voice brought me back to Erika's porch.

---

3   The decree was introduced on April 16, 1944, less than a month after the Nazi invasion of Hungary, mandating "the reporting and sequestration of all properties owned by members of the Jewish faith including jewelry, bank accounts, and safety deposits." http://www.lootedart.com/MFEU4G20953.

> We do not have a table, so the standing mirror in the bedroom is used for writing,

Laci relates in his letter. Then, he continues to describe the house:

> I moved in two days ago. I fired the janitor who was hired by the congregation and whom I could not use to do anything and hired a woman with four children and also a cranky maid. While the maid's apartment is still occupied, or until you or the family arrives, they will live in my old room and in the family room. You will probably think of them as being too numerous but I deliberately chose them taking into an account the current security conditions and the lack of security hardware in the house (there is no fence, and windows and locks are missing). I wanted a woman who is physically attached to the house by her family.
>
> The house was in a terrible situation. With the help of that woman we cleaned it up by and large, plugged the mouse holes, and then I moved in. I repaired the windows using glass panes from windows with double-glazing so that each one has at least one pane. I got a door handle and a lock mounted only on the front door. All the door handles and light switches were looted; the faucets and the fence were taken too. The house is being restored to the condition of an average Jewish household in Gyula. You can come with Tóni, and Ágica[4] can also come for a vacation. I moved into the old living room, and I got the two yellow beds, the nightstand, the big yellow three piece wardrobe, and the standing mirror. Your room next to mine is going to be the sitting room. There are only four armchairs in there now, but tomorrow your combination cupboard and desk will arrive. We still do not have a table, but there is going to be one soon with chairs, too. I am having the bathtub and the stove transported tomorrow by a butcher, the tap may be brought over from Károlyi Sándor Street.
>
> The Jewish Council mishandled much of our property. They investigated Papp Mihály and took back [from him] some of our white furniture, bed, cupboard, chairs, kitchen cabinet, but then they probably gave them away to someone else and then lost track of them. I have no choice but to start visiting all the Jewish homes one by one. By the way, I also have a dispute with them [the Jewish Council]. I would like to get carpets to replace ours but it does not work that easily because the Forced Labor men here [who returned earlier] already took for themselves the "recovered" Jewish property. The deportees who are returning now are finding nothing is here.

---

4   Ágica is the endearment name for Ági (Ágnes) Palócz.

> It would be better if you were here because it is easier to get things for a family [rather than for a single man]. Our carpets are surely around here somewhere, used by someone else, but I will need you to find them because I would not recognize them. I have got a cooking stove, it is the hardest thing to get nowadays. I located through my own investigation Schmer Dénes's [stove] and therefore he could give me his stove allowance. I already have a lamp, and will get another one or two. We have eight paintings. I gave one of them as a gift to the person who found them.

I looked around the room. Dan and Liora were immersed in their thoughts. Molly was taking pictures of us and of the documents scattered on the table. I was grateful to her for recording this unique event. For a brief moment we transcended time and we were with Laci as he entered his looted home and with Sándor, Lili, and Judit as they were leaving their home for the last time.

> I have settled with Kovács. When I arrived in Gyula, Lebovits Ernő and Békés Gyurka told me that Kovács claimed to have been robbed [of our jewelry that he was guarding for us]. But they also said they do not believe that he was. I had a delicate situation in my hands. If I confront Kovács, he may never recant his story again. But if I bring the police with me and they cannot find the jewelry—which I was quite certain would happen—I may get myself into trouble.
>
> I came up with a third approach. I sent him one of my detective friends with a story that while he was investigating another case, he [the detective] discovered that Mr. Kovács must have guarded the Laufer jewelry well. Then he [the detective] met me on a tram in Pest and relayed the good news to me. Now I am here at Gyula and would like to come by to thank him in person for this great service. We will never find out if Kovács really intended to steal the jewelry, as I have heard, or all along had honest intentions. The fact is that—as he [Kovács] later told me—the visit of the detective felt like a slap on his face. He told the detective that he had everything, not in Gyula but at Túrkeve. He brought [the jewelry] back last week.

Tomi stopped his reading with a grin on his face. "It is so typical of your dad. He was truly something. He out-maneuvered Kovács. I heard many stories about people who received valuables to guard and then found ways not to return them when their owners returned."

> I got back approximately 220 grams [of gold] out of my own items. I am missing a double-bottomed gold watch weighing 30 gr, and the following things: a necklace, a bracelet that my dear Lili surely took with her!

I stopped Tomi's reading. Did Laci write "my dear Lili?" This is how Hungarians often refer to the dead. Did this mean that Laci already knew that Lili was not coming back?

Tomi could not tell.

> From Mama's things,

Tomi continued,

> I got back the silver purse, our father's IWC gold watch, a gold pin, and a silver box. Two items are missing. One is the diamond earrings. They must have been taken to the Gyula pawnshop. According to Kovács, he never received them. But you itemized for me a 'diamond earring, ring, and watch.' Kovács showed me a one carat diamond earring but he claimed it belonged to his wife. The other item is the watch. According to mother's notes, she took the watch to the Gyula pawnshop. But that was the one I got back from Kovács. At the same time one of my own watches is missing. Is it possible that mother switched between the watches and put my lower quality watch in pawn instead of father's? Or maybe father had two gold watches? In that case the question is: where is my watch? Did Kovács really not get it? You noted a ring too. What kind of ring is it? Is it possible that mother had a precious diamond ring? Because Kovács gave me some tiny thing when I asked for the ring but I still do not know whether she had had a diamond ring too? Please let me know as soon as possible. The jeweler Gál thinks that father might have had some jewelry too. What do you know about that?

My mind was back again with Böske. The proud, once wealthy woman was forced, according to this letter, to pawn her jewelry. Only desperation could bring her to the pawnshop. I could imagine her entering the pawnshop, looking left and right to make certain no one saw her.

When did she pawn that watch? She could not do that after April 16, 1944 when the Nazis issued the decree ordering Hungarian Jews to surrender their valuables. That means that their fortune was lost even before the occupation. Did she get a good price? Probably not.

The other question I had was when did Böske commission Kovács, who lived in Gyula, to safeguard the family jewelry? She had to do so before the Nazi occupation in March because within a day of the occupation Böske, along with all Hungarian Jews, was not allowed to travel. That means that on the day of the occupation she was in Budapest and remained there until her death in the hands of the Arrow Cross thugs. Otherwise she would have been deported to Auschwitz with the rest of her family in Gyula. But then what caused her, even before the Nazi occupation, to suspect that the family jewelry was at risk and needed to be hidden?

I could not answer these questions but I had to admire Böske's resolve and foresight.

Tomi continued reading the letter aloud.

> I already informed you about Simon. Did you get the letter that I sent with Emandity Kató, the 5,000 pengő and the 1 kg butter? And my messages [that were] sent with Spielman? As I wrote, I will accept money as compensation for the stolen rails. Could I get an option on a real estate in Pest, for example the one on Molnár utca? I asked that you send me a telegram about it, but I still did not receive one. Please let me know immediately by mail or telegram what is the final price for the Molnár utca apartment and how long will that price be held. Keep me informed whether there is gold available, whether you are able to buy it, how much you can buy and at what price. Or should I accept for my cash high quality soap instead?
>
> With this letter I am also sending you 80 eggs, 1.5 kg lard and potato-sugar. About the latter: let me know if you can use it for canning or as a sweetener. Should I send more of it?[5]

---

5   The letter prompted some of my own memories. I was a young child when the nascent state of Israel went through a depression. Though no one suffered hunger, basic staples such as eggs, flour, sugar, milk, and meat were rationed. Common fruits like apples or peaches were unavailable to most Israelis.

"Farm Eggs" in those days did not mean "organic" as it would today, but eggs acquired directly from a farm, outside the official food distribution chain. They could be a gift from a friend or a relative who had a farm, or purchased in the black market at double or triple their official price but without surrendering coupons from the ration coupon book. It is quite likely that some of the eighty eggs that Évi received from Laci became the Hungarian equivalent of "Farm Eggs."

I also lived in Israel through runaway inflation, not like the inflation in Hungary, but disastrous nevertheless. A salary paid at the beginning of the month lost nearly sixteen percent of its value by the end of that month. Prices changed so often that they lost any meaning. Only hard assets such as gold, real estate, or foreign currency were considered as keeping their value.

If you need more money, tell me soon so I can send it when I find an opportunity. I rarely get some eggs. Should I buy fat? How much? Here it costs 700 pengő.

Any news from Laci [Évi's husband.]?

Dear Évi, please check occasionally on Molnár utca to prevent others from claiming it as an empty apartment while I am spending my time here. Settle the rent and communal work!

This letter is being carried to you by Mrs. Nyitrai, she is the new house custodian.

God bless you. Lots of kisses and hugs to Böske [of course this is not their mother Böske], Ágica, and Andris, too.

Your loving,

Laci

Gyula, 1945. VIII/11.[6]

But with all its detail, Laci's letter does not discuss the only one item that truly mattered to him: that Lili and Judit were not coming back!

My mind drifted to Laci returning to what was once his home. I could imagine him entering the looted house. No one met him in the Gyula station. He walked the short distance along Béke sugárút to the house, carrying his small bag. Every day for the last three years he dreamed about this moment. And now when it arrived he was terribly lonely, sad and anxious.

Gyula was spared the destruction suffered by Budapest. It was liberated by the Red Army on October 6, 1944, (82) after less than seven months of Nazi occupation. But that was sufficient time to eliminate the Jews and steal their property. Less than four months separated Sándor, Lili, and Judit from freedom. They were deported from the Gyula ghetto on Friday June 16, 1944 (83) to a tobacco warehouse in the nearby town Békécsaba and from there to Auschwitz on June 26.

As if recognizing how little time they had, the city elders of Gyula rushed on June 22, 1944 to declare the deportees as absentees and their property abandoned. The City Council minutes read: "The Board of Trustees of the city of Gyula—as according to the notification of Mayor, the Jews of Gyula have been interned and their present residence is unknown and they have also failed to set up a trust administering their property—pursuant to Section D, Paragraph 28 of Act XX, 1877 and executive order 231300/1944 BM—has decided to give control of the administration of the property of the following absentee Jewish residents to trustees obliged

---

6 Gyula, August 11, 1945.

to administer such property for the purposes specified..." (84) Török József, resident of Gyula, was delegated to act as trustee for Sándor.

The Council was "gracious" enough though to allow the absentees to appeal their decision within fifteen days of its delivery.

How cynical and malicious. The council knew well where the "absentee deportees" were! Six days earlier, two trucks and forty horse-drawn wagons, all provided by the mayor, waited on Kossuth tér for the deportees and carried them ten miles away to the tobacco warehouse in Békéscsaba. (85) The convoy was accompanied by an armed police guard, also dispatched by the city. Anyone who cared could find the "absentee deportees" waiting in inhumane conditions for the trains that would take them to the crematoria.

The Gyula city councilmen knew very well that no one would appeal their decision. Even if Sándor received the notification, he was too preoccupied with finding some water and a slice of bread for his infant granddaughter and her mother or a shady corner to hide from the scorching sun. But the troubled leaders were more concerned in "legalizing" their looting than visiting their colleague Sándor, who had served on the same council for many years, to offer him or his family a hand, or just a kind parting word, and, of course, to ask for his instructions regarding the disposition of his property. Such courtesies were not necessary; they knew he would not be coming back.

But some Jews did return much sooner than expected. On November 7, 1944, the Gyula City Council issued a new order annulling the previous order and placing many of the seized Jewish goods under the protection the newly established Jewish Council. (86)

When Laci arrived, the Jewish Council already had records showing that Sándor, Lili, and Judit were deported from Békéscsaba and after three days in a scorching hot cattle car, their train reached Auschwitz. Within minutes, they were lined up in two lines, men in one and women and children in the other, for the infamous selection process; Judit and Lili were waved to the left, Sándor to the right.

By sunset, Lili and Judit along with most of their train's passengers were dead, their bodies cremated. Their names are engraved on a marble memorial in the Gyula Jewish cemetery.

Sándor was waved to the right, to forced labor. At age 59 he became a slave. His brother Feri, who was deported from his hometown Babócsa, met him there. Both Feri and Sándor survived until January 17, 1945, Auschwitz's last day as an active concentration camp. With the Red Army approaching, Berlin ordered the camp evacuated and all evidence of the crimes committed erased. The crematoria and gas chambers were blown up months earlier, damning documents burned, and KZs able to walk were lined up and ordered to march west. Those unable to walk were shot. However, some prisoners in the infirmary were overlooked and abandoned without medicine, food or water. A few survived for ten days, until the arrival or the Soviet army. (42 pp. 151-173) Sándor was too weak to march but not sick enough to be in the sick bay. He was shot at Auschwitz's gate, collapsing at Feri's feet. Feri survived the infamous "death march." He died in Babócsa in 1975.

Laci's letter describing the state of the house was factual, unemotional. He lost his mother, father, wife, and little daughter. Would a looted house seem like an insult to injury, the final straw that would make one give up? Maybe for some people, but not for Laci.

Liora, Dan, Molly, and I visited that house a few days earlier. Its image was still fresh in my mind when Tomi read Laci's letter. I could easily envision the house as Laci found it: red tile roof, yellow front, broken glass in the four large windows facing the street. The fences along the side and back yards missing, shrubs and trees overgrown, the yard filled with weeds, and the large piles of timber in the backyard that once were taller than the house were gone.

But when we saw it the house was old and had aged well. Three signs by the front door announced that two lawyers and one event coordinator shared the space. The house had been turned into an office.[7]

As we were taking pictures, trying to peek along the sides of the house and over its fence into the yard, a window opened and a man leaned out. Here was our opportunity! I greeted the man in Hungarian, introduced myself as the grandson of the man who built the house and asked for his permission to come in. Mr. Sándor Lovász, as he introduced himself, gladly showed us in. The sign by the door reminded me that Mr. Lovász was the event coordinator.

We walked through the front door and a short corridor into a large anteroom. Chairs lined up along the walls implied that this was a waiting room.

I looked around the room. I could picture the large heavy cherry-wood dining table surrounded by eight matching chairs that once made this space a dining room. The table would be covered with a white crocheted tablecloth and with large bowl of fresh apricots in the middle. I could hear the sounds of a large family gathering for a Sabbath lunch. I could smell the aroma of the chilled sour cherry soup brought from the kitchen, the goulash still bubbling gently on the stove and the finely chopped dill ready to be added to the cucumber salad.

---

7   I visited the house again in 2016. A large sign at the front pronounced "LAUFER HÁZ ANNO 1929" (Laufer House year 1929). It was posted by its new owner, who also posted its history in the anteroom.

Three rooms opened from the facing wall of the anteroom and another one from its side wall. "This must have been the parents' bedroom," Lovász explained, pointing to the door opening from the side wall to our right. "It was the corner room, the best room of the house. The other rooms were the children's room, and over there, behind you were the kitchen and the bathroom."

We finished touring the main house and its rooms and were ready to leave, when Lovász asked us to follow him to the back of the house. "Uncle Pista, look, I am bringing you guests," he yelled as we emerged from a back door into a little patio overlooking a wonderful yard filled with mature fruit trees, apricots, yellow plums, purple plums, grape vines, blooming rose bushes. It was a little heaven.

Lovász opened a door off the patio and led us into a small room. My eyes were drawn to the facing wall that was decorated with many large skulls of bucks with larger antlers. At least ten smaller skulls and antlers were mounted on the wall to our left. Medals were hanging from several of the trophies on green, white and red ribbons. An old lady sat in a large armchair beneath the large skulls. To our left in another armchair and with a walker next to him sat an old man. This had to be "Uncle Pista," the champion hunter and winner of the medals.

Mr. Farkas and his wife, as Lovász introduced them, had lived in this small apartment for more than fifty years. This had to be the maid's apartment that Laci mentioned in his letter.

We were invited to sit on the couch next to Mrs. Farkas. Mr. Farkas remembered that Mr. Laufer once lived in this house. He had never met him; he was too young when Mr. Laufer lived there.

A thought flashed through my mind that Farkas would have been a teenager when Sándor, Lili, and Judit were marched through the streets of Gyula on their way to the tobacco warehouse in Békéscsaba from where they were deported to Auschwitz. He might have not remembered Sándor, but he must have remembered that Friday morning on June 1944 when the Jews were paraded through Kossuth tér, Gyula's central square. He had to have been there. It was not an event a teenager would miss. I looked at the old man wondering, did he jeer like the others when he saw Sándor pass? Did he taunt Lili when he saw her walk by, carrying Judit in her arms, trying to calm her from the terrifying vile words shouted by the crowd? But then I shook off these dark thoughts. There was no use in thinking them.

But then another thought flashed through my mind: how did Laci look at his Gyula neighbors when he met them? Did he wonder, just like I did, which of them heckled his daughter, wife, and father when they walked for the last time through the streets of their own town? Who among those on the streets of Gyula had sullied his house?

Farkas remembered that Sándor was a timber merchant. *"Only a timber merchant would put such heavy rafters on the roof of a one-story building. His son came back in 1947 and sold the house."*

I doubted Farkas when he said that Laci sold the house. But the letter that Tomi read to us a few days later confirmed that Farkas was telling the truth after all.

1945-1949: Budapest

Nine years after graduating law school, Laci still did not have a law license. Other than the little he could recover from his parents' fortune, he had no assets. He had no family and hardly any friends. He was a loner by nature, but in the summer of 1945 he was extremely lonely. Though he was smart, hardworking, honest, and from a good family, all the ingredients necessary for a successful life, he had the terrible misfortune of growing up and living in the wrong time and the wrong country.

Back in Budapest after a month in Gyula, he must have considered leaving Hungary. There was nothing to keep him there, no family, career, or property. But he had no other country to go to. America did not welcome Holocaust survivors; neither did the rest of Europe. Israel did not exist yet and Palestine, under British rule, was closed to Jewish immigration. Australia might have welcomed him, but it was far away and remote.

Many Hungarian and Eastern European refugees chose to permanently leave their homelands. Those in the territories controlled by Western allies were interned in DP camps, waiting indefinitely, often for years,[1] (7 pp. 340-341) for an opportunity to emigrate. Laci was eager to launch his career. He was not willing to be trapped indefinitely in a refugee camp.

Laci's new life in Hungary started in an economically depressed environment. Hungary's infrastructure had been destroyed by some of the heaviest battles of the war, its factories looted by the Germans, the Fascist Arrow Cross government, and the Soviets. The final blow was the onerous Armistice agreement that imposed on Hungary heavy reparations in cash, products, and food that slowed recovery for many years. (6 pp. 61-80) Lacking machinery and basic supplies like fertilizers, harvests were shrinking while demands by the occupying Soviet forces still had to be met. By 1946, famine spread throughout the civilian population, even to the farmers themselves.

---

1   For example, one refugee had to wait in a DP camp in Bremen Germany until September 1947 to immigrate to the US.

To make matters worse, civil liberties were limited by the heavy-handed Soviets. Even book burnings that were typical of the Nazi and Fascist regimes were back, (6 pp. 66-70) except that now the destroyed books were anti-Communist rather than Communist.

And yet, despite these difficulties, the summer of 1945 was remembered as a time of great hope and optimism. Official Hungary denounced the Jewish Laws[2] (7 p. 342) and restored all rights to the survivors. People's courts were established to try war criminals, many of them for murdering or mistreating Jews. Within a year, more than 27,000 war criminals were tried. Although some notorious criminals escaped with light sentences, 332 received death sentences, and of those, 146 were executed. (23) Laci told me that during that period he grew a menacing moustache and with a group of survivors, hunted down war criminals and even witnessed some of the hangings.

Along with the war crimes trials, Hungary engaged in other forms of retribution. 40,000 people were interned in the following five years without any legal conviction and 62,000 public servants were dismissed. 200,000 ethnic Germans, known as Svábs,[3] were held collectively guilty of war crimes and deported. This massive reprisal was certainly a political cleansing process that often had nothing to do with past anti-Semitism, the Holocaust, or any war crimes. Nevertheless, it still carried a sense of retribution and further enhanced the sense that justice was being served. (7 p. 344)

Adding to the sense of new possibilities were the political liberties never experienced before which at the time could not be foreseen as short-lived. Despite restrictions imposed by the occupying Soviets, several non-Communist parties were permitted to form. Many Jews became politically active and quickly reached dominant roles both in the Communist Party and the more centrist Small Holders' party. In August 1945, the head of the Armistice Control Commission notified the provisional Hungarian Government that free elections should be held as soon as possible. (6 p. 95) These would become the first free elections in Hungary's thousand-year history, and the last for more than another four decades. All citizens ages twenty and older were allowed to vote without gender discrimination or educational requirement. These might seem trivial in Western democracies but were revolutionary for Hungarians.

---

2 Although Act XXV of 1946 restored all rights to Hungarian Jews, it was the first step in a process that continues today of deflecting all blame to the Holocaust of Hungarian Jews to foreign intervention claiming that the Hungarian nation resisted the persecution fiercely.

3 Sváb is the Hungarian spelling for "Schwab." It is pronounced as Schwab.

Laci despised Communism. If his political activity in Israel decades later is any indication, he must have been an active member of the Small Holders' Party. In the November 1945 elections that saw a remarkable participation of 92 percent of all eligible voters this party won 57% of the ballots. (6 p. 101) Hungarians felt that a page was closing on an old world and a new page of hope and liberalism was opening.

In September Laci applied for admission to the Budapest Bar Association.[4] The correspondence was already conducted from his new apartment on 16 Molnár utca, a two-bedroom apartment on the second floor of a five-story building that doubled as his office. Three years later, one of these bedrooms was turned into my nursery.

In his letter to the Bar, Laci explained the six-year delay since he first became eligible to apply. In concise language he stated that he had been drafted to the Hungarian Forced Labor service in 1942, sent to Russia, and from there in October 1944 he was deported to Dachau. But even more importantly, he had to explain a felony conviction in 1942 that resulted in a one-year jail sentence, stating that his crime of assisting a Jew escape persecution was not a crime under the current law and therefore his conviction should not be considered a felony. Without rehabilitation Laci would remain a felon, ineligible for admission to the Bar.

Under the personal data line of "Married" and "Children" on the application form he wrote "Died in Auschwitz."

Laci passed the Bar exam on February 1946 and was admitted to the Bar. He stated criminal defense as his main focus. A copy of his Lawyer ID card printed in Hungarian and French certifies that on March 1, 1946, Dr. Laufer László was registered as a lawyer on Page 8662 of the Association of Lawyers' list.

I found another round of correspondence between Laci and the Bar Association amusing. A year after being admitted, he requested that the effective date of his admission be moved up from 1946 to 1940, the date in which he could have been admitted had there not been the restrictions of the Jewish Laws. I could not tell if this additional seniority would have provided him with any advantage. It might have been just his sense of justice and fairness. His request was approved.

The zeal for life of Holocaust survivors is astonishing. Despite the traumas, many were eager to quickly rebuild their lives. Some married within weeks after

---

4 Copy of that letter was found by Dr. Tibor Várkonyi in the Association's archive

Laci and Zsuzsi's wedding, Budapest, December 14, 1946

their liberation, often for the simple reason of wanting children of their own. Laci was no different. He married my mother, Dénes Zsuzsana, on December 14, 1946 after a brief six-week courtship.

Judging by the few pictures I found, their wedding was a small affair, probably no more than a family dinner. In one picture, Zsuzsi and Laci are seated at a beautiful dinner table holding up their wine glasses facing each other. Zsuzsi is dressed in a dark jacket showing some cleavage. On her right arm she was wearing a heavy gold bracelet that I still have. By her plate is a bouquet of flowers. Laci is wearing a double-breasted pinstriped jacket and a dark tie. His black hair, combed backwards, is shiny with brilliantine. He strikes me as being exceptionally thin, much thinner than I remember him. Could it be that he had still not regained his pre-war weight?

Unfortunately, the optimism that resulted from the free elections in 1945 and the wide spread of war crime trials gave way to a regrowth in anti-Semitism, even pogroms, (6 pp. 141-163 and 217-239) and the rise of a totalitarian Communist regime. Life for liberal Jews like Laci was getting worse.

Resentment by Christians over the demands of Jews who were trying to restore ownership of their property, a sense that the new government was controlled by Jews, and overall disappointment led in 1946 to anti-Jewish demonstrations and looting in dozens of towns such as Ózd and a lynching of a police officer in Miskolc. In Kunmadaras, where only seventy-three Jews survived the Holocaust, a pogrom was motivated by an ancient blood libel that claimed that Jews were using Christian children to make sausages. It became clear that the war and the Holocaust had not removed deep-seated prejudice.[5]

Despite the wide support that the Small Holders' Party enjoyed in the 1945 elections, its power eroded quickly, partly because of the presence of the Soviet army in Hungary, partly as a result of the rifts within the party itself, and partly due to mismanagement of the political power it had won. Consequently, in the elections in August 1947, though still nominally democratic, they lost their power to the Communist party. (6 p. 262)

Aided by the Soviets, the Communist party started to resort to tactics, often outside the law, aimed at destroying the other parties. Strategically, the party developed a strong national organization while the other parties concentrated their efforts on parliamentary work. Changes introduced by the Communists were small, but persistent and consistent. Most of the population did not recognize the trend and its consequences until it was too late.

For example, through a slow process of increased supervision of the banks, the Communist Party succeeded in nationalizing them by the end of 1947. In an opinion survey, 53 percent of the respondents did not understand the enormous impact of this action and supported it. (6 p. 268) The natural progression from the nationalization of the banks was nationalization of the factories that depended on bank credit. This too was supported by most workers who expected their wages to increase. That did not happen. Just the opposite, with factories nationalized, strikes were outlawed, and the disappointed workers lost their most potent weapon.

Schools were nationalized on June 1948. (6 p. 286) Now children, and by extension their parents, could be indoctrinated by a central authority. Beginning in 1949, most major companies in Hungary were nationalized, including small businesses. (6 p. 294) Almost everyone in the country fell in one way or another under government control; be it as a wage earner, a student

---

5   A recent Hungarian movie, *1945*, directed by Ferenc Török, depicts brilliantly the sense of fear and resentment arising in a small Hungarian village when two Jews arrive on the morning of August 12, 1945 to the small train station. Speculations that these two Jews returned to reclaim Jewish property taken by the villagers cause within hours rifts in and between families and even one suicide. Ironically, Laci's letter from Gyula describing his efforts of reclaiming his family's property was dated August 11, 1945.

or simply a consumer of information. Free opinions and new ideas were no longer welcome. The years of Stalinist terror had begun.

In December 1948 the borders were closed. Leaving Hungary without authorization was no longer permitted. This was justified by the shortage of manpower brought about by the war's heavy losses[6] and the post-war emigration. (87)

In May 1949, Rákosi Mátyás, the "Great Leader of the Working Nation," (88) won the national elections by a sweeping margin of 95.6 percent or 5,730,519 of the nationwide votes. More than 165,000 courageous opposition voters voted against him. They had no opposition party to vote for.

Rákosi Mátyás, a Stalin disciple, took his cues from the Moscow regime. After consolidating power in 1949, his administration began implementing purges in Stalin's style.

Rákosi's commitment to Stalin earned Hungary the dubious distinction of having the highest percentage of political purge victims of any Soviet satellite nation. Most dissidents were exiled to remote villages in Hungary where living standards were poor; many were imprisoned and some executed.

One of the casualties was the Hungarian Zionist Association. The Association formed before the war to help Jews escape deportation and the Arrow Cross murderers, and after the establishment of Israel it worked to promote and aid emigration to Israel. Between October 1948 and March 1949 its membership grew from 15,000 to 41,000 (89) with many registering to get help to escape Hungary and immigrate to Israel. (87 p. 143)

Initially the Soviet and Hungarian governments supported the establishment of Israel both in the UN vote in 1947 that ended the British mandate in Palestine and partitioned the land between the Jews and the Arabs, and immediately after Israel's Declaration of independence. Both governments expected that the left-leaning Israeli leadership would align itself with the Soviet bloc. They even helped to arm the newly formed IDF.[7] But late in 1948, when Israel appeared to align with the Anglo-American axis, the Soviet Union and most of its satellite states, including Hungary, turned hostile.

---

6   More than 700,000 lives lost, of which nearly 500,000 were Jews.
7   Israel received large quantities of WWII surplus arms from Czechoslovakia. Some of those arms were shipped on trains through Hungary to a Romanian port on the Black Sea where they were loaded on Israel-bound ships.

Hungary's hostility towards Zionism might have also derived from Rákosi's desire to demonstrate that his Jewish background would not compromise his loyalty to Hungary. But without a doubt, the organization's role of supporting illegal emigration provided the legal excuse. When the Austrian border was closed both to incoming and outgoing traffic, the Zionist movement stood out among the few groups that still could organize large-scale illegal immigration. They had the financial backing of Jewish philanthropic organizations, access to reliable human smugglers, and the facilities to handle the immigrants once they crossed the border. (87 p. 141)

On March 13, 1949, sensing the displeasure of Rákosi and his party, the Zionist Association's Management Committee met and decided that: "Since the State of Israel is now established, the main objective of the organization was met, and since there are now normal diplomatic relationships between Israel and Hungary, the working of the Management Committee and the Association can be terminated..." (89 p. 168)

Despite the official dissolution of the Zionist Association and termination of its activities, at least officially, its leaders were arrested in May and accused of supporting emigration from Hungary. (87 p. 163) Obviously, the true motivation for these arrests was political rather than operational.

On June 18, 1949, barely five weeks after Rákosi's landslide victory, eleven Zionist leaders were arrested in Budapest, charged with organizing illegal emigration of Jews and tried. (90) Three of the accused were acquitted and the other eight received varying jail terms. (91)

Laci was one of the defense lawyers in that trial. He and I never discussed the trial in detail or the crimes of the accused. We both knew that their only crime was being on the wrong side of political currents.

I reviewed several Hungarian newspapers from those days looking for any record of what seemed to be a show trial. But the papers were preoccupied in praising Rákosi and his new government. Two cartoons showed hundreds of excited voters casting their ballots in a polling station and scores of others dancing, (92) demonstrating the sweeping joy of the "workers' nation." Four years after ridding itself of the Nazi regime, Hungary was once again a totalitarian nation. Once again, papers reported only government-approved news. Except that now, positive news happened in Hungary and its "socialist" sister nations while negative news happened in the "imperialist" nations.

The headline of one paper on the day of the Zionists trial announced that a crowd of 100,000 gathered in Kossuth tér, just behind the Hungarian Parliament, for a peace demonstration; another headline reported a new wave of terror in Spain. Another paper proudly reported that a new paper product made of straw was developed and introduced in Hungary. It also reported that Hungarian workers sent a letter to Comrade Stalin urging him to protect the peace against threats by the hateful Imperialist nations. Two commercial advertisements recommend buying canned food because it was cheaper than home cooking. (93)

There was no mention of the Zionist trial. To nearly all Hungarians the trial did not occur.

July-August 1949: Escape from Hungary

Purges and retributions by the Rákosi's regime were extensive and sweeping. Between 1948 and 1953 approximately 1.3 million people, in a nation of ten million, went before tribunals. Nearly half of the accused were sentenced from capital punishment to losing their jobs. Many others were deported to the countryside without trial and their apartments and belongings given to party elite. (6 p. 295)

So when a few weeks after the Zionist trial, the custodian of Laci's apartment building whispered to him that while no one was home, *"they came to measure your apartment,"* where "they" meant government agents, Laci had to believe that the government was already preparing to turn over his apartment to someone else while he and his family were planned to be "relocated".[1]

That evening Laci and Zsuzsi decided to flee Hungary—without delay and without raising suspicion of their plans.

Only three people knew of this decision: Zsuzsi's parents, János and Margit, and Laci's sister, Évi. [2] Until their escape in a few days, Laci had to continue his routine work; he could not notify his clients of his imminent departure; nor could he and Zsuzsi sell any of their belongings, however small and irrelevant.

In the few days they had, Zsuzsi smuggled some of their portable valuables to my grandparents' apartment. Shuttling between the two apartments with me in my stroller she carried in her purse jewelry, cash and gold and in my stroller, neatly folded Persian rugs and artwork. Even their wedding bands were left

---

1. What went through Laci's mind at that moment? Did he even weigh alternative explanations to this unsolicited visit? He had to be worried after the Zionist trial that he would suffer retributions. He had to be terrified when the custodian warned him. Laci never admitted that there could be other reasons to the search of his apartment. But he knew too well the consequences of "relocation." Once again, he had a family. Finally, he had a flourishing career. I can see his grey eyes turning into steel and his jaws clenching. They did not need words to convey their meaning.
2. Sixty years later, my uncle Pista (Dénes, István) told me that János offered Laci to help him re-establish himself as a lawyer in another European country. Laci turned him down. He saw no place for himself and his family in Europe. He was determined to go to Israel.

behind knowing that if they were caught at the border with them, they would also be tried as gold smugglers.[3]

Zsuzsi and me, Budapest, December 1948

The archives of the Budapest Bar Association had a record of this quick escape—in a letter from Dr. Bárány Gyula, a Budapest attorney, stating that "due to his departure abroad, Dr. Laufer László, a Budapest attorney and member of the Bar can no longer handle his cases." The letter is dated August 19, 1949, two months after the Zionist trial. It had intended to tie up the loose ends left by the sudden and unannounced departure of Laci, Zsuzsi and, of course, me, their one-year-old baby.

The letter continues:

> The office of my colleague Dr. Laufer László and my own office are in the same building and on the same floor, and until now we often filled in for each other in our cases, and his clients could turn to me for help in his absence.
>
> The authorities have taken over Dr. Laufer's apartment and its contents. In fact, its contents have already been hauled away and his legal files and, his case-books were scattered on the hardwood floor in his office.[4]

---

3 They received those wedding bands twenty years later when my grandparents visited Israel.
4 So the authorities found out about Laci's departure even before his colleague and next door neighbor did. How did they learn about it so quickly? After all, he left illegally, in secrecy and without leaving any record at a border crossing. Did the "authorities" come to arrest him soon after his departure only to discover that their prey had fled? Perhaps, Laci's suspicions were well-founded and he was slated to be "purged."

> In the interest of his clients, I request the Bar to allow me to take over the cases and representations of my colleague, Dr. Laufer László, who has departed abroad.
>
> My colleague, Dr. Laufer László, left at the end of last month with his wife and his one-year-old son and on the sixth of this month, his sister Mrs. Gróf who resides in Budapest received a sign of life from Vienna from him and his family.

The last paragraph reads as an afterthought. Dr. Bárány must have already typed the entire letter on his typewriter when he realized that he should call Évi to find out what she knew.

Attached to the letter was a list of the client files that Bárány found. It did not include any of the Zionist trial defendants. It could mean that Laci was not their attorney after all. But it might also mean that Laci destroyed those files and the confidential information they must have held, or that the "authorities" carried away those files exactly because they contained confidential information and names of new targets for their purges.

Among my own records I found a certificate dated August 8, 1949, bearing the picture of Laci and Zsuzsi holding me in her arms. It was issued by the International Committee of Jewish Refugees in Austria certifying that we registered there as refugees, number 1690/49. Another document issued by the Vienna police department on August 14, 1949 granted me a temporary permit to stay in Austria.

But neither Bárány nor the certificates could tell how we reached Vienna. How a survivor of concentration camps, his new wife and their one-year-old baby crossed a hostile border in the middle of the night, leaving behind their old way of life, careers and possessions, even their gold wedding bands.

Hungary is a land-locked country. In 1949 Austria was its only neighbor that remained under Western influence. The rest, Romania to the west, Slovakia to the north, and Yugoslavia in the south already fell under Soviet influence.

In the first years after the war, departure from Hungary was as easy as a short train ride to Vienna. But soon after emigration was declared illegal, the Austrian border was sealed by a fence, watchtowers and a 50-meter-wide strip of land along the border clear of trees. In addition, all west-bound trains were stopped at the border crossing and searched. (91 p. 124)

Nevertheless, for most of 1949, the Hungarian border with Slovakia remained loosely protected and the Slovakian border with Austria mostly open. During a short period of seven to eight months, 12,000 Jews escaped

Hungary through Slovakia. In a typical transit, immigrants who successfully crossed into Slovakia were taken to Bratislava on the Austrian border, issued a temporary Slovakian immigration passport that was stamped by an Israeli entry visa, allowed to cross by train to Austria and transported to Venice or Bari for departure to Israel. (91 pp. 122-124)

As the number of these escapees grew, Hungary started to demand that Slovakia close this indirect escape route and meanwhile, Hungary tightened its own security along the Slovak border. Soon after, on April 1949, a young group of 34 Zionists, pretending to be on an outing, departed by train from Budapest to Nagymaros, a small town on the Danube facing Visegrád, a historic medieval castle. There they planned to meet with a smuggler who was to take them by truck to the nearby border crossing point. Instead, they were captured by the Hungarian National Protection authorities and imprisoned in Vác. (89, p. 299, note 836)

In July, barely a month before we were to take a similar route, Slovakia yielded to the continuing Hungarian pressure and sealed its Austrian borders. Hungarians who reached Slovakia were still taken to Bratislava but were detained there. Some were kept in jail and upon their release returned to Hungary. (87 p. 144) But some were still allowed to continue to Austria. After mid-August no one was allowed to proceed from Bratislava to Austria. That border was sealed as well. (91 p. 125)

Although the Zionist organization no longer existed, it still operated a clandestine escape organization, facilitating the crossing of an inhospitable country to a third country and supporting transfer to the final destination. Laci must have turned to that clandestine organization. They arranged for a reliable smuggler to guide us across the Danube to Slovakia, they found a Slovakian contact to meet us on the other side of the border, generated the travel documents needed to reach Austria, and they certainly tipped the scales in our favor when the Czechoslovakian authorities weighed our fate, deciding whether to turn us back to Hungary, to a long prison term for Laci and Zsuzsi and an orphanage for me, or to let us continue to Austria.

Late afternoon on the day of our departure Laci left his office for the last time, locked the door and before walking to our apartment stopped by Bárány's office and as he had done every evening, waved goodnight. He ate a light dinner with Zsuzsi, packed in her small backpack their rations and powdered milk for me; drugged me with sleeping pills and packed me into his large backpack. With me sound asleep, they walked to the train station and purchased round trip tickets to Esztergom, one of the oldest towns in Hungary, the seat of the Hungarian Catholic church, and most importantly, on the banks of the River Danube. When the train departed, they took one last look at Budapest. They would not see it again for more than forty years.[5]

They reached Esztergom shortly after dark. Several tourists got off the train with them. The Danube was less than a mile away and Slovakia, on its opposite bank, just a short boat ride.

They found their smuggler's house at the end of a side street near the Danube. They knocked on the door with a pre-arranged signal. The door was opened by a young, solidly built man. He let them in and closed the door quickly. There were no introductions. Laci did not know the man's name and he did not know theirs. Two other "clients" whom Laci did not recognize were already waiting.

The smuggler led them to an adjacent room where he asked for their credentials. Laci handed him a sealed, unaddressed envelope. The smuggler opened it and pulled out a business card and half of his fee. The other half was to be paid by his Budapest contact after Laci met his Slovakian contact. The smuggler inspected their bags to confirm that they did not carry any contraband and ordered them to drug me again with another sleeping pill.

They left the house near midnight. The neighborhood was quiet. Even the cicadas found their mates and went to sleep. The only sound was that of ten hiking boots hitting the street pavement. The night was moonless but the outline of the massive Catholic basilica on the castle hill above them was clearly visible against the dark skies. Laci looked at the stars. The North Star was just ahead of them, perched above the cross on the main dome of the Basilica of Esztergom like a shiny diamond. The Danube was to their left.

Despite the late hour, the hot air felt like a furnace. A heat wave that took hold over Central Europe turned that walk into a torture. But thanks to the dry weather that came with it, the water level in the Danube was low and its flow slowed. Crossing the river promised to be easy and quick.

They passed the basilica at the foot of the hill and continued on a dirt road along the Danube. Light breezes coming off the river helped cool them slightly. When the road curved behind the hill that now blocked the city lights, the smuggler stopped, reached under a bush and pulled out two oars. Then he asked the two men to join him and on his knees crawled under another bush where he uncovered a wooden boat. The three men then pulled it out and

---

5 According to Ági Palócz, Laci told her that we reached Slovakia by crossing the Danube near Esztergom in a smuggler's boat.

carried it into the water. Within minutes, five adults and one baby were floating on the Danube with the smuggler rowing them towards Slovakia.

It must have seemed like a miracle but when the boat's bottom scraped the opposite bank its bow was pointing to a barely visible narrow dirt road that entered a forest. Without getting out of the boat, the smuggler instructed them to follow the road for two miles until they reached a small town. Their Slovakian contact would meet them there at first light and would transport them to Bratislava. They jumped out of the boat into ankle high water and before they reached the road, the darkness already swallowed the smuggler who was rowing back to Esztergom.

When they reached the first houses at the edge of a little town, the black sky was giving way to a pale early dawn. They stepped back into the woods to wait for their guide. *"If all goes as planned, we could be in Bratislava by noon,"* Laci thought.

They found an isolated spot surrounded by pine trees. The thick layer of pine needles provided them with an inviting mattress. Three of the adults lay down and fell asleep, exhausted from a tense, sleepless night. Only Laci remained awake watching the road.

Dawn turned into morning, morning into noon, and noon into evening. No one came for them. Their rations, designed for a day, were running out. The little water they carried was used to mix my powdered milk into my breakfast. Soon, all turned hungry, thirsty, and restless. They could not go into the Slovak town for the risk of being discovered, nor could they go down to the river. They were illegal in a foreign country with no money, provisions, or alternative instructions—and with a baby. The best they could do was to wait patiently, hoping that their contact was late or that another guide would arrive.

Their guide arrived two days late.[6]

They were brought by the Slovakian contact to a large building near downtown Bratislava. It might have been an old school but now served as a dormitory. A receptionist in the lobby was expecting them, they were on her list. She assigned Laci, Zsuzsi, and me to a room that was already occupied by another couple. She could not tell when the transfer to Vienna would take place, nor if it would ever take place. But she did know that the Slovaks were becoming tougher on immigration to the West and asked that we not draw attention to our presence. We were to remain in the building.

---

[6] Laci's personal account to Ági Palócz.

So we did. We remained in the building for ten days. Every day Laci saw small groups arriving, mostly from Hungary, and others leaving by car or by train. He could not determine if those who left were headed to Vienna or back to Hungary. But rumors estimated that at least half of the new arrivals were deported back.[7] The overcrowded living conditions, lack of privacy, summer heat, and noise added to the tensions that were fueled by the uncertainty and lack of any control over the residents' fate.

On the morning of the tenth day, Laci was called to the receptionist desk to get our travel documents that had just arrived. We were cleared for immediate departure to Vienna.

That afternoon we boarded the train. The ride to Vienna should have taken less than two hours. But shortly after leaving the station the train was stopped at the border. At least twenty border policemen, some holding dogs on their leashes, stood along the track. Two of them boarded our car and started inspecting travel documents. Zsuzsi recounted to me that moment. She knew we had valid travel documents but she also knew that these officers could be arbitrary even if our documents were good.

One of the policemen approached Laci. Zsuzsi remembered his *"blue eyes, cold like a fish."* He took our documents, inspected them for a few minutes and looked at us with his *"cold fish eyes."* I smiled at him with a baby smile and he smiled back. Then he pulled out his stamp, stamped our papers and wished us a pleasant trip. We were finally safe.

We reached Vienna early that evening. A woman at the station exit was holding a sign with several names on it including "Laufer." We became the guests of the World Jewish Congress in the Arzbergerstrasse camp in the American zone of Vienna.

Among old family documents I found our Israeli immigration certificate issued by the Austrian branch of the Israeli Immigration Bureau four days after our arrival. Laci and Zsuzsi's pictures are on the front page with their names handwritten in Hebrew by the issuing clerk along the signature line below their pictures. But at the top of the document that same clerk inserted their last name as "Tauber." Obviously, Israeli immigration clerks were just as arbitrary as their colleagues in Ellis Island, inventing, whether intentionally or not, new names for the immigrants.

---

7   A similar account is given by Albrich and Zweig. (91 p. 127) Though they do not provide a clear picture of the numbers and dates, at least on one occasion a train with six hundred and fifty refugees was returned to Hungary without letting anyone off.

Two weeks later, another entry was added to that certificate. This time by Prof. Dr. Vittorio Sengoli from the Verona City Hospital, declaring that "Tauber Laszlo, Tauber Zsuzsanna, and Gabriel are in good health."

I remember Zsuzsi telling me that while on the train from Vienna to our Italian port of departure I became seriously ill and had to be taken off the train in Verona and hospitalized. I never understood why, but I had to receive a blood transfusion. The blood was donated by an Italian policeman. Zsuzsi loved to tease me that my temper was determined by the Italian cop's blood that was flowing in my veins.

We reached Israel in October 1949: nearly three months after our escape.

June 1982: A War of Deception[1]

*B*orn of the ambition of one willful, reckless man, Israel's 1982 invasion of Lebanon was anchored in delusion, propelled by deceit, and bound to end in calamity. It was a war for whose meager gains Israel had paid an enormous price that has yet to be altogether reckoned. (94)

On Sunday, June 13, 1982 Israeli tanks rolled into the streets of Ba'abda, an eastern suburb of Beirut. It was the first time Israeli forces entered the capital of a neighboring country. It was in sharp contrast to Israel's long-standing policy of not capturing foreign capitals or meddling with their government.

That policy had been strictly followed in previous wars. Capturing an Arab capital was an easy option at the end of the Yom Kippur War. Damascus was within the range of Israeli cannons and all that separated IDF forces and Cairo was 65 miles of an empty desert road. Yet, the Israeli government chose, rightly so, to stay away. But on that day in 1982 that policy was thrown by the wayside.

Yasser Arafat, the Chairman of the Palestinian Liberation Organization, stood that morning by the window of his office in a Beirut high rise with binoculars and watched in disbelief Israeli military vehicles and soldiers moving about in the city only a mile away. For a while he thought that the vehicles belonged to the Phalangists, an armed Christian minority that was known to have ties to Israel. But he was soon convinced that these were indeed Israelis.

Israeli television broadcast carried live images of Israeli soldiers and vehicles in the streets of Ba'abda. Earlier that morning it quoted the Israeli Prime Minister Menachem Begin stating that Israel had no intention of entering Beirut and that at the present time there were no Israeli soldiers in Beirut. A TV report that was prepared the day before and banned for

---

[1] The Hebrew title of a book by Schiff and Ya'ari (94) describing the events that led up to the Lebanon War, the war itself and its aftermath. The English translation of that book is referenced below.

broadcast by the military censor stated that Israeli forces already controlled the runways of Beirut's airport and were at the edge of the Christian-controlled section of Beirut.

It seems that as the Israeli public and most of the world were introduced to a new reality, the only people who were still unaware of this dramatic development and the departure from a long-standing Israeli policy were Prime Minister Menachem Begin and much of his cabinet. Unbelievable as it was, the capture of a Beirut suburb and the departure from an important policy were never discussed, let alone approved, by the Israeli government. (94 p. 193)

To add to the irony, Begin met that morning with the US Envoy Phillip Habib, who was dispatched earlier by President Reagan to the Middle East in an attempt to avoid the war, and after it started, to contain it. True to his belief, Begin insisted the IDF had no plans of entering Beirut. Habib retorted in anger "Your tanks are already in Ba'abda! Our Ambassador in Beirut has already reported the presence of Israeli tanks next to the presidential palace." (94 p. 193)

That morning I sat in my armored personal carrier (APC) that was parked on the meticulously manicured putting green of a golf course south of the Lebanese coastal city Sidon. It was unfortunate for Aramco, the Saudi oil company that owned the golf course, that we chose it as the site of our brigade's headquarters and an artillery battalion. But this was the only flat space along the narrow coastal plain in the area that was large enough to accommodate cannons, trucks, and armored vehicles without interfering with the heavy traffic that headed north towards Beirut, barely 30 miles away.

Just across the coastal highway separating us from the Mediterranean was Aramco's Zaharani oil terminal. It was at the terminus of the Trans Arabia Pipeline (Tapline) that carried oil from Saudi Arabia through Jordan, Syria, the Israeli-held Golan Heights and Lebanon to the Mediterranean Sea. Although Tapline was inactive for more than six years, the gigantic tanks in the terminal still contained crude oil. Stray bullets or tank shells, fired a few days earlier during the heavy battles between IDF forces and PLO terrorists along the road, ignited several of them and started huge fires that were still burning, billowing giant columns of black smoke that were visible as far south as Haifa.

Listening to an Israeli radio broadcast describing the incursion to Ba'abda, I matched the reported locations of our advancing forces with targets that our artillery brigade engaged that morning. Unlike Begin and most of his cabinet, I did know IDF's objectives months before the launch of this new war that was named euphemistically "Peace of the Galilee War." I knew months in advance that when—not "if"—the war was launched, our brigade's destination would be Beirut. Months earlier I even toured southern Lebanon, an enemy territory, in broad daylight to select positions for our invading artillery battalions. The only information I missed was the pretext that would be used to launch this war and the start date.

When I heard Begin's denial that Israeli soldiers were present in Beirut I was certain that this was merely a clever political maneuver. I never suspected that a week after launching this war, our Prime Minister and much of his cabinet still did not know its true objectives, let alone its true status.

But I had no doubt on that Sunday morning that much of the Israeli public was fooled in believing that our incursion deep into a foreign country and its capital, the heavy losses we already suffered, and the enormous economic cost were necessary for our national security. I was upset that less than nine years after the terrible experience of the Yom Kippur War, Israeli soldiers, and I among them, were once again ordered to risk our lives, this time without a credible threat or a convincing justification.

Liora, our two American-born children, and I had returned to Israel two years earlier, after five years in Princeton. Those were wonderful years of growth and learning. Our family expanded: Aharon was born in 1975, barely two months after we settled in the University's graduate student housing. Tammar was born two years later in the nearby town of Trenton, in a Catholic hospital run by nuns, because my meager stipend could not bear the costs of labor and delivery in Princeton's more elegant hospital.

Years later Liora recalled how uncomfortable she was in that hospital bed under the large cross on the wall. That is, until her friend suggested that she should imagine that these were two giant crossed mezuzahs.[2]

After earning my Ph.D. in Mechanical and Aerospace Engineering, I worked for Western Electric's research center near Princeton and spent a delightful year developing laser techniques to study chemical processes on metal surfaces.

Liora remembered our time in Princeton fondly. She loved the simple life of a stay-at-home mom, living among graduate students and their families and providing a loving home to our children and me.

---

[2] A mezuzah is a decorative case containing a parchment inscribed with Hebrew verses from Deuteronomy 6:4-9 and 11:13-21. The mezuzah is mounted on the right side of a house doorframe to mark it as Jewish.

We enjoyed Princeton and America, but we missed Israel. When I was offered a faculty position in Technion we knew we had to return. Western Electric tried to lure me with a large raise, promotion, and a Green Card. But home was calling and in 1980 we were back in Israel, happy to be united with our family and old friends.

Liora joined the office of a prominent Israeli graphologist who became her mentor and taught her the craft. Graphology would become her passion, second only to her family. It would accompany her through her life and bring her joy, satisfaction, and pride. It inspired her to start her own business, Callirobics, that over twenty-five years helped thousands of children worldwide with learning difficulties improve their self-esteem, motor skills, eye-hand coordination, and of course, handwriting.

My work at the Technion was gratifying and intellectually nourishing too. Lasers were starting to be introduced into medicine as a surgical tool. The ability to focus the beam into small spots promised that surgeons would be able to remove small tumors or perform sharp incisions with hardly any damage to the surrounding tissues. Unfortunately, the heat generated by the laser beam at the point of impact damaged the living tissue and the outcome was often much worse than expected. I began to study the thermal effects of these beams on living tissues, and my work won me national and international recognition. Combined with my teaching work, my academic career was flourishing.

We enrolled Aharon and Tammar in Israeli kindergarten. Having been isolated in America from Israeli children, their Hebrew vocabulary was lacking all the forbidden words, and their knowledge of Israeli children's antics was limited. But within weeks they caught up. They quickly got used to the freedoms Israeli children took for granted and were roaming with their new friends in the open fields near our house, in the parks, or in the street. But most of all, they enjoyed the family they had not known, their two grandmothers and two grandfathers, many aunts and uncles, cousins and second cousins.

We spent our weekends and vacations touring our old-new country, visiting nearby places like Mount Carmel or distant places such as Nuweibaa on the Sinai shores of the Red Sea. We stopped for meals in long-forgotten restaurants and bought freshly pressed olive oil from little presses in the Galilee. We climbed mountains and dipped in the Dead Sea, we marvelled at the dazzling bloom of spring wild flowers and the emptiness and silence of the Negev Desert. We became re-acquainted with Israeli theatre and shows, and became supporters of the Israeli Philharmonic Orchestra. We felt like tourists in our own country.

We loved our new life in Israel, and Israel loved us. But it was a very different country from the one we remembered. For better and worse, the effects of the Yom Kippur War were still playing out politically, economically, and militarily. Egypt signed a peace treaty with Israel. Jordan, while still not friendly, turned away from open hostility. Syria, while still hostile, chose to scale back its military and ease the tension along its border with Israel.

By contrast, the Lebanese border, which until the Six-Day War was peaceful, turned into the hottest front. PLO[3] terrorists settled in Southern Lebanon, wrestling control of the area from the weak Lebanese army and started attacking Israeli settlements along that border. One of the most heinous attacks took place on May 22, 1970. A school bus from the border settlement of Avivim was ambushed by PLO terrorists who killed twelve passengers, among them eight children.

The hold of the PLO over southern Lebanon increased significantly after their attempt on September 1970 to overthrow Jordan's King Hussein. The attempt was quashed and the PLO leadership was pushed out and resettled in Lebanon.[4] Southern Lebanon, and particularly the area at the base of Mount Hermon, turned into a quasi-state that was nicknamed Fatahland.[5]

Fatahland turned into a vast terrorist base that spread terror along the Lebanese border, deep into Israel and overseas. Attacks by terrorists became the norm. A massacre in Kiryat Shmona cost the lives of eighteen Israelis, of whom eight were children. Another attack in Ma'alot claimed the lives of thirty-one Israelis, including twenty-two high school students, and an attack on an El Al plane in Athens shook the Israeli public and the world opinion. Despite massive IDF retaliations that leveled some towns and Palestinian camps in Southern Lebanon, Israelis, and in particular the inhabitants of northern towns and settlements, felt vulnerable and anxious. The IDF's overwhelming might failed to guarantee the safety of Israelis.

Meanwhile, Israel was also grappling with the economic fallout of the Yom Kippur War. Its enormous cost that was largely funded by debt, combined with international inflationary pressures, produced hyperinflation in Israel. In 1980, our first year back in Israel, the average monthly inflation was 7.3 percent (yes, per month), rising to nearly 16 percent per month in 1984.

---

3   PLO—Palestinian Liberation Organization.
4   September 1970 is remembered in Palestinian history as Black September.
5   Though the PLO and the Fatah movement are not the same, the two were often considered in Israel as one.

This rapid inflation forced the government and the public to develop clever coping mechanisms. To protect their value: savings, salaries, and nearly all long-term transactions were indexed to the cost of living that was gauged regularly by the government. Thanks to this indexing, I got an automatic raise every month. But this was a fool's raise. The index, as I soon realized, reflected price increases of the previous month whereas my salary was paying the costs of the coming month. In a month where inflation exceeded 10 percent, my inflation-adjusted salary fell short by at least 10 percent. Nevertheless, the adjustment brought some sense of stability.

To benefit from the galloping inflation, Israelis delayed payments. Utility bills, mortgages, medical bills were paid directly to the payees' bank accounts on their due day. On certain days of the month, lines of last-minute payers stretched from the bank teller's window out to the street and around the block.

Jokes from the hyperinflationary days in Germany and Hungary such as *"in the old days, one could go to the market with a wallet of money to pay for a basket of goods whereas now, one needs to go the market with a basket of money to buy a wallet of goods,"* were brought back to life.

Out of curiosity, I calculated the cost of covering a wall with Israeli currency notes in circulation compared with the cost of wallpaper. One shekel notes were more economical. The double-sided notes also offered the opportunity to create clever patterns by alternating sides.[6]

The hyperinflation was brought to a rapid end in July 1985 by the Economic Stabilization Policy, which was a bold Israeli government action. The prices of more than two thousand goods and services were fixed by that policy and a small army of inspectors was retained to monitor those prices nationwide and to impose draconian fines on violators. Within a year, the annual inflation rate dropped to 19 percent. Though still high, Israelis viewed it as stability.

Along with the economy and national security, the political landscape also changed dramatically. What seemed to be impossible before the Yom Kippur War became a reality on May 1977. The left-leaning Alignment Party—Ma'arach in Hebrew—that included leaders and parties which controlled the Israeli politics since the early days of Zionism lost control to the right wing

---

6 Inflation rewards borrowers by eroding their debt and consequently punishes savers. Laci was a saver. His Bar Association pension, to which he contributed for nearly thirty years, was invested conservatively in government bonds that paid a fixed rate of interest that was too low to compensate for the rapid erosion of the principal. When he retired in 1984, his pension eroded to the equivalent of 25 dollars a month. Ironically, he survived on German social security benefits that were paid to him as reparations for being a slave in Mühldorf.

Likud Party that combined the right wing Herut party with several liberal and centrist parties. The power shift was labeled by the television anchor who first announced the election results as a *Mahapach*, or "upheaval." That term stuck in the Israeli collective memory.

The truly revolutionary nature of the *Mahapach* was best represented by the new prime minister, Menachem Begin, who a few years earlier was derided as a demagogue, terrorist or potentially a dictator. He was now the new Israeli leader. He defeated Shimon Peres, one of Israel's most prominent politicians. Through a decades-long public service career, Peres was responsible for the buildup of the Israeli military force as well as the development of Israel's nuclear capabilities. But on May 1977 it was Menachem Begin who was the prime minister.

The historic elections of 1977 that demonstrated the strength of Israel's democracy also included a bizarre affair that demonstrated one of its serious weaknesses. Two years before the election, a French-Jewish businessman, Flatto Sharon, arrived in Israel and requested citizenship based on the Law of Return that guarantees such citizenship to all Jews who wish to settle in the country.

Flatto Sharon (unrelated to the future Minister of Defense Ariel Sharon) was fleeing French authorities after being charged with a 60 million dollar tax evasion. When it appeared that the newly acquired Israeli citizenship might not shield him from French extradition request, Sharon decided to run for the Israeli Knesset hoping to gain parliamentary immunity. Despite being unable to speak Hebrew and without a political platform, his one-person party won two percent of the national votes, enough to seat two members. Some observers noted after the elections that most of his votes came from Dimonah, a small development town in the Negev, comprising mostly of French-speaking immigrants. Rumors of a massive bribery scheme were not far behind. In 1984 Flatto Sharon was convicted of bribery in that election campaign and sentenced to three months of community service. He was never elected to the Knesset again and never extradited to France either.

The newly elected government also won the right to appoint new ministers and high-level officials. Having never been part of the establishment, their pool of experienced candidates was perilously thin and numerous unqualified persons found themselves in positions of power. One of my high-school friends, who until the election served as a low-level clerk for one of Likud's smallest components, became at the age of twenty-nine the director of one of the ministries.

Begin and his government will be remembered for negotiating and signing the Israel-Egypt Peace Treaty. That agreement, signed on March 26, 1979, legitimized the State of Israel, at least in the eyes of one neighboring country, and stabilized its southern border. Eventually, this agreement paved the way to a peace treaty with Jordan and some normalization with other Arab nations such as Morocco and even Saudi Arabia.

But while the peace treaty with Egypt was being negotiated and the south turned calm, the border with Lebanon boiled over and on March 14, 1978, following an attack on an Israeli bus traveling along the coastal highway between Haifa and Tel Aviv by terrorists originating in Lebanon, a large IDF force entered Southern Lebanon and captured territory up to the Litani River.

The objectives of what was later called Operation Litani were to clear Southern Lebanon and Fatahland of PLO terrorists and restore calm along that border. Two weeks later, Israel and Lebanon adopted a UN Security Council resolution calling for a cease-fire and allowing a UN Interim Force in Lebanon (UNIFIL) to monitor the border and the area evacuated by Israel. Later, Yasser Arafat, the PLO's Chairman, added his signature to the agreement and effectively made it the first cease-fire agreement with Israel endorsed by an official Palestinian body. (95)

But for all its remarkable successes, the first Begin government is also remembered for the runaway inflation that was accelerated by its questionable economic policies, multiple scandals, bickering among ministers from different factions, and defections of some ministers and members of parliament from the coalition. By its fourth year, the coalition supporting the government in the Knesset was severely thinned. Responding to popular pressure, the Knesset legislated on January 1981 early elections for June 30, 1981, ahead of the November 1981 schedule. (96)

Opinion polls of that time suggested that Begin's government was regarded as Israel's worst. Polls held in December 1980 showed that if elections were held then, the Likud would win 18 out of 120 the Knesset seats, whereas the left-leaning Alignment party would win 56 seats. (96 p. 506) By comparison, in the 1977 elections the Likud won 45 seats against the Alignment's 32.

From a low point of only 18 Knesset seats in December, monthly polls showed steady growth to 31 seats in March, 43 seats just before the June elections and finally 48 seats in the elections themselves versus 47 seats won by the Alignment party. Although still a thin margin, this was seen by the Likud as a huge victory. Once again Begin was called by the Israeli President to form a new government.

The rapid turnaround in public opinion was viewed as nothing less than a miracle. It was attributed in large part to Begin's extraordinary oratory gift that made his opponent, Shimon Peres, look pale. (96 p. 511) But other factors might have contributed too. A smear campaign against Peres made unsubstantiated claims that while in power he benefited members of his family with preferential treatment. Even more outrageous was a claim that his mother was an Arab. The latter is reminiscent of modern day allegations that President Obama is a Muslim or that he was not born in the US.

Another peculiar event that possibly earned votes for the Likud Party was a claim made days before the elections by Yaakov Meridor. A wealthy Likud candidate for the Knesset, Meridor announced that an Israeli scientist working for him invented a thermodynamic process that would allow the energy needed to power a single light bulb to illuminate a city the size of Ramat Gan.[7] Although the details of the process had to be kept secret, Meridor promised that if the Likud was re-elected, he would make it available to the nation at no cost.

When my colleagues in the Technion and other Israeli experts cried out publicly that such a process could not possibly exist, Meridor offered to retain an independent scientist to review the invention and determine if it violated any law of physics. Surprisingly, one such scientist was found at the Technion. After review, the quite reputable soft-spoken professor declared that indeed, the invention did not contradict any laws of physics.

After the elections, with the Likud's victory in hand, Meridor's scientist disclosed his "invention." As the Technion professor stated, it was well within the boundaries of known physics. Except that the "invention" was not new. It offered a method of capturing waste energy in the form of heat dumped by power plants into lakes, rivers, or the atmosphere. Dumping heat is an unavoidable part of the power generation process. Many prior inventors, motivated by the prospect of significant economic and environmental gains, proposed methods of re-using that waste energy. Unfortunately, the "new" process, like many others before it, was possible but not practical economically; using waste energy to generate electricity still remains more expensive than the fuel used in the primary process.

Meridor was ridiculed for this affair. Nevertheless, he was appointed Minister of Economics and Inter-Ministry Coordination, a post he retained until the following elections in 1984. (97)

---

7   Ramat Gan—a Tel Aviv suburb with an approximate population of 100,000.

As if all that was not enough, three weeks before the elections, Begin ordered an air raid on the nuclear reactor in Baghdad. This was a risky and daring operation whose necessity was never disputed in Israel, though it was heavily criticized by the US, Europe and, of course, by the Arab world. Its remarkable success, most likely, added votes to the Likud. Begin was accused of timing the raid close to the elections to gain that exact advantage. But in retrospect, this timing could have also backfired had the risky mission gone badly.

Looking back at Begin's second term, two things stand out. The first was the razor-thin margin of support in the Knesset. For fear that the opposition might use the absence of even one member of the Knesset to launch a vote of non-confidence, coalition members of the Knesset were required to obtain approval for any foreign travel. I could recall at least one occasion where the government survived on a tied non-confidence vote.

The second element was the lack of moderate representation in the cabinet. Begin's first cabinet included three moderate ministers with military experience, Moshe Dayan, Chaim Weitzman and Yigael Yadin, who helped drive him and his government towards signing the peace treaty with Egypt and possibly away from military adventures. (94 p. 38) There were no such moderates to counteract the aggressive and often irresponsible drive of its new extremist right-wing ministers, particularly his Defense Minister, Ariel Sharon.

Despite its inherent political weakness and tepid public support, Begin and his new government entangled Israel in its most disastrous war, the War for the Peace of Galilee. The lack of moderating voices allowed Sharon to push Begin and the government into this war by gradually weakening the checks and balances that kept previous governments from dangerous conflicts. (94 pp. 38-39)

One of the factors that helped Sharon push through his agenda was that all military and foreign relations matters were concentrated in the hands of five, highly monolithic figures: Begin, the prime minister, Sharon, the minister of defense, Yitzhak Shamir, the foreign minister, Lt. General Rafael Eitan, the battle-hardened Chief of Staff and Moshe Arens, a Technion Aeronautical Engineering professor, who was appointed as the Israeli ambassador to the US. This government, unlike previous governments, was looking for opportunities to make war rather than avoid it. There was no one with stature and experience to moderate this impulse. The few dovish ministers such as Mordechai Zippori and Yosef Burg who could potentially oppose the pro-war government were too weak, and they were often kept in the dark by Sharon, his defense ministry, and by the IDF.

The progress towards war in Lebanon was imperceptible. Even ministers of Begin's cabinet were not fully aware of the trajectory that Sharon had set with Begin's consent. But when analyzed in historic perspective, the process was clearly premeditated and planned.

December 14, 1981 might be remembered as the date of Israel's descent towards war. On that day, the Knesset passed a law annexing the Golan Heights that was captured in the Six-Day War and defended in the Yom Kippur War. The annexation by itself was probably not part of the plan but it was nevertheless an excellent excuse to concentrate Israeli forces in the north along the Syrian and Lebanese borders.

Less than a week after the annexation, and while the US was already implementing sanctions against Israel and chastising it for the move, Begin invited his cabinet to his home where he was recuperating from a bad fall that had shattered his hip. At that meeting he asked Sharon to describe his plans for a vast military operation that was code named Operation Big Pines. The word "Big" was used to distinguish it from a more modest plan, Operation Little Pines, which would be discussed at a later time.[8]

---

8   History often provides an interesting perspective. The US presidential election in 2000 between Al Gore and George W. Bush ended in a nearly perfect tie. The tie was eventually decided by the Supreme Court in favor of President Bush. Similar to Begin, Bush chose two strong hawkish men to advise him on defense and policy matters, Vice President Dick Cheney and Defense Secretary Donald Rumsfeld, but with no significant moderating voice in the cabinet to counter them. Following the September 11, 2001 attacks, under their strong influence, Bush chose to invade Iraq, a country that bore no direct responsibility to these events but was portrayed as harboring terrorists and weapons of mass destruction.

The military operation in Iraq was initially successful. Despite the vast distance from the US, Iraq was occupied within weeks and its dictator Sadam Hussein removed from power. Soon after the invasion, President Bush, standing proudly on an aircraft carrier under a banner "mission accomplished" declared victory. But with Sadam Hussein gone, the country was destabilized, its various religious and ethnic factions turned on each other and against the American forces. More than a decade later, the vacuum created by toppling Sadam Hussein and the subsequent retreat of the US from Iraq was filled by new and far more violent terrorist organizations.

Ironically, the War for the Peace of Galilee was a preview of the Iraq War or Operation Iraqi Freedom as it was dubbed. The similarities are striking: poorly justified or unsubstantiated explanations for the invasions, immediate military success by a strong army fighting a weak regular army, followed by the rapid collapse of the invaded nation and the rise of new terrorist organizations that continue to this day to terrorize Israel and the world and finally, belated public recognition of the disastrous results. A clear distinction between the two wars was their scale.

"Our objective is Lebanon, not Syria," Sharon explained. "If the Syrians start anything, we'll respond in Lebanon and solve the problem there." (94 p. 47) Sharon then presented a map to the stunned cabinet ministers that showed black arrows pointing to the Beirut-Damascus highway, the road connecting the two capitals. Israel had no intention of capturing Beirut, Sharon reassured his colleagues. The plan was only to cut off Syrian access to the Lebanese capital.

But cutting off the road would still have required capturing at least half of the Lebanese territory, some of the dovish ministers responded. That for sure would require engaging the Syrian forces stationed in Lebanon. Without hesitation, Sharon promised that such engagement with the Syrians could be avoided and then asked for approval of the plan. Several ministers from the Liberal party objected, and rather than sustaining a rejection, Begin simply adjourned the meeting.

The thought of reaching the Beirut-Damascus highway might have been conceived as early as March 1976 during the first direct contact between representatives of Israel and the Phalangists. This small group asked for Israeli support, arguing that like the Jews, they were a persecuted minority and therefore shared a common interest and fate. In the years that followed, the Phalangists suggested joint military operations intended to replace the regime in Lebanon with one that would be accommodating to both Israel and the Christians. Though earlier Israeli governments, most notably Rabin's, declined to get involved, the Phalangists found more sympathetic ears in Begin and Sharon.

When presenting his plan on December 1981, Sharon hinted that while Israel may not actively capture Beirut, the Phalangists might do so; particularly if the IDF reached as far north as the Beirut-Damascus highway and connected with them there.

Although the Israeli cabinet did not approve his plan, two weeks later Sharon and a large entourage traveled to Beirut to discuss it with Bashir Gemayel, one of the Phalangists leaders. At one point during the visit, Sharon, his aides and his hosts climbed to the roof of a seventeen-story building to survey the city. A month later, Lt. Gen. Eitan visited Gemayel in Beirut to further refine the yet unapproved plan. (94 pp. 49-51) Of course, no one in Israel, other than those directly involved, knew about the clandestine visits by two top defense officers to the very heart of enemy territory.

Approximately at that time, I was called in for a one-day military reserve duty. It was not a routine call but not unusual either. As an IDF reserve officer,

I could expect one-day calls for briefings or to inspect the equipment in our emergency depot. That particular call was to the headquarters of the Chief of Artillery at the Northern Command in Nazareth.

The large conference room in the massive fort dating back to the period of the British Mandate was filled with artillery officers. I recognized many brigade and battalion commanders with whom I had worked in the past. I was the most junior officer in that room. We all jumped to our feet when the IDF Chief of Artillery, a brigadier general, entered the room.

"Tension along the Lebanese border is rising" the general stated, "and we are planning to take Beirut and eliminate all the PLO terrorists there." I was overwhelmed by the occasion and even more so by the general's statement. We were going to occupy the capital of another country. This was not a small matter. I could barely follow the details when the general displayed a large map of Lebanon showing our planned movements. My brigade was to proceed along the coastal road, pass through the biblical cities of Tyre and Sidon and by Beirut's international airport, to the outskirts of Beirut where we would be able to cover the entire city with our cannons.

I was perplexed. I could not recall any recent event along the Lebanese border that would justify such a far-reaching reaction. The previous summer, the PLO had shelled northern Israeli settlements. It was a reaction to IDF aerial raids of targets in Beirut and Fatahland. The PLO fired more than 1200 shells on nearly every settlement between Naharia on the Mediterranean coast and Kiryat Shmona at the tip of the upper Galilee in the east, causing casualties, damage and panic. Nearly half of Kiryat Shmona's population abandoned the town. It was unusual for so many Israelis to abandon their homes in the face of such attacks. But rather than ordering an invasion of Lebanon to root out the PLO as the general was describing now, Begin agreed to a cease-fire agreement with the PLO, a significant concession that amounted to recognition and legitimization of the terrorist organization. The agreement compelled the PLO to refrain from attacks along the Lebanese border. That border remained quiet since, though the PLO continued to conduct operations overseas and along the Jordanian border.

What could possibly now justify such a vast operation, when the events of the previous summer led to only a cease-fire agreement? If the other officers in the room were pondering the same question, their faces did not betray it.

Spring arrived early in Israel that year. By early March, the hills of Mount Carmel, saturated by the plentiful winter rains, turned a lush green speckled by patches of pink and white cyclamen flowers, white daffodils, pink irises, red

June 1982: A War of Deception

anemones and even tiny orchids. The gray winter skies gave way to a sunny deep blue. It was just such a magnificent spring day that framed my next introduction to the upcoming war.

A call the night before from my reserve unit's clerk interrupted our family dinner. Apologizing for the short notice, he requested that I be available the next day for an unspecified tour of a possible deployment site. Early the following morning, he told me, I was to wait for my colleague to pick me up at home. That colleague would bring my side arm, ammunition and rations for the day.

At 6 am, a black Ford Bronco with an Israeli civilian license plate pulled up at the front door of my apartment building. Shimon, a battery commander in my brigade, was at the wheel. He was driving his own truck. Two other officers whom I did not recognize were with him. Neither was wearing their rank insignia and Shimon asked me to remove mine as well. We were going to a place where we were better off not being recognized as IDF officers, he explained, without elaborating further.

We turned towards the coast and drove north passing Acre at the opposite end of the Haifa Bay and Nahariya. Just before the white lime cliffs of Rosh HaNikrah that marked the border with Lebanon, Shimon turned east along the Northern highway. After a few miles he turned north once again, climbing the steep hill towards Kibbutz Hanita and the border road. We were soon driving along the border fence.

Lebanese villages only a mile or two to our north dotted the landscape. Occasional shepherds herded their sheep up to the border fence to graze the last inch of Lebanese grass.

Before Zar'it, a small Israeli communal border settlement, Shimon turned onto the freshly swept dirt road running alongside the fence and stopped abruptly in front of a gate. Without a word he jumped out of the idling car, pulled a key from his pocket, unlocked the gate and swung it open. He then returned to the car, drove through the open gate, stopped, got out and locked it. Four IDF officers in military uniforms were now riding on a Lebanese road in a single civilian vehicle with Israeli license plates. Strangely, Shimon made no attempt to disguise our nationality or at least have a well-armed escort accompany us.

The Lebanese road was no different from the Israeli. We encountered only two Lebanese cars. Their drivers were either unsurprised by our vehicle or concealed their emotions well. Soon we got off the road and climbed a green hill. Just like hills in the Israeli side of the Galilee, this too was green but without wild flowers. Flowers either don't grow in Lebanon, I thought, or the sheep had already grazed the hill. Yet, it was beautiful. The blue Mediterranean, barely ten miles to our west, was shimmering under the midday sun.

"*We will be there within a day of entering Lebanon,*" Shimon explained while pointing to Tyre, a small coastal city on a peninsula north west of our location. "*Our brigade headquarter will be on this hill,*" he continued. I agreed with his choice. It offered us an excellent vantage point, while at the same time our cannons could be hidden from enemy view in the many valleys surrounding us. After marking the location on our topographic maps and assigning positions to our firing units, we proceeded to inspect the positions we would take at the next stage of our planned invasion.

Late afternoon, after touring the southwestern corner of Lebanon for several hours, we headed back to Israel. We reached the UN check point of Rosh HaNikrah which lay at the top of the white lime cliff we saw that morning from the Israeli side. A bored UN soldier waved us through without checking any of our documents. A military police soldier on the Israeli side stopped us just long enough to exchange a few greetings, sufficient to convince him we were genuine Israelis.

We were back in Israel. I regretted not stopping at a Lebanese restaurant for lunch. But we were under orders. We stopped instead at Abu Christo, an Arab restaurant on the Mediterranean side of the walls of Acre. The hummus, augmented by the magnificent view of the Haifa Bay, tasted wonderful. In three months' time, I would have lunch in a Lebanese restaurant.

Planning for the war continued outside public view. In April, high-ranking IDF officers visited Beirut to coordinate plans with the Phalangists. One of the outcomes Israel expected to achieve was the installation of a Phalangist leader as the president of Lebanon, preferably Bashir Gemayel. But as the visiting IDF officers discovered, the Phalangists had bigger plans: to have Israel uproot the Syrians from Lebanon. (94 p. 54) Rather than being alarmed by this divergence in expectations, Israel continued planning as if they were aligned.

Meanwhile, Begin met with his IDF Chief of Intelligence and with the head of the Israeli Mossad, the secret service. These two spymasters rarely agreed, but in that meeting they concurred that Israel should not go into a war whose objective was the installation of a Phalangist president. The Phalangist military is unreliable, they warned. Israel could not count on any help from that group. These strong opinions helped Begin change his favorable views of the grand plans of Operation Big Pines. Instead, he started leaning towards the much smaller operation—Little Pines—that would uproot the PLO from a strip of land 25 miles north of the border (94 pp. 53-54) and put Israel's settlements out of PLO's artillery range.

The shift in Begin's views of the war's objectives and its scale did not deter Sharon from continuing to plot Operation Big Pines. By then he had successfully isolated the cabinet from the IDF General Staff. The prime minister and his cabinet were effectively cut off from any meaningful stream of information. (94 p. 55) Most striking was that while the cabinet's May 10 meeting ended with an understanding that the upcoming war would be limited in scope, the generals discussed on May 13 a large operation with one of its objectives being the link-up with the Christian Phalangists in Beirut. Whereas the cabinet discussed the removal of the PLO from a 25-mile strip in South Lebanon while steering clear of any clashes with Syrian forces in Lebanon, the General Staff discussed cutting off the Beirut-Damascus highway that, without a doubt, would trigger clashes with the Syrian army.

I find it surprising that in a country where the military is an "army of the people" the cabinet could remain so effectively isolated. Thousands of IDF officers, many of them reservists like me, must have known the upcoming war's true objectives. Though the briefings they attended were classified, secrets held by so many inevitably leak out. Even Begin's son, a reserve army officer, must have known these plans. Did he not talk to his father?

With the cabinet, and often Begin himself, isolated from information and clear reports from the IDF command, Sharon effectively took control over that information and used it to drive his own agenda. On the eve of the war he presented to the cabinet an operation that would be limited to a 25-mile strip north of Israel and would not last more than forty-eight hours. Then, after the start of the war, he kept returning with requests to approve slight movements beyond that range, often stating that those movements were necessary to protect the forces in the field. Step by step, he dragged the cabinet to a broader operation under the pretense of new and developing needs, whereas in fact his true objectives, and the objectives assumed by the IDF (and known even to junior officers like myself), were aligned with Operation Big Pines all along.

Sharon's ability to wrestle the authority from the Prime Minister to run a significant military operation even as the majority of his cabinet rejected it was comparable to a putsch or a coup. By the time the cabinet took full control back two months later it was too late. (94 p. 227)[9]

---

9 On August 12 Sharon ordered the air force to bomb Beirut. The savage bombing that was later dubbed as "Black Thursday" resulted in an unofficial estimate of 300 dead civilians.

The first outward sign of the imminent war was an Israeli bombing of southern Lebanon on April 21 and then a second bombing mission on May 9. The first was a response to the death of an Israeli soldier in Southern Lebanon in territory held by an Israeli ally, and the second was a response to the discovery of an explosive device in a school in Ashkelon, in southern Israel. The PLO did not respond to the first bombing raid, clearly hoping to preserve the ceasefire from the previous summer. It did however respond to the second raid by firing more than 100 Katyusha rockets without hitting any Israeli settlement, an obvious attempt to warn Israel without actually pushing it into a further escalation. (94 p. 55)

The pretext for war came late at night on June 3. Shlomo Argov, the Israeli ambassador to the UK, was shot in the head, outside the Dorchester Hotel in London, by a terrorist who fired from a short range using a small, easily concealed Polish-made machine gun. (94 p. 98) The make of this unique weapon was relevant because Israeli intelligence knew that it was supplied exclusively to the terrorist organization headed by Abu Nidal, a sworn enemy of the PLO, and its chair, Yasser Arafat. Therefore, Israeli intelligence knew that this attempt on Argov was not ordered or executed by the PLO.

The following morning, Begin convened an emergency meeting and declared that Israel would not stand for an attack on an Israeli ambassador and announced that he already decided with the Chief of Staff Eitan on Israel's response. But before Eitan was allowed to spell out the details of the response, the head of the General Security Services described what happened and although details were still sketchy, he suggested that the assailants were from Abu Nidal's organization. Begin stopped him and responded angrily, "They are all PLO."

When Eitan got the floor, he too sneered *"Abu Nidal, Abu Shmidal, we have to strike at the PLO."* The ministers did not hear that the assault on Argov was supported by Iraq, whose leaders not only wanted a revenge for the bombing of their nuclear reactor the previous year, but more importantly, wanted to drag Israel into a war in Lebanon in the hope that Israel would clash with Iraq's rival, Syria.

Eitan's proposal was to bomb sensitive targets in West Beirut in the hope that with some luck, PLO leadership might also get hit. Although Eitan stated

---

The bombing mission was ordered while an agreement of the evacuation of the PLO from Beirut was nearly finalized. In response to worldwide rage, the Israeli cabinet divested Sharon of his authority to activate the air force.

that this attack would draw a PLO response, no one in the cabinet asked if he had an alternative plan. And so the attack on PLO targets in West Beirut was approved. (94 pp. 100-101)

That evening, like on every Friday, we gathered at Laci and Zsuzsi's apartment for a light supper. Safta Suzi (Grandma Suzi), as her grandchildren called her, prepared a tray of cold cuts, cheese, sliced challah bread and her signature apple cake. Expecting to hear important news, Saba Laci (Grandpa Laci) turned on the radio for the evening broadcast that started with a report of the Israeli air force attack on PLO targets in West Beirut, and the almost immediate PLO response of heavy shelling along the northern Israeli border from Nahariya to Kiryat Shmona.

"*I'm about to be mobilized for another war,*" I said when the broadcast ended. Laci and Zsuzsi listened, astonished when I told them about my briefings at the Northern Command and the tour of Southern Lebanon. The children, though hearing our conversation, did not understand its implications. But we, the adults did: I was going to a war, leaving behind a wife and two children. It would be my fourth war.

When we reached home later that evening, an emergency draft notice was already posted on our door. I was ordered to report by the following morning to my unit in Kurdany, an old military base south of Acre.

My unit was ready for departure that afternoon. It was not the same unit with which I fought in 1973. But like my old unit, its soldiers were experienced and the lessons of the Yom Kippur War had been studied and implemented. The depots were in excellent shape, the role of each member well understood. Preparing for departure to a new war was easy. But overcoming our emotions and frustrations was not. To many of us this was the fourth war and to a handful it was the fifth. We needed more explanation why this war was necessary. But none were forthcoming.

We headed out on our half-tracks. Unlike the Yom Kippur War, our trip to the front was only thirty miles long. We did not need transporters. We knew we would ride these half-tracks all the way to the outskirts of Beirut, most probably on the same tank of gas. I could not help but notice that it was the fifteenth anniversary of the Six-Day War.

I stood on the seat next to my driver, half of my body exposed; leading our column along the same coastal highway I had traveled only three months earlier in Shimon's Ford Bronco. We passed through the suburbs of Acre and Nahariya. Civilians lining up along the road cheered as if it was a military parade. Some even threw flowers and candy at us. Getting injured by a hard candy on the way to war, I thought, would be embarrassing. I sat down, hiding behind the half-track's steel plates.

In a very different time and place other jubilant armies headed to war. In 1914, the commanders, soldiers, marching bands and the cheering civilians of the Austro-Hungarian Empire celebrated a sure victory even before the second shot was fired. The first shot that killed the Archduke Franz Ferdinand in Sarajevo and triggered the First World War had been fired a month earlier.

Many of the jubilant soldiers in the First World War did not return and those who did four years later were changed forever. Many in the jubilant crowds died of hunger and disease; many lost a relative or everything they owned. It was the last time the Austro-Hungarian army went to war. The cheers and the greedy desire for an easy victory were the sparks that ignited that war. My sinking heart feared that we too might not be headed to an easy victory. I wished I was not part of the parade and I envied those on the sideline who would be sleeping that night in their own beds while I would be setting up camp on a desolate hill in enemy territory.

We reached the border fence near Zar'it before dark. The gate was missing; tanks leading the invasion had already torn off an entire section. The hill had changed too; spring had given way to summer turning the lush green to brown. But the sky was still deep blue and the setting sun, plunging into the Mediterranean, painted the horizon red.

I am sure that all master sergeants are made of the same substance. Shushu, my new master sergeant, was dark-skinned, slim and had no mustache. By his appearance alone no one could mistake him for Kupy. But like Kupy, he was energetic, resourceful, and authoritative. He did not have a magic trunk like Kupy's, but somehow he always produced what no one else could. From the first day we had the best rations the Army issued and more than we could consume, the best halftracks, more blankets and tents than the army intended to issue. And when a few days later we left the hill towards populated areas, he bought from local street merchants counterfeit Scottish whiskey, fresh cherries from the mountains of Lebanon, and American cigarettes—counterfeit too. Like Kupy, he set up a unit piggy bank to fund these clandestine procurements. I knew that, like Kupy, he wanted me to stay out of his way and let him run the unit's discipline, equipment maintenance, and supply. I was happy to leave it all in his capable hands. We trusted each other and did all we could to bring our soldiers and ourselves back to our families alive and healthy. We succeeded in doing that.

We started firing our cannons shortly after sunset aiming at the refugee camps near Tyre where PLO terrorists chose to hide and to fire their anti-tank weapons against our advancing tanks. The war would not officially start until 11 am the next day, but six PLO battalions entrenched in these camps had to be "softened" before the paratroopers could go in. The following morning the air force joined in the assault. (94 p. 118) The PLO was not sitting idle either. Their cannons and Katyusha launchers fired that night more than 500 shells at 29 northern settlements. They did not bother aiming at us. Aiming at civilians was far more valuable in their eyes than destroying a cannon or an army command post.

About the time we started to fire, Begin convened his cabinet in his residence in Tel Aviv for an emergency meeting. Having ignited the Lebanese border there was no doubt that the cabinet would now approve a full-scale military operation. The only remaining question was the extent. When the Minister of Defense and his Chief of Staff took the floor, they asked for an incursion of no more than twenty-five miles that would push PLO cannons out of range of Israeli settlements. There was no mention in that meeting of linking up with the Phalangists, engaging the Syrian forces in Lebanon or entering Beirut. (94 pp. 102-105)

Only the Minister of Communications, Mordechai Zippori, questioned the plans in that meeting and asked specifically how far exactly the line would reach. It would be just south of Sidon in the west, Sharon promised, and north of Lake Quaraoun in the east. It would be reached in twelve hours though, given the uncertainties of battle, it might take twenty-four hours. The cabinet was promised by both Begin and Sharon that there was no intention of reaching Beirut.

The limited plan was approved with only two ministers abstaining. The only minister to raise objections voted in favor of the limited plan, satisfied that his questions were answered. The mission that Zippori and the cabinet approved was in sharp contrast to my orders.

I never found out if the Chief of Staff knew that evening that his orders diverged from the cabinet's approved plan. But without a doubt, Sharon knew. (98)[10]

---

10 Benziman, a *Ha'aretz* reporter, stated in an article unrelated to the Lebanon war that Begin knew that Sharon was lying to him during that war. Sharon sued Benziman and *Ha'aretz* for slander. The courts determined that Sharon lied to Begin, the cabinet, and the Knesset, and that Begin knew about it but chose to take responsibility for that war alone rather than blaming Sharon.

The war that was to last twelve, twenty-four hours at most, lasted much longer. It took four days just to subdue the PLO resistance in Tyre, barely twelve miles from the border. We continued firing our cannons at the refugee camps for three days. Fortunately no one fired at us. But Israeli settlements near the border were not as fortunate. The PLO continued firing at Nahariya and Kiryat Shmona.

On the fourth day we left the hill towards Sidon. We rolled down to the coast and then turned north on the historically significant coastal road. Before Israel's War of Independence one could start at Kantara on the Suez Canal and drive on this road through Gaza City, Tel Aviv, Haifa, Tyre, Sidon, and Beirut to Latakia in Syria. Ancient Pharaohs traveled on this road to conquer and control their vast empire. King Solomon traveled on this road to meet his friend Hiram, King of Tyre, and along this road cedars of Lebanon were transported to build the ancient Temple in Jerusalem.

The road that once resembled the French Riviera, lined with beach resorts, inns, tavernas, and restaurants that attracted wealthy Arabs was now turned into a devastated war zone. Buildings were damaged, stores burned and looted; panoramic restaurants sitting on the edge of cliffs overlooking the Mediterranean were reduced to empty shells. Uncollected human and animal corpses lying along the road for days began decomposing. The stench of death combined with smoke and gunpowder brought back memories from Geneifa Hills, in the land of Goshen on the other side of the Suez Canal.

Late that afternoon we reached the Aramco golf course south of Sidon and our lead units started toward Damour, a small village along the coast that controlled the road to Beirut. Damour was a Maronite Christian village until the Lebanon Civil War in 1976 when PLO units raided it and took it over, massacring its Christian inhabitants and forcing the survivors to flee. Damour needed to be captured before IDF forces could continue north to Beirut. But as our front unit found out, the village was abandoned before their arrival. The shelling did not make much difference.

We also turned our heavy mortars on Ein Hilweh, a Palestinian refugee camp across the road from the port of Sidon. It too was critical for the free flow of military traffic northward. But unlike Damour, the leaders of Ein Hilweh chose to put up a suicidal fight, fighting to the last person, including civilians, like a second Masada. It would take us eight days to eliminate all resistance there.

On Friday, the sixth day of the war, at noon, a ceasefire agreement with Syria was to take place. The agreement, however, did not seem to apply to my artillery brigade. Orders for support kept coming in. Several Israeli Skyhawk bombers also showed up overhead and started diving towards Ein Hilweh releasing their bombs. (94 p. 146) Occasionally, a shoulder-held ground-to-air missile rose towards the planes but flares released by the pilots easily deflected them.

Hoping to minimize the loss of lives, the IDF command sent three delegations into the camp to convince its leaders that they were surrounded and heavily outnumbered, and asked them to lay down their arms, promising that unarmed fighters would be freed unharmed. Two of the delegations were not even allowed in; the third delegation returned shaken after observing civilians who tried to leave the camp being executed. Two additional delegations followed. Even a psychologist was flown in from Tel Aviv to advise the command on negotiating tactics. But the camp would not surrender. For days, Israeli planes and artillery pulverized it. Clouds of black smoke and dust rose, signaling a new and terrible kind of war forced on us without any obvious reason or benefit.

Later that Friday, well after the ceasefire deadline, I heard exchanges over the radio that suggested that several Israeli units were clashing with a Syrian brigade near Beirut. I noted that these Israeli units were heading to Beirut, and like us, they were well outside the twenty-five mile range, well outside the promised duration of twenty-four hours and well outside the ceasefire deadline. I could not have possibly known then that the cabinet was still unaware of these digressions. The fog of war, like in 1967 and 1973, was again hovering over the battlefield. But this time it was spread to confuse us, the soldiers, the Israeli public, and most importantly, the highest levels of our government.

Nevertheless, several ministers started suspecting that the reports they received were not the entire truth. That Friday, Energy Minister Yitzhak Berman asked Sharon somewhat mockingly: "Arik, perhaps you will be good enough to tell us what you're going to ask for approval of the day after tomorrow, so that you can secure what you are going to ask us to approve tomorrow morning." (94 p. 187)

Sharon, while stung by Berman's remark and repeating his promise not to enter Beirut or link-up with the Phalangists, neglected to tell his colleagues that a helicopter was waiting outside the building to fly him to Junieh, north of Beirut, for a meeting with Bashir Gemayel to iron out the last details of the link-up that the cabinet had just been assured would not happen. (94 p. 189)

When Israeli forces connected the following Sunday with Phalangist forces north of Beirut, the PLO headquarters in the city and its forces were effectively encircled. When it dawned on Arafat that he was under siege, he told a representative of the Lebanese army that he might consider ordering his forces to leave the city if safe passage were to be granted. But the following day he changed his mind and words like "a second Stalingrad" were mentioned. (94 p. 198) When it also became clear that the Phalangists would not keep their promise to clear out the PLO from Beirut, Israel was left with only two options: to remove the PLO themselves or keep the PLO under siege until they agreed to leave. It was the start of a nine-week siege that no one predicted and certainly no one had planned.

Instead of returning home from Sidon by the end of the first week, my unit was moved once again to an area southeast of Beirut's international airport. From the hill I had selected for our headquarters we could see the idled runway. Numerous Boeing 707 planes, bearing on their tails the green symbol of the cedar of Lebanon, were parked in a straight row alongside the abandoned terminal. Aiming our shots from that hill at the PLO positions in Beirut was like shooting fish in a barrel.

At the bottom of the hill stood several abandoned apartment buildings. I kept worrying that a terrorist might be hiding in one of them. One morning our watch saw a suspicious movement near one of the buildings and opened fire. No one returned fire but we did not see suspicious movements again.

By the second week of the siege, our artillery brigade was joined by several new reserve brigades. When all the new brigades were in place, our headquarters was ordered to coordinate a massive night shelling of the PLO positions. By one estimate, we deployed more guns around Beirut than the German army did around Stalingrad. We fired all our guns in what was mostly a one-sided shelling. The PLO inside the city managed to launch only several Katyusha rockets. Unfortunately a handful of those rockets hit Israeli positions and killed several soldiers. Our massive shelling on the other hand resulted in significant property damage, approximately fifty PLO casualties.[11] But the PLO resisted our calls to surrender.

A new ceasefire was declared on June 25th, when sections of the Beirut-Damascus highway were in Israeli hands. But the Lebanese war did not end with that ceasefire. It would officially end three years later, on June 1985, after a gradual withdrawal of Israel from most of its territories in Lebanon into

---

11 Nearly thirty years, later an American friend told me that he was in Beirut during that night of heavy shelling. As a staff member of the CBS news team, he stayed in a luxury hotel in the city that CBS thought was known to the IDF as the headquarters of foreign correspondents and therefore safe from Israeli shelling. But on his very first night in Beirut, hundreds of shells landed in the city, many near his hotel.

a small security zone in the south that it held until 2000. (99)[12] Other than the siege on Beirut, much of the fighting in Lebanon ended. It was time to allow reservists to go on leave.

On the third Friday of my deployment it was my turn to go on leave. A command car took me down the hill and dropped me off on the Beirut-Rosh HaNikra highway to hitchhike my way to Haifa.

It might seem unthinkable today that an individual soldier would hitchhike home out of a war zone. It turned unthinkable two months later. But in the immediate days after the ceasefire much of Lebanon south of Beirut was peaceful. The Lebanese army was never adversarial to the invading IDF forces and the terrorists were either trapped in Beirut or remained out of sight trying to reorganize. Local entrepreneurs set up roadside stands to sell souvenirs, cherries, whiskey, fake American cigarettes and on occasion even real American cigarettes. Sections of the highway looked like a long stretch of an open air market. An abundance of military vehicles, carrying supplies and troops along the highway, guaranteed that hitchhiking would not be difficult. I was in Nahariya within an hour and at home three hours later.

A picture in our family album shows my six-year old son Aharon dressed in my military fatigues, aiming my Uzi towards the camera. He must have thought that war was a fun game. He even offered to return with me to my unit when my leave was over.

I was much less excited. I tried telling my friends at home that the Peace of Galilee, the presumable cause of this war, was a fallacy, that reaching Beirut was a mistake that had already cost us hundreds of lives, that drafting soldiers who survived the Yom Kippur War into a new and clearly unnecessary war amounted to a betrayal. Some agreed, but many called me a traitor. Liora suggested I keep these sentiments to myself. She was right; there was nothing for me to gain other than heartbreak and angry disagreements. It would take many months before the Israeli public would understand the true nature of the war. Surprisingly, the Israeli press remained supportive of the war. The normally critical press chose to carry the official line with hardly any opposition or criticism.

I hitchhiked back to my unit at the end of that weekend.

Most of my unit's work was completed when we reached our last position near Beirut's airport; response to the endless calls for artillery support

---

12 Because the end of the war was marked by a gradual withdrawal of IDF forces, there is no fixed date to mark that end, though June 1985 is considered as the end date. The last Israeli soldiers left the buffer zone in Southern Lebanon on May 24, 2000, nearly eighteen years after the start of the war.

was mostly in the hands of the cannon battalions. I was now free to allocate manpower and my own time to tour the area to scope out potential artillery positions.

On one clear early July day we drove from the outskirts of Beirut south toward Sidon where we turned east towards Mount Lebanon, the biblical mountain range where the cedars of Lebanon grow.

The winding road climbed up the steep mountain range. In contrast with the hills of Mount Carmel and the Galilee which were forested by early settlers, the hills of Mount Lebanon were mostly barren. Near the top we stopped at an overlook. The entire coastline was visible through the crystal clear mountain air. I could even see Mount Carmel, far south, and Haifa on its slope.

Behind us, across the road, stood a gigantic cedar of Lebanon. The heavy limbs, each the size of a tree, were stretched out horizontally like welcoming arms. To measure its large trunk, four of us joined hands trying to hug it. We barely closed the circle with our arms and fingers fully stretched out.

I tried to imagine King Hiram's slaves cutting down a giant cedar like this one; muscular men, naked from the waist up, their sweating torsos glistening in the sun, beating their axes against the giant tree. The iron axes were dull in comparison to modern steel axes, and their overseer would have been impatient and angry. It must have taken days to topple the giant tree and then many more to cut off its limbs and branches. Once cut, the heavy trunk and limbs were tied to oxen and hauled down to the coast on their way to Jerusalem to build King Solomon's temple.

We listened to the quiet breeze blowing through the cedar's needles when one of us noted that he could not see or hear birds. He already noticed that there were no birds near Beirut but assumed that the birds there were startled by the sounds and smoke of the recent war. We continued looking for birds throughout our stay in Lebanon but hardly saw any. We could not understand this phenomenon because across the Israeli border, a short distance away, birds were plentiful and diverse.

We drove over the peaks of Mount Lebanon and down a steep and curving road to the Beka'a Valley. Just in time for lunch, we found a Lebanese restaurant on the shores of Lake Quaraoun, a large artificial lake in the valley. This time I was determined not to miss the opportunity to sample authentic Lebanese cuisine.

We parked our command cars in the large parking lot next to luxury cars carrying Lebanese license plates and entered the restaurant. Several men wearing jackets and ties sat by a large round table having what seemed to be a business lunch. The restaurant owner ran from behind the counter and with hand motions directed us to the deck overlooking the lake. Before a menu was even offered, a waiter arrived carrying a large tray of small plates with Lebanese falafel,[13] hummus, labne,[14] baba ghannouj,[15] and freshly baked pita. We ordered platters of delicious shashlik and kebab.[16]

Paying our bill with Israeli Shekels was just as surrealistic as the lunch itself on that glorious deck, the formally dressed businessmen in this remote location, the luxury cars parked next to our dusty command cars and our faith that the restaurant and the food we ate were safe.

When we left, the businessmen celebrated the conclusion of their meeting with glasses of cloudy white drink, Arak Zahlawi[17] mixed with water and ice.

On our drive back we stopped at an orchard. Branches of its large trees were bent under the weight of red cherries. A little boy, barely six years old, managed a roadside stand filled with bags of cherries. The young boy proved to be a shrewd and hardnosed negotiator. But even more surprising, he spoke sufficient Hebrew to haggle with us, and knew enough arithmetic to compute his prices in Israeli Shekels. Either the schools in the Beka'a Valley were excellent, or all one needs to succeed in business can be learned at a Lebanese cherry stand.

The last three weeks of our deployment in Lebanon also marked the last days of calm there. Within days after our departure, terrorists emerged from their hiding places and began ambushing Israeli soldiers and vehicles along the roads and shelling Israeli army posts, often with short range mortars. Life and travel in Lebanon turned dangerous. Posts were fortified; military travel in Lebanon was conducted only in convoys escorted by tanks and APCs. By all accounts, the days of the War of Attrition along the Bar-Lev line were back. Nearly every passing day brought new headlines with names of casualties.

The approaching winter brought new hardships: muddy impassable roads, unbearable cold in posts that were not designed for winter, endlessly long nights and, worst of all, more terrorist attacks.

---

13 Lebanese falafel is made of chickpeas and fava beans. By contrast, Egyptian falafel is made of fava beans only.
14 Labne—a tart yogurt cheese.
15 Baba ghannouj—a Lebanese eggplant salad.
16 The Lebanese terminology distinguishes between shashlik—skewered chunks of meat and kebab—skewered minced meat. They both are typically grilled over charcoal.
17 Arak—an anise-flavored Lebanese spirit, similar to the Greek ouzo or the French pastis. El Zahlawi is one of the better known distilleries.

Holding the new territory fell mostly on the reserve force. Men were taken from their homes and families for weeks in a cold and dangerous land. They were fighting a war that soon everyone in Israel started questioning.

It would be eighteen years before Israel would withdraw from the remaining narrow strip in southern Lebanon it held for security purposes. Thousands would pay with their lives, maimed bodies and traumatized souls thanks to the follies of their vain and thoughtless leaders.

Twenty-four years after that Lebanon war, Israel would fight another Lebanon war that would be aptly called the Second Lebanon War. The new war would be against Hezbollah, a Shi'a terrorist organization that was formed by the amalgamation of various other organizations and armed soon after the First Lebanon War. (100) One of its declared objectives was to expel the invaders, and when Israel chose in 2000 to unilaterally abandon its remaining positions in southern Lebanon, Hezbollah declared victory. One could debate the legitimacy of the claim. But without a doubt, their stated objective was achieved, Israel left Lebanon, whether under Hezbollah pressure or not. Encouraged by its perceived victory, Hezbollah vowed to push the Jews out of the entire State of Israel. In 2015, more than thirty years after the War of the Peace of the Galilee, most of Israel's population was under the threat of Hezbollah rockets. Israel's largest cities, Haifa, Tel Aviv, and Jerusalem, together with large industries, air fields, and ports were in the sights of Hezbollah's crosshairs. What was started in 1982 as an effort to bring calm to settlements along a narrow strip on the Lebanese border grew into a threat to the entire nation.

Back at home at the end of my deployment, Liora and I heard Begin boast in a radio address about the great victory. He gloated with pride for presiding over a war that he described as "war of choice."[18]

We were stunned.

For the first time in Israel's history and less than nine years after the Yom Kippur War, an Israeli leader "chose" to take our country to war. He could also "choose" not to send to war the men who were still licking their physical and emotional wounds suffered in earlier wars. Of course, the Prime Minister did not discuss with those who would be called to pay the price if that was their choice as well. His choice ignored the moral foundations of Israel and the sanctity of human life: both ours and our enemy's. His choice created a new

---

18 By contrast, on May 28, 1967 after his fumbled speech Eshkol visited the Pit—the IDF command bunker. After being criticized by the generals for waiting too long he said that the IDF was not established to conduct a "war of choice."

economic cost that would pile on top of the still unpaid costs of the Yom Kippur War. The army that was named the Israeli Defense Force was tasked to wage an offensive "war of choice."

At the age of 34 I could expect sixteen additional years of reserve duties. I also had a son who in eleven years' time would be called to serve his turn. How many wars of choice or wars of necessity would I still face? Would I be fighting another war of choice side by side with my son or my daughter's husband? Would there be another phenomenal leadership failure like the Yom Kippur War?

We loved Israel; we loved living near our extended family. We loved our work and were satisfied with our living standards. But we could no longer stomach the dangers of elective wars or reckless neglect. We already paid the price for the existence of Israel. Our parents paid the price for being Jews.

That evening Liora and I decided that our place was in America.

When we left Israel in 1986 to settle in America, we were already a family of five. Our youngest son Dan was born in Haifa in July 1984. We felt blessed for having such a wonderful family and for being offered opportunities in America, but were saddened for leaving behind the country that we loved and where many of our memories were formed.

Works Cited

1. Wiesel, Elie. *Night*, XV. New York: Bantam Books, 1982.
2. "Kamianets-Podilskyi massacre." *Wikipedia, the Free Encyclopedia*. Accessed November 16, 2016, https://en.wikipedia.org/wiki/Kamianets-Podilskyi_massacre.
3. Dantsig, Hillel. *Be-tsel Susim, Im Pelugat Haavoda shel Yahadut Hungaria Ba'Hazit Ha'Rusit* [in Hebrew]. Bet Loḥame ha'Geṭaot: Hotsaat Ha'kibuts ha'meuḥad, 1976.
4. Diósi, Imre. *Munkaszolgálat és hadifogság, egy gyulai zsidó visszaemlékezése* [in Hungarian]. Budapest: Gabbiano Print Kft., 2009.
5. Braham, Randolph. "The Hungarian Labor Service System, 1939-1945." *East European Quarterly*, 35-36. Boulder, CO, and New York: Columbia University Press, 1977.
6. Kenez, Peter. *Hungary from the Nazis to the Soviets*, 77. Cambridge: Cambridge University Press, 2006.
7. Vági, Zoltán, László Csősz, and Gábor Kádár. *The Holocaust in Hungary, Evolution of a Genocid*. Edited by Jürgen Matthäus and Jan Lambertz, 348. Lanham, MD: Alta Mitra Press in Association with the United States Holocaust Memorial Museum, 2013.
8. Cornelius, Deborah S. *Hungary in World War II, Caught in the Cauldron*, 216. New York: Fordham University Press, 2011.
9. Braham, Randolph L. *The Politics of Genocide*, 309. New York: Columbia University Press, 1981.
10. "István Horthy." *Wikipedia, the Free Encyclopedia*. Accessed November 10, 2016, https://en.wikipedia.org/wiki/Istv%C3%A1n_Horthy.
11. Braham, Randolph L. *The Wartime System of Labor Service in Hungary, Variety of Experiences*, 22. New York : Columbia University Press, 1995.
12. Rozzett, Robert. *Conscripted Slaves. Hungarian Jewish Forced Laborers on the Eastern Front during the Second World War*, 75-76. Jerusalem : Yad Vashem, 2013.
13. Herzog, Chaim, comp., *Kol Israel Radio Commentaries Broadcast During the Six-Day War*. LP Recording. S. l.: CBS, 1968.
14. Dunstan, Simon. *The Six Days War, 1967: Jordan and Syria*, 88. Oxford, UK, and Long Island City, NY: Osprey Publishing, 2009.
15. Oren, Michael B. *Six Days of War, June 1967 and the Making of Modern Middle East*, 283-4. New York: Ballantine Books, 2002.
16. Shirer, William L. *The Nightmare Years 1930-1940*, 531-2. Boston, Toronto: Little Brown and Company, 1984.
17. Herzog, Chaim. *The Arab-Israeli Wars, War and Peace in the Middle East* [in Hebrew], 152. Jerusalem: Edanim Publisher, 1983.

18. "Khartoum Resolution." *Wikipedia, the Free Encyclopedia.* Accessed November 10, 2016, https://en.wikipedia.org/wiki/Khartoum_Resolution.
19. Leibowitz, Yeshayahu. *Judaism, Human Values, and the Jewish State,* 225-6. Edited by Eliezer Goldman, translated by Eliezer Goldman Yoram Navon, and by Zvi Jacobson, Gershon Levi, and Raphael Levy. Cambridge, Massachusetts: Harvard University Press, 1992.
20. Dayan, Yael. *Sinai, June 1967, Personal Diary* [in Hebrew], 68. Tel Aviv: Am Oved Publishers, 1967.
21. Karsai, Elek A. *Fegyvertelen Álltak Az Aknamezökön...* [They Stood Unarmed in the Minefields...] [in Hungarian]. Vol. 1 of *Dokumentumok a Munkaszolgálat történetéhez Magyarországon.* Budapest: Magyar Izraeliták Orzságos Képviselete Kiadása, 1962.
22. Reiner, Moshe. *Loyalty and its Tragic Reward* [in Hebrew], 121. Haifa: Private edition, 2004.
23. Karsai, László. "The People's Courts and Revolutionary Justice in Hungary." *The Politics of Retribution in Europe: World War II and Its Aftermath, 1939-1948,* 233-251. Edited by István Deák, Jan T. Gross and Tony Judt. Princeton: Princeton University Press, 2000.
24. "Pinsk." *Wikipedia. The Free Encyclopedia.* Accessed November 11, 2016, http://en.wikipedia.org/wiki/Pinsk.
25. "Brest Ghetto." *Wikipedia. The Free Encyclopedia.* Accessed November 10, 2016, http://en.wikipedia.org/wiki/Brest_Ghetto.
26. Laufer, Dov (László). "Childhood Memories: The Changed Letters" [in Hebrew]. *Magazine of the Liberal Workers Union of the GAHAL representation in the Histadtrut* 17/5 (May 1973): 61-63. Tel Aviv: The Liberal Workers Union. Special issue for Israel's 25th Independence Day.
27. Dunstan, Simon. *Israeli Fortifications of the October War, 1973,* 9. Oxford, UK and New York, NY: Osprey Publishing, 2008.
28. "Bar Lev Line." *Wikipedia. The Free Encyclopedia.* Accessed November 10, 2016, http://en.wikipedia.org/wiki/Bar_Lev_Line.
29. Bar-Siman-Tov, Yaacov. *The Israeli-Egyptian War of Attrition 1969-1970, A Case Study of Limited Local War,* 63. New York: Columbia University Press, 1980.
30. Exodus 17:1-7.
31. Rabinovich, Abraham. *The Yom Kippur War,* 11. New York: Shocken Books, 2004.
32. El Shazly, Saad. *The Crossing of the Suez,* 232. San Francisco, CA: American Mideast Research, 2003.
33. Golan, Matti. *The Secret Conversations of Henry Kissinger* [in Hebrew], 68. Tel Aviv: Shoken Publishing, 1976.
34. Exodus 14:6-9.
35. Genesis 46:34.
36. Dunstan, Simon. *The Sinai,* Vol. 2 of *The Yom Kippur War, 1973,* 89. Oxford, UK, and Long Island City, NY: Osprey Publishing, 2003.
37. Sandberg, Moshe. *My Longest Year* [in Hebrew], 54-114. Jerusalem: Yad Vashem, 1968.
38. "International Tracing Service Abbreviations." *ITS—International Tracing Service.* Accessed September 9, 2016, https://www.its-arolsen.org/en/information-center/abbreviations/.
39. Levi, Primo. *The Drowned and the Saved,* 93. New York: Vintage International, A division of Random House, 1989.

40. Magdolna Diósi, née Magdolna Fodor. *Reminiscences by Mrs Diósi née Magdolna Fodor from 1994*. Accessed September 9, 2016, http://bekes.archivportal.hu/id-437-reminiscences_by_mrs_diosi_nee_magdolna.html.
41. "Totenliste(Excel)—KZ-Gedenkstätte Mühldorfer Hart." *KZ-Gedenkstätte Mühldorfer Hart*. Accessed September 9, 2016, http://www.kz-gedenk-mdf.de/totenlisteexcel.
42. Levi, Primo. *Survival in Auschwitz*, 22-37. New York: Touchstone, 1986.
43. 135633, Ka-Tzetnik. *Sunrise Over Hell*, 158-161. Translated by Nina De-Nur. London: W. H. Allen, A Howard & Wyndham Company, 1977. Originally published in Hebrew as *Salamandra*.
44. Pavelec, Sterling Michael. *The Jet Race and the Second World War*, 91-109. Annapolis: Naval Institute Press, 2007.
45. Schoonbrood, Lou. "The Kassel Underground." *TIGHAR Tracks* 11/4 (December 31, 1995). Accessed January 4, 2018, http://tighar.org/Publications/TTracks/1995 Vol_11/1104.pdf.
46. Joint Intelligence Objective Agency, Washington, D.C. *German Underground Installations. Part One of Three: Unique Design and Construction Methods*. CIOS Section Intelligence Division Office, Chief Engineer, USFET, APO 887, USFET APO. Brooklyn, NY: British Intelligence Objectives Sub-Committee, September 20, 1945. Distributed by Mapleton House (Book Dept.). Code No. 51-269-1.
47. Müller, Peter. "The Bunker Complex in the Mühldorf Hart: An Arms Race and Human Suffering." *Mühldorf a. Inn*. Accessed September 12, 2016, http://www.muehldorf.de/files/the_bunker_complex_in_the_muhldorfer_hart.pdf.
48. Stolpmann, Herb. "Sattelite Camp Kaufering." *Dachau KZ*, November 6, 2011. Accessed September 12, 2016, http://dachaukz.blogspot.com/2011/11/prologue-dachau-kz-satellite-camp.html.
49. Bankel, Hansgeorg. "A German War Plant from 1944/45: The Aircraft Factory Weingut I and the Concentration Camp Waldlager 6 Near Muhdlorf/Inn." Proc. 3rd Intnl. Cong. On Construction History. Cottbus: s. n., May 2009.
50. Hibbeler, R.C. *Engineering Mechanics, Statics*, 377. Upper Saddle River: Pearson Prentice Hall, 2013.
51. "Organisation Todt." *Wikipedia, the Free Encyclopedia*. Accessed September 13, 2016, https://en.wikipedia.org/wiki/Organisation_Todt.
52. Charmatz, Konrad. *Nightmares, Memoirs of the Years of Horror Under Nazi Rule in Europe, 1939-1945*, 174. Edited by Matthew Kudelka, translated by Miriam Dashkin Beckerman. Syracuse: Syracuse University Press, 2003.
53. "Battle of the Bulge." *Wikipedia, the Free Encyclopedia*.Accessed October 5, 2016, https://en.wikipedia.org/wiki/Battle_of_the_Bulge.
54. Neutzling, Bill. "Recollections of 19 MAR 1945." *Bill Neutzling's B-24 Liberator Web Site*. Accessed October 6, 2016, http://www.angelfire.com/wv/liberator/franz.html.
55. Diem, Veronika. *Die Freiheitsaktion Bayern: Ein Aufstand in der Endphase des NS-Regimes*, 520. Kallmünz:Verlag Michael Laßleben, 2013. [Germ.]
56. "99th Infantry Division (United States)." *Wikipedia, the Free Encyclopedia*.Accessed October 17, 2016, http://en.wikipedia.org/wiki/99th_Infantry_Division_%28United_States%29.

57. "The 99th Infantry Division." *Holocaust Encyclopedia*. United States Holocaust Memorial Museum. Accessed October 17, 2016, http://www.ushmm.org/wlc/en/article.php?ModuleId=10006153.
58. Shimkin, Michael B. "An Incident in Ampfing." *Scientific Monthly* 63/4 (October 1946), 281-292.
59. "Displaced persons camp." *Wikipedia, the Free Encyclopedia.* Accessed October 21, 2016, http://en.wikipedia.org/wiki/Displaced_persons_camp.
60. "Feldafing displaced persons camp." *Wikipedia, the Free Encyclopedia.* Accessed October 21, 2016, http://en.wikipedia.org/wiki/Feldafing_displaced_persons_camp.
61. Schochet, Simon. *Feldafing*, 21. Vancouver: November House, 1983. ISBN 0-920156-12-6.
62. *Papendorf, Germany. Jews from Feldafing DP Camp, who travelled on the illegal immigrant ship Exodus, 1947 (President Warfield), postwar.* Yad Vashem. Accessed October 24, 2016, http://collections1.yadvashem.org/arch_srika/1001-1500/1461-1500/1486_1036.jpg. Item ID 11905, Archival Signature 1486/1036.
63. Uris, Leon. *Exodus*. New York: Doubleday and Company, 1958.
64. "SS Exodus." *Wikipedia, the Free Encyclopedia.* Accessed October 24, 2016, http://en.wikipedia.org/wiki/SS_Exodus.
65. *Photograph—Lyrics to Jewish national anthem and portriats of Zionist leaders hang in a classroom.* Holocaust Encyclopedia photograph. United States Holocaust Memorial Museum. Accessed November 2, 2016, https://www.ushmm.org/wlc/en/media_ph.php?MediaId=2134.
66. *Feldafing, Bavaria, Germany, Vocational school for tailoring in the DP camp.* Yad Vashem. Accessed October 25, 2016, http://collections1.yadvashem.org/arch_srika/Albums/26-48/26_38.jpg. Item ID 55271, Album Number FA26/38.
67. *Feldafing, Bavaria, Germany, Workers with a printing press in a DP camp.* Yad Vashem. Accessed October 25, 2016, http://collections1.yadvashem.org/arch_srika/Albums/26-48/26_22.jpg. Item ID 57838, Album Number FA26/22.
68. *Feldafing, Bavaria, Germany, Vehicle repair in the DP camp.* Yad Vashem. Accessed October 25, 2016, http://collections1.yadvashem.org/arch_srika/Albums/26-48/26_29.jpg. Item ID 56552, Album number FA26/29.
69. *Feldafing, Bavaria, Germany, Vocational school for shoemakers in the DP camp.* Yad Vashem. Accessed October 25, 2016, http://collections1.yadvashem.org/arch_srika/Albums/26-48/26_39.jpg. Item ID 56698, Album number FA26/39.
70. *Feldafing, Bavaria, Germany, Metalwork vocational training in a DP camp.* Yad Vashem. Accessed October 25, 2016, http://collections1.yadvashem.org/arch_srika/Albums/26-48/26_24.jpg. Item ID 60729, Album numberFA26/24.
71. *Feldafing, Bavaria, Germany, Vocational school for carpentry in the DP camp.* Yad Vashem. Accessed October 25, 2016, http://collections1.yadvashem.org/arch_srika/Albums/26-48/26_32.jpg. Item ID 60872, Album Number FA26/32.
72. *Feldafing, Bavaria, Germany, Hairdressing school and salon in the DP camp.* Yad Vashem. Accessed October 25, 2016, http://collections1.yadvashem.org/arch_srika/Albums/26-48/26_45.jpg. Item ID 65341, Album number FA26/45.
73. *Feldafing, Bavaria, Germany, Vocational school for logging in a DP camp.* Yad Vashem. Accessed October 25, 2016, http://collections1.yadvashem.org/arch_srika/Albums/26-48/26_43.jpg. Item ID 62457, Album number FA26/43.

74. "Feldafing Displaced Persons Camp, 25 Cents." *World and Military Notes.com*. Accessed October 25, 2016, http://worldandmilitarynotes.com/displaced-persons-camps/feldafing-displaced-persons-camp-25-cents.
75. *Feldafing, Bavaria, Germany, Trucks in the DP camp yard*. Yad Vashem. Accessed October 25, 2016, http://collections1.yadvashem.org/arch_srika/Albums/26-48/26_2.jpg. Item ID 56132, Album Number FA26/2.
76. *Feldafing, Bavaria, Germany, A group of survivors repatriating to Rumania, at the train station*. Yad Vashem. Accessed October 26, 2016, http://collections1.yadvashem.org/arch_srika/Albums/26-48/26_13.jpg. Item ID 57701, Album Number FA26/13.
77. *Feldafing, Bavaria, Germany, A group of survivors repatriating to Rumania, boarding a train*. Yad Vashem. Accessed October 26, 2016, http://collections1.yadvashem.org/arch_srika/Albums/26-48/26_14.jpg. Item ID 59141, Album Number FA26/14.
78. Horváth, Rita. "Jews in Hungary after the Holocaust: The National relief Committee of Deportees 1945-1950." *Journal of Israeli History* 19 (Frank Cass, Summer 1998): 69-91.
79. Frojimovics, Kinga, Géza Komoróczy, Pusztai Viktória, and Strbik, Andrea. *Jewish Budapest. Monuments, Rites, History*, 403. Edited by Géza Komoróczy. Budapest: Central European University Press, 1999.
80. Zweig, Ronald W. *The Gold Train: The Destruction of the Jews and the Looting of Hungary*. London: Penguin, 2002.
81. *Irving Rosner et al, vs. United States of America*. 01-1859-CIV/Seitz. S. I. United States District Court Southern District of Florida, May 7, 2001.
82. "Békécsaba." *Wikipedia, the Free Encyclopedia*. Accessed October 2016, https://en.wikipedia.org/wiki/B%C3%A9k%C3%A9scsaba.
83. Balogh, István. *Békés Békétlenség, A Békés Megyei Zsidók Története* [in Hungarian], 145. Budapest: Tótkomlós, 2007.
84. "Decision of the Board of Trustees to place Jews in charge of trustees. Final decision. Gyula City hall Minutes: 36/b Gyula, June 22, 1944." *Magyar Nemzeti Levéltár Békés Megyei Levéltára*. Accessed October 28, 2016. http://www.bekes-archiv.hu/id-747-36_b_gyula_june_22_1944_the_decision.html.
85. "Introduction, history of the local Jewish community." *Magyar Nemzeti Levéltár Békés Megyei Levéltára*. Accessed October 28, 2016. http://www.bekes-archiv.hu/id-422-introduction_history_of_the_local.html.
86. "The reorganization of the Judenrat. The announcement of Artúr Licht and colleagues regarding the reorganization of the Judenrat. Gyula City hall Minutes: November 7, 1944." *Magyar Nemzeti Levéltár Békés Megyei Levéltára*. Accessed October 28, 2016, http://www.bekes-archiv.hu/id-759-44_gyula_november_7_1944_the.html.
87. Garai, George. *The Policy Towards the Jews, Zionism, and Israel of the Hungarian Communist Party, 1945-1953*, 140. London School of Economics, 1979. Ph.D. Thesis. Thesis number DX203358.
88. Headline in a daily newspaper [in Hungarian]. *Szabad Szo* [Free Word] 51 (May 15, 1949): 112.
89. Novák, Attila. *Átmenetben: A cionista mozgalom négy éve Magarországon* [in Hungarian], 167. S. l.: Magyar Zsidó Történelem, Múlt és Jövö Kiadó, 2000. ISBN 963 9171 51 4.

90. Israeli Consul to Act As Observer at Budapest Trial of 11 Former Zionist Leaders. *JTA-Jewish Telegraphic Agency*, June 15, 1949. Accessed: November 1, 2016, http://www.jta.org/1949/06/15/archive/israeli-consul-to-act-as-observer-at-budapest-trial-of-11-former-zionist-leaders.
91. Albrich, Thomas and Ronald W. Zweig, editors. *Escape Through Austria, Jewish Refugees and the Austrian Route to Palestine*, 124. London and Portland, OR: Frank Cass, 2002.
92. *Világosság* [Clarity] [in Hungarian], May 17, 1949, 113.
93. *Magyar Nemzet* [Hungarian Nation] [in Hungarian], June 19, 1949, 140.
94. Schiff, Ze'ev and Ehud Ya'ari. *Israel's Lebanon War*, 301. New York: Simon and Schuster, 1984. ISBN 0-671-47991-1.
95. Cobban, Helena. *The Palestinian Liberation Organization: People, Power and Politics*, 95-96. Cambridge: Cambridge University Press, 1985.
96. Peretz, Don and Sammy Smooha "Israel's Tenth Knesset Elections: Ethnic Upsurgence and Decline of Ideology." *The Middle East Journal* 35 (Middle East Institute, Automn 1981): 506-526.
97. "Ya'akov Meridor." *Wikipedia, the Free Encyclopedia*. Accessed November 7, 2016, https://en.wikipedia.org/wiki/Ya'akov_Meridor.
98. Benziman, Uzi. *Nothing but the Truth* [in Hebrew]. Jerusalem: Keter Publishing House Ltd., 2002. ISBN 965-07-1110-4.
99. "1982 Lebanon War." *Wikipedia, the Free Encyclopedia*. Accessed November 9, 2016, https://en.wikipedia.org/wiki/1982_Lebanon_War.
100. "History of Hezbollah." *Wikipedia, the Free Encyclopedia*. Accessed November 9, 2016, https://en.wikipedia.org/wiki/History_of_Hezbollah.

Index

Academic Reserves (AR) corps, 87, 92, 94, 100, 102–103, 106–107, 110, 112, 115, 118, 122, 124, 135, 143, 187, 189, 192, 197
Adabiya, 252
Adan, Avraham "Bren", 213, 233, 241
Adler Rabbi, Ignác, 54
Akavish, 235–236, 247
Akavish Road, 227, 229–232, 235
Alexeyevka, 81, 161–162, 169
Ampfing, 275, 275n12, 280, 304–305, 314–315, 317–319, 324
anti-Semitism, 4, 28, 30, 41, 58, 96, 154, 349
Appell, *or* Appellplatz 274–275, 283–286, 289–290, 293, 303, 307–308
Arafat, Yasser, 362, 369, 378, 283
Ardennes, 298
Argov, Shlomo, 378
Arrow Cross Party, 28, 30, 39n14, 333, 334, 340, 346, 351
Arzbergerstrasse camp, 360
Ataqa, Mount 246–247, 261
Attrition War, 182–209, 228, 235, 257, 387
Auschwitz, 39n14, 58, 100, 110, 154, 271, 271, 274, 277, 305, 315, 324, 336, 340–344, 348

B

Ba'abda, 362–363
Babócsa, 29, 342–343
Bárdossy, László, 4, 8, 156–157
Bar Lev, Haim, 185, 186, 233
Bar-Lev line, 185–187, 189, 202, 202n5, 206, 208, 217, 229, 387
Begin, Menachem, 123, 128, 129, 148, 148n2, 362–364, 368–374, 376–378, 381, 388
Beirut, 362–364, 373–374, 376–379, 381–386

Beirut-Damascus highway, 373, 377, 384
Békéscsaba, 42, 54, 282, 341–342, 344
Béke sugárút, 18, 33, 75, 323, 336, 341
Belgorod, 169, 171–173
Ben-Gurion, David, 120
Beth Oren, 114
Big Pines, Operation, 372, 376–377
Bir Gifgafa, *see* Rephidim
Blitzkrieg, 19, 60–61, 141–142
Böske, *see* Laufer, Berta
Bratislava, 357, 359
Brest, 180–181
Bronna Góra, 181
Buchenwald, 311, 313–314
Budapest, 181, 267, 270, 305, 308, 311, 324, 330–332, 334–336, 339, 341, 346–353, 355–358
    siege of, 331
    Budapest Bar Association, 2, 348, 355
    Budapest Keleti pályaudvar, 2, 27, 330
Burg, Yosef, 371
Bush, George W., 372n8

C

Carmel Center, 101, 106
Carpathian Group, 156–158
Chernyanka, 80
Chinese Farm, 228–234, 247
Czinczár family, 31–32

D

Dachau, 266–267, 269n5, 269–270, 272–277, 280–281, 283, 297, 303, 305, 311–313, 329, 348
Damour, 382
Dayan, Moshe, 120–121, 125–126, 128–129, 140, 182, 185, 208, 223, 233, 261, 371

Debrecen, 39–40, 43, 45, 179
Degania, 114, 127, 131–133, 143
De Gaulle, Charles, 109–110
Dénes, István "Pista," 354
Deversoir Airbase, 239–241, 243–244, 247, 249–250, 252, 258
Dischinger, Franz, 277–278, 280
Don River, 19, 160
Doroshich, 177
Dunkirk, 102, 142, 298

E
Eban, Abba, 109
Economic Stabilization Policy (1985), 367
Egyptian-Israeli General Armistice Agreement, 90, 92, 95–96, 99, 101
Egyptian-Syrian defense pact (1966), 91
Egyptian Second Army, 220–221, 229–230, 252
Egyptian Third Army, 229, 246–250, 252–255, 257, 260–261, 263
Ein-Gev, 135–136
Ein Hilweh, 382–383
Eisenhower, Dwight D., 110
Eitan, Rafael, 371, 373, 378
El Arish, 136, 146, 188, 202, 216
SHEKEM, 188–189, 195
Elazar, David "Dado", 219, 224, 233
el-Sadat, Anwar, 98
el-Shazly, Saad, 219
Eshkol, Levi, 86, 88–89, 118–126, 128–129, 133, 138
Esther, Queen, 75, 134
Esztergom, 357–359

F
Farhud, 154
Feldafing (DP camp), 324–330, 332, 336
Ferdinand, Archduke Franz, 380
First Lebanon War, see Lebanon War (1982)
Flatto-Sharon, Shmuel, 368

G
GALATZ (radio), 90, 95, 124, 136, 210, 256
Galilee, 103, 143, 209, 365, 374–375, 386
  Sea of, 111, 135, 145, 217
Gaza, 95, 101, 106, 150, 188, 202, 216, 254, 382
Gemayel, Bashir, 373, 376, 383

Geneifa, 245–246, 248–252, 256, 260, 262, 382
Gerbeaud (café), 23–25
Goebbels, Joseph, 309
Göncöl Szekér (the Big Dipper constellation), 67
Golan Heights, 88–89, 111, 118, 135, 39–141, 143, 144n1, 145, 147, 183, 206, 210, 212, 216–217, 220–221, 223–224, 252, 363, 372
  Sha'ar HaGolan, 112–115, 119–121, 123, 127, 132–135, 140, 143–145, 153, 192
Gomel, 26, 35, 59–64, 77–79, 272
Göring, Hermann, 276, 309
Goshen, Land of, 245, 248, 250, 258, 260, 262, 264, 382
Great Bitter Lake, 190, 200, 227–231, 233–234, 236, 238, 243, 247, 258
Gyula, 17–22, 25–39, 43, 50, 54, 56, 67, 74–75, 139, 179, 270, 282, 309, 321, 323, 332, 334, 336–342, 344–346

H
Habib, Phillip, 363
Hadow, Michael, 147
Haifa, 86, 91, 102–104, 112, 123–124, 126, 132, 135, 137–138, 146, 148, 154, 187, 202, 205, 209 211, 221, 225, 260, 304n37, 326–327, 363, 369, 382, 385–386, 388–389
Haifa Bay, 91, 102, 209, 375–376
HaKotel HaMa'aravi, (also the Wailing Wall) 89, 135, 137, 153
Hatzar-Mavet, 237–239, 241, 243–244, 247, 252, 255, 260
Hebrew Song Festival, 89
Hermon, Mount, 103, 208, 366
Herut Party, 128, 148, 368
Herzl, Theodor, 327
Herzog, Chaim, 105, 125, 129–130, 133–134, 136
Hezbollah, 388
Hitler, Adolf, 61, 102, 156–158, 173, 179, 276, 278, 298, 307, 309, 324–325, 331
Hitler Youth (Hitlerjugend), 325
Holocaust, 2, 85–86, 110, 121, 266, 270, 310, 313–314, 330, 334, 347

Holocaust survivors, 37n12, 85–87, 94–95, 97, 100, 105, 110, 121, 137, 139, 153, 253, 313, 316n3, 327–328, 330, 346, 348, 350
Horthy, Miklós, 8, 50, 61, 65n2, 156–157
Hovav, Moshe, 90, 95–96
Hungarian Army, 18–19, 36, 39, 41, 43, 45, 49, 60–61, 64, 74, 80–81, 84, 155–158, 161, 163–164, 166, 174, 177, 280
    Hungarian Forced Labor Battalions, see MUSZ
    Hungarian Second Army, 19, 41n1, 59, 81, 142, 155, 158–161, 165
Hungarian Zionist Association, 351–352
Hungarian Zionist trial (1949), 353–356
Hussein of Jordan, King, 126, 132, 147, 182, 184, 366

I
International Committee of Jewish Refugees, Austria, 356
Ipolyság, 9–11, 13–14
Ismailia, 151, 244, 258
Israel-Egypt Peace Treaty (1979), 254, 366, 369
Israeli Defense Force (IDF), 86, 89, 93–94, 101, 104–105, 107, 111–112, 117, 120, 125–127, 130, 132, 133, 134, 136–138, 141, 143, 145, 150–151, 153, 184, 186, 188–189, 191, 195–196, 199, 203, 206–208, 210, 212–213, 216–218, 220, 225, 232, 236, 239, 242, 245, 248–250, 253, 255–259, 351, 362–363, 366, 369, 372–377, 382–385, 388n18
Israeli Air Force, 89, 92, 134, 136, 139, 142, 212, 216–217, 221, 230, 247, 379
Israeli–Egyptian Disengagement Treaty of 1974, 261
Israeli–Egyptian negotiations, 255
Israeli-Palestinian conflict, 128n15
Israeli Philharmonic Orchestra, 365
Israeli War of Independence, 86, 112–113, 154, 254, 382
    Israel's Declaration of independence, 112, 351
    Israel's 19th Independence Day, 85–90

J
Jerusalem, 85–87, 89–90, 125–126, 128, 132–133, 135, 137, 139, 146, 153–154, 182, 187, 193, 214, 382, 386, 388

Jewish Laws, 3, 3n6, 4, 35, 58, 347–348
Johnson, B. Lyndon, 109
Jordan, 87, 89, 92, 94, 102–103, 112, 115, 121, 126, 128, 132–137, 140, 142, 146, 148–149, 184, 205, 206, 209, 254, 363, 366, 369, 374
Jordan River, 91, 117, 122, 184
Jordan Valley, 111–113, 116, 118, 145, 154, 184

K
Kamianets-Podilskyi, 4
Kassa, 36, 55, 156
Kaufering, 277
Kecskemét, 33
Keitel, Wilhelm, 158
Kharkov, 170, 172–173, 176, 179–180
Khartoum Resolution, see "Three No's" resolution
Kiev, 121, 176–177, 180, 269
Kiryat Shmona, 366, 374, 379, 382,
Kissinger, Henry, 247, 254–255
Kol Israel (radio), 130, 137
Kolozsvár, 26, 166
Korosten, 177, 179–180

L
Laci, see Laufer, László
Lánchíd, 55, 331
Laufer, Aharon, 265, 364–365, 385
Laufer, Berta "Böske," (neé Neumann), 17–18, 20–23, 25–31, 75, 179–180, 332–336, 339–341
Laufer, Dan, 265, 332, 338, 343, 389
Laufer, Éva "Évi," 21, 29, 75, 332–334, 336, 341, 354, 356
Laufer, Judit, 9, 12–13, 16–18, 20–25, 27–30, 32–35, 37–38, 40, 53, 55, 67, 139, 154, 179–180, 269, 271, 290, 305, 307, 309, 320, 322–323, 331–332, 336, 338, 341–342, 344
Laufer, László "Laci," 1–4, 7–57, 59–75, 78–79, 86, 88, 95–99, 101–102, 104–105, 107–110, 121, 131, 137–139, 142, 146, 148–149, 154–155, 161–164, 167, 169, 174–179, 210–211, 226, 251, 266–271, 275, 280–297, 299–314, 316, 319–325, 328–333, 336, 338–339, 341–349, 352, 354–361, 379

Laufer, Liora, 187, 209–211, 218, 225–226, 260, 265, 267, 332, 335, 338, 343, 364–365, 385, 388–389

Laufer Liliá "Lili," (neé Rozenzweig), 3, 3n7, 9, 11–14, 16–18, 20–30, 33–34, 37–38, 39n14, 42, 50, 53, 55, 67, 139, 154, 179–180, 269–271, 305, 307, 320, 322, 331–332, 336, 338–339, 341–342, 344

Laufer, Noemi, 94, 98–99, 102, 108–109, 146, 148, 333

Laufer, Sándor, 14, 17–18, 20–21, 25, 28–38, 39n14, 40, 50, 53–54, 75, 154, 179–180, 270, 287, 305, 332–333, 335–336, 338, 341–345

Laufer, Tammar, 265, 266, 267n2, 364–365

Laufer, Zsuzsánna "Zsuzsi" (neé Dénes), 86, 95–97, 99, 102, 105, 107, 109, 137, 139, 146, 148, 226, 349, 354–357, 359–361, 379

Lebanon, 102–103, 122n11, 123, 126, 206, 208, 362–364, 366, 369, 372–382, 384–388

Lebanon, Mount 386

Lebanon War (1982), 122n11, 363–364, 371, 372n8, 385, 388

Leibowitz, Yeshayahu, 150

Levi, Primo, 275, 285

Likud Party, 368–371

Litani, Operation, 369

Little Pines Operation, 372

Lutz, Carl, 334n2

M

Ma'arach, 367, 369

Mahapach, 368

Maozim, also Maoz 186–190, 195, 202–204, 206–207, 217

Maoz Lituf, 190–205, 207, 217

Maoz Matsmed, 229, 237

Masada (kibbutz), 112, 115, 127, 140, 145, 382

Mauthausen-Gusen, 313, 335–336

Meir, Golda, 223, 232, 255, 261

Meridor, Yaakov, 370

Merkaz, *see* Carmel Center

Mettenheim, 300–301, 303–305

Mineo, Salvatore "Sal", 326

Mirdafim, 184

Mitla Pass, 208, 262

Mohács, 181

Mosonyi utcai toloncház (the detention center on Mosonyi Street), 1–2, 4, 16–17

Mühldorf, 265–266, 277–282, 292, 295, 299, 300n31, 300–301n33, 301, 304, 307, 309–310, 312–314, 317–319, 323–324, 329

Munich Agreement, 102

MUSZ (Munkaszolgálat, *also* Hungarian Forced Labor Battalions), 3, 18–19, 25, 26n11, 26–27, 32, 38, 42–43, 46–63, 65–69, 71–74, 77, 79–84, 98, 142, 155, 159, 161–174, 176–178, 180–181, 267, 272, 280, 303, 323, 268, 270, 272, 274, 280, 285, 292, 348

N

Nablus Casbah, 149–150

Nasser, Gamal Abdel, 97, 101, 103, 120, 124, 126, 129, 130, 134, 184–185, 189, 208

Nathan, Shuli, 89, 94

Naveh Sha'anan, 90

Nazi National Redoubt, 309, 309n42

Negev, 105–106, 126, 150–151, 212, 365, 368

Newman, Paul, 326

Nickel Grass, Operation, 248, 248n13, 259

Nixon, Richard, 254

Nizhyn, 77

Normandy, 181, 267, 276, 298–299

Novy Oskol, 80

Numerus Clausus Act of September 22, 1920, 41n2

O

Organisation Todt (OT), 274, 278–280, 317–319, 322

P

Palestinian Liberation Organization (PLO), 128, 184, 362–363, 366, 369, 374, 376–379, 381–384

Papendorf, 326–327

Patton, George S., 313–314

Peres, Shimon, 368, 370

Phalangists, 362, 373, 376-377, 381, 383-384

Pinsk, 180

Polensky and Zöllner (P&Z), 279–280, 295–297, 297n27, 299, 301

Püspökladány, 34–36, 39, 41–59, 63, 179, 272

R
Rabin, Yitzhak, 86, 89, 91, 120, 136, 183, 373
Radio Cairo, 90–91, 125, 134
Rákosi, Mátyás, 351–354
Red Army, 52, 61, 78, 160–161, 163–164, 166, 169, 171–173, 176, 180–181, 276, 276, 298, 305, 331, 341–343, 350
Red Cross Family Tracing Service, 323
Rephidim, 188–189, 222
Rikhye, Indar Jit, 95
Rosh HaNikrah, 102, 375–376

S
Sabra (Tzabar), 85, 85n2, 102, 120
Sadat, Anwar, 98, 208–209, 254–255, 261
Saint, Eva Marie, 326
Schwartz, Endre, 42, 42n5, 45–46, 53–54, 56, 60, 62–71, 74, 78–80, 161–165, 167, 171, 174–179, 287
Second Lebanon War, 388
Sha'ar HaGai, 153–154
Sha'ar HaGolan, *see* Golan Heights
SHABAZAN, 195–198
SHACHPATZ, 199, 201–202
Shamir, Yitzhak, 371
Sharm-El-Sheikh, 101, 103, 139
Sharon, Ariel, 123, 151, 225, 229–230, 233, 233n9, 252, 368, 371–373, 377, 377n9, 381, 381n10, 383
Shazar, Zalman, 85, 88
Shebekino, 168–169
Shemer, Naomi, 89–90
Shimkin, Michael, 314–319, 322
Shivta, 150–151, 153
    Shivta battalion, 151–152
Shoah, *see* Holocaust
Shukairy, Ahmad, 128
Sinai, 90–92, 95–96, 99, 101–102, 104, 106–107, 121, 123, 133–134, 136–139, 147–148, 151, 183–185, 188–189, 207–208, 210–212, 216, 219, 222, 223–225, 227–228, 232–233, 235, 247–248, 251, 255, 257–259, 261–262, 365
Sinai Campaign (1956), 86, 90, 110, 120, 138, 148, 214, 253, 304n37
Six-Day War, 60n2, 109–142, 148n2, 150, 182, 184–185, 187, 189, 200, 206, 208–209, 211, 214–215, 218, 228, 242, 245, 253–254, 366, 372, 379

Small Bitter Lake, 190, 200
Small Holders' Party, 347–348, 350
Song for Peace, 182–183
SS *Einsatzgruppen* (killing squads), 4, 181
Stalingrad Battle, 155
Star of David, 31–32, 130
Stary Oskol, 77, 79, 169
Szeged Law School,
Szombathelyi, Ferenc 156–158

T
Tasa, 208, 226–227, 232
Tawfiq (village), 113, 115–119, 130–133, 135, 137, 140–141, 143–145
Technion, Israel Institute of Technology, 87, 90, 99, 101–102, 106, 119, 146, 187, 205, 209, 255, 262, 365, 370–371
Tel Aviv, 106, 125–126, 132, 134, 148, 183–184, 187–188, 202, 211–212, 221, 233, 255, 260, 326, 369, 381–383, 388
Tel Katzir, 143, 145
Tel Megiddo, 148
"Tembel" sunhats, 85
Thant, *also* U Thant, 95, 101–102, 106
"Three No's" resolution, 147, 150, 183
Tiran, Straits of, 101, 109–110, 120, 139, 147
Tolerance Tax, 32
Trans-Arabia Pipeline (Tapline), 363
Treblinka, 305
Tzemach, 111, 127

U
Umm Qatef, 146, 151
Umm Qatef, battle of, 151–153
United Nations, 87, 90–91, 95–96, 98–99, 101–102, 104, 106–107, 140, 144, 248, 252, 255, 257–258, 261, 263, 327–328, 351, 376
UN Interim Force in Lebanon (UNIFIL), 369
UN Relief and Rehabilitation Administration (UNRRA), 325, 329
UN Security Council, 95, 248, 369
US Army 99th Infantry Division, 299, 313–314
Uris, Leon, 326
Uryv, 160, 166
US military operation in Iraq, 372n8

V
Várkonyi, Tibor, 2n5, 348n4

Verebély (*now* Vrable), 11–12, 14, 38, 305
Volokonovka, 80–81, 165, 168
Voronezh, 19, 142, 159–160, 169

W
Waldlager 5 ("Forest Camp 5"), 280–281
Wallenberg, Raoul, 334, 334n2
War for the Peace of Galilee, *see* Lebanon War (1982)
Weitzman, Chaim, 327, 371
Werth, Henrik, 157
West Bank, 128n15, 139, 147–148, 148n2, 150, 182–184, 187, 254

Wings of Eagles, Operation, 154, 154n6

Y
Yadin, Yigael, 371
Yaguri, Assaf, 219
Yetziat Europa, 327
Yom Kippur War, 75, 186, 206–264, 299n29, 362, 364, 366–367, 372, 379, 385, 388–389

Z
Zippori, Mordechai, 371, 381